T0224045

Communications
in Computer and Information Science

879

Commenced Publication in 2007
Founding and Former Series Editors:
Phoebe Chen, Alfredo Cuzzocrea, Xiaoyong Du, Orhun Kara, Ting Liu,
Dominik Ślęzak, and Xiaokang Yang

Fagen Li · Tsuyoshi Takagi
Chunxiang Xu · Xiaosong Zhang (Eds.)

Frontiers in Cyber Security

First International Conference, FCS 2018
Chengdu, China, November 5–7, 2018
Proceedings

 Springer

Editors
Fagen Li [iD]
University of Electronic Science
and Technology of China
Chengdu, China

Chunxiang Xu
University of Electronic Science
and Technology of China
Chengdu, China

Tsuyoshi Takagi
University of Tokyo
Tokyo, Japan

Xiaosong Zhang
University of Electronic Science
and Technology of China
Chengdu, China

ISSN 1865-0929   ISSN 1865-0937   (electronic)
Communications in Computer and Information Science
ISBN 978-981-13-3094-0   ISBN 978-981-13-3095-7   (eBook)
https://doi.org/10.1007/978-981-13-3095-7

Library of Congress Control Number: 2018959233

This Springer imprint is published by the registered company Springer Nature Singapore Pte Ltd.
The registered company address is: 152 Beach Road, #21-01/04 Gateway East, Singapore 189721,
Singapore

Preface

The First International Conference on Frontiers in Cyber Security (FCS 2018) was held in Chengdu, P.R. China, November 5–7, 2018. The conference was organized by the Center for Cyber Security, University of Electronic Science and Technology of China (UESTC) and supported by the University of Tokyo, Hubei University of Technology, and Xidian University. As a new interdisciplinary subject, cyber security has attracted more and more attention from researchers and practitioners in academia and industry. The main goal of the FCS conference is to provide a good platform for researchers and practitioners to exchange the latest research results on new frontiers in cyber security.

This year we received 62 submissions. All the submissions were anonymous and only the Program Committee chairs knew the authors' information. Each submission was allocated to at least three Program Committee members and each paper received on average 2.98 reviews. The submission and review process was supported by the EasyChair conference management system. In the first phase, the Program Committee members individually evaluated the papers and did not know the review opinions of others. In the second phase, the papers were carefully checked in an extensive discussion. Finally, the committee decided to accept 18 full papers and three short papers, leading to an overall acceptance rate of 33.9%.

The program included three keynote speeches, given by Prof. Jian Weng (Jinan University) titled "How Did the Grinch Steal Smart Christmas", Prof. Sherman S. M. Chow (The Chinese University of Hong Kong) titled "Privacy-Preserving Machine Learning" and Prof. Boris Düdder (University of Copenhagen) titled "Blockchain Applications in Edge Computing-Based Logistics".

We would like to thank the Program Committee members and the external reviewers for their careful reviews and post-review discussions. The review work is very tough and time-consuming. We also want to deeply thank the members of the Organizing Committee for their excellent service and help for the organization of this conference. We are very grateful to the staff at Springer for their help in producing the proceedings. Finally, and most importantly, we want to thank all the authors who submitted to the conference and helped make the event a success.

November 2018

Fagen Li
Tsuyoshi Takagi
Chunxiang Xu
Xiaosong Zhang

Organization

General Co-chairs

Chunxiang Xu   University of Electronic Science and Technology of China, China

Xiaosong Zhang   University of Electronic Science and Technology of China, China

Program Co-chairs

Fagen Li   University of Electronic Science and Technology of China, China

Tsuyoshi Takagi   The University of Tokyo, Japan

Publicity Chair

Qi Xia   University of Electronic Science and Technology of China, China

Organizing Committee

Changchun Li   University of Electronic Science and Technology of China, China

Jingqi Li   University of Electronic Science and Technology of China, China

Xiaozhen Liu   University of Electronic Science and Technology of China, China

Program Committee

Ruhul Amin   International Institute of Information Technology-Naya Raipur, India

Man Ho Au   Hong Kong Polytechnic University, Hong Kong, SAR China

Zhenfu Cao   East China Normal University, China

Kim-Kwang Raymond Choo   University of Texas at San Antonio, USA

Jintai Ding   University of Cincinnati, USA

Shaojing Fu   National University of Defense Technology, China

Debasis Giri   Haldia Institute of Technology, India

Fuchun Guo   University of Wollongong, Australia

Jinguang Han   University of Surrey, UK

Additional Reviewers

Chen, Long
Dai, Elim
Gao, Juntao
Hesamifard, Ehsan
Hu, Jiaxi
Jiang, Linzhi
Larangeira, Mario
Li, Ming
Liao, Xin
Liao, Xiaojuan
Liu, Jianan
Lu, Zhenliang
Ning, Jianting

Qu, Longjiang
Sakurai, Kouichi
Sun, Aiying
Sun, Lixue
Wang, Xingfeng
Weng, Jiasi
Wu, Ge
Zhang Yinghui
Zhang, Yue
Zhou, Yuyang
Zhu, Hui
Zhu, Yanmin

Keynote Speech Abstracts

How Did the Grinch Steal Smart Christmas

Jian Weng

College of Information Science and Technology, Jinan University, Guangzhou,
China
cryptjweng@gmail.com

Abstract. In this talk, we show how Grinch, the bad guy, could ruin our Christmas in the era of Internet of Things (IoT). Particularly, we target a known manufacturer, APPLights. Their products include C9 lights, icicle light-strings, spotlight projectors, candy cane pathway markers and Kaleidoscope spotlights. They can often be seen in a local Home Depot store in the US during the winter holiday season. APPLights' Android or iOS app can be used to control these lights through Bluetooth Low Energy (BLE). The app protects its source code using encryption by Qihoo 360 jiagubao, Java Native Interface (JNI) techniques, code obfuscation and supports password based user authentication at the application layer. We systematically perform static analysis and dynamic analysis of the app, and conduct traffic analysis of the BLE traffic to understand the security measures of the lighting system. With our replay attack, brute force attack and spoofing attack, we can control any product that uses the APPLights app. Extensive real world experiments are performed to validate the feasibility of these attacks. We have also investigated 8 lights in total and two medical devices we can find on market from different vendors to prove that the results and observations from this study can be extended to other similar BLE applications. To defend against these attacks, we design an application layer BLE-based secure IoT communication protocol and implement it on the TI CC2640R2F chip. Our evaluation shows that the defense strategy effectively thwarts all attacks.

Blockchain Applications in Edge Computing-Based Logistics

Boris Düdder

Department of Computer Science, University of Copenhagen, Copenhagen, Denmark
boris@di.ku.dk

Abstract. Many blockchain projects have been deployed or are field tested in various industries. Industries with a high degree of organizational centralization benefit most of the blockchain's decentralized architecture and security properties. Logistics is such an industry which is transformed by digitalization. The shipping industry transports 90% of all commodities worldwide. Logistics have well-defined business processes which can be supported by smart contracts and smart payment systems. We will discuss prevailing security risks and challenges of blockchain-based logistics with edge-based computing including secure cash flows.

Contents

Security Design

Invited Paper

Privacy-Preserving Machine Learning

Sherman S. M. Chow[✉]

Department of Information Engineering, The Chinese University of Hong Kong,
Shatin, N.T., Hong Kong
sherman@ie.cuhk.edu.hk

Abstract. The popularization of cloud computing and machine learning algorithms facilitates ranges of complex analytic services, such as medical or financial assessments. This allows a computationally-limited client to get predictions or classification results by paying for the analytic services. These services often involve sensitive data which should be kept private. Ideally, we hope for privacy-preserving machine learning services. The clients can learn the results of the model from a service provider without revealing their inputs and the results. Meanwhile, the trained model is kept confidential from the clients with as minimal leakage as possible. This keynote focuses on how cryptography can enable privacy-preserving machine learning services, in particular, decision tree evaluation.

Keywords: Machine learning · Processing encrypted data
Decision tree

1 Privacy Concerns in Machine Learning

Machine learning analyzes the statistics of past data to devise complex models for making predictions for new data as a query. It has wide applications, *e.g.*, medical diagnosis, object recognition, recommender system, risk assessment, *etc.*

Typical machine learning algorithms make predictions by processing the query in plaintext. Yet, the querying clients (or users) using machine learning services may not want to reveal their sensitive information or corresponding classification result to the server. Leakage of sensitive information (*e.g.*, food allergy, whereabouts) can be a life-or-death issue, especially when they are in the hand of those with criminal intent. Of course, if the server is willing to give the model to the clients. The client can then compute locally without leaking anything. However, the clients may not want to spend so much computation resources for processing a complex model. From another perspective, training a complex model can be costly. Moreover, a model may leak information about the sensitive data used to train the model. Revealing the model means compromising the privacy of the individuals who contributed their data. Giving the model to the clients thus hurts the profit and reputation of the service provider, and may even violate regulations like the Health Insurance Portability and Accountability Act.

F. Li et al. (Eds.): FCS 2018, CCIS 879, pp. 3–6, 2018.
https://doi.org/10.1007/978-981-13-3095-7_1

2   Decision Tree

Here, we focus on privacy-preserving classification of decision trees, a commonly used classification algorithm for its effectiveness and simplicity. A decision tree model takes as input a vector of client attribute, called a feature vector, and outputs the classification result. A decision tree consists of two types of nodes, decision (internal) nodes, and leaf nodes. Each decision node denotes a test on the input attributes, while each leaf node corresponds to a classification result. When evaluating a decision tree, starting from the root node, the classifier compares one attribute in the feature vector with a node-specific threshold, and traverse to the left or right subtree based on the comparison result. The process is repeated at each level until it reaches a leaf node, and the output is the classification result associated with that leaf node.

Comparing to deep learning approaches which are more powerful, decision tree approach is more efficient when the data has a hierarchical structure and requires less parameter tuning as well as training cost. Furthermore, in general, the more complicated the underlying (non-privacy-preserving) machine learning it is, the less efficient will be the corresponding privacy-preserving version.

To preserve privacy in the above scenario is actually a specific instance of the secure two-party computation (2PC) problem. This thus can be solved by cryptographic primitives such as homomorphic encryption (HE) and garbled circuits.

3   Privacy-Preserving Decision Trees Evaluation

Apply the generic cryptographic primitives directly on top of the whole machine learning evaluation algorithm incurs a high cost in computation and communication. Tailor-made approaches, some for specific machine learning models, can be far more efficient [1,10]. It does not mean 2PC are HE not necessary, but those are for specific basic functionalities such as integers comparison [3,8].

Bost et al. [1] used additive homomorphic encryption (AHE) and fully homomorphic encryption (FHE) to build privacy-preserving protocols for hyperplane decision, naïve Bayes, and decision tree classifiers. Their construction treats the decision trees as high-degree polynomials, hence it requires the usage of FHE.

Wu et al. [10] proposed an improved protocol for decision trees by using only AHE and oblivious transfer (OT). For hiding the tree structure, their protocol transforms a decision tree into a complete and randomized tree. So its server computation and communication complexities are exponential in the depth d of the decision tree. This increases the workload "unnecessarily" especially when the decision tree is sparse, i.e., when $m \ll d$ where m is the number of nodes.

Tai et al. [6] avoided the exponential blow-up in both time and space complexities by reducing the evaluation of a decision tree to the paths of the tree. The server can then compute the encrypted results by evaluating linear functions. The server complexity is linear in the number of nodes. For all five datasets in

UCI machine learning repository[1] considered in the experiment of Wu *et al.* [10], this shows an improvement of the protocol of Wu *et al.* [10].

4   Recent Works

Recently, there are two follow-up works of Tai *et al.* [6]. Both of them require the client and the server communicate for at least $4d$ rounds, while the protocol of Tai *et al.* requires only 4 rounds, yet with m secure comparisons.

Joye and Salehi [4] proposed an improved secure comparison protocol and also a new privacy-preserving decision tree evaluation protocol using OT. It only requires a single comparison for each level of a complete tree.

Tueno, Kerschbaum, and Katzenbeisser [7] flattened the tree into an array. In this way, using either OT, oblivious RAM (ORAM), oblivious data structure, or function-secret-sharing linear ORAM (see the references within [7]), the number of secure comparisons is also reduced to d. Moreover, their protocol achieves sub-linear (in m) communication complexity (except the OT-based instantiation).

Tai [5] also proposed secure evaluation protocols for decision tree which requires $O(d)$ number of rounds and $O(d)$ secure comparisons. With the increased number of interactions, the protocols also aim to support outsourcing both the decision tree model and its computation to untrusted cloud servers. It even does not require homomorphic encryption but just symmetric-key encryption. Yet, it relies on the non-colluding assumption of two cloud servers [2,9].

5   Concluding Remarks

We mostly discussed decision tree evaluation. There are cryptographic approaches which support training or other models such as neural network. They are still relatively heavyweight and research works are still ongoing.

Acknowledgement. Sherman S. M. Chow is supported by the General Research Fund (CUHK 14210217) of the Research Grants Council, University Grant Committee of Hong Kong.

References

1. Bost, R., Popa, R.A., Tu, S., Goldwasser, S.: Machine learning classification over encrypted data. In: 22nd Annual Network and Distributed System Security Symposium, NDSS 2015, San Diego, California, USA, 8–11 February 2015. The Internet Society (2015)
2. Chow, S.S.M., Lee, J., Subramanian, L.: Two-party computation model for privacy-preserving queries over distributed databases. In: Proceedings of the Network and Distributed System Security Symposium, NDSS 2009, San Diego, California, USA, 8th February - 11th February 2009. The Internet Society (2009)

---

[1] https://archive.ics.uci.edu/ml.

3. Damgård, I., Geisler, M., Krøigaard, M.: A correction to 'efficient and secure comparison for on-line auctions'. IJACT **1**(4), 323–324 (2009)
4. Joye, M., Salehi, F.: Private yet efficient decision tree evaluation. In: Kerschbaum, F., Paraboschi, S. (eds.) DBSec 2018. LNCS, vol. 10980, pp. 243–259. Springer, Cham (2018). https://doi.org/10.1007/978-3-319-95729-6_16
5. Tai, R.K.H.: Privacy-preserving decision trees evaluation protocols. Master's thesis, Department of Information Engineering, The Chinese University of Hong Kong, Shatin, N.T., Hong Kong (2018). Supervised by S.S.M. Chow
6. Tai, R.K.H., Ma, J.P.K., Zhao, Y., Chow, S.S.M.: Privacy-preserving decision trees evaluation via linear functions. In: Foley, S.N., Gollmann, D., Snekkenes, E. (eds.) ESORICS 2017. LNCS, vol. 10493, pp. 494–512. Springer, Cham (2017). https://doi.org/10.1007/978-3-319-66399-9_27
7. Tueno, A., Kerschbaum, F., Katzenbeisser, S.: Private evaluation of decision trees using sublinear cost. PoPETs **1**, 1–21 (2019)
8. Veugen, T.: Improving the DGK comparison protocol. In: 2012 IEEE International Workshop on Information Forensics and Security, WIFS 2012, Costa Adeje, Tenerife, Spain, 2–5 December 2012, pp. 49–54. IEEE (2012)
9. Wang, B., Li, M., Chow, S.S.M., Li, H.: A tale of two clouds: computing on data encrypted under multiple keys. In: IEEE Conference on Communications and Network Security, CNS 2014, San Francisco, CA, USA, 29–31 October 2014, pp. 337–345. IEEE (2014)
10. Wu, D.J., Feng, T., Naehrig, M., Lauter, K.E.: Privately evaluating decision trees and random forests. PoPETs **2016**(4), 335–355 (2016)

Symmetric Key Cryptography

On k–error Linear Complexity
of Zeng-Cai-Tang-Yang Generalized
Cyclotomic Binary Sequences of Period p^2

Chenhuang Wu[1,2] and Chunxiang Xu[1(✉)]

[1] Center for Cyber Security, School of Computer Science and Engineering,
University of Electronic Science and Technology of China,
Chengdu 611731, Sichuan, People's Republic of China
ptuwch@163.com, chxxu@uestc.edu.cn
[2] Provincial Key Laboratory of Applied Mathematics, Putian University,
Putian 351100, Fujian, People's Republic of China

Abstract. Due to good pseudorandom properties, generalized cyclotomic sequences have been widely used in simulation, radar systems, cryptography, and so on. In this paper, we consider the k-error linear complexity of Zeng-Cai-Tang-Yang generalized cyclotomic binary sequences of period p^2, proposed in the recent paper "New generalized cyclotomic binary sequences of period p^2", by Z. Xiao et al., who calculated the linear complexity of the sequence (Designs, Codes and Cryptography, 2018, 86(7): 1483–1497). More exactly, we determine the values of k-error linear complexity over $\mathbb{F}_2$ for $f = 2$ and almost $k > 0$ in terms of the theory of Fermat quotients. Results indicate that such sequences have good stability.

Keywords: Cryptography · Pseudorandom sequences
k-error linear complexity · Generalized cyclotomic classes
Fermat quotients

1 Introduction

Pseudorandom sequences have been widely used in modern communications, such as simulation, radar systems, bluetooth, coding theory, cryptography, and so on [14]. Cyclotomic classes over $\mathbb{Z}_n^*$ play an important role in the design of pseudorandom sequences [8], where $\mathbb{Z}_n = \{0, 1, 2, \ldots, n - 1\}$ be the residue class ring of integers modulo n and $\mathbb{Z}_n^*$ be the multiplicative group consisting

An extended version of this work will be submitted to Elsevier. This work supported by the National Natural Science Foundation of China under grant No. 61772292, 61872060, by the National Key R&D Program of China under grant No. 2017YFB0802000, by the Provincial Natural Science Foundation of Fujian under grant No. 2018J01425 and by the Program for Innovative Research Team in Science and Technology in Fujian Province University.

F. Li et al. (Eds.): FCS 2018, CCIS 879, pp. 9–22, 2018.
https://doi.org/10.1007/978-981-13-3095-7_2

of all invertible elements in $\mathbb{Z}_n$. In the literature, cyclotomic classes are classified into two kinds, namely classical cyclotomic classes for n is prime and generalized cyclotomic classes for n is composite, respectively. To the best of our knowledge, there are mainly five classes of cyclotomy: Classical cyclotomy [13], Whitemans generalized cyclotomy [20], Ding-Helleseth generalized cyclotomy [9], k-fold cyclotomy [6], and Zeng-Cai-Tang-Yang generalized cyclotomy [22]. Using classical cyclotomic classes and generalized cyclotomic classes to construct binary sequences which are called classical cyclotomic sequences [10,11,16] and generalized cyclotomic sequences [7,9,19,21], respectively.

In [22], Zeng, Cai, Tang and Yang introduced a new kind of generalized cyclotomy in order to construct optimal frequency hopping sequences. In this paper, we called such generalized cyclotomy as Zeng-Cai-Tang-Yang generalized cyclotomy. Very recently, Xiao, Zeng, Li and Helleseth proposed a new family of binary sequences based on Zeng-Cai-Tang-Yang generalized cyclotomy, by defining the generalized cyclotomic classes modulo p^2, where p is an odd prime [21].

Suppose that $p-1 = ef$ and g is a primitive root[1] modulo p^2, the generalized cyclotomic classes for $1 \leq j \leq 2$ were defined as follows:

$$D_0^{(p^j)} \triangleq \{g^{kfp^{j-1}} \pmod{p^j} : 0 \leq k < e\}$$

and

$$D_l^{(p^j)} \triangleq g^l D_0^{(p^j)} = \{g^l \cdot g^{kfp^{j-1}} \pmod{p^j} : 0 \leq k < e\}, \ 1 \leq l < fp^{j-1}.$$

Then they defined a new p^2-periodic binary sequence (s_n):

$$s_n = \begin{cases} 0, \text{ if } n \pmod{p^2} \in C_0, \\ 1, \text{ if } n \pmod{p^2} \in C_1, \end{cases} \tag{1}$$

where

$$C_0 = \bigcup_{i=f/2}^{f-1} pD_{i+b}^{(p)} \pmod{f} \cup \bigcup_{i=pf/2}^{pf-1} D_{i+b}^{(p^2)} \pmod{pf}$$

and

$$C_1 = \bigcup_{i=0}^{f/2-1} pD_{i+b}^{(p)} \pmod{f} \cup \bigcup_{i=0}^{pf/2-1} D_{i+b}^{(p^2)} \pmod{pf} \cup \{0\}$$

for $b \in \mathbb{Z} : 0 \leq b < fp$. They considered the linear complexity of the proposed sequences for $f = 2^r$ for some integer $r \geq 1$ and proved that the linear complexity $LC^{\mathbb{F}_2}((s_n))$ of (s_n) satisfied

$$LC^{\mathbb{F}_2}((s_n)) = \begin{cases} p^2 - (p-1)/2, \text{ if } 2 \in D_0^{(p)}, \\ p^2, \qquad\qquad \text{ if } 2 \notin D_0^{(p)}, \end{cases}$$

---

[1] For our purpose, we will choose g such that the fermat quotient $q_p(g) = 1$, see the notion in Sect. 2.

if $f = 2^r$ (integer $r > 0$) and $2^{(p-1)/f} \not\equiv 1 \pmod{p^2}$.

As a significant cryptographic feature of sequences, the linear complexity provides information on the predictability. In other words, sequences with small linear complexity are unsuitable for cryptographic applications. In the following, we review the definition of the linear complexity of a periodic sequences. Assume that $\mathbb{F}$ is a field. The *linear complexity* of a T-periodic sequence (s_n) over $\mathbb{F}$, denoted by $LC^{\mathbb{F}}((s_n))$, is the smallest order L of a linear recurrence relation over $\mathbb{F}$ that is satisfied by (s_n)

$$s_{n+L} = c_{L-1}s_{n+L-1} + \ldots + c_1 s_{n+1} + c_0 s_n \quad \text{for } n \geq 0,$$

where $c_0 \neq 0, c_1, \ldots, c_{L-1} \in \mathbb{F}$. The *generating polynomial* of (s_n) is defined as

$$S(X) = s_0 + s_1 X + s_2 X^2 + \ldots + s_{T-1}X^{T-1} \in \mathbb{F}[X].$$

Then, as showed in [8], the linear complexity over $\mathbb{F}$ of (s_n) can be computed by

$$LC^{\mathbb{F}}((s_n)) = T - \deg\left(\gcd(X^T - 1, \ S(X))\right). \tag{2}$$

From the point of cryptographic application, the linear complexity of a sequence should be large, and should not be significantly reduced when a few terms of the sequence are changed. This leads to the concept of the k-error linear complexity. For an integer $k \geq 0$, the *k-error linear complexity* over $\mathbb{F}$ of a sequence (s_n), denoted by $LC_k^{\mathbb{F}}((s_n))$, is the smallest linear complexity (over $\mathbb{F}$) of the sequence (s_n) which is changed at most k terms per period. The k-error linear complexity was even earlier defined as sphere complexity in [12,18]. It is clear that $LC_0^{\mathbb{F}}((s_n)) = LC^{\mathbb{F}}((s_n))$ and

$$T \geq LC_0^{\mathbb{F}}((s_n)) \geq LC_1^{\mathbb{F}}((s_n)) \geq \ldots \geq LC_w^{\mathbb{F}}((s_n)) = 0$$

when w is the hamming weight, i.e., the number of nonzero terms, of (s_n) per period. The main purpose of this work is to determine the k-error linear complexity of (s_n) in Eq. (1) for $f = 2$.

The paper is organized as follows. As a useful technique for the proof of our main result, the notation of *Fermat quotients* and some necessary lemmas are showed in Sect. 2. In Sect. 3, the main result and its proof are presented in Theorem 1, and two examples used to illustrate the correctness of the main result are presented. In the last Section, we give some concluding remarks.

2   Tools and Auxiliary Lemmas

We find that the construction of (s_n) in Eq. (1) has close relation with Fermat quotients. In the following part, we briefly review the concept of Fermat quotient, and interpret the relations of the construction (s_n) and Fermat quotients. Then, we show some necessary lemmas for proving our main result.

For integers $u \geq 0$, the *Fermat quotient* $q_p(u)$ at u is defined by

$$q_p(u) \equiv \frac{u^{p-1} - 1}{p} \pmod{p} \in \{0, 1, \ldots, p-1\},$$

where $\gcd(u, p) = 1$, if $\gcd(u, p) = p$ we set $q_p(u) = 0$, see [17]. We have

$$\begin{cases} q_p(u + \ell p) \equiv q_p(u) - \ell u^{-1} \pmod{p}, \\ q_p(uv) \equiv q_p(u) + q_p(v) \pmod{p}. \end{cases} \tag{3}$$

Then for $\gcd(u, p) = 1$ and $\gcd(v, p) = 1$, it is easy to see that $q_p : \mathbb{Z}_{p^2}^* \to \mathbb{F}_p$ is an epimorphism. Now, we define

$$D_l = \{u : 0 \le u < p^2, \gcd(u, p) = 1, q_p(u) = l\}, \quad 0 \le l < p,$$

which makes a partition of $\mathbb{Z}_{p^2}^*$. Together with the second equation in (3) and the primitive root g modulo p^2 with $q_p(g) = 1^2$, it is easy to know that

$$D_l = \{g^{l+ip} \pmod{p^2} : 0 \le i < p - 1\}, \quad 0 \le l < p.$$

Therefore, according to the definition of $D_l^{(p^2)}$ in Sect. 1, it is clear that

$$D_l = \bigcup_{i=0}^{f-1} D_{ip+l}^{(p^2)}, \quad 0 \le l < p.$$

Specially, $D_l = D_l^{(p^2)}$ if $f = 1$.

Several sequences have been defined from Fermat quotients in the literature, see [1–3, 5, 15]. For example, the binary threshold sequence (s_n) is defined by

$$s_n = \begin{cases} 0, \text{ if } 0 \le q_p(n)/p < \frac{1}{2}, \\ 1, \text{ if } \frac{1}{2} \le q_p(n)/p < 1, \end{cases} \quad n \ge 0.$$

The Legendre-Fermat sequence (s_n) is defined by

$$s_n = \begin{cases} 0, \text{ if } \left(\frac{q_p(n)}{p}\right) = 1 \text{ or } q_p(n) = 0, \\ 1, \text{ otherwise}, \end{cases} \quad u \ge 0.$$

Here and hereafter $\left(\frac{\cdot}{p}\right)$ is the Legendre symbol.

Indeed, both sequences above can be characterized by D_l for $0 \le l < p$. In particular, their k-error linear complexity has been investigated in [4]. The way of [4] helps us to study the k-error linear complexity of (s_n) in Eq. (1) in this work.

Now we first prove some necessary lemmas. From now on, we denote by $\mathcal{Q} \subset \{1, 2, \ldots, p-1\}$ the set of quadratic residue modulo p and by $\mathcal{N} \subset \{1, 2, \ldots, p-1\}$ the set of quadratic non-residue modulo p, respectively. The notation $|Z|$ denotes the cardinality of the set Z.

Lemma 1. Let $D_l^{(p^2)}$ be defined for $0 \le l < 2p$ with $f = 2$ as in Sect. 1. For $0 \le l < p$, we have

$$\{n \bmod p : n \in D_{2l}^{(p^2)}\} = \mathcal{Q}, \quad \text{and} \quad \{n \bmod p : n \in D_{2l+1}^{(p^2)}\} = \mathcal{N}.$$

---

[2] Such g always exists.

Proof. From the definition of $D_{2l}^{(p^2)}$, each element in $D_{2l}^{(p^2)}$ is of the form g^{2l+2kp} modulo p^2 for $k \geq 0$. So

$$g^{2l+2kp} \equiv g^{2l+2k} \pmod{p},$$

which is a quadratic residue modulo p. The second can be proved similarly.   □

Lemma 2. *Let D_l be defined for $0 \leq l < p$ as in Sect. 2 using Fermat quotients, $v \in \{1, 2, \ldots, p-1\}$ and $V_v = \{v, v+p, v+2p, \ldots, v+(p-1)p\}$. Then, we get $|V_v \cap D_l| = 1$ for each $0 \leq l < p$.*

Proof. According to the first equation in Eq. (3), if $q_p(v + i_1 p) = q_p(v + i_2 p) = l$ for $0 \leq i_1, i_2 < p$, in other words, $q_p(v) - i_1 v^{-1} \equiv q_p(v) - i_2 v^{-1} \pmod{p}$. Then, it derives $i_1 = i_2$.   □

Lemma 3. *Let $D_l^{(p^2)}$ be defined for $0 \leq l < 2p$ with $f = 2$ as in Sect. 1. Let $v \in \{1, 2, \ldots, p-1\}$ and $V_v = \{v, v+p, v+2p, \ldots, v+(p-1)p\}$.*

(1). If $v \in Q$, then for each $0 \leq l < p$, we have

$$|V_v \cap D_{2l}^{(p^2)}| = 1, \quad |V_v \cap D_{2l+1}^{(p^2)}| = 0.$$

(2). If $v \in N$, then for each $0 \leq l < p$, we have

$$|V_v \cap D_{2l}^{(p^2)}| = 0, \quad |V_v \cap D_{2l+1}^{(p^2)}| = 1.$$

Proof. If $v \in Q$, then all numbers in V_v are quadratic residues modulo p. Lemma 2, together with $D_l = D_l^{(p^2)} \cup D_{l+p}^{(p^2)}$ for $0 \leq l < p$, implies the first statement in this lemma. Similar argument holds for $v \in N$.   □

Lemma 4. *Let C_0 and C_1 be defined with $f = 2$ as in Sect. 1. Let $v \in \{1, 2, \ldots, p-1\}$ and $V_v = \{v, v+p, v+2p, \ldots, v+(p-1)p\}$.*
  (1). For even $0 \leq b < 2p$, we have

$$|V_v \cap C_0| = (p-1)/2, \quad |V_v \cap C_1| = (p+1)/2,$$

if $v \in Q$, and

$$|V_v \cap C_0| = (p+1)/2, \quad |V_v \cap C_1| = (p-1)/2,$$

if $v \in N$.
  (2). For odd $0 \leq b < 2p$, we have

$$|V_v \cap C_0| = (p+1)/2, \quad |V_v \cap C_1| = (p-1)/2,$$

if $v \in Q$, and

$$|V_v \cap C_0| = (p-1)/2, \quad |V_v \cap C_1| = (p+1)/2,$$

if $v \in N$.

Proof. For even b, there are $(p+1)/2$ many even numbers and $(p-1)/2$ many odd numbers in the set $\{b, b+1, \ldots, b+p-1\}$, respectively. By Lemma 3, if $v \in \mathcal{Q}$, we see that

$$\mathcal{V}_v \subseteq \bigcup_{l=0}^{p-1} D_{2l}^{(p^2)}.$$

From the constructions of C_0 and C_1, we see that there are $(p+1)/2$ many $D_{2l}^{(p^2)}$ and $(p-1)/2$ many $D_{2l+1}^{(p^2)}$ contained in C_1 for $0 \leq l < p$. With $|\mathcal{V}_v \cap D_{2l}^{(p^2)}| = 1$ and $|\mathcal{V}_v \cap D_{2l+1}^{(p^2)}| = 0$ in Lemma 3(1) again for $v \in \mathcal{Q}$, we get that $|\mathcal{V}_v \cap C_1| = (p+1)/2$ and $|\mathcal{V}_v \cap C_0| = (p-1)/2$.

The rest of statements can be proved similarly. $\qquad\qquad\square$

Lemma 5. *Let $\theta \in \overline{\mathbb{F}}_2$ be a fixed primitive p-th root of unity. We have*

(1). $\displaystyle\sum_{n\in\mathcal{Q}} \theta^{in} = \sum_{n\in\mathcal{Q}} \theta^n, \quad \sum_{n\in\mathcal{N}} \theta^{in} = \sum_{n\in\mathcal{N}} \theta^n \quad$ *if $\left(\frac{i}{p}\right) = 1.$*

(2). $\displaystyle\sum_{n\in\mathcal{Q}} \theta^{in} = \sum_{n\in\mathcal{N}} \theta^n, \quad \sum_{n\in\mathcal{N}} \theta^{in} = \sum_{n\in\mathcal{Q}} \theta^n \quad$ *if $\left(\frac{i}{p}\right) = -1.$*

(3) $\displaystyle\sum_{n\in\mathcal{Q}} \theta^n \in \mathbb{F}_4 \setminus \mathbb{F}_2 \quad$ *if $\left(\frac{2}{p}\right) = -1.$*

Proof. It is clear. $\qquad\qquad\square$

Lemma 6. *Let $D_l^{(p^2)}$ be defined for $0 \leq l < 2p$ with $f = 2$ as in Sect. 1 and $d_l^{(p^2)}(X) = \displaystyle\sum_{n \in D_l^{(p^2)}} X^n$. Let $\theta \in \overline{\mathbb{F}}_2$ be a fixed primitive p-th root of unity and $\xi = \displaystyle\sum_{n\in\mathcal{Q}} \theta^n$. For $1 \leq i < p$ we have*

$$d_{2l}^{(p^2)}(\theta^i) = \begin{cases} \xi, & \text{if } \left(\frac{i}{p}\right) = 1, \\ 1 + \xi, & \text{if } \left(\frac{i}{p}\right) = -1, \end{cases}$$

and

$$d_{2l+1}^{(p^2)}(\theta^i) = \begin{cases} 1 + \xi, & \text{if } \left(\frac{i}{p}\right) = 1, \\ \xi, & \text{if } \left(\frac{i}{p}\right) = -1, \end{cases}$$

for $0 \leq l < p$.

Proof. Since $d_{2l}^{(p^2)}(X) \equiv \displaystyle\sum_{n\in\mathcal{Q}} X^n \pmod{X^p - 1}$ by Lemma 1, we derive

$$d_{2l}^{(p^2)}(\theta^i) = \sum_{n\in\mathcal{Q}} \theta^{ni} = \begin{cases} \displaystyle\sum_{n\in\mathcal{Q}} \theta^n, & \text{if } \left(\frac{i}{p}\right) = 1, \\ \displaystyle\sum_{n\in\mathcal{N}} \theta^n, & \text{if } \left(\frac{i}{p}\right) = -1. \end{cases}$$

The second can be proved similarly. $\qquad\qquad\square$

Here we say, the *weight* of a polynomial $h(X) \in \mathbb{F}_2[X]$ means the number of non-zero coefficients of $h(X)$, denoted by $wt(h(X))$.

Lemma 7. *Assume that 2 is a primitive root modulo p, $\theta \in \overline{\mathbb{F}}_2$ is a primitive p-th root of unity and $\omega \in \mathbb{F}_4 \backslash \mathbb{F}_2$. For any non-constant polynomial $h(X) \in \mathbb{F}_2[X]$ with $h(\theta) = \omega$, we have $wt(h(X)) \geq (p-1)/2$.*

Proof. Let $\xi = \sum\limits_{n \in Q} \theta^n$. By Lemma 5(3) we get $\xi \in \mathbb{F}_4 \backslash \mathbb{F}_2$, since 2 is a primitive root modulo p.

Now for $\omega \in \mathbb{F}_4 \backslash \mathbb{F}_2$, we see that $\omega = \xi = \sum\limits_{n \in Q} \theta^n$ or $\omega = \xi^2 = 1 + \xi = \sum\limits_{n \in N} \theta^n$.

We only prove the case when $\omega = \xi$, the latter can follow in a similar way.

First, we select $h(X) \in \mathbb{F}_2[X]$ such that $h(X) \equiv \sum\limits_{n \in Q} X^n \pmod{X^p - 1}$, or directly, let $h(X) = \sum\limits_{n \in Q} X^n$, we have $h(\theta) = \sum\limits_{n \in Q} \theta^n = \xi = \omega$. Then $wt(h(X)) \geq (p-1)/2$.

Second, let $h_0(X) \in \mathbb{F}_2[X]$ such that $wt(h_0(X)) < (p-1)/2$ and $h_0(\theta) = \omega$. Let $\overline{h}_0(X) \equiv h_0(X) \pmod{X^p - 1}$ with $\deg(\overline{h}_0) < p$ and let $H_0(X) = \overline{h}_0(X) + \sum\limits_{n \in Q} X^n$ whose degree is also less than p. Obviously, $H_0(X)$ is non-zero because $\overline{h}_0(X) \neq \sum\limits_{n \in Q} X^n$, where the weight of $\sum\limits_{n \in Q} X^n$ is $(p-1)/2$. Then, it is easy to get that $H_0(\theta) = 0$ and $H_0(\theta^{2^j}) = 0$ for $1 \leq j < p-1$ because of 2 is a primitive root modulo p. Thus,

$$(1 + X + X^2 + \ldots + X^{p-1}) | H_0(X),$$

i.e., $H_0(X) = 1 + X + X^2 + \ldots + X^{p-1}$, which derives that $\overline{h}_0(X) = 1 + \sum\limits_{n \in N} X^n$ and $wt(\overline{h}_0(X)) = (p+1)/2$. Therefore, $wt(h_0) \geq wt(\overline{h}_0) = (p+1)/2$ which leads to a contradiction. This completes the proof.   □

3   Main Result and Examples

In this section, we show the main result in the following Theorem with a detailed proof. Then, two examples verified by Magma program are used to illustrate the correctness of our main result.

3.1   Main Result

Theorem 1. *Let (s_n) is the binary sequence of period p^2 defined in Eq. (1) with $f = 2$ and even $b : 0 \leq b < fp$ in the definition of C_0 and C_1. If 2 is a primitive root modulo p^2, then the k-error linear complexity over $\mathbb{F}_2$ of (s_n) satisfies*

$$LC_k^{\mathbb{F}_2}((s_n)) = \begin{cases} p^2, & \text{if } k = 0, \\ p^2 - 1, & \text{if } 1 \leq k < (p-1)/2, \\ p^2 - p, & \text{if } (p-1)/2 \leq k < (p^2 - p)/2, \\ p - 1, & \text{if } k = (p^2 - p)/2, \\ 1, & \text{if } k = (p^2 - 1)/2, \\ 0, & \text{if } k > (p^2 - 1)/2, \end{cases}$$

if $p \equiv 3 \pmod{8}$, *and*

$$LC_k^{\mathbb{F}_2}((s_n)) = \begin{cases} p^2, & \text{if } k = 0, \\ p^2 - 1, & \text{if } 1 \le k < (p-1)/2, \\ p^2 - p + 1, & \text{if } k = (p-1)/2, \\ p^2 - p, & \text{if } (p+1)/2 \le k < (p^2 - p)/2, \\ p, & \text{if } k = (p^2 - p)/2, \\ 1, & \text{if } k = (p^2 - 1)/2, \\ 0, & \text{if } k > (p^2 - 1)/2, \end{cases}$$

if $p \equiv 5 \pmod{8}$.

For odd b, we have a similar result according to Lemma 4. We note here that for $k = 0$, it comes from [21].

Proof. It is clear that the weight of (s_n) is $(p^2 - 1)/2 + 1$. So we always suppose $k < (p^2 - 1)/2$.

Note that the generating polynomial of (s_n) is

$$S(X) = 1 + \sum_{j=0}^{p-1} d_{b+j}^{(p^2)}(X) + \sum_{j \in \mathcal{Q}} X^{jp} \in \mathbb{F}_2[X], \tag{4}$$

where $d_l^{(p^2)}(X) = \sum_{n \in D_l^{(p^2)}} X^n$ for $0 \le l < 2p$. Let

$$S_k(X) = S(X) + e(X) \in \mathbb{F}_2[X] \tag{5}$$

be the generating polynomial of the sequence gained from (s_n) with exactly k terms are changed per period. The $e(X)$ is called as the corresponding error polynomial which has k many monomials. It is clear that $S_k(X)$ is a nonzero polynomial because $k < (p^2 - 1)/2$.

Then we need to consider the common roots of $S_k(X)$ and $X^{p^2} - 1$. In other words, consider the roots of the form $\beta^n (n \in \mathbb{Z}_{p^2})$ for $S_k(X)$, in which $\beta \in \overline{\mathbb{F}}_2$ is a primitive p^2-th root of unity. Equation (2) can help us to derive the values of k-error linear complexity of (s_n) if we know the number of the common roots.

Now, we deduce the remaining proof in the following cases.

The first case is $k < (p^2 - p)/2$.

Firstly, we suppose that $S_k(\beta^{n_0}) = 0$ for some $n_0 \in \mathbb{Z}_{p^2}^*$. Because 2 is a primitive root modulo p^2, for each $n \in \mathbb{Z}_{p^2}^*$, there is a $0 \le j_n < (p-1)p$ such that $n \equiv n_0 2^{j_n} \bmod p^2$. Then

$$S_k(\beta^n) = S_k(\beta^{n_0 2^{j_n}}) = S_k(\beta^{n_0})^{2^{j_n}} = 0,$$

that is, all $(p^2 - p)$ many elements β^n for $n \in \mathbb{Z}_{p^2}^*$ are roots of $S_k(X)$. Hence,

$$\Phi(X) | S_k(X) \text{ in } \overline{\mathbb{F}}_2[X],$$

for the reason that the roots of

$$\Phi(X) = 1 + X^p + X^{2p} + \ldots + X^{(p-1)p} \in \mathbb{F}_2[X],$$

are exactly β^n for $n \in \mathbb{Z}_{p^2}^*$. Then, we set

$$S_k(X) \equiv \Phi(X)\pi(X) \pmod{X^{p^2} - 1}. \tag{6}$$

Because $\deg(S_k(X)) = \deg(\Phi(X)) + \deg(\pi(X)) < p^2$, it is apparent that $\pi(X)$ should be one of the following:

$$\pi(X) = 1;$$
$$\pi(X) = X^{v_1} + X^{v_2} + \ldots + X^{v_t};$$
$$\pi(X) = 1 + X^{v_1} + X^{v_2} + \ldots + X^{v_t};$$

where $1 \le t < p$ and $1 \le v_1 < v_2 < \ldots < v_t < p$. It is easy to see that, the exponent of each monomial in $\Phi(X)\pi(X)$ forms the set $\{lp : 0 \le l \le p - 1\}$ or $\{v_j + lp : 1 \le j \le t, 0 \le l \le p - 1\}$ or $\{lp, v_j + lp : 1 \le j \le t, 0 \le l \le p - 1\}$ for above different $\pi(X)$, respectively.

(i). If $\pi(X) = 1$, it is easy to see that by (4)–(6)

$$e(X) = \sum_{j=0}^{p-1} d_{b+j}^{(p^2)}(X) + \sum_{j \in \mathcal{N}} X^{jp},$$

which implies that $k = (p^2 - 1)/2$.

(ii). If $\pi(X) = X^{v_1} + X^{v_2} + \ldots + X^{v_t}$, let

$$\mathcal{I} = \{v_1, v_2, \ldots, v_t\}, \quad \mathcal{J} = \{1, 2, \ldots, p - 1\} \setminus \mathcal{I}$$

and let $z = |\mathcal{I} \cap \mathcal{Q}|$. This yields $|\mathcal{J} \cap \mathcal{Q}| = (p-1)/2 - z$, $|\mathcal{I} \cap \mathcal{N}| = t - z$ and $|\mathcal{J} \cap \mathcal{N}| = (p-1)/2 - t + z$. For $\mathcal{V}_v = \{v + \ell p : 0 \le \ell < p\}$, by Lemma 4 it can be derived that

$$e(X) = \sum_{v \in \mathcal{I} \cap \mathcal{Q}} \sum_{j \in \mathcal{V}_v \cap C_0} X^j + \sum_{v \in \mathcal{J} \cap \mathcal{Q}} \sum_{j \in \mathcal{V}_v \cap C_1} X^j$$
$$+ \sum_{v \in \mathcal{I} \cap \mathcal{N}} \sum_{j \in \mathcal{V}_v \cap C_0} X^j + \sum_{v \in \mathcal{J} \cap \mathcal{N}} \sum_{j \in \mathcal{V}_v \cap C_1} X^j + 1 + \sum_{j \in \mathcal{Q}} X^{jp},$$

which indicates that

$$k = z \cdot (p-1)/2 + ((p-1)/2 - z) \cdot (p+1)/2 + (t - z) \cdot (p+1)/2$$
$$+ ((p-1)/2 - t + z) \cdot (p-1)/2 + 1 + (p-1)/2$$
$$= (p^2 - 1)/2 + 1 + t - 2z.$$

It can be verified that $-(p-1)/2 \le t - 2z \le (p-1)/2$. Then $k \ge (p^2 - p)/2 + 1$.

(iii). Similarly, for $\pi(X) = 1 + X^{v_1} + X^{v_2} + \ldots + X^{v_t}$, it can be obtained that

$$e(X) = \sum_{v \in \mathcal{I} \cap \mathcal{Q}} \sum_{j \in \mathcal{V}_v \cap C_0} X^j + \sum_{v \in \mathcal{J} \cap \mathcal{Q}} \sum_{j \in \mathcal{V}_v \cap C_1} X^j$$
$$+ \sum_{v \in \mathcal{I} \cap \mathcal{N}} \sum_{j \in \mathcal{V}_v \cap C_0} X^j + \sum_{v \in \mathcal{J} \cap \mathcal{N}} \sum_{j \in \mathcal{V}_v \cap C_1} X^j + \sum_{j \in \mathcal{N}} X^{jp},$$

and $k = (p^2 - 1)/2 + t - 2z$. As in (ii), $k \geq (p^2 - p)/2$.

From the above, if $k < (p^2 - p)/2$, it is always true that $S_k(\beta^n) \neq 0$ for all $n \in \mathbb{Z}_{p^2}^*$.

Secondly, let $\theta = \beta^p$, by Lemmas 5 and 6, we get from Eq. (4) for $0 \leq i < p$

$$S_k(\beta^{ip}) = S_k(\theta^i) = e(\theta^i) + S(\theta^i)$$

$$= e(\theta^i) + \begin{cases} (p^2+1)/2, & \text{if } i = 0, \\ \omega \frac{p+1}{2} + (1+\omega)\frac{p-1}{2} + 1 + \frac{p-1}{2}, & \text{if } \left(\frac{i}{p}\right) = 1, \\ \omega \frac{p-1}{2} + (1+\omega)\frac{p+1}{2} + 1 + \frac{p-1}{2}, & \text{if } \left(\frac{i}{p}\right) = -1, \end{cases} \quad (7)$$

$$= \begin{cases} e(1) + 1, & \text{if } i = 0, \\ e(\theta^i) + 1 + \omega, & \text{if } \left(\frac{i}{p}\right) = 1, \\ e(\theta^i) + \omega, & \text{if } \left(\frac{i}{p}\right) = -1, \end{cases}$$

where $\omega = \sum_{n \in Q} \theta^n \in \mathbb{F}_4 \setminus \mathbb{F}_2$ and $\left(\frac{\cdot}{p}\right)$ is the Legendre symbol. In the following, we need to look for $e(X)$ with the smallest $wt(e(X))$ such that $e(1) = 1$, or $e(\theta^i) = 1 + \omega$ for $\left(\frac{i}{p}\right) = 1$, or $e(\theta^i) = \omega$ for $\left(\frac{i}{p}\right) = -1$. These play an important role in calculating the number of roots of the form β^{ip} $(0 \leq i < p)$ for $S_k(X)$.

If $e(X)$ with $1 \leq wt(e(X)) < (p-1)/2$, then $e(1) = wt(e(X))$ and $e(\theta^i) \notin \mathbb{F}_4$ for $1 \leq i < p$ by Lemma 7. Therefore, any monomial $e(X)$ (i.e., $wt(e(X)) = 1$) can be used to deduce $S_k(\beta^0) = 0$ but $S_k(\beta^{ip}) \neq 0$ for $1 \leq i < p$. Thus, by Eq. (2),

$$LC_{(p-3)/2}^{\mathbb{F}_2}((s_n)) = LC_1^{\mathbb{F}_2}((s_n)) = p^2 - 1.$$

Let $e(X)$ satisfy $wt(e(X)) = (p-1)/2$ and $e(X) \equiv \sum_{n \in \mathcal{N}} X^n \pmod{X^p - 1}$. Then, $e(1) = (p-1)/2$ and by Lemma 5

$$e(\theta^i) = \begin{cases} \sum_{n \in \mathcal{N}} \theta^{in} = \sum_{n \in \mathcal{N}} \theta^n = 1 + \omega, & \text{if } \left(\frac{i}{p}\right) = 1, \\ \sum_{n \in \mathcal{N}} \theta^{in} = \sum_{n \in Q} \theta^n = \omega, & \text{if } \left(\frac{i}{p}\right) = -1, \end{cases} \quad 1 \leq i < p,$$

which imply that $S_k(\beta^0) = (p+1)/2$ and $S_k(\beta^{ip}) = 0$ for $1 \leq i < p$ and hence

$$LC_{(p-1)/2}^{\mathbb{F}_2}((s_n)) = \begin{cases} p^2 - p + 1, & \text{if } p \equiv 5 \pmod 8, \\ p^2 - p, & \text{if } p \equiv 3 \pmod 8. \end{cases}$$

We note that $p \equiv 5 \pmod 8$ or $p \equiv 3 \pmod 8$ since 2 is a primitive root modulo p^2.

For the case as $p \equiv 5 \pmod 8$, we select $e(X)$ satisfying $wt(e(X)) = (p+1)/2$ and $e(X) \equiv 1 + \sum_{n \in Q} X^n \pmod{X^p - 1}$. Then, it can be derived that $S_k(\beta^{ip}) = 0$ for $0 \leq i < p$, and hence,

$$LC_{(p+1)/2}^{\mathbb{F}_2}((s_n)) = p^2 - p.$$

The second case is $k = (p^2 - p)/2$.

Now consider $k = (p^2 - p)/2$. From the above (iii), only cases where $\mathcal{I} = \mathcal{Q}$ are useful; in this case, $t = z = (p-1)/2$, and

$$e(X) = \sum_{v \in \mathcal{Q}} \sum_{j \in V_v \cap C_0} X^j + \sum_{v \in \mathcal{N}} \sum_{j \in V_v \cap C_1} X^j + \sum_{j \in \mathcal{N}} X^{jp},$$

then it is easy to verify that $S_k(\beta^n) = 0$ for all $n \in \mathbb{Z}_{p^2}^*$. It can be checked that by Lemmas 5 and 6

$$e(\beta^{ip}) = e(\theta^i) = \tfrac{p-1}{2} \sum_{v \in \mathcal{Q}} \theta^{iv} + \tfrac{p-1}{2} \sum_{v \in \mathcal{N}} \theta^{iv} + \tfrac{p-1}{2}$$

$$= \tfrac{p-1}{2} \left(\sum_{v \in \mathcal{Q}} \theta^{iv} + \sum_{v \in \mathcal{N}} \theta^{iv} \right) + \tfrac{p-1}{2}$$

$$= \tfrac{p-1}{2} + \tfrac{p-1}{2} = p - 1 = 0$$

for $1 \le i < p$ and $e(\beta^0) = e(1) = (p-1)/2$. Then from Eq. (7), $S_k(\beta^0) = (p+1)/2$ and $S_k(\beta^{ip}) \neq 0$ for $1 \le i < p$. Therefore,

$$LC_{(p^2-p)/2}^{\mathbb{F}_2}((s_n)) = p - \delta,$$

where $\delta = 1$ if $p \equiv 3 \pmod 8$ and $\delta = 0$ if $p \equiv 5 \pmod 8$.

Finally, if $k = (p^2 - 1)/2$, the 1-sequence can be derived after changing the k many 0's in (s_n). Clearly, the linear complexity of 1-sequence is 1. Similarly, if $k > (p^2 - 1)/2$, the 0-sequence can be obtained, and the linear complexity of 0-sequence is 0. This completes the proof.   □

3.2   Two Examples

Here, we give two examples to illustrate the correctness of our main result, both of which have been verified by Magma program.

Example 1. Let $p = 3, f = 2$ and $e = 1$. We note that 2 is a primitive root modulo $p^2 = 9$. Then, one period of the sequence (s_n) is $[1, 1, 1, 1, 1, 0, 0, 0, 0]$ with the period of 9. Note that k-error linear complexity of a sequence is the smallest linear complexity that can be obtained by changing at most k terms of the sequence per period. The data are listed in the Table 1. In Table 1, k denotes the number of errors, $(s_n)'_k$ denotes a sequence that reach the smallest linear complexity among all the sequences generated from (s_n) by changing exactly k items, $LC((s_n)'_k)$ denotes the linear complexity of the sequence $(s_n)'_k$, and $LC_k^{\mathbb{F}_2}((s_n))$ denotes the k-error linear complexity of the sequence (s_n). The elements of $(s_n)'_k$ in red denotes the error positions comparing with (s_n).

It is clear that the results listed in Table 1 are consistent with the results described in Theorem 1 where $p = 3$.

Table 1. The k-error linear complexity of (s_n) with $p = 3$

k	$LC((s_n)'_k)$	$(s_n)'_k$	$LC_k^{\mathbb{F}_2}((s_n))$
0	9	[1, 1, 1, 1, 1, 0, 0, 0, 0]	9
1	6	[1, 1, 0, 1, 1, 0, 0, 0, 0]	6
2	7	[0, 0, 1, 1, 1, 0, 0, 0, 0]	6
3	2	[1, 1, 0, 1, 1, 0, 1, 1, 0]	2
4	1	[1, 1, 1, 1, 1, 1, 1, 1, 1]	1
5	0	[0, 0, 0, 0, 0, 0, 0, 0, 0]	0

Example 2. Let $p = 5, f = 2$ and $e = 2$. We note that 2 is a primitive root modulo $p^2 = 25$. Then, one period of the sequence (s_n) is [1, 1, 1, 0, 1, 1, 0, 0, 1, 1, 0, 0, 0, 0, 0, 0, 1, 1, 0, 0, 1, 1, 0, 1, 1] with the period of 25. As discussed in Example 1., the data are listed in Table 2. The meanings of the symbols k, $(s_n)'_k$, $LC((s_n)'_k)$ and $LC_k^{\mathbb{F}_2}((s_n))$ are the same as in Table 1.

Table 2. The k-error linear complexity of (s_n) with $p = 5$

k	$LC((s_n)'_k)$	$(s_n)'_k$	$LC_k^{\mathbb{F}_2}((s_n))$
0	25	[1,1,1,0,1,1,0,0,1,1,0,0,0,0,0,0,1,1,0,0,1,1,0,1,1]	25
1	24	[0,1,1,0,1,1,0,0,1,1,0,0,0,0,0,0,1,1,0,0,1,1,0,1,1]	24
2	21	[1,1,0,1,1,1,0,0,1,1,0,0,0,0,0,0,1,1,0,0,1,1,0,1,1]	21
3	20	[0,0,1,0,0,1,0,0,1,1,0,0,0,0,0,0,1,1,0,0,1,1,0,1,1]	20
4	21	[0,1,0,1,1,0,0,0,1,1,0,0,0,0,0,0,1,1,0,0,1,1,0,1,1]	20
5	20	[0,0,0,0,0,1,0,1,1,1,0,0,0,0,0,0,1,1,0,0,1,1,0,1,1]	20
6	21	[0,0,0,1,1,0,1,0,1,1,0,0,0,0,0,0,1,1,0,0,1,1,0,1,1]	20
7	20	[0,0,0,1,0,1,0,1,0,1,0,0,0,0,0,0,1,1,0,0,1,1,0,1,1]	20
8	21	[0,0,0,1,0,0,1,0,1,0,0,0,0,0,0,0,1,1,0,0,1,1,0,1,1]	20
9	20	[0,0,0,1,0,0,0,1,0,1,1,0,0,0,0,0,1,1,0,0,1,1,0,1,1]	20
10	5	[1,1,0,0,1,1,1,0,0,1,1,1,0,0,1,1,1,0,0,1,1,1,0,0,1]	5

It is easy to verify the 12-error and 13-error linear complexity of the sequence (s_n) with the period of 25, since it can result in the 1-sequence and 0-sequence, respectively. Obviously, the results listed in Table 2 are consistent with the results described in Theorem 1 where $p = 5$.

4   Conclusions

For $f = 2$, we have determined the values of the k-error linear complexity of a Zeng-Cai-Tang-Yang generalized cyclotomic binary sequence of period p^2 published recently on the journal Designs, Codes and Cryptography. Results suggest that such sequences possess very large linear complexity and the linear complexity does not decrease greatly by changing a few terms. However, for the case $f = 2^r(r > 1)$ and other even f, the discussion becomes more complicated and it seems that the way used in this paper does not work well without more knowledge. This will be our next work.

References

1. Chen, Z.: Trace representation and linear complexity of binary sequences derived from Fermat quotients. Sci. China Inf. Sci. **57**(11), 1–10 (2014)
2. Chen, Z., Du, X.: On the linear complexity of binary threshold sequences derived from Fermat quotients. Des. Codes Cryptogr. **67**(3), 317–323 (2013)
3. Chen, Z., Gómez-Pérez, D.: Linear complexity of binary sequences derived from polynomial quotients. In: Helleseth, T., Jedwab, J. (eds.) SETA 2012. LNCS, vol. 7280, pp. 181–189. Springer, Heidelberg (2012). https://doi.org/10.1007/978-3-642-30615-0_17
4. Chen Z., Niu Z., Wu C.: On the k-error linear complexity of binary sequences derived from polynomial quotients. Sci. China Inf. Sci. **58**(9), 092107:1–092107:15 (2015)
5. Chen, Z., Ostafe, A., Winterhof, A.: Structure of pseudorandom numbers derived from Fermat quotients. In: Hasan, M.A., Helleseth, T. (eds.) WAIFI 2010. LNCS, vol. 6087, pp. 73–85. Springer, Heidelberg (2010). https://doi.org/10.1007/978-3-642-13797-6_6
6. Chung, J., Yang, K.: k-fold cyclotomy and its application to frequency-hopping sequences. IEEE Trans. Inf. Theory. **57**(4), 2306–2317 (2011)
7. Ding, C.: Binary cyclotomic generators. In: Preneel, B. (ed.) FSE 1994. LNCS, vol. 1008, pp. 29–60. Springer, Heidelberg (1995). https://doi.org/10.1007/3-540-60590-8_4
8. Cusick, T., Ding, C., Renvall, A.: Stream Ciphers and Number Theory. Gulf Professional Publishing, Houston (2004)
9. Ding, C., Helleseth, T.: New generalized cyclotomy and its application. Finite Fields Appl. **4**(2), 140–166 (1998)
10. Ding, C., Helleseth, T., Lam, K.: Several classes of binary sequences with three-level autocorrelation. IEEE Trans. Inf. Theory **45**(7), 2606–2612 (1999)
11. Ding, C., Hesseseth, T., Shan, W.: On the linear complexity of Legendre sequences. IEEE Trans. Inf. Theory **44**(3), 1276–1278 (1998)
12. Ding, C., Xiao, G., Shan, W.: The Stability Theory of Stream Ciphers. Springer, Berlin (1991). https://doi.org/10.1007/3-540-54973-0
13. Gauss, C.: Disquisitiones Arithmeticae, 1801; English translation: Yale University Press, New Haven (1966). Reprinted by Springer, Berlin (1986)
14. Golomb, S., Gong, G.: Signal Design for Good Correlation: for Wireless Communication, Cryptography, and Radar. Cambridge University Press, Cambridge (2005)
15. Gómez-Pérez, D., Winterhof, A.: Multiplicative character sums of Fermat quotients and pseudorandom sequences. Period. Math. Hungar. **64**(2), 161–168 (2012)
16. Kim, J., Song, H.: On the linear complexity of Hall's sextic residue sequences. IEEE Trans. Inf. Theory **47**(5), 2094–2096 (2001)
17. Ostafe, A., Shparlinski, I.: Pseudorandomness and dynamics of Fermat quotients. SIAM J. Discr. Math. **25**(1), 50–71 (2011)

18. Stamp, M., Martin, C.: An algorithm for the k-error linear complexity of binary sequences with period 2^n. IEEE Trans. Inform. Theory **39**(4), 1398–1401 (1993)
19. Sun, Y., Ren, W.: Linear complexity of binary sequences based on two-fold cyclotomy. J. Sichuan Univ. (Nat. Sci. Edn.) **52**(4), 748–754 (2015). (in chinese)
20. Whiteman, A.: A family of difference sets. Illinois J. Math. **1**, 107–121 (1962)
21. Xiao, Z., Zeng, X., Li, C., Helleseth, T.: New generalized cyclotomic binary sequences of period p^2. Des. Codes Crypt. **86**(7), 1483–1497 (2018)
22. Zeng, X., Cai, H., Tang, X., Yang, Y.: Optimal frequency hopping sequences of odd length. IEEE Trans. Inf. Theory **59**(5), 3237–3248 (2013)

Novel Analysis of Stream Cipher Combing LFSR and FCSR

Lihua Dong[1(✉)], Jie Wang[1], and Shuo Zhang[2]

[1] Xidian University, Xi'an 710071, China
lih_dong@mail.xidian.edu.cn
[2] No. 722 Research Institute of CSIC, Wuhan 430205, China

Abstract. At Indocrypt'2002, a new pseudorandom generator based on linear feedback shift register (LFSR) and feedback with carry shift registers (FCSR) was proposed by Arnault. And at Indocrypt'2004, Bin Zhang et al. showed that the self-synchronizing stream cipher constructed by Arnault's pseudorandom generator was extremely weak against a chosen ciphertext attack. In this paper, we show that the synchronizing stream cipher constructed by Arnault's pseudorandom generator bear good immunities to the attack proposed by Bin Zhang et al., but can not resist the LFSRization attack proposed by Martin Hell and Thomas Johansson. Then we propose a modification to the synchronizing stream cipher, and show that it inherits of the nice statistical properties of the pseudorandom generator and provided a resistant to the known attacks. The new architecture still has high throughput and low implementation cost.

Keywords: Stream cipher · FCSR · Chosen ciphertext attack
VFCSR · Ring FCSR

1 Introduction

Stream ciphers are an important class of private-key encryption algorithms which are extremely fast and usually have very minimal memory and hardware source requirements. Therefore, stream ciphers are widely used in different areas of national economy: digital signal processing, entertainment, music and graphics composition, simulation and testing, equation-solving, cryptography devices, etc. [1]. However, the objective for designing a perfect stream cipher that might become suitable for widespread adoption has been far from coming true.

There are different methods to develop keystream generators, but one of the most popular is based on the shift register. Previously, the designers widely used LFSR as a basic component of such generators [2,3]. Yet, over the years, few proposals have withstood cryptanalysis. Many of the attacks exploit the mathematical structure of LFSR. To avoid these pitfalls, alternative constructions have been proposed recently. One of these suggestions is to replace LFSR with FCSR.

© Springer Nature Singapore Pte Ltd. 2018
F. Li et al. (Eds.): FCS 2018, CCIS 879, pp. 23–38, 2018.
https://doi.org/10.1007/978-981-13-3095-7_3

Based on the fact that an FCSR can be combined with a linear component, and an LFSR has to be combined with a nonlinear component, a pseudorandom generator and a self- synchronizing stream cipher were proposed in 2002, combining an LFSR and an FCSR [4]. The new architecture was very fast and had a low implementation cost. However, in [5], Zhang et al. showed that such a simple design is extremely weak under a chosen ciphertext attack. By the 60-bit chosen ciphertext, they can recover the secret keys in 1 s on a Pentium 4 processor. Thus, they suggested that this cipher should not be used in practice.

In this paper, we considered the security of the synchronizing stream cipher composed of the pseudorandom generator proposed by Arnault [4]. We showed that the synchronizing stream cipher bore good immunities to the attack proposed by Bin Zhang et al., but could not resist the LFSRization attack proposed by Hell and Johansson [6]. The weakness used in the LFSRization attack is that the carries are driven by the content of a single cell in a Galois FCSR. To prevent the weakness, generic FCSR called ring FCSR is presented in [7]. Another approach is Vectorial FCSR (VFCSR) proposed in [8]. In 2012, Thierry P. Berger and Marine Minier showed that Vectorial FCSRs used in Galois mode stay sensitive to the LFSRization attack of FCSRs and the hardware implementations of V-FCSRs in Galois mode were less efficient than those based on FCSRs in ring mode.

In this paper, we replace the FCSR in the synchronizing stream cipher given in [7] by the ring FCSR. We show that the modification inherits of the nice statistical properties of the pseudorandom generator and provide a resistant to the known attacks. And the new architecture is still very fast and has a low implementation cost also.

The paper is organized as follows. In Sect. 2, a brief description of the self-synchronizing stream cipher and synchronous stream ciphers constructed by the Arnault's pseudorandom generator is given. Then an introduction to the chosen cipher attack on the self-synchronous stream ciphers is presented in Sect. 3. The security of the synchronizing stream cipher is analyzed in Sect. 4. A modification of the synchronizing stream cipher is given in Sect. 5, and the security analysis is also given in this section. Finally, some conclusions are given in Sect. 6.

2   Recalling the Synchronizing Stream Cipher and Self-synchronous Stream Ciphers

In this section, some backgrounds on the FCSR are first reviewed. And a brief description of the self-synchronizing stream cipher and the synchronizing stream cipher is given.

2.1   FCSR

FCSR introduced by Goresky and Klapper in [9,10] is a binary register, shares many of good properties of classical LFSRs, except that it performs operations with carries. FCSR also has both Fibonacci and Galois structures [11]. The

Galois architecture is more efficient due to the parallel computation of feedbacks. In [7], a new structure called ring FCSR gradually grabs researchers' attention. An FCSR can be used to generate a binary sequence $S=\{s_i\}_{i\geq0}$ which corresponding to a 2-adic integer. Here the so called 2-adic integer is a formal power series $S(2) = \sum_{i=0}^{\infty} s_i 2^i$ with $s_i \in \{0,1\}$ The set of 2-adic integers is denoted as Z_2. The addition and multiplication in Z_2 is done according to $2^i+2^i=2^{i+1}$ for all $i \geq 0$, i.e. taking the carry to the higher order term.

The following lemmas give a complete characterization of eventually periodic 2-adic binary sequences in terms of 2-adic integers.

Lemma 1 [9]. *Let $S(2) = \sum_{i=0}^{\infty} s_i 2^i$ be the 2-adic integer corresponding to a binary sequence $S=\{s_i\}_{i\geq0}$. S is eventually periodic if and only if there exists two integers p and q in Z such that $S_2=p/q$ with q odd. Further, S is strictly periodic if and only if $pq \leq 0$ and $|p| \leq |q|$.*

Lemma 2 [9]. *If sequence $S=s_0, s_1 \ldots s_2, \ldots$ is a periodic binary sequence, and $-p/q$ is the fraction in lowest terms whose 2-adic expansion agrees with the sequence S, then the 2-adic complexity $\Phi(S)$ of S is the real number $log2(max(p,q))$. If S is strictly periodic with minimal period $T \geq 2$, then*

$$\Phi(S) = log_2(q) = log_2((2^T - 1)/gcd(S^T(2), 2^T - 1)) \tag{1}$$

Lemma 3 [9]. *Let S be an eventually periodic binary sequence, $S(2)=p/q$, with q odd and p and q co-prime, be the corresponding 2-adic number in its rational representation. The period of S is the order of 2 modulo q, i.e., the smallest integer t such that $2^t \equiv 1(mod\ q)$.*

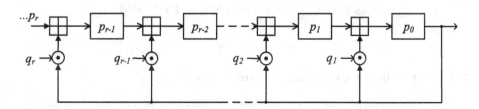

Fig. 1. Galois representation of a modified FCSR.

A slight modification of the FCSR leads to the division of a 2-adic number by an integer, which is shown in the above Fig. 1. Here $\boxplus$ denotes the addition with carry, i.e. the output of a $\boxplus$ b is $a \oplus b \oplus c_{n-1}$ and the carry is $c_n = ab \oplus ac_{n-1} \oplus bc_{n-1}$. $\odot$ is the binary multiplication. As in [5], we always assume $p = \sum_{i=0}^{r} p_i 2^i + p_{r+1} 2^{r+1} + \ldots \geq 0$ and $q = 1 - 2d = 1 - \sum_{i=1}^{r} q_i 2^i$ with p_i and $q_i \in \{0,1\}$, r is the bit length of d, and the binary expansion of d is $d = \sum_{i=0}^{r-1} d_i 2^i$. Put $I_d=\{i\ |0 \leq i \leq r$-2 and $d_i=1\}$ and call the cells of the carry register in the set I_d as active cells. Note that the active cells are the ones in the interval $0 \leq i \leq r$-2, and $d_{r-1}=1$ always hold. The number of the active cells l plus one is the Hamming weight of d. We write the contents of carry register C at time t as $c(t) = (c_0(t),\ldots,c_{r-2}(t))$ and the content of main register M with r binary memories as $m(t) = (m_0(t),\ldots,m_{r-1}(t))$. The contents at time t of the individual cells in the carry register C and main register M are denoted as $c_i(t)$ and $m_i(t)$ respectively. Then the FCSR fulfills the 2-adic division of p/q.

At time $t+1$, the state $(m(t+1), c(t+1))$ is updated in the following way:

1. for $0 \leq i \leq r\text{-}2$
   if $i \notin I_d$, $m_i(t+1) := m_{i+1}(t)$
   if $i \in I_d$, $m_i(t+1) := m_{i+1}(t)+c_i(t)+m_0(t)$
   $\quad\quad c_i(t+1) := m_{i+1}(t)c_i(t)+c_i(t)m_0(t)+m_0(t)m_{i+1}(t)$
2. for $i=r\text{-}1$, $m_{r-1}(t+1) := m_r(t)+q_r m_0(t)$

where $+$ denotes the bitwise XOR, and the content of $m_r(t)$ is the external input.

Similarly, a slight modification of the Galois representation of a LFSR leads to the division of a series by a polynomial, which is shown in Fig. 2 [5]. Here $\oplus$ and $\odot$ denote the binary addition and the binary multiplication respectively. And the input of the circuit is $S(x) = \sum_{i=0}^{\infty} s_i x^i$ and the output is $S'(x) = S(x)/f(x)$ with $f(x) = 1 + \sum_{i=0}^{r} f_i x^i$.

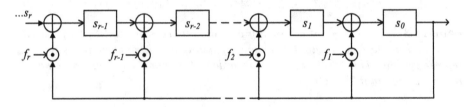

Fig. 2. Galois representation of a modified LFSR.

2.2 The Self-synchronizing Stream Cipher

The self-synchronizing stream cipher given in [4] is a concatenation of one slightly modified LFSR and one slightly modified FCSR as shown in Fig. 3.

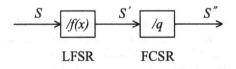

Fig. 3. The self-synchronizing stream cipher.

Let S of the length less than k be the message to be encrypted, and $S(x) = \sum_{i=0}^{l} s_i x^i$, $l < k$, be the corresponding formal power series. The connection polynomial $f(x)$ of the LFSR and the connection integer q of the FCSR are the secret parameters used in the cipher. And $f(x)$ is a primitive polynomial of degree k, while q of the size k, i.e. $q \approx 2^k$, is a negative prime. Initialize LFSR and FCSR randomly, then the encryption scheme is:

1. Compute $S'(x) = S(x)/f(x)$ by the LFSR divisor-box.
2. Convert $S'(x)$ into the 2-adic integer $S'(2)$.
3. Compute the ciphertext $S''(2) = S'(2)/q$ by the FCSR divisor-box.
   Upon decrypting, initialize all the LFSR and FCSR cells (including the carries) to be zero. The corresponding decryption scheme is:
1. Compute $S'(2) = qS''(2)$.
2. Convert $S'(2)$ into the formal power series $S'(x)$.
3. Compute the plaintext S by $S(x) = f(x)S'(x)$.

It is shown in [4] that this generator has high throughput and low implementation cost. However, this cipher can be attacked by a chosen ciphertext attack as shown in [5]. The attack is introduced in the following Sect. 3.

2.3   The Synchronizing Stream Cipher

The structure of the synchronizing stream cipher as shown in Fig. 4 is still based on the pseudorandom generator proposed by Arnault which is a concatenation of a LFSR and a slightly modified FCSR. The difference with the self-synchronizing stream cipher is that

1. The circuit for generating the m-sequence S is not the modification one, that is the circuit is self-feedback and no outside input.
2. The secret parameter of the synchronizing stream cipher is just the initial state of the LFSR.
3. The public parameters of the synchronizing stream cipher are the primitive feedback polynomial $f(x)$ of the LFSR and the prime connection integer q of the FCSR.

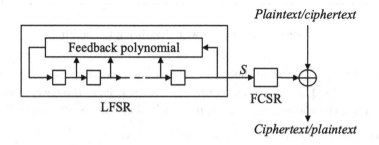

Fig. 4. Synchronizing stream cipher.

The encryption/decryption scheme is:

1. Generate the m-sequence S by the LFSR.
2. Feed the output m-sequence S into the modified FCSR divisor-box.
3. Compute the output $S(2)/q$ by the modified FCSR divisor-box.
4. The output S' of the modified FCSR divisor-box is the key stream.
5. XOR the key stream with the plaintext/ciphertext.

Here the degree k of the primitive connection polynomial $f(x)$ of the LFSR is a prime such that $T = 2^k$-1 is also a prime and the negative prime connection integer q of size k, i.e. $q \approx 2^k$, is chosen to satisfy the following conditions [4]:

1. $T = 2^k$-1 is co-prime to $|q|$-1.
2. The order of 2 modulo q is exactly $|q|$-1.

3   The Chosen Ciphertext Attack

In [5], the decrypt circuit is composed by the two circuits depicted in Figs. 5 and 6 proposed to fulfill the multiplication by q and $f(x)$, respectively.

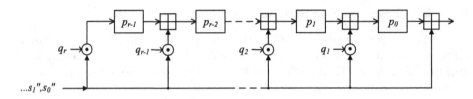

Fig. 5. Multiplication circuit with q being the multiplier.

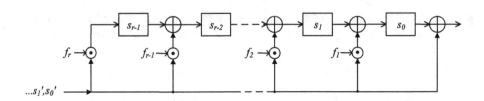

Fig. 6. Multiplication circuit with $f(x)$ being the multiplier.

Let $S''(2) = \sum_{i=0}^{\infty} s_i'' 2^i$ be the 2-adic integer corresponding to the ciphertext sequence $S'' = \{s_i''\}_{i \geq 0}$. Upon decrypting, let all the cells in the decrypt circuits be zero. Then the computation of the first multiplication $qS''(2)$ is as follows

$$
\begin{aligned}
qS''(2) &= (s_0'' + s_1'' 2 + s_2'' 2^2 + \ldots)(1 - q_1 2 + q_2 2^2 - \ldots - q_k 2^k) \\
&= -(s_0'' + s_1'' 2 + s_2'' 2^2 + \ldots)(q_1 2 + q_2 2^2 + \ldots + q_k 2^k - 1) \\
&= -(s_0'' + s_1'' 2 + s_2'' 2^2 + \ldots)(q_1 2 + q_2 2^2 + \ldots + q_k 2^k) + (s_0'' + s_1'' 2 + s_2'' 2^2 + \ldots)
\end{aligned}
$$

$$(2)$$

A special ciphertext with the following form is chosen in [5],

$$\underbrace{(*, *, \ldots, *,}_{A} \underbrace{1, 1, \ldots, 1, 1)}_{B} \tag{3}$$

Where A is a randomly chosen binary prefix of certain length and B is an all-1 string of certain length. Feed the chosen ciphertext into the multiplication circuit shown in Fig. 5, then

$$
\begin{aligned}
S'(2) &= (s_0'' + s_1''2 + s_2''2^2 + \ldots + s_l''2^l + 1.2^{l+1} + 1.2^{l+2} + \ldots)q \\
&= (s_0'' + s_1''2 + s_2''2^2 + \ldots + s_l''2^l)q + (1.2^{l+1} + 1.2^{l+2} + \ldots)q \\
&= (s_0'' + s_1''2 + s_2''2^2 + \ldots + s_l''2^l)q + \frac{2^{l+1}}{1-2}q \\
&= (s_0'' + s_1''2 + s_2''2^2 + \ldots + s_l''2^l)q + 2^{l+1}(-q)
\end{aligned}
\tag{4}
$$

Then feed the corresponding polynomial $S'(x)$ into the multiplication circuit 6. The final output of the circuit is the decrypted message $f(x)S'(x)$. Since the secret q is a negative prime, the decrypted message $f(x)S'(x)$ is of finite length. Thus, the decrypted message $f(x)S'(x)$ can be factored [5]. After factoring, both $f(x)$ and $S'(x)$ can be obtained. Keeping in mind that $S'(x)$ is the polynomial corresponding to the 2-adic integer $(s_0'' + s_1''2 + s_2''2^2 + \ldots + s_l''2^l)q + 2^{l+1}(-q)$. Therefore, the secret q can be retrieved by factoring the integer. A full description of the attack is as follows.

1. Choose a string as shown in (2) and feed it into the decryption circuits.

2. Convert the decrypted message into polynomial form and factor it to get $f(x)$ and the size less than k be the message to be encrypted.

3. Transform $S'(x)$ into the integer form and factor the integer to recover q.

4   The Security Analysis of the Synchronizing Stream Ciphers

So far, the security of the self-synchronizing stream ciphers given in [4] is just endangered by the chosen ciphertext attack presented by [5]. In this section, we show that the synchronizing stream cipher provides a resistant to the attacks similar to that given in [5], but cannot provide a resistant to the M. Hell and T. Johansson's real-time cryptanalysis [6].

4.1   Chosen Plaintext Attack on the Synchronizing Stream Ciphers

The reason that the chosen ciphertext attack on the self-synchronizing stream ciphers works well is mainly due to the fact that once selecting the special ciphertext $(*,*,\ldots, *,1,1\ldots,1,1)$, the decrypted message $f(x)S'(x)$ is of finite length, which makes it is possible to factor $f(x)S'(x))$. Then the secret parameters used in the cipher including the connection polynomial $f(x)$ of the LFSR and the connection integer q of the FCSR can be determined. After obtaining the secret parameters, the corresponding plaintext can be obtained by the decrypted circuit.

Nevertheless, for the synchronizing stream cipher, 2-adic integer corresponding to the output key stream sequence S' is $S'(2) = S(2)/q = p'/qq'$. This is an l-sequence. In this case, we cannot select a special key stream $(*,*,\ldots,*,1,1\ldots,1,1)$ such that the length of "1,1,...,1,1" is infinite. While the length of "1,1,...,1,1" is m, and m is finite, then

$$
\begin{aligned}
S'(2) &= (s_0'' + s_1''2 + s_2''2^2 + \ldots + s_l''2^l + 1.2^{l+1} + 1.2^{l+2} + \ldots + 1.2^{l+m})q \\
&= (s_0'' + s_1''2 + s_2''2^2 + \ldots + s_l''2^l)q + (1.2^{l+1} + 1.2^{l+2} + \ldots + 1.2^{l+m})q \\
&= (s_0'' + s_1''2 + s_2''2^2 + \ldots + s_l''2^l)q + \frac{2^{l+1} - 2^{l+m+1}}{1 - 2}q \\
&= (s_0'' + s_1''2 + s_2''2^2 + \ldots + s_l''2^l)q + (2^{l+m+1} - 2^{l+m})q
\end{aligned}
$$

$$(5)$$

Since the secret q is a negative prime, the 2-adic integer $S'(2)$ is of infinite length. Thus, the decrypted message $f(x)S'(x)$ is of infinite length. The attack will not work for the new construction.

4.2   M. Hell and T. Johansson's Real-Time Cryptanalysis

The Threat to the F-FCSR. F. Arnault and T. P. Berger proposed to add a linear filter to FCSR and made a stream cipher proposal, called F-FCSR [12]. The hardware-oriented version F-FCSR-H v2 was selected as one of the four final hardware-oriented stream cipher candidates in the eSTREAM portfolio [13]. Unfortunately, at ASIACRYPT 2008, M. Hell and T. Johansson presented a real time attack on the F-FCSR stream cipher family by using the bias in the carry cells of the FCSR. Recently, Haixin Song et al. proved in theory that the probability distribution of the carry cells of F-FCSR-H v2 and F-FCSR-H v3 is not uniform, which provides a theoretical support to M.Hell and T.Johansson's cryptanalysis of F-FCSR-H [14].

The main observation of the M.Hell and T.Johansson's cryptanalysis of F-FCSR-H is that every time the feedback bit is zero: all cells in carry vector C that are zero must remain zero, whereas those with value one has a 50% chance of becoming zero. So, a zero feedback bit at time t gives a carries vector at time $t + 1$ of roughly half the weight compared to time t. The all zero feedback sequence can appear if the main register input to the last carry addition is the all one sequence and start with setting the carry bit to one.

$$EventEzero : C(t) = C(t + 1) = \ldots = C(t + 19) = (0, 0, \ldots, 0, 1, 0). \quad (6)$$

When the event Ezero happens, there would be 20 consecutive zeros in the feedback and that the carry would have remained constant for 20 cycles. It need about $log_2 82$ zeros in the feedback to push the weight of carry vector C to 1 and an additional 19 zeros in the feedback to keep carry vector C constant for 20 cycles. Assuming a uniform distribution on the feedback bits, this would lead to a probability of very roughly 2^{-26} for the event Ezero to happen.

Assuming that event Ezero occurs, the remaining part is to recover the main register from the given keystream bytes $z(t), z(t+1), , z(t+19)$. At the time t, the contents of the main register and carry register are

$$(M, C)(t) = (xx...xx011...1100, 000...0010) \tag{7}$$

Here, "x" represents unknown element, the length of the string "11...11" is 16. And the state is updated as $(M, C)(t+1) = (xx...xx011...1100, 000...0010)$. Here the length of the string "11...11" is 15. $(M, C)(t+2)=(xx...xx011...1100, 000...0010)$. Here the length of the string "11...11" is 14.

$$\begin{aligned}
&..\\
(M,C)(t+15) &= (xxxxxxxx...xx0100, 000...0010)\\
(M,C)(t+16) &= (xxxxxxxx...xxx000, 000...0010)\\
(M,C)(t+17) &= (\ xxxxxxxx...xxxx10, 000...0010)\\
(M,C)(t+18) &= (\ xxxxxxxx...xxxxx1, 000...0010)\\
(M,C)(t+19) &= (\ xxxxxxxx...xxxxxx, ??????????)
\end{aligned}$$

This will lead to a linear system of equations with 160 equations in 160 unknowns. And this could basically be solved through Gaussian elimination, costing something like 1603 operations. The detail analysis can be seen in [6].

The Threat to the Synchronizing Stream Ciphers. In the synchronizing stream cipher, similar to the theorem 1 and theorem 3 given in [14], we have:

Proposition 1. *The active carry cell sequence $(c_{jk}(0), c_{jk}(1),...)$ of the FCSR in the synchronizing stream cipher is still a homogeneous Markov chain, which satisfies*

$$prob(c_{jk}(t+1) = a|c_{jk}(t) = b) = \begin{cases} 3/4 & \text{if } a \oplus b=0 \\ 1/4 & \text{if } a \oplus b=1 \end{cases}, where\ a, b \in \{0,1\}. \tag{8}$$

Proof. First for the active carry cell sequence $(c_{jk}(0), c_{jk}(1),...)$, we have

$$c_{jk}(t+1) = m_0(t)c_{jk}(t) \oplus m_{jk}(t)c_{jk}(t) \oplus m_0(t)m_{jk}(t). \tag{9}$$

This means that the state c_{jk} at time $t+1$ only depends on the states m_0, m_{jk} and c_{jk} at time t.

And we know that the input of the synchronizing stream cipher is an m-equence. According to the update function of the synchronizing stream cipher, the main register cells of the synchronizing stream cipher are independent and uniformly distributed binary random variables. Thus m_0, m_{jk} are independent of c_{jk}, and the sequence $(c_{jk}(0), c_{jk}(1),...)$ is a Markov chain.

1. If $c_{jk}(t) = b = 0$, then $c_{jk}(t+1) = m_0(t)m_{jk}(t)$.
   And $prob(c_{jk}(t+1) = 1|c_{jk}(t)=b) = 1/4$, $prob(c_{jk}(t+1) = 0$
   $c_{jk}(t) = b) = 3/4$.

2. If $c_{jk}(t) = b = 1$, then $c_{jk}(t+1) = m_0(t) \oplus m_{jk}(t) \oplus m_0(t)m_{jk}(t)$.
   And $prob(c_{jk}(t+1) = 0|c_{jk}(t) = b) = 1/4$, $prob(c_{jk}(t + 1) = 1$
   $c_{jk}(t) = b) = 3/4$

Therefore,

$$prob(c_{jk}(t+1) = a|c_{jk}(t) = b) = \begin{cases} 3/4 & \text{if a} \oplus \text{b=0} \\ 1/4 & \text{if a} \oplus \text{b=1} \end{cases}, where\ a, b \in \{0, 1\}. \quad (10)$$

The proof is finished.

Proposition 2. *The probability of the homogeneous Markov chain* $(c_{j1}(0),$ $c_{j2}(1),\dots)$ *to be zero for l consecutive clocks is:*

$$prob(c_{jk}(t) = 0, c_{jk}(t + 1) = 0, \dots, c_{jk}(t + l - 1) = 0) = \frac{1}{2}(\frac{3}{4})^{l-1} \quad (11)$$

Proof. If $l = 1$, $prob(c_{jk}(t) = 0) = 1/2$, the proposition holds.
   Suppose the proposition holds for l-1 consecutive clocks, then

$$prob(c_{jk}(t) = 0, c_{jk}(t + 1) = 0, \dots, c_{jk}(t + l - 1) = 0)$$
$$= prob(c_{jk}(t + l - 1) = 0|c_{jk}(t) = 0, c_{jk}(t + 1) = 0, \dots, c_{jk}(t + l - 2) = 0)$$
$$\times\ prob(c_{jk}(t) = 0, c_{jk}(t + 1) = 0, \dots, c_{jk}(t + l - 2) = 0)$$
$$\quad (12)$$

Since $(c_{j1}(0), c_{j2}(1), \dots)$ is a homogeneous Markov chain, we have

$$prob(c_{jk}(t) = 0, c_{jk}(t + 1) = 0, \dots, c_{jk}(t + l - 1) = 0$$
$$= prob(c_{jk}(t + l - 1) = 0|c_{jk}(t + l - 2) = 0) \quad (13)$$
$$\times\ prob(c_{jk}(t) = 0, c_{jk}(t + 1) = 0, \dots, c_{jk}(t + l - 2) = 0)$$

By the Proposition 1 and the inductive hypothesis

$$prob(c_{jk}(t) = 0, c_{jk}(t+1) = 0, \dots, c_{jk}(t+l-1) = 0) = 3/4 \cdot 1/2 \cdot 3/4^{l-2} = \frac{1}{2}(\frac{3}{4})^{l-1}$$
$$\quad (14)$$

The proof is completed.
   This shows that the output sequence of a single carry cell of FCSR in the synchronizing stream ciphers has poor randomness, and it can be distinguished from an independent and uniformly distributed binary random sequence.
   So the bias in the carry cells of the FCSR can't be avoided. The event Ezero has to occur. Thus the synchronizing stream ciphers can't against the M. Hell and T. Johansson's attack.

5   A Modification of the Synchronizing Stream Cipher

In this section, to explore more possibilities of the application for FSCR in key stream generators, we proposed a modification of the synchronizing stream cipher given in [7] by a ring FCSR. Theoretical analysis and practical verification show that the modification is considered reasonable. And the most importance is the attacks introduced in [6] are thus totally discarded when this new mode is used.

A ring FCSR is a new FCSR representation given in [7] by Arnault et al. as the respondence to LFSRization of FCSR. The ring structure can be viewed as a generalization of the Fibonacci and Galois representations. In a ring FCSR, any binary cell can be used as a feedback bit for any other cell and it has multiple feedback functions with different inputs. An example of a ring FCSR is shown in Fig. 7.

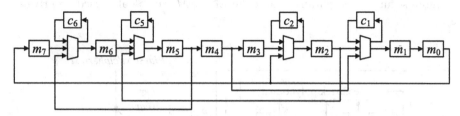

Fig. 7. An example of a ring FCSR (q = -347).

Figure 7 can be described using the following transition matrix A (with q = -347):

$$A = \begin{bmatrix} 0\,1\,0\,0\,0\,0\,0\,0 \\ 0\,0\,1\,0\,1\,0\,0\,0 \\ 1\,0\,0\,1\,0\,0\,0\,0 \\ 0\,0\,0\,0\,1\,0\,0\,0 \\ 0\,0\,0\,0\,0\,1\,0\,0 \\ 0\,0\,1\,0\,0\,0\,1\,0 \\ 0\,0\,0\,0\,0\,1\,0\,1 \\ 1\,0\,0\,0\,0\,0\,0\,0 \end{bmatrix} \tag{15}$$

$a_{i,j}$ is the element at $i - th$ row and $j - th$ column, $m_i(m_j)$represents the $i - th(j - th)$ main register of the ring FCSR:

$$A = (a_{i,j})_{0 \le i,j \le n} with a_{i,j} = \begin{bmatrix} 1 & if\ cell\ m_j\ is\ used\ to\ update\ cell\ m_i \\ 0 & otherwise. \end{bmatrix} \tag{16}$$

For the modified synchronizing stream cipher in Fig. 8:
Private key:

1. A polynomial $p(x)$ which the degree is less than k, where k is a prime such that 2^k is also a prime.

2. A negative prime q, $q \approx 2^k$ satisfying the two following conditions:
   $2^k - 1$ is co-prime to $|q| - 1$.
   The order of 2 modulo q is exactly $|q| - 1$.

Public key:

1. An irreducible primitive polynomial $f(x)$ of degree k.

The encryption/decryption scheme is:

1. Generate the m-sequence S by the LFSR.
2. Feed the output m-sequence S into the ring FCSR divisor-box.
3. Compute the output $S(2)/q$ by the ring FCSR divisor-box.
4. The output S' of the ring FCSR divisor-box is the key stream.
5. XOR the key stream with the plaintext/ciphertext.

For more security, the parameters of the LFSR M can be also used as private key.

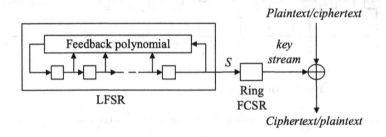

Fig. 8. The modified synchronizing stream cipher

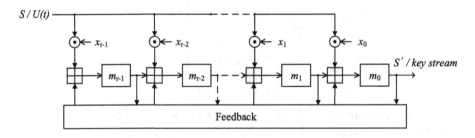

Fig. 9. The ring FCSR with an input S or $U(t)$

5.1 Resistant to M. Hell and T. Johansson's Real-Time Cryptanalysis

The attack presented in [6] against F-FCSR, depends on correlations between carry values and feedback values. More precisely, all feedback values are controlled by the right-most register m_0 bit. When m_0 bit be forced to 0 or 1 during t consecutive clocks, the carry register is kept in the constant sequence $c = (0, \ldots, 1, 0)$, the behavior of stream cipher becomes linear. According to the nature of l-sequence, the probability of such occurrence is approximately 2^{-t}. However, if a ring FCSR is used, all carry registers are no longer affected by the same bit register, so the probability of ring FCSR being linearized will be greatly reduced, this probability decreases to $2^{-t \cdot k}$ [7], where k is the number of units of the main register controlling a feedback. In practice, the number of main registers with feedback tends to exceed half of the number of main registers, so the probability of linearization of the ring FCSR becomes so small that the cost of such an attack is often almost higher than the exhaustive search.

5.2   Statistical Properties

The modified synchronizing stream cipher inherits the excellent statistical properties of the pseudorandom generator given in [4]. The details of the statistical analysis are given as follows.

Periodicity of the Key Stream Sequence. As shown in Fig. 8, analyzing the cycle of the key stream is equivalent to analyzing the period of the ring FCSR output sequence S' with input S or $U(t)$ in Fig. 9. Firstly, we need to explain some of the symbolic meaning in Fig. 9. Let $m_i(t)$ denote the content of each cell of the main register at time t, $M_i(t) = \sum_{k \in N} m_i(t+k)2^k$ is the series observed in the $i-th$ cell and $c_i(t)$ denote the content of each cell of the carry register at t. Define vector $m(t) = (m_0(t), \ldots, m_{r-1}(t))^t$, $M(t) = (M_0(t), \ldots, M_{r-1}(t))^t$, $c(t) = (c_0(t), \ldots, c_{r-1}(t))^t$. $u(t)$ is the input bit of the ring FCSR. Similarly, $U(t) = \sum_{k \in N} u(t+k)2^k$ is the series of input $u(t)$ and X is a input vector $(x_0, \ldots, x_{r-1})^t$, where $x_0, \ldots, x_{r-2} = 0$, only $x_{r-1} = 1$. The reason for converting to vector format is to analyze based on a matrix.

Lemma 4 *([15] Theorem). The series $M_i(t)$ observed in the cells of the main register are 2-adic expansion of p_i/q with and with $q = det(I - 2A)$.*

Lemma 5 *([15] Proposition 5). Assume there is no input. The 2-adic integers $M_i(t)$ can be written p_i/q where $p_i \in Z_2$ and $q = det(I - 2A)$ is odd (so $p_i(t)/q \in Z_2$). More precisely, $(p_1(t), \ldots, p_{r-1}(t))^t = (I - 2A)^*(m(t) + 2c(t))$ where $(I - 2A)^*$ denotes the adjacent of $I - 2A$.*

Using the above two lemmas, we can derive the periodic nature of the modification of the synchronizing stream cipher.

Proposition 3. *The sequence S' is periodic of period $T' = (2^k - 1)(|q| - 1)$ with a heuristic probability p greater than $1 - 2^{-k}$.*

Proof. Proof From lemma 5, we get

$$qM(t) = (I - 2A)^*(m(t) + 2c(t) + 2XU(t)) \tag{17}$$

as $(I - 2A)(I - 2A)^* = qI$, A and I are the transition matrix and the identity matrix, respectively. When assumed input $XU(t) = 0$, the right hand simplifies to $(I - 2A)^*(m(t)+2c(t))$. It is a vector $(p_0(t), \ldots, p_{r-1}(t))^t$ of 2-adic integers and $M_i(t) = p_i(t)/q$ for each i. Moreover $(I - 2A)(I - 2A)^* = det(I - 2A)I$, this indicates $q = det(I - 2A)$. Notice that in order to generate the l-sequence, q requires a prime number, and 2 is the root of modulo q. Constructing the ring FCSR that satisfies the conditions is still under further research, seeing [16,17] for some more effective methods.

In our design, we can see that input $XU(t)$ is not equal to 0, here $U(t) = S$ which is output m-sequence of LFSR, so the period of $U(t)$ is $T = 2^k - 1$. Let $U_t = \sum_{t=0}^{T-1} u(t)2^t$, $N = 2^T - 1$, according to the one-to-one correspondence between periodic sequence of period T and 2-adic representation, the 2-adic expression of $U(t)$:

$$U(t) = \frac{\sum_{t=0}^{T-1} u(t)2^t}{2^T - 1} = \frac{U_t}{N} = \frac{p'h}{q'h} = \frac{p'}{q'} \tag{18}$$

where h be the greatest common divisor of U_t and N, set $U_t = p'h$ and $N = q'h (p'q' \leq 0, |p'| \leq |q'|$ and q' odd, owing to the fact that $U(t)$ is a m-sequence), thus 2-adic reduced form $U(t)$ is $U(t) = p'/q'$, then

$$M(t) = \frac{(I - 2A)^*(m(t) + 2c(t))}{q} + \frac{(I - 2A)^*(2XU(t))}{q} \tag{19}$$

$$= \frac{(I - 2A)^*(m(t) + 2c(t))}{q} + \frac{(I - 2A)^*(2X)}{q} \cdot \frac{p'}{q'} \tag{20}$$

$$= \frac{p}{q} + \frac{R}{q} \cdot \frac{p'}{q'} = \frac{pq' + Rp'}{qq'} \tag{21}$$

$$= \frac{Rp'}{qq'} = \frac{P}{Q} \tag{22}$$

Equation (20) is the result of substituting Eq. (18) into Eq. (19). Set $p = (I - 2A)^*(m(t)+2c(t)) = (p_0(t), \ldots, p_{r-1}(t))^t$, $R = (I-2A)^*(2X) = (R_0, \ldots, R_{r-1})^t$, R and p have similar product formulas, $P = Rp'$, $Q = qq'$, $P/Q \in Z_{(2)}$. In order to simplify the analysis, notice the fact that the initial values of the ring FCSR main and carry registers are all 0 in our modification of the synchronizing stream cipher. So $p = (0, \ldots, 0)^t$, which explains from Eq. (21) to Eq. (22). We choose a prime k such that $2^k - 1$ is also a prime. Obviously, $2^k - 1$ is a Mersenne number. The period of $U(t)$ is $T = 2^k - 1$, this implies that the order of 2 module q' is $T = 2^k - 1$. The order of 2 module q is $|q| - 1$ which is co-prime to T, thus the order of 2 module $Q = q'q$ is then $T' = (2^k - 1)(|q| - 1)$. We tried to pick a prime q satisfies $2^k <= q <= 2^{k+1}$, so p' will not be divisible by q, as in [4], we can also get a similar conclusion that the heuristic probability of q' divides R is less than 2^{-k}. Otherwise, R is only related to the structure of the ring FCSR, let $|R| \leq |q|$, $Rq \geq 0$ in design, a strict periodic sequence can be obtained.

2-Adic Complexity of the Key Stream Sequence. Let the output binary sequence of the LFSR denote as $S=\{s_i\}_{i\geq0}$, and the output sequence of the 2-adic division box by a prime q as $S'(t)$, then we have $S(2) = qS'(2)$. Similar to [4], we have the following results:

Proposition 4. *The 2-adic complexity of* $P/Q \in Z_{(2)}$, *where we assume* $gcd(P,Q) = 1$, $P < Q$, *is* $\pounds\,(P/Q)=log_2(max(|P|,|Q|)) = k + 2^k - log_2 h$.

Proof. According to the definition of complexity of Z_2 elements. We obtain:

$$
\begin{aligned}
\pounds(P/Q) &= log_2(max(|P|,|Q|)) \\
&= log_2(|qq'|) \\
&= log_2(|q|) + log_2(|q'|) \\
&\approx log_2(2^k) + log_2(N/h) \quad\quad\quad (23) \\
&= k + log_2((2^T - 1)/h) \\
&\approx k + T - log_2 h \\
&\approx k + 2^k - log_2 h
\end{aligned}
$$

As shown above, the derivation process of Eq. (23) is based on such assumptions and facts that the period of the LFSR output sequence is a Mersenne number, the cycle q of the independent ring FCSR is approximately equal to 2^k and the output sequence of modified synchronizing stream cipher is strictly periodic.

Linear Complexity of the Key Stream Sequence. The main principle of the new construction is still base on the fact that 2-adic operations and linear operations are not related. And thus, we can expect that the linear complexity of our new construction is about 2^{2k-2} as given in [4].

6   Conclusions

In this paper, we have analyzed the security of the synchronizing stream ciphers constructed based on the pseudorandom generator proposed by Arnault. The synchronizing stream ciphers can circumvent the security weaknesses of the self-synchronizing stream ciphers design, but cannot resist the M. Hell and T. Johansson's real-time cryptanalysis. To obtain better security properties, the FCSR is substituted by the ring FCSR. The new construction has preserved the excellent statistical properties and can prevent the M. Hell and T. Johansson's real-time cryptanalysis and other known attacks.

References

1. Shyrochin, V.P., Vasyltsov, I.V., Karpinskij, B.Z.: Investigations of the basic component of FCSR-generator. In: Proceedings of the Second IEEE International Workshop on Intelligent Data Acquisition and Advanced Computing Systems: Technology and Applications, pp. 132–135. IEEE (2003)

2. Golić, J.D.: On the security of shift register based keystream generators. In: Anderson, R. (ed.) FSE 1993. LNCS, vol. 809, pp. 90–100. Springer, Heidelberg (1994). https://doi.org/10.1007/3-540-58108-1_12

3. Rueppel, R.A.: Analysis and Design of Stream Ciphers. Springer, Heidelberg (1986). https://doi.org/10.1007/978-3-642-82865-2

4. Arnault, F., Berger, T.P., Necer, A.: A new class of stream ciphers combining LFSR and FCSR architectures. In: Menezes, A., Sarkar, P. (eds.) INDOCRYPT 2002. LNCS, vol. 2551, pp. 22–33. Springer, Heidelberg (2002). https://doi.org/10.1007/3-540-36231-2_3

5. Zhang, B., Wu, H., Feng, D., Bao, F.: Chosen ciphertext attack on a new class of self-synchronizing stream ciphers. In: Canteaut, A., Viswanathan, K. (eds.) INDOCRYPT 2004. LNCS, vol. 3348, pp. 73–83. Springer, Heidelberg (2004). https://doi.org/10.1007/978-3-540-30556-9_7

6. Hell, M., Johansson, T.: Breaking the F-FCSR-H stream cipher in real time. In: Pieprzyk, J. (ed.) ASIACRYPT 2008. LNCS, vol. 5350, pp. 557–569. Springer, Heidelberg (2008). https://doi.org/10.1007/978-3-540-89255-7_34

7. Arnault, F., Berger, T., Lauradoux, C., Minier, M., Pousse, B.: A new approach for FCSRs. In: Jacobson, M.J., Rijmen, V., Safavi-Naini, R. (eds.) SAC 2009. LNCS, vol. 5867, pp. 433–448. Springer, Heidelberg (2009). https://doi.org/10.1007/978-3-642-05445-7_27

8. Allailou, B., Marjane, A., Mokrane, A.: Design of a novel pseudo-random generator based on vectorial FCSRs. In: Chung, Y., Yung, M. (eds.) WISA 2010. LNCS, vol. 6513, pp. 76–91. Springer, Heidelberg (2011). https://doi.org/10.1007/978-3-642-17955-6_6

9. Klapper, A., Goresky, M.: 2-Adic shift registers. In: Anderson, R. (ed.) FSE 1993. LNCS, vol. 809, pp. 174–178. Springer, Heidelberg (1994). https://doi.org/10.1007/3-540-58108-1_21

10. Klapper, A., Goresky, M.: Feedback shift registers, 2-Adic span, and combiners with memory. J. Cryptol. $\mathbf{10}(2)$, 111–147 (1997)

11. Klapper, A., Goresky, M.: Fibonacci and galois representations of feedback-with-carry shift registers. IEEE Trans. Inf. Theory $\mathbf{48}(11)$, 2826–2836 (2002)

12. Arnault, F., Berger, T.P.: Design and properties of a new pseudo-random generator based on a filtered FCSR automaton. IEEE Trans. Comput. $\mathbf{54}(11)$, 1374–1383 (2005)

13. The eSTREAM Project. http://www.ecrypt.eu.org/stream/endofphase3.html

14. Song, H., Fan, X., Wu, C., Feng, D.: On the probability distribution of the carry cells of stream ciphers F-FCSR-H v2 and F-FCSR-H v3. In: Wu, C.-K., Yung, M., Lin, D. (eds.) Inscrypt 2011. LNCS, vol. 7537, pp. 160–178. Springer, Heidelberg (2012). https://doi.org/10.1007/978-3-642-34704-7_13

15. Arnault, F., Berger, T.P., Pousse, B.: A matrix approach for FCSR automata. Cryptogr. Commun. $\mathbf{3}(2)$, 109–139 (2011)

16. Lin, Z., Pei, D., Lin, D., et al: Fast construction of binary ring FCSRs for hardware stream ciphers. Designs Codes Cryptography, (2), 1–15 (2017)

17. Pei, D., Lin, Z., Zhang, X.: Construction of transition matrices for ternary ring feedback with carry shift registers. IEEE Trans. Inf. Theory $\mathbf{61}(5)$, 2942–2951 (2015)

Public Key Cryptography

Heterogeneous Deniable Authentication
for E-Voting Systems

Chunhua Jin$^{(\boxtimes)}$, Guanhua Chen, Changhui Yu, and Jianyang Zhao

Faculty of Computer and Software Engineering, Huaiyin Institute of Technology,
Huai'an 233003, China
xajch0206@163.com, 0206501301@163.com, hayuchanghui@163.com,
jszhaojy@163.com

Abstract. An electronic voting (e-voting) system allows voters to cast their votes secretly and securely over a public channel. Security is the critical issue that should be considered in such a system. In this paper, we propose a heterogeneous deniable authentication (HDA) protocol for e-voting systems. The proposed protocol allows a sender in a certificate-less (CL) cryptography system to transmit a message to a receiver in a public key infrastructure (PKI) system. Our protocol is provably secure in the random oracle model under the bilinear Diffie-Hellman (BDH) and computational Diffie-Hellman (CDH) assumptions. Additionally, our protocol provides batch verification, which can accelerate the verification of authenticators. Based on these features, our protocol is highly suitable for practical e-voting systems.

Keywords: E-voting system · Security · Heterogeneous system
Deniable authentication

1 Introduction

Electronic voting (e-voting) is an online voting system that is structured on a cryptography technique, and it has been gradually implemented and advocated by people. The system supports full-function online voting using general household devices, and all the polling results will be counted automatically and anonymously. Compared with traditional voting, e-voting is a more economic system that addresses transparency and impartiality. Although an e-voting system provides considerable convenience for voters to cast their votes, it also brings many challenges. One of the main reasons for such challenges is the security due to the uncontrolled and unsupervised Internet environment. A deniable authentication protocol can be applied in an e-voting system to achieve its security requirements, such as uncoercibility, efficiency, deniable authentication and verifiability. A deniable authentication protocol has two characteristics: (1) it enables an

Supported by the Natural Science Foundation of Jiangsu Province (Grant No. BK20161302), Electric Power Company Technology Project of Jiangsu Province (Grant No. J2017123).

© Springer Nature Singapore Pte Ltd. 2018
F. Li et al. (Eds.): FCS 2018, CCIS 879, pp. 41–54, 2018.
https://doi.org/10.1007/978-981-13-3095-7_4

intended receiver to identify the source of a given message, and (2) the intended receiver cannot prove the source of a given message to any third party. Such characteristics are important for e-voting systems. Li et al. [1] showed that deniable authentication has important applications in e-voting systems, and they provided the following example. In an e-voting system, let Alice be a voter and Bob be a tally authority. Suppose that Carol, a third party, forces Alice to vote for a candidate, but Alice does not want to vote for that candidate. Alice is asked to send her ballot m with the authenticator to Bob such that Bob believes that this ballot is from Alice and not from anyone else. In addition, Bob cannot prove the source of the ballot m to Carol even if Bob and Carol cooperate together. If there is cooperation between Bob and Carol, then Carol may question the validity of the proof given by Bob. In this example, Carol cannot force Alice to vote for this candidate. Therefore, to protect a voter from coercion in e-voting systems, we need a protocol that enables a tally authority to identify the source of a given ballot but not prove the source of a given ballot to a third party. The objective of this paper is to design an efficient deniable authentication protocol based on a heterogeneous system for practical e-voting systems.

1.1   Related Work

There are three public key cryptosystems: public key infrastructure (PKI), identity-based cryptosystem (IBC) and certificateless cryptosystem (CLC). In a PKI, a certificate authority (CA) issues a public key certificate. The purpose of this certificate is to bind the public key and the identity of a user by the signature of the CA. By verifying the public key certificate, we can verify the validity of a public key. If the certificate is valid, then the public key is also valid. However, the main difficulty in PKI is how to manage the public key certificates, including their distribution, storage, revocation, and the computational cost of certificate verification. To eliminate the reliance on public key certificates and simplify public key management, IBC emerged at the right moment [2]. In an IBC, a user's public key can be computed directly from its identity information, such as telephone number, IP address and e-mail address. The authenticity of a public key is explicitly verified without a public key certificate. The corresponding private key is computed by a trusted third party called a private key generator (PKG). However, there is a weakness in IBC called the key escrow problem. With this weakness, the PKG is unconditionally trustable, and it knows all the users' private keys. Consequently, CLC was proposed to solve the key escrow problem in IBC [3]. In CLC, a trusted third party called a key generator center (KGC) only generates a partial private key using the master private key. A user's full private key is produced by combining the partial private key with a secret key chosen by the user. The corresponding public key is produced by combining the secret key with system parameters. Note that the KGC has no knowledge of the full private key because it does not know the secret key chosen by the user. Hence, CLC has neither a public key certificate management problem nor a key escrow problem.

According to the aforementioned three public key cryptosystems, many efficient PKI-based deniable authentication protocols [4–9], IBC-based deniable authentication protocols [10–12] and CLC-based deniable authentication protocols [13,14] have been proposed. In [4], Wang and Song proposed a non-interactive deniable authentication protocol based on designated verifier proofs. They proved the security of their protocol under the decisional Diffie-Hellman (DDH) assumption. In [5], Raimondo and Gennaro proposed two additional approaches for deniable authentication. Their schemes do not require the use of CCA-secure encryption; thus, they demonstrated a different generic approach to the problem of deniable authentication. Tian et al. [6] presented a new paradigm to construct a non-interactive deniable authentication protocol and proved its security in a security model that they defined. Li and Takagi [7] proposed a deniable authentication protocol that satisfies the deniable authentication, mutual authentication and confidentiality. Gambs et al. [8] proposed a prover-anonymous and deniable distance-bounding authentication protocol. They formally modeled and defined prover anonymity. To achieve deniability, they ensured that the back-end server cannot distinguish prover behavior from malicious verifier behavior. Zeng et al. [9] proposed a deniable ring authentication protocol to handle concurrent scenarios. They constructed a CCA2-secure multi-receiver encryption scheme to support this protocol that requires only 2 communication rounds, which is round-optimal in fully deniable ring authentications. Lu et al. [10] proposed an ID-based deniable authentication protocol under the RSA assumption, and they used the provable security technique to analyze its security. Li et al. [11] proposed an efficient deniable authentication protocol using bilinear pairings, and they proved its security in the random oracle model. Yao and Zhao [12] designed two deniable Internet key-exchange protocols: one is in the traditional PKI setting, and the other is in the identity-based setting. Jin et al. [13] proposed a CL deniable authentication protocol using pairings under the BDH and CDH assumptions (henceforth called JXLZ). Jin et al. [14] developed a CL deniable authentication protocol without pairings, and they provided its formal security in the random oracle model (henceforth called JXZL).

There is a common characteristic for the aforementioned deniable authentication protocols, that is, the communication entities of these protocols are all in the same environment. For example, in these protocols [4–9], the communication entities are all in the PKI setting; in these protocols [10–12], the communication entities are all in the IBC setting; and in these protocols [13,14], the communication entities are all in the CLC setting. This characteristic makes these protocols unsound in heterogeneous e-voting systems. Li et al. [15] proposed two heterogeneous deniable authentication (HDA) protocols for pervasive computing environments using bilinear pairings. The first protocol allows a sender in a PKI environment to send a message to a receiver in an IBC environment. The second protocol allows a sender in an IBC environment to send a message to a receiver in a PKI environment.

1.2 Contribution

Because almost all of the existing deniable authentication protocols are homogeneous, they are not suitable for practical e-voting systems. The contribution of this paper is to address the design problem for HDA. Specifically, we propose an HDA protocol that allows a sender in a CLC environment to transmit a message to a receiver in a PKI environment. We present a formal security model for the HDA protocol and prove its security in the random oracle model under the BDH and CDH assumptions. In addition, our protocol provides batch verification, which can accelerate the verification of authenticators. The proposed protocol is very sound for practical e-voting systems.

1.3 Organization

The remainder of this paper is arranged as follows. Preliminaries are introduced in Sect. 2. Then, an HSC scheme is designed in Sect. 3. We discuss its security and performance in Sect. 4. Finally, Sect. 5 provides conclusions.

2 Preliminaries

In this section, the bilinear pairings are outlined.

2.1 Bilinear Pairings

Let G_1 and G_T be a cyclic additive group and a cyclic multiplicative group, respectively. The generator of G_1 is P. G_1 and G_T have the same order q. A bilinear pairing is a map $\hat{e} : G_1 \times G_1 \to G_T$ with the following three properties:

1. Bilinear: Upon inputting $P, Q \in G_1, a, b \in Z_q^*$, we have $\hat{e}(aP, bQ) = \hat{e}(P, Q)^{ab}$.
2. Non-degeneracy: A $P, Q \in G_1$ exists such that $\hat{e}(P, Q) \neq 1$.
3. Computability: Upon inputting $P, Q \in G_1$, an efficient algorithm exists to compute $\hat{e}(P, Q)$.

A bilinear pairing that satisfies the aforementioned properties is called an admissible bilinear pairing. The modified Weil pairing and Tate pairing are admissible maps of this type. For more details, readers can refer to [16,17].

Upon inputting a cyclic addition group G_1, its prime order q and generator P, the CDH problem in G_1 involves computing abP given $(P, aP, bP) \in G_1$.

Definition 1. The (ϵ, t)-CDH assumption holds when no t-polynomial time adversary $\mathcal{F}$ exists who has an advantage of at least ϵ in solving the CDH problem.

Upon inputting a cyclic addition group G_1 and a cyclic multiplicative group G_2 of the same prime order q, P is a generator of G_1, and $\hat{e} : G_1 \times G_1 \to G_T$ is a bilinear map. The BDH problem is to compute $\hat{e}(P, P)^{abc}$ given (P, aP, bP, cP) with $a, b, c \in Z_q^*$.

Definition 2. The (ϵ, t)-BDH assumption holds when no t-polynomial time adversary $\mathcal{F}$ exists who has an advantage of at least ϵ in solving the BDH problem.

3 An HSC Scheme

In this section, we first provide the syntax and security concepts for an HDA scheme that enables a sender that belongs to a CLC system to transmit a message to a receiver that belongs to a PKI system. Here, we employ CLP-HSC to denote the following DA, in which "CL" denotes CLC and "P" denotes PKI. Then, we describe our proposed HDA scheme.

3.1 Syntax

A generic CLP-HDA scheme consists of the following eight algorithms.

Setup: Upon inputting a security parameter k, this algorithm, which executes on a KGC, outputs a master private key s and the system parameters *params*. For simplicity, we omit *params* in the other algorithms.

$CLC - PPKE$: Upon inputting the master key s and the identity ID of a user, this partial private extraction algorithm, which executes on a KGC, outputs a partial private key D_{ID}. The KGC securely transmits the partial private key to the corresponding user.

$CLC - UKG$: Upon inputting the identity ID of a user, this user key generation algorithm, which executes on a user, outputs a secret value x_{ID}.

$CLC - PRKS$: Upon inputting a user's partial private key D_{ID} and its secret value x_{ID}, this private key setup algorithm, which executes on a user, outputs a full private key S_{ID}.

$CLC - PUKS$: Upon inputting a user's secret value x_{ID}, this public key setup algorithm, which executes on a user, outputs a public key PK_{ID}.

$PKI - KG$: This key generation algorithm is executed by PKI users. The user selects a secret key sk and calculates a corresponding public key pk, which is signed by its CA.

Authenticate: Upon inputting a message m; a sender's full private key S_{ID}, identity ID and public key PK_{ID}; and a receiver's public key pk, this deniable authentication algorithm (executed by the sender) returns a ciphertext σ.

$Verify$: Upon inputting a ciphertext σ, a message m, a sender's identity ID_s and public key PK_{ID}, and a receiver's private key sk, this verify algorithm (executed by the receiver) returns a symbol $\top$ when σ is valid or a symbol $\bot$ when σ is not valid.

For consistency, the algorithm should satisfy the following requirement: if

$$\sigma = Authenticate(m, S_{ID}, ID, PK_{ID}, pk),$$

then we have

$$m = Verify(\sigma, ID, PK_{ID}, sk).$$

3.2 Security Concepts

Compared with traditional authentication protocols, a deniable authentication protocol has the following two security requirements: (1) it enables a designated receiver to identify the source of a given message, and (2) the designated receiver cannot prove the source of a given message to any third party. Li et al. [11] presented a security concept called deniable authentication against adaptive chosen message attacks (DA-CMA). However, this security concept is not suitable for our proposed CLP-DA protocol. Here, we slightly amend the concept in Li et al. [11]'s protocol to adjust the CLP-DA protocol.

In the CLP-DA protocol, the sender is in the CLC system. We should consider two types of adversaries [3], Type I and Type II, with different capabilities. A Type I adversary simulates an attacker, which is a user who does not have access to the master private key. However, it can replace any user's public key with a valid value of its choice. A Type II adversary simulates a trusted third party that has access to the master private key, but it cannot replace any user's public key.

First, we present the following game (Game I) performed between a Type I adversary $\mathcal{F}_{\mathcal{I}}$ and a challenger $\mathcal{C}$.

Initial: Upon inputting a security parameter k, $\mathcal{C}$ executes the *Setup* algorithm and sends the system parameters *params* to the adversary $\mathcal{F}_{\mathcal{I}}$. Additionally, $\mathcal{C}$ also runs the $PKI - KG$ algorithm to generate a receiver's private key sk^* and the corresponding public key pk^*. It transmits pk^* to $\mathcal{F}_{\mathcal{I}}$.

Attack: $\mathcal{F}_{\mathcal{I}}$ requests a polynomially bounded number of queries adaptively.

- Partial private key extraction queries: $\mathcal{F}_{\mathcal{I}}$ first chooses an identity ID and transmits it to $\mathcal{C}$. Then, $\mathcal{C}$ executes the $CLC - PPKE$ algorithm and transmits the partial private key D_{ID} to $\mathcal{F}_{\mathcal{I}}$.
- Private key setup queries: $\mathcal{F}_{\mathcal{I}}$ first chooses an identity ID and transmits it to $\mathcal{C}$. Then, $\mathcal{C}$ executes the $CLC - PRKE$ algorithm and transmits the full private key S_{ID} to $\mathcal{F}_{\mathcal{I}}$ ($\mathcal{C}$ may run the $CLC - PPKE$ and $CLC - UKG$ algorithms if necessary).
- Public key queries: $\mathcal{F}_{\mathcal{I}}$ first chooses an identity ID and transmits it to $\mathcal{C}$. Then, $\mathcal{C}$ executes the $CLC - PUKE$ algorithm and transmits the public key PK_{ID} to $\mathcal{F}_{\mathcal{I}}$.
- Public key replacement queries: $\mathcal{F}_{\mathcal{I}}$ replaces a public key PK_{ID} with a new value of its choice.
- Authentication queries: $\mathcal{F}_{\mathcal{I}}$ submits the identity ID of a sender and a message m. $\mathcal{C}$ first runs the $CLC - PRKE$ and $CLC - PUKE$ algorithms to obtain the private key S_{ID} and public key PK_{ID} of the sender, respectively. Then, $\mathcal{C}$ runs the *Authentication* $(m, S_{ID}, ID, PK_{ID}, pk^*)$ algorithm and sends the obtained result σ to $\mathcal{F}_{\mathcal{I}}$. If the public key has been replaced, then $\mathcal{C}$ cannot compute the sender's secret value. In this case, $\mathcal{F}_{\mathcal{I}}$ must additionally supply it.
- Verify queries: $\mathcal{F}_{\mathcal{I}}$ submits the identity ID of a sender, a message m and a deniable authenticator σ to $\mathcal{C}$. $\mathcal{C}$ first runs the $PKI - KE$ algorithm to obtain the private key sk^* of the receiver. Then, $\mathcal{C}$ runs the $Verify((m, \sigma, ID, PK_{ID}, sk^*)$ algorithm and sends the obtained result to $\mathcal{F}_{\mathcal{I}}$. The result is either a symbol $\top$ or a symbol $\bot$.

Forgery: $\mathcal{F}_I$ generates a deniable authentication σ^*, the identity ID^* of a sender and a message m^*. It succeeds if the following conditions hold:

1. $Verify(m^*, ID^*, sk^*) = \top$.
2. $\mathcal{F}_I$ has not requested a key extraction query on identity ID_S^*.
3. $\mathcal{F}_I$ has not requested an authentication query on (m^*, ID_s^*).

The advantage of $\mathcal{F}_I$ is defined as the probability that it wins.

Definition 3. A CLP-HDA scheme is $(\epsilon_{da}, t, q_k, q_d, q_v)$-Type-I-DA-CMA secure if no probabilistic polynomial time (PPT) adversary $\mathcal{F}_I$ succeeds with an advantage of at least ϵ_{da} after at most q_k key extraction queries, q_d authentication queries and q_v verify queries.

Second, we present the following game (Game II) performed between a Type II adversary $\mathcal{F}_{II}$ and a challenger $\mathcal{C}$.

Initial: Upon inputting a security parameter k, $\mathcal{C}$ executes the *Setup* algorithm and sends both the system parameters *params* and the master private key s to the adversary $\mathcal{F}_{II}$. Additionally, $\mathcal{C}$ also runs the $PKI - KG$ algorithm to generate a receiver's private key sk^* and the corresponding public key pk^*. It transmits pk^* to $\mathcal{F}_{II}$.

Attack: $\mathcal{F}_{II}$ requests a polynomially bounded number of private key setup queries, public key queries, authentication queries and verify queries as in Game I. Here, we do not need partial private key extraction queries because $\mathcal{F}_{II}$ can compute it by itself.

Forgery: $\mathcal{F}_{II}$ generates a deniable authentication σ^*, the identity ID^* of a sender and a message m^*. It succeeds if the following conditions hold:

1. $Verify(m^*, ID^*, sk^*) = \top$.
2. $\mathcal{F}_{II}$ has not requested a key extraction query on identity ID_S^*.
3. $\mathcal{F}_{II}$ has not requested an authentication query on (m^*, ID_S^*).

The advantage of $\mathcal{F}_{II}$ is defined as the probability that it wins.

Definition 4. A CLP-HDA scheme is $(\epsilon_{da}, t, q_k, q_d, q_v)$-Type-II-DA-CMA secure if no PPT adversary $\mathcal{F}_{II}$ succeeds with an advantage of at least ϵ_{da} after at most q_k key extraction queries, q_d authentication queries and q_v verify queries.

Definition 5. A CLP-HDA scheme is $(\epsilon_{da}, t, q_k, q_d, q_v)$-DA-CMA secure if it is both Type I DA-CMA secure and Type II DA-CMA secure.

In Game I and Game II, note that the adversary is unaware of the receiver's private key sk^*. This corresponds to the deniability property. The sender can deny its action because the receiver can also generate a valid deniable authenticator. This is the main difference between deniable authentication and undeniable authentication in digital signature schemes.

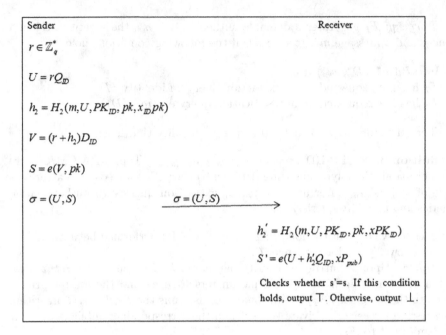

Fig. 1. A CLP-HSC scheme

3.3 Proposed CLP-HSC Scheme

In this section, we present an efficient CLP-HSC scheme using bilinear pairings that mainly consists of eight algorithms: *Setup, CLC − PPKE, CLC − UKG, CLC − PKS, PKI − KG, Authenticate* and *Verify*. Then, we present the design of CLP-HSC. We list the main notations of our scheme in Table 1.

Setup: Upon inputting a security parameter k, the PKG selects the bilinear map groups (G_1, G_2) of prime order q, a generator P for G_1 and a bilinear map $G_1 \times G_1 \to G_2$. It then chooses a master private key $s \in Z_q^*$, a master public key $P_{pub} = sP$, and the hash functions $H_1 : \{0,1\}^* \to G_1$ and $H_2 : \{0,1\}^* \times G_1 \to Z_q^*$. The public parameters are $\{G_1, G_2, e, q, P, P_{pub}, H_1, H_2\}$.

CLC − PPKE: A sender submits its identity ID to KGC. The KGC calculates the partial private key $Q_{ID_S} = H_1(ID_S)$ and sends it to the sender.

CLC − UKG: A sender with identity ID chooses a random value $x_{ID} \in Z_q^*$ as the secret value.

CLC − PRKS: Given a partial private key D_{ID} and a secret value x_{ID}, this algorithm returns a full private key $S_{ID} = (D_{ID}, x_{ID})$.

CLC − PUKS: Given a secret value x_{ID}, this algorithm returns a public key $PK_{ID} = x_{ID}P$.

PKI − KG: A receiver in a PKI system selects a random value $x \in Z_q^*$ as its private key and computes $pk = xP$ as the corresponding public key.

Table 1. Notations

Notation	Description
k	A security parameter
G_1	A cyclic addition group
G_2	A cyclic multiplicative group
e	A bilinear map $e : G_1 \times G_1 \rightarrow G_2$
P	A generator of group G_1
q	The order of groups G_1 and G_2
s	A master private key of PKG
P_{pub}	A master public key of PKG
$H_i()$	A collision-resistant hash function $(i = 1, 2)$
ID	An identity of a sender
Q_{ID}	A hash value of a sender's identity
D_{ID}	A partial private key of a sender with identity ID_s
S_{ID}	A full private key of a sender with identity ID_s
PK_{ID}	A public key of a sender
x_{ID}	A secret value of a sender
sk	A private key of a receiver
pk	A public key of a receiver

Authenticate: Upon inputting a message m, the sender's private key S_{ID}, identity ID and public key PK_{ID} and the receiver's public key pk, the sender executes the following procedures.

1. Choose $r \in Z_q^*$ randomly and compute $U = rQ_{ID}$.
2. Compute $h_2 = H_2(m, U, PK_{ID}, pk, x_{ID}pk)$.
3. Compute $V = (r + h_2)D_{ID}$.
4. Compute $S = e(V, pk)$.
5. Output a deniable authenticator $\sigma = (U, S)$.

USC: Upon inputting a message m, a deniable authenticator σ, a sender's identity ID and public key PK_{ID}, a receiver's private key sk and public key pk, the receiver executes the following procedures.

1. Compute $h_2' = H_2(m, U, PK_{ID}, pk, xPK_{ID})$.
2. Compute $S' = e(U + h_2'Q_{ID}, xP_{pub})$
3. Check whether $S' = S$. If this equation holds, output $\top$; otherwise, output $\bot$.

Now, we verify the consistency of the proposed CLP-HDA protocol. Because $V = (r + h_2)D_{ID}$ and $P_{pub} = sP$, we have

$$\begin{aligned}
S' &= e(U + h_2'Q_{ID}, xP_{pub}) \\
&= e(rQ_{ID} + h_2'Q_{ID}, xsP) \\
&= e((r + h_2')Q_{ID}, xsP) \\
&= e((r + h_2')D_{ID}, xP) \\
&= e(V, pk) \\
&= S
\end{aligned}$$

The proposed CLP-HDA protocol also supports batch verification. Given n deniable authenticators

$$(ID_1, m_1, \sigma_1), ..., (ID_n, m_n, \sigma_n),$$

where $\sigma_i = (U_i, S_i)$ (i $=$ 1,...,n), the receiver with secret key x selects $n - 1$ randomizing factors $\alpha_2, ..., \alpha_n$ from Z_q^* and verifies these authenticators simultaneously by computing $h_i = H_2(m_i, U_i, PK_{ID_i}, pk, x_{ID_i}pk)$ for $i = 1, 2, ..., n$ and checking whether

$$S_1 \cdot \prod_{i=2}^{n} S_i = e(U_1 + h_1Q_{ID_1} + \sum_{i=2}^{n} \alpha_iU_i + \sum_{i=2}^{n} \alpha_ih_iQ_{ID_i}, xP_{pub})$$

holds. If this equation holds, output ⊤; otherwise, output ⊥.

4   Analysis of the Protocol

In this section, we analyze the security and performance of our proposed CLP-HSC scheme.

4.1   Security

We show that the proposed CLP-HDA protocol is deniable by Theorem 1 and is DA-CMA secure by Theorem 2.

Theorem 1 (Deniability): The proposed CLP-HDA protocol is deniable.

Proof: After receiving a deniable authenticator $\sigma = (U, S)$, the receiver can identify the source of a message m with its private key sk. To simulate the transcripts on a message m, the receiver follows the steps below.

1. Choose $\bar{r} \in Z_q^*$ randomly and compute $\bar{U} = \bar{r}Q_{ID}$.
2. Compute $\bar{h}_2 = H_2(m, \bar{U}, PK_{ID}, pk, x_{ID}pk)$.
3. Compute $\bar{S} = e(\bar{U} + \bar{h}_2Q_{ID}, xP_{pub})$.

$\bar{\sigma} = (\bar{U}, \bar{S})$ generated by the receiver is indistinguishable from $\sigma = (U, S)$ generated by the sender according to the *Authenticate* algorithm in Sect. 3. Let $\sigma' = (U', S')$ be a deniable authenticator that is selected randomly from the set of all valid sender's deniable authenticators. The probability is $\Pr[\bar{\sigma} = \sigma'] = 1/(q-1)$ because $\bar{\sigma}$ is generated from a randomly selected value $\bar{r} \in Z_q^*$. Similarly, the probability $\Pr[\sigma = \sigma']$ has the same value $1/(q-1)$ because σ is also generated from a randomly selected value $r \in Z_q^*$. According to the above statement, we find that both of them have the same probability distribution.

Theorem 2. Under the random oracle model, our scheme is DA-CMA secure under the BDH and CDH assumptions.

Lemma 1. Under the random oracle model, if an adversary $\mathcal{F}_I$ exists that can break the Type-I-DA-CMA security of our proposed CLP-HSC scheme, running in a given time t and making at most q_{ppk} partial private key extraction queries, q_{sk} private key setup queries, q_{pk} public key queries, q_{pkr} public key replacement queries, q_a authenticate queries, q_v verify queries and q_{H_i} oracle H_i ($i = 1, 2$) queries with an advantage $\epsilon \geq 10(q_a + 1)(q_a + q_{H_2})q_{H_1}/(2_1^k)$, then an algorithm $\mathcal{C}$ exists that resolves the BDH problem in expected time $t' \leq 120686 q_{H_2} q_{H_1} 2^k t / \epsilon (2^k - 1)$.

Proof: This proof is omitted because of page limitation. Please contact the corresponding author for the full version.

Lemma 2. Under the random oracle model, if an adversary $\mathcal{F}_{II}$ exists that can break the Type-II-DA-CMA security of our proposed CLP-HSC scheme, running in a given time t and making at most q_{sk} private key setup queries, q_{pk} public key queries, q_a authenticate queries, q_v verify queries and q_{H_i} oracle H_i ($i = 1, 2$) queries with an advantage ϵ, then an algorithm $\mathcal{C}$ exists that resolves the CDH problem with probability $\epsilon' > \epsilon - 1/q_{sk} - (q_a(q_a + q_{H_2}))/2^k$ in time $t' < t + (2(q_a + q_{H_2}) + q_v)t_e$, where t_e denotes the time to compute one pairing.

Proof: This proof is omitted because of page limitation. Please contact the corresponding author for the full version.

4.2 Performance Evaluation

In this section, Table 2 shows the performance of the proposed scheme, which is evaluated based on comparing the major computational cost, communication overhead, and cryptographic environment of our scheme with those of the existing schemes JXLZ [13] and JXZL [14]. We denote the point multiplication in G_1, the exponentiation in G_2, and the pairing operation in G_2 as PM, E, and PC, respectively. The other operations are omitted because they are trivial. We should verify the public key certificate before using the public key since JXZL [14] is based on the traditional PKI environment. It is assumed that the public key certificates are signed using the elliptic curve digital signature algorithm (ECDSA)[18]. ECDSA needs one point multiplication operation to sign a message and two point multiplication operations to verify a signature. We note that the modular exponentiation operation in a finite field is equivalent to point multiplication operation in elliptic curve cryptosystem (ECC) (i.e., $E = PM$). As shown in Table 2, the computational costs of JXLZ [13] and our scheme are the same in the *Authenticate* and *Verify* algorithms, which are slightly higher than JXZL [14] because the pairing evaluation is the most time-consuming operation. In addition, note that JXZL [14] and JXLZ [13] are not HDA protocols and are not suitable for e-voting systems. Clearly, the communication overheads of JXZL [14] and our scheme are somewhat high because an element S that belongs to G_2 needs to be transmitted to the receiver.

As shown in Table 2 JXZL [14] and JXLZ [13] do not support batch verification. When receiving n authenticators, these two schemes need to verify each authenticator one by one. Our scheme supports batch verification, which can accelerate the process of verification. We implement the three protocols on an MNT curve with an embedding degree of 6 and 160 bits q on an Intel Pentium IV 3.0 GHz machine [18]. From [19], the time for computing a pairing is 4.5 ms, and the time for computing a point multiplication is 0.6 ms. Figure 1 shows the

Table 2. Performance comparison

Scheme	Computational cost			Communication overhead	Environment
	Authenticate	Verify	Batch verify		
JXLZ [13]	3PM+1P	2PM+1P	-	$|m| + |Z_q^*| + |G_2|$	CLC $\longrightarrow$ CLC
JXZL [14]	7PM	6PM	-	$|m| + 2|Z_q^*|$	CLC $\longrightarrow$ CLC
Ours	3PM+1P	2PM+1P	(2n-1)PM+1P	$|m| + |Z_q^*| + |G_2|$	CLC $\longrightarrow$ PKI

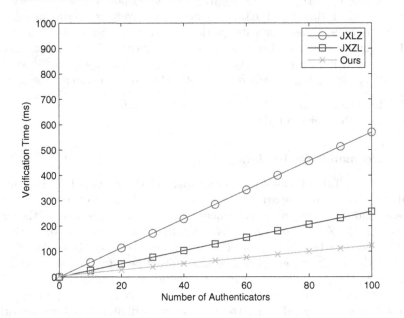

Fig. 2. Number of authenticators versus verification time

relationship between the verification time and the number of authenticators in these three schemes. JXLZ [13] needs 2PM+1P (5.7 ms) to verify an authenticator and $2n$PM+1nP (5.7n ms) to verify n authenticators. JXZL [14] needs 3PM+1MM (2.58 ms) to verify an authenticator and $3n$PM+1nMM (2.58n) to verify n authenticators. Our scheme needs 2PM+1P (5.7 ms) to verify an authenticator and $(2n-1)$PM+1P ($1.2n+3.9$ ms) to verify n authenticators. If $n=100$, our protocol is $\frac{570-123.9}{570} = 78\%$ faster than JXLZ [13] and $\frac{250-123.9}{250} = 52\%$ faster than JXZL [14]. Therefore, our scheme is very suitable for practical e-voting systems.

5   Conclusion

In this paper, we proposed an efficient HSC scheme for e-voting systems that allows a sender to belong to a CLC environment but to transmit a message to a receiver that belongs to a PKI environment. The proposed scheme is proven to be DA-CMA secure under the BDH and CDH problems in the random oracle model. In addition, the proposed scheme supports batch verification, which accelerates the verification of authenticators. This characteristic of our scheme can be applied well in e-voting systems.

References

1. Li, C., Hwang, M., Liu, C.: An electronic voting protocol with deniable authentication for mobile ad hoc networks. Comput. Commun. **31**(10), 2534–2540 (2008)
2. Shamir, A.: Identity-based cryptosystems and signature schemes. In: Blakley, G.R., Chaum, D. (eds.) CRYPTO 1984. LNCS, vol. 196, pp. 47–53. Springer, Heidelberg (1985). https://doi.org/10.1007/3-540-39568-7_5
3. Al-Riyami, S.S., Paterson, K.G.: Certificateless public key cryptography. In: Laih, C.-S. (ed.) ASIACRYPT 2003. LNCS, vol. 2894, pp. 452–473. Springer, Heidelberg (2003). https://doi.org/10.1007/978-3-540-40061-5_29
4. Wang, B., Song, Z.: A non-interactive deniable authentication scheme based on designated verifier proofs. Inf. Sci. **179**(6), 858–865 (2009)
5. Di Raimondo, M., Gennaro, R.: New approaches for deniable authentication. In: 12th ACM Conference on Computer and Communications Security, pp. 112–121. ACM, Maryland (2005)
6. Tian, H., Chen, X., Jiang, Z.: Non-interactive deniable authentication protocols. In: Wu, C.-K., Yung, M., Lin, D. (eds.) Inscrypt 2011. LNCS, vol. 7537, pp. 142–159. Springer, Heidelberg (2012). https://doi.org/10.1007/978-3-642-34704-7_12
7. Li, F., Takagi, T.: Cryptanalysis and improvement of robust deniable authentication protocol. Wirel. Pers. Commun. **69**(4), 1391–1398 (2013)
8. Gambs, S., Onete, C., Robert, J.: Prover anonymous and deniable distance-bounding authentication. In: 9th ACM Symposium on Information Computer and Communications Security, pp. 501–506. ACM, Kyoto (2014)
9. Zeng, S., Chen, Y., Tan, S., He, M.: Concurrently deniable ring authentication and its application to LBS in VANETs. Peer-to-Peer Netw. Appl. **10**(4), 844–856 (2017)

10. Lu, R., Cao, Z., Wang, S., Bao, H.: A new ID-based deniable authentication protocol. Informatica **18**(1), 67–78 (2007)
11. Li, F., Xiong, P., Jin, C.: Identity-based deniable authentication for ad hoc networks. Computing **96**(9), 843–853 (2014)
12. Yao, A., Zhao, Y.: Privacy-preserving authenticated key-exchange over Internet. IEEE Trans. Inf. Forensics Secur. **9**(1), 125–140 (2014)
13. Jin, C., Xu, C., Li, F., Zhang, X.: A novel certificateless deniable authentication protocol. Int. J. Comput. Appl. **37**(3–4), 181–192 (2015)
14. Jin, C., Xu, C., Zhang, X., Li, F.: An efficient certificateless deniable authentication protocol without pairings. Int. J. Electron. Secur. Digit. Forensics **7**(2), 179–196 (2015)
15. Li, F., Hong, J., Omala, A.: Practical deniable authentication for pervasive computing environments. Wirel. Netw. **24**(1), 139–149 (2018)
16. Choon, J.C., Hee Cheon, J.: An identity-based signature from gap Diffie-Hellman groups. In: Desmedt, Y.G. (ed.) PKC 2003. LNCS, vol. 2567, pp. 18–30. Springer, Heidelberg (2003). https://doi.org/10.1007/3-540-36288-6_2
17. Boneh, D., Franklin, M.: Identity-based encryption from the Weil pairing. In: Kilian, J. (ed.) CRYPTO 2001. LNCS, vol. 2139, pp. 213–229. Springer, Heidelberg (2001). https://doi.org/10.1007/3-540-44647-8_13
18. Johnson, D., Menezes, A., Vanstone, S.: The elliptic curve digital signature algorithm (ECDSA). Int. J. Inf. Secur. **1**(1), 36–63 (2001)
19. Scott, M.: Efficient implementation of cryptographic pairings (2007). http://www.pairing-conference.org/2007/invited/Scottslide.pdf

One-Round Authenticated Group Key Establishment Using Multilinear Maps

Kashi Neupane[✉]

Department of Mathematics, University of North Georgia,
Oakwood, GA, USA
knneupane@ung.edu

Abstract. In this paper, we propose a one-round authenticated group key establishment protocol. Our protocol is based on Graded Decisional Diffie-Hellman assumption, and it requires timestamps. The resulting solution is in the random oracle model, builds on a multilinear map, and offers integrity as well as strong entity authentication. This proposed construction can also be viewed as a compiler that can transform a passively secure one-round group key establishment protocol to an actively secure one without an additional round.

Keywords: Group key establishment · Multilinear maps · Timestamps

1 Introduction

Group Key Establishment protocols allow a group of people to establish a common secret in presence of adversaries. Once a common secret is established, members of the group can exchange large amount of data securely as desired. Most commonly used tools for group key establishment protocols are two-party Diffie-Hellman assumption [7] and Joux's 3-party key agreement protocol [9]. On the other hand, Wu et al. [12] reconsidered the definition of group key agreement and introduced the notion of asymmetric group key agreement. They also proposed an asymmetric GKA protocol which is secure under the decision BDHE assumption without using random oracles. Zhang et al. [13] proposed a security model for identity-based authenticated asymmetric group key agreement (IB-AAGKA) protocols. Then, they proposed an IB-AAGKA protocol which is proven secure under the Bilinear Diffie-Hellman Exponent assumption. One of the major goals in establishing a secure key is communication efficiency. Boneh and Silverberg [3] argued that multilinear mapping would have very interesting applications in cryptographic protocols in order to reduce the number of rounds. Construction of multilinear mapping was a long-standing problems. In 2013, multilinear mappings proposed by Garg et al. [8] and Coron et al. [6] based on ideal lattice and over the integers respectively. Moreover, Garg et al. also proposed a one-round group key exchange protocol as its one of the most fascinating applications.

© Springer Nature Singapore Pte Ltd. 2018
F. Li et al. (Eds.): FCS 2018, CCIS 879, pp. 55–65, 2018.
https://doi.org/10.1007/978-981-13-3095-7_5

Garg et al. [8] proposed one-round group key establishment protocol which is unauthenticated i.e. secure against passive eavesdroppers only which is far less than what we want from a key exchange protocol. Most of the authenticated symmetric group key agreement protocols based on these common tools require at least two rounds. It is a very common practice to achieve an actively secure protocol from passively secure one with the use of a compiler [2,10]. The major drawback of this technique is that it costs one more additional round. The additional round certainly limits the use of protocols for many applications in which each users get only one chance to send their messages. In this research, we construct a compiler that can transform a passively secure protocol to an actively secure one without an additional round, and present an actively secure one-round group key establishment protocol. More specifically, we extend the existing one-round unauthenticated group key exchange protocol to an authenticated one without the cost of one additional round. We use multilinear mapping proposed by Garg et al. [8], and make use of timestamps proposed by Barbosa and Farshim [1]. With our techniques, we not only construct an actively secure protocol, we also provide some additional features, such as entity authentication and integrity of the protocol in one round.

2   Preliminaries

As a mathematical tool we use Approximate Multilinear Mappings, proposed by Garg et al. [8], which have been used to derive a Graded Encoding System. In this section, we briefly review the notion of Graded Encoding System. For more detailed information, we refer to [6,8]. We also review the standard definition of signature scheme at the end of the section.

2.1   Brief Overview

Consider an integer n which is large enough to ensure the security and a polynomial ring $R = \mathbb{Z}[x]/x^n + 1$. One generates a principal ideal $I = \langle g \rangle \subset R$ by generating a secret short ring element $g \in R$. An integer parameter q and another random secret $z \in R/qR$ are also generated. With the use of such parameters, each coset $e + I$ of the quotient ring R/I is encoded in multiple levels. If c is an element from $e + I$, then the level-i encoding of the element $e + I$ is an element of the form $[c/z^i]_q$. Such encodings can be added and multiplied, as long as the norm of the numerator remains shorter than q; the encoding of an element in the level κ can be obtained by taking the product of κ encoding of level 1. For such level-κ encodings, one can then define a zero-testing parameter, $p_{zt} = [hz^\kappa/g]_q$, for some small $h \in R$. This zero-testing parameter is used to determine whether a level-κ encoding c is zero or not by computing $[p_{zt} \cdot c/z^\kappa]_q = [hc/g]_q$. More specifically, zero from non-zero can be distinguished by using zero-testing parameter since the product $[p_{zt} \cdot c/z^\kappa]_q$ is small whenever c is small, and the product $[p_{zt} \cdot c/z^\kappa]_q$ is large whenever c is large. Additionally, two encodings of the two different elements from two encodings of the same element can be distinguished by subtraction with the help of this zero-testing parameter.

In this notion graded encoding system, there are levels of encodings to generate ciphertexts from plaintexts. Ring elements $\alpha \in R$ are considered as plaintexts, $\alpha.g$ in the source group are considered as level-1 elements, and a product of i level encodings represents level-i encodings. So, level-κ encodings corresponds to the target group from multilinear maps. Now we review the definition of κ-graded encoding system and then GDDH assumption from [6, 8].

Definition 1 (κ-Graded Encoding System). *A κ-Graded Encoding System for a ring R is a system of sets $\mathbb{S} = \{S_i^{(\alpha)} \subset \{0,1\}^* : \alpha \in R, 0 \leq i \leq \kappa\}$, with the following properties:*

- *For every fixed i, the sets $\{S_i^{(\alpha)} : \alpha \in R\}$ are disjoint.*
- *There are binary operations $+$ and $-$ (on $\{0,1\}^*$) such that for every $\alpha_1, \alpha_2 \in R$, every index $i \leq \kappa$, and every $u_1 \in S_i^{(\alpha_1)}$ and $u_2 \in S_i^{(\alpha_2)}$, it holds that $u_1 + u_2 \in S_i^{(\alpha_1 + \alpha_2)}$ and $-u_1 \in S_i^{(-\alpha_1)}$, where $\alpha_1 + \alpha_2$ and $-\alpha_1$ are addition and negation in R.*
- *There is an associative binary association $\times$ on (on $\{0,1\}^*$) such that for every $\alpha_1, \alpha_2 \in R$, every i_1, i_2 with $i_1 + i_2 \leq \kappa$, and $u_1 \in S_{i_1}^{(\alpha_1)}$ and $u_2 \in S_{i_2}^{(\alpha_2)}$, it holds that $u_1 \times u_2 \in S_{i_1+i_2}^{(\alpha_1 \cdot \alpha_2)}$. Here $\alpha_1 \cdot \alpha_2$ is multiplication in R, and $i_1 + i_2$ is integer addition.*

2.2 Multilinear Map Procedures

Instance Generation. The randomized algorithm $\mathsf{InstGen}(1^\lambda, 1^\kappa)$ takes the security parameters λ and κ as it inputs and returns $(\mathsf{params}, p_{zt})$, where params is a description of a κ-Graded Encoding System and p_{zt} is a zero-testing parameter.

Ring Sampler. The randomized algorithm $\mathsf{samp}(\mathsf{params})$ takes a nearly uniform element $\alpha \in_R R$ as its input and returns a level-zero encoding $a \in S_0^{(\alpha)}$, but the encoding of a does not have to be uniform in $S_0^{(\alpha)}$.

Encoding. The $\mathsf{Enc}(\mathsf{params}, i, a)$ takes a level-zero encoding $a \in S_0^{(\alpha)}$ for some $\alpha \in R$ and index $i \leq \kappa$ as its inputs and returns the level-i encoding $u \in S_i^{(\alpha)}$ for some α.

Re-randomization. The randomized $\mathsf{reRand}(\mathsf{params}, i, u)$ rerandomizes encodings to the same level i, as long as the initial encoding u is under a given noise bound.

Addition and negation. Given params and two encodings relative to the same level, $u_1 \in S_i^{(\alpha_1)}$ and $u_2 \in S_i^{(\alpha_2)}$, we have $\mathsf{add}(\mathsf{params}, u_1, u_2) \in S_i^{(\alpha_1 + \alpha_2)}$ and $\mathsf{neg}(\mathsf{params}, u_1) \in S_i^{(-\alpha_1)}$, subject to bounds on the noise.

Multiplication. For $u_1 \in S_i^{(\alpha_1)}$ and $u_2 \in S_j^{(\alpha_2)}$, there is $\mathsf{mul}(\mathsf{params}, u_1, u_2) = u_1 \times u_2 \in S_{i+j}^{(\alpha_1 \cdot \alpha_2)}$.

Zero-Test. The procedure Zero(params, p_{zt}, u) outputs 1 if $u \in S_\kappa^{(0)}$ and 0 otherwise.

Extraction. This procedure extracts a "canonical" and "random" representation of ring elements from their level-κ encoding. More precisely, ext(params, p_{zt}, u) outputs, say $s \in \{0, 1\}^\lambda$ such that:

- ext(params, p_{zt}, u_1) = ext(params, p_{zt}, u_2), for every $\alpha \in R$ and $u_1, u_2 \in S_\kappa^{(\alpha)}$,
- The distribution $\{$ext(params, p_{zt}, u) $: \alpha \in_R R, u \in S_\kappa^{(\alpha)}\}$ is nearly uniform over $\{0, 1\}^\lambda$.

2.3   Hardness Assumptions

Graded Decisional Diffie-Hellman Problem. Garg et al. [8] modeled their hardness assumptions based on the discrete logarithm and DDH assumptions in multilinear groups. Here we review the concepts of graded DDH problem (GDDH problem) as defined by [6,8] which they formalized as the following process:

- (params, p_{zt}) $\leftarrow$ InstGen(1^λ, 1^κ)
- Choose $a_j \leftarrow$ samp(params) for all $1 \leq j \leq \kappa + 1$, a_j is a randomly and uniformly generated element in R
- set $u_j \leftarrow$ reRand(params, 1, enc(params, 1, a_j)) for all $1 \leq j \leq \kappa + 1$, u_j is an encoding at level 1
- Set $\tilde{u} = $ reRand(params, κ, enc(params, κ, $\prod_{i=1}^{\kappa+1} a_i$)), $\tilde{u}$ is an encoding of the right product at level κ
- Set $\hat{u} = $ reRand(params, κ, enc(params, κ, r)), $\hat{u}$ is an encoding of a random product r at level κ

The GDDH distinguisher is given as input either $\tilde{u}$ (encoding of the right product) or $\hat{u}$ (encoding of a random product), along with the $\kappa+1$ level-one encodings u_j, and must decide which is the case.

Graded Decisional Diffie-Hellman GDDH Assumption. The Graded Decisional Diffie-Hellman Assumption is that the advantage of any efficient adversary is negligible in the security parameter against Graded Decisional Diffie-Hellman Problem.

2.4   Digital Signature Scheme

A digital signature is a method to sign a message electronically by a user which can be verified by anybody later. A digital signature protects data from being altered, respectively enables the detection of modification. We quickly review the definition of a signature scheme—for more details we refer to [11].

Definition 2 (Signature scheme). *A signature scheme $S = (\mathcal{K}, \mathcal{S}, \mathcal{V})$ is a triple of polynomial-time algorithms:*

- *A probabilistic key generation algorithm $\mathcal{K}$ which takes the security parameter 1^k as its input, and returns a key pair (pk, sk)—a public verification key pk and matching secret signing key sk;*
- *A probabilistic signing algorithm $\mathcal{S}$ which takes message $M \in \{0,1\}^*$ and secret signing key sk as its inputs, and returns a signature σ on M;*
- *A deterministic verification algorithm $\mathcal{V}$ which takes a public key pk, a message M, and a signature σ for M as its inputs, and returns 1 or 0, indicating whether σ is a valid signature for M under the public key pk.*

For pairs (sk, pk) output by $\mathcal{K}$, we require that with overwhelming probability the following condition holds: $\mathcal{V}_{pk}(M, \mathcal{S}_{sk}(M)) = 1$, for all messages M.

Definition 3 (Existentially unforgeable signature scheme under chosen message attacks (UF–CMA)). *A signature scheme $\mathcal{S}$ is said to be existentially unforgeable under chosen message attacks if for all probabilistic polynomial time adversaries $\mathcal{A}$ the following probability is negligible (in k):*

$$Pr[(pk, sk) \leftarrow \mathcal{K}; (M, \sigma) \leftarrow \mathcal{A}^{\mathcal{S}_{sk}(\cdot)} : \mathcal{V}_{pk}(M, \sigma) = 1 \wedge (M, \sigma) \neq (M_i, \sigma_i)],$$

where M_i denotes a message submitted by $\mathcal{A}$ to $\mathcal{S}_{sk}(\cdot)$.

3 Security Model

Our security analysis is based on the model used by Katz and Yung [10], which was based on Bresson et al. [4,5]. Additionally, we extend the security model by using timestamps as proposed by Barbosa and Farshim [1] to capture the notion of timeliness. In this model, each user is given a local clock at the beginning.

Protocol Participants. We denote by $\mathcal{U} = \{U_0, ..., U_n\}$ a polynomial size set of *users*, which are modeled as ppt algorithms, and each $U \in \mathcal{U}$ can execute a polynomial number of protocol instances Π_U^s concurrently ($s \in \mathbb{N}$). User identities are assumed to be bitstrings of identical length k and to keep notation simple, throughout we will not distinguish between the bitstring identifying a user U and the algorithm U itself. To a protocol instance Π_U^s, the following seven variables are associated:

acc_U^s: a Boolean variable, which is set to TRUE if and only if the session key stored in sk_U^s has been accepted;

pid_U^s: stores the identities of those users in $\mathcal{U}$ with which a key is to be established, including U;

sk_U^s: is initialized with a distinguished NULL value and after a successful protocol execution stores the session key;

sid_U^s: stores a non-secret session identifier that can be used as public reference to the session key stored in sk_U^s;

$state_U^s$: stores state information;

$term_U^s$: a Boolean variable, which is set to TRUE if and only if the protocol execution has terminated;

$used_U^s$: indicates if this instance is involved in a protocol run.

Initialization. In this timestamps model, local clocks are introduced, we provide each party with a clock variable, which is initially set to zero. Before actual protocol executions take place, a trusted initialization phase *without adversarial interference* is allowed. In this phase, for each $U \in \mathcal{U}$ a (verification key, signing key)-pair $(pk_U, sk_U^{\mathsf{sig}})$ for an existentially unforgeable (EUF-CMA secure) signature scheme is generated, sk_U^{sig} is given to U only, and pk_U is handed to all users in $\mathcal{U}$ and to the adversary.

Adversarial Capabilities and Communication Network. The network is non-private, fully asynchronous and allows arbitrary point-to-point connections among users. The adversary $\mathcal{A}$ is modeled as ppt algorithm with full control over the communication network. More specifically, $\mathcal{A}$'s capabilities are captured by the following *oracles*:

$\mathsf{Send}(U, s, M)$: sends the message M to instance Π_U^s of user U and returns the protocol message output by that instance after receiving M. The Send oracle also enables $\mathcal{A}$ to initialize a protocol execution by sending a special message $M = \{U_{i_1}, \ldots, U_{i_r}\}$ to an unused instance Π_U^s. After such a query, Π_U^s sets $\mathsf{pid}_U^s := \{U_{i_1}, \ldots, U_{i_r}\}$, $\mathsf{used}_U^s := \mathrm{TRUE}$, and processes the first step of the protocol.

$\mathsf{Reveal}(U, s)$: returns the session key sk_U^s if $\mathsf{acc}_U^s = \mathrm{TRUE}$ and a NULL value otherwise.

$\mathsf{Corrupt}(U)$: for a user $U \in \mathcal{U}$ this query returns U's long term signing key sk_U^{sig}.

$\mathsf{Tick}(U)$: increment the clock variable at user $U \in \mathcal{U}$ and its new value is returned.

In order to achieve any short of timeliness guarantee by capturing the notion of synchronization of clocks, we define the following:

Definition 4 (δ-synchronization). *An adversary in the timed BCPQ model satisfies δ-synchronization if it never causes the* clock *variables of any two honest parties to differ by more than δ.*

Now we review the concept of entity authentication based on timestamps from [1]. Let $t_B(E)$ be the function returning the value of the local clock at B when the event E occurred. Let $\mathsf{acc}(\mathsf{A}, \mathsf{i})$ and $\mathsf{term}(\mathsf{B}, \mathsf{j})$ denote that the event Π_A^i accepted and the event that Π_B^j terminated respectively. Let Π_A^i and Π_B^j be two partnered oracles where the latter has terminated.

Definition 5 (β-recent Entity Authentication ($\beta - \mathrm{REA}$)). *We say that a key exchange protocol provides β-recent initiator-to-responder authentication if it provides initiator-to-responder authentication, and furthermore for any honest responder oracle Π_B^j which has terminated with partner Π_A^i, with A honest, we have*

$$|t_B(\mathsf{term}(\mathsf{B}, \mathsf{j})) - t_A(\mathsf{acc}(\mathsf{A}, \mathsf{i}))| \leq \beta.$$

In addition to the mentioned oracles, $\mathcal{A}$ has access to a Test oracle, which can be queried only once: the query $\mathsf{Test}(U, s)$ can be made with an instance Π_U^s that has accepted a session key. Then a bit $b \leftarrow \{0, 1\}$ is chosen uniformly at random; for $b = 0$, the session key stored in sk_U^s is returned, and for $b = 1$ a uniformly at random chosen element from the space of session keys is returned.

Definition 6 (Partnering). *Two instances* $\prod_{U_i}^{s_i}$ *and* $\prod_{U_j}^{s_j}$ *are* partnered *if* $\mathsf{sid}_{U_i}^{s_i} = \mathsf{sid}_{U_j}^{s_j}$, $\mathsf{pid}_{U_i}^{s_i} = \mathsf{pid}_{U_j}^{s_j}$ *and* $\mathsf{acc}_{U_i}^{s_i} = \mathsf{acc}_{U_j}^{s_j} = \mathrm{TRUE}$.

Based on this notion of partnering, we can specify what we mean by a *fresh* instance, i.e., an instance where the adversary should not know the session key:

Definition 7 (Freshness). *An instance* $\prod_{U_i}^{s_i}$ *is said to be* fresh *if the adversary queried neither* $\mathsf{Corrupt}(U_j)$ *for some* $U_j \in \mathsf{pid}_{U_i}^{s_i}$ *before a query of the form* $\mathsf{Send}(U_k, s_k, *)$ *with* $U_k \in \mathsf{pid}_{U_i}^{s_i}$ *has taken place, nor* $\mathsf{Reveal}(U_j, s_j)$ *for an instance* $\prod_{U_j}^{s_j}$ *that is partnered with* $\prod_{U_i}^{s_i}$.

It is worth noting that the above definition allows an adversary $\mathcal{A}$ to reveal *all* secret signing keys without violating freshness, provided $\mathcal{A}$ does not send any messages after having received the signing keys. As a consequence security in the sense of Definition 8 below implies forward secrecy: We write $\mathsf{Succ}_{\mathcal{A}}$ for the event $\mathcal{A}$ queries Test with a fresh instance and outputs a correct guess for the Test oracle's bit b. By

$$\mathsf{Adv}_{\mathcal{A}}^{\mathsf{ke}} = \mathsf{Adv}_{\mathcal{A}}^{\mathsf{ke}}(k) := \left| \Pr[\mathsf{Succ}] - \frac{1}{2} \right|$$

we denote the *advantage* of $\mathcal{A}$.

Definition 8 (Semantic security). *A key establishment protocol is said to be* (semantically) secure, *if* $\mathsf{Adv}_{\mathcal{A}}^{\mathsf{ke}} = \mathsf{Adv}_{\mathcal{A}}^{\mathsf{ke}}(k)$ *is negligible for all ppt algorithms* $\mathcal{A}$.

In addition to the above standard security goal, we are also interested in *integrity* (which may be interpreted a form of "worst case correctness") and *strong entity authentication*:

Definition 9 (Integrity). *A key establishment protocol fulfills* integrity *if with overwhelming probability for all instances* $\prod_{U_i}^{s_i}$, $\prod_{U_j}^{s_j}$ *of uncorrupted users the following holds: if* $\mathsf{acc}_{U_i}^{s_i} = \mathsf{acc}_{U_j}^{s_j} = \mathrm{TRUE}$ *and* $\mathsf{sid}_{U_i}^{s_i} = \mathsf{sid}_{U_j}^{s_j}$, *then* $\mathsf{sk}_{U_i}^{s_i} = \mathsf{sk}_{U_j}^{s_j}$ *and* $\mathsf{pid}_{U_i}^{s_i} = \mathsf{pid}_{U_j}^{s_j}$.

Definition 10 (Strong entity authentication). *We say that* strong entity authentication *for an instance* $\Pi_{U_i}^{s_i}$ *is provided if* $\mathsf{acc}_{U_i}^{s_i} = \mathrm{TRUE}$ *implies that for all uncorrupted* $U_j \in \mathsf{pid}_{U_i}^{s_i}$ *there exists with overwhelming probability an instance* $\Pi_{U_j}^{s_j}$ *with* $\mathsf{sid}_{U_j}^{s_j} = \mathsf{sid}_{U_i}^{s_i}$ *and* $U_i \in \mathsf{pid}_{U_j}^{s_j}$.

4   The Proposed Group Key Establishment Protocol

4.1   Description of the Protocol

The proposed protocol is an authenticated one-round group key exchange protocol. The protocol makes use of a polynomial ring, timestamps, and random oracle $H : \{0,1\}^* \to \{0,1\}^\kappa$. In this protocol, all parties are allowed to broadcast only one message simultaneously. Once each party broadcast their messages, each party will be able to compute a common master key after successful verification of signatures and timestamps. The proposed protocol for establishing a common session key among users $U_0, \ldots, U_N$ with $\kappa = N - 1$, is described in Fig. 1 Finally, each user computes a session key and a session id using the same master key. Here P_{zt} is a level $N - 1$ zero-test parameter. In this construction, we insist that the order of the quotient ring R/I be a large prime.

Round 1:

Setup($1^\lambda, 1^N$) - Takes a security parameter $\lambda \in Z^+$ and the number of participants N. It runs InstGen algorithm (params, P_{zt}) $\leftarrow$ InstGen($1^\lambda, 1^{N-1}$) and outputs (params, P_{zt}) as the public parameter.

Publish(params, P_{zt}, i) - Each party U_i chooses a random level-zero encoding $d_i \leftarrow$ Samp(Params) as a secret key and publishes the corresponding level-one public-key $w_i \leftarrow$ Enc(params, $1, d_i$). Each party U_i checks the local time value t_i, constructs a messages $m_i = w_i \| t_i \| \sigma_i(w_i \| t_i \| \text{pid})$, and broadcasts it.

KeyGen(params, $P_{zt}, d_i, \{m_i\}_{i \neq j}$) - Upon receipt of m_i from each party, U_j accepts the message m_i from U_i if:

- the signature σ_i is successfully verified
- $t_i \in [t_j - \delta, t_j + \delta]$
- List L does not contain the pair (m, t)
- U_j updates the list L adding pair (m, t_j)

If all the verifications are successful, then each party U_i multiplies its secret key d_i by the public keys of all its peers $v_j \leftarrow d_j \prod_{i \neq j} w_i$. Thus, each user gets a level $N - 1$ encoding of the product coset $\prod (d_i + I)$. Finally, each party uses the extraction routine to compute the master key $K \leftarrow$ ext(params, P_{zt}, v_j) and sets $\text{sk}_{U_i} := H(K\|0)$ and $\text{sid}_{U_i} := H(K\|1)$.

Fig. 1. Secure group key establishment.

4.2   Security Analysis

The security of the protocol in Fig. 1 can be ensured secure provided that the Graded Decisional Diffie-Hellman assumption holds on a polynomial ring $\mathbb{Z}[x]/x^n + 1$ and the underlying signature scheme is existentially unforgeable. More specifically, we have the following:

Proposition 1. *Suppose the GDDH assumption holds and the underlying signature scheme holds in the sense of UF-CMA. Then the protocol in Fig. 1 is semantically secure, fulfills integrity, and strong entity authentication holds to all involved instances in the timed BCPQ model.*

Proof. Let q_{send} and q_{ro} denote the polynomial upper bounds for the number of the adversary $\mathcal{A}$'s queries to the Send oracle and random oracle H respectively. First, we address two events that each of them can occur with negligible probability only:

Let Forge be the event that $\mathcal{A}$ succeeds in forging a signature σ_i of a protocol participant U_i on a message without having queried Corrupt(U_i). During the protocol's initialization phase, a challenge verification key can be assigned to a user $U \in \mathcal{U}$ uniformly at random, and with probability at least $1/|\mathcal{U}|$, the event Forge results in a successful forgery for the challenge verification key. As $|\mathcal{U}|$ is a polynomial, Forge can occur with negligible probability only.

Let Collision be the event of a collision in the random oracle H, i.e., H produces the same output value for two different input values. As a Send query causes one random oracle query, we can bound the number of queries to H by $q_{\mathsf{send}} + q_{\mathsf{ro}}$. Hence,

$$\Pr[\mathsf{Collision}] \leq (q_{\mathsf{send}} + q_{\mathsf{ro}})^2/2^{\kappa}$$

is negligible.

As each of the events Forge, and Collision occurs with negligible probability only, subsequently we may assume they do not occur. To establish semantic security, we use 'game hopping' and let a given adversary $\mathcal{A}$ interact with a simulator. For the advantage of $\mathcal{A}$ in Game i we write $\mathrm{Adv}_{\mathcal{A}}^{\mathrm{Game}\ i}$. Similarly, $\Pr[\mathrm{Succ}_{\mathcal{A}}^{\mathrm{Game}\ i}]$ denotes the probability of success of $\mathcal{A}$ in Game i. The event of $\mathcal{A}$ to succeed in Game i and the advantage of $\mathcal{A}$ in Game i will be denoted by $\mathrm{Succ}_{\mathcal{A}}^{\mathrm{Game}\ i}$ and $\mathrm{Adv}_{\mathcal{A}}^{\mathrm{Game}}\ i$, respectively.

With this we are ready for the main part of the proof:

Game 0: This game is identical to the original attack game for the adversary, with all oracles being simulated faithfully. In particular,

$$\mathrm{Adv}_{\mathcal{A}} = \mathrm{Adv}_{\mathcal{A}}^{\mathrm{Game}\ 0}.$$

Game 1: This game differs from Game 0 in the simulator's response in Round 1. Instead of computing v_j from d_i's as specified in Round 1, the simulator replaces v_j with a uniformly at random chosen element. We have $|\mathrm{Adv}_{\mathcal{A}}^{\mathrm{Game}\ 1} - \mathrm{Adv}_{\mathcal{A}}^{\mathrm{Game}\ 0}| \leq |\Pr(\mathrm{Succ}_{\mathcal{A}}^{\mathrm{Game}\ 1}) - \Pr(\mathrm{Succ}_{\mathcal{A}}^{\mathrm{Game}\ 0})|$, and to recognize the latter as negligible consider the following algorithm $\mathcal{B}$ to solve the GDDH problem: $\mathcal{B}$ faithfully simulates all parties and oracles as faced by $\mathcal{A}$ in Game 0 with one exception. Namely, let u be the GDDH challenge received by $\mathcal{B}$. Then

– the n-party key common element v_j is not computed as specified in the protocol but replaced with the value u in the GDDH challenge.

Whenever $\mathcal{A}$ correctly identifies the secret bit of the (simulated) Test oracle, $\mathcal{B}$ outputs a 1, i.e., claims $u = v_j$. By construction we have

$$\mathrm{Adv}_{\mathcal{B}}^{\mathrm{gddh}} = \left| \frac{1}{2} \cdot \Pr[\mathrm{Succ}_{\mathcal{A}}^{\mathrm{Game}\ 0}] + \frac{1}{2} \cdot (1 - \Pr[\mathrm{Succ}_{\mathcal{A}}^{\mathrm{Game}\ 1}])] - \frac{1}{2} \right|$$

$$= \frac{1}{2} \cdot \left| \Pr[\mathrm{Succ}_{\mathcal{A}}^{\mathrm{Game}\ 1}] - \Pr[\mathrm{Succ}_{\mathcal{A}}^{\mathrm{Game}\ 0}] \right|,$$

and with the GDDH assumption we recognize $|\mathrm{Adv}_{\mathcal{A}}^{\mathrm{Game}\ 1} - \mathrm{Adv}_{\mathcal{A}}^{\mathrm{Game}\ 0}|$ as negligible.

Game 2: Here we replace the session key sk_{U_i} with a uniformly at random chosen bitstring in $\{0,1\}^{\kappa}$. Game 1 and Game 2 only differ if the adversary queries the random oracle H with the extracted key K. With no information about K other than $H(K\|0)$ and $H(K\|1)$ being available to $\mathcal{A}$, we obtain

$$\left|\mathrm{Adv}_{\mathcal{A}}^{\mathrm{Game}\ 3} - \mathrm{Adv}_{\mathcal{A}}^{\mathrm{Game}\ 1}\right| \leq \frac{q_{\mathsf{ro}} + q_{\mathsf{send}}}{2^{\kappa}}.$$

By construction $\mathrm{Adv}_{\mathcal{A}}^{\mathrm{Game}\ 2} = 0$, and we recognize the protocol in Fig. 1 as secure, provided that the GDDH assumption holds.

Integrity. If all the instances of honest users agree on a common session identifier $H(K \| 1)$, unless the event Collision occurs they have obtained the same "master key" K—and therewith partner identifier. With the session key being computed as $H(K \| 0)$, we see that equality of session identifiers with overwhelming probability ensures identical session keys too.

Entity Authentication. Successful verification of the signatures and successful verification of validity of timestamps on the Round 1 messages, ensure the existence of a used instance for each intended communication partner and that the respective v_i values are identical. The latter implies equality of both the pid_i- and the sid_i-values.

□

5 Conclusion

In this paper, we proposed a one-round authenticated group key establishment protocol in the random oracle model. Our work can also transform a passively secure protocol to an actively secure one without an additional round. For applications where communication cost is high, this seems an attractive feature. The above proposed protocol is based on Graded Diffie-Hellman assumption and makes use of timestamps. Additionally, the protocol ensures the entity authentication and integrity of the protocol.

References

1. Barbosa, M., Farshim, P.: Security analysis of standard authentication and key agreement protocols utilising timestamps. In: Preneel, B. (ed.) AFRICACRYPT 2009. LNCS, vol. 5580, pp. 235–253. Springer, Heidelberg (2009). https://doi.org/10.1007/978-3-642-02384-2_15
2. Bohli, J.-M.: A framework for robust group key agreement. In: Gavrilova, M., et al. (eds.) ICCSA 2006. LNCS, vol. 3982, pp. 355–364. Springer, Heidelberg (2006). https://doi.org/10.1007/11751595_39

3. Boneh, D., Silverberg, A.: Application of multilinear forms to cryptography. Contemp. Math. **324**, 71–90 (2003)
4. Bresson, E., Chevassut, O., Pointcheval, D.: Provably authenticated group Diffie-Hellman key exchange — the dynamic case. In: Boyd, C. (ed.) ASIACRYPT 2001. LNCS, vol. 2248, pp. 290–309. Springer, Heidelberg (2001). https://doi.org/10.1007/3-540-45682-1_18
5. Bresson, E., Chevassut, O., Pointcheval, D., Quisquater, J.-J.: Provably authenticated group Diffie-Hellman key exchange. In: Proceedings of the 8th ACM Conference on Computer and Communications Security CCS 2001, pp. 255–264. ACM (2001)
6. Coron, J.-S., Lepoint, T., Tibouchi, M.: Practical multilinear maps over the integers. In: Canetti, R., Garay, J.A. (eds.) CRYPTO 2013. LNCS, vol. 8042, pp. 476–493. Springer, Heidelberg (2013). https://doi.org/10.1007/978-3-642-40041-4_26
7. Diffie, W., Hellman, M.E.: New direction in cryptography. IEEE Trans. Inf. Theory **22**, 644–654 (1976)
8. Garg, S., Gentry, C., Halevi, S.: Candidate multilinear maps from ideal lattices. In: Johansson, T., Nguyen, P.Q. (eds.) EUROCRYPT 2013. LNCS, vol. 7881, pp. 1–17. Springer, Heidelberg (2013). https://doi.org/10.1007/978-3-642-38348-9_1
9. Joux, A.: A one round protocol for tripartite DiffieHellman. J. Cryptol. **17**(4), 263–276 (2004)
10. Katz, J., Yung, M.: Scalable protocols for authenticated group key exchange. In: Boneh, D. (ed.) CRYPTO 2003. LNCS, vol. 2729, pp. 110–125. Springer, Heidelberg (2003). https://doi.org/10.1007/978-3-540-45146-4_7
11. Menezes, A., Van Oorschot, P., Vanstone, S.: Handbook of Applied Cryptography. CRC Press, Boca Raton (1996)
12. Wu, Q., Mu, Y., Susilo, W., Qin, B., Domingo-Ferrer, J.: Asymmetric group key agreement. In: Joux, A. (ed.) EUROCRYPT 2009. LNCS, vol. 5479, pp. 153–170. Springer, Heidelberg (2009). https://doi.org/10.1007/978-3-642-01001-9_9
13. Zhang, L., Wu, Q., Qin, B., Domingo-Ferrer, J.: Identity-based authenticated asymmetric group key agreement protocol. In: Thai, M.T., Sahni, S. (eds.) COCOON 2010. LNCS, vol. 6196, pp. 510–519. Springer, Heidelberg (2010). https://doi.org/10.1007/978-3-642-14031-0_54

Novel Secure Privacy-Preserving Decentralized Attribute-Based Encryption

Pengfei Liang[✉], Leyou Zhang, and Yujie Shang

School of Mathematics and Statistics, Xidian University, Xi'an 710126, China
pengfeixdsecure@163.com

Abstract. Decentralized attribute-based encryption (DABE) is an efficient multi-authority attribute-based encryption system. But most of the available are shown there are security vulnerabilities. How to construct secure DABE is still a challenging problem at present. In this paper, based on Lewko and Waters's scheme, a decentralized attribute-based encryption with preserving the privacy of the identifies and attributes in access structure is proposed. The presented scheme keeps the security of the original one and removes the random oracle. In addition, the proposed scheme achieves the user collusion avoidance. Finally, we show that the security of the proposed scheme is reduced to static assumptions based on dual system encryption instead of other strong assumptions.

Keywords: Decentralized ABE · Privacy-preserving
Resistance collusion

1 Introduction

ABE has been fully concerned [1–9] since it was issued by Sahai and Waters in 2005 [10]. In ABE, the private key was generated by a single central authority (CA). CA not only interacts with all users in the system but verifies identities and attributes for them, which brings the problem of overburden and disproportionate power. However, the emergence of multiple authorities (MAs) can solve the above problems, where MAs can lighten the burden of user authentication and concentration of power. Since then, the open problem is how to construct an ABE system in which a user can extract his own private key from multiple authorities so as to reduce the trust and burden of the central authority. To address this open question, Chase proposed the first multi-authority attribute-based encryption (MA-ABE) in scheme [6]. There are polynomial number of authorities of independence to monitor attributes and distribute private keys for users in [6]. It can tolerate any number of corrupt authorities. However, Chase's scheme did not consider the protection of user's privacy. In addition, multiple authorities in his scheme are supervised by a central authority, which means it needs central authority to distribute secret keys for multiple authorities, users' GIDs and private keys for them. Chase and Chow improved the scheme [6] and first proposed

© Springer Nature Singapore Pte Ltd. 2018
F. Li et al. (Eds.): FCS 2018, CCIS 879, pp. 66–80, 2018.
https://doi.org/10.1007/978-981-13-3095-7_6

a privacy-preserving multi-authority attribute-based encryption (PPMA-ABE) scheme [7]. In their works, they removed the need for central authority but required the interaction among multiple attribute authorities. Then Li et al. [11] proposed a multi-authority ciphertext-policy ABE (MA-CP-ABE) scheme that access structure employs an AND gate with wildcards. In [11], authors use an anonymous key distribution protocol to hide the user's GID. This scheme allows tracking identity of the misbehaved users who leak the decryption key, and it also requires the interaction among multiple authorities. Scheme [7] leaves an open challenge to construct a PPMA-ABE scheme where it does not require interaction among multiple authorities.

In 2011, Lewko and Waters [12] proposed a novel multi-authority attribute-based encryption system. As shown in Fig. 1, the central authority was removed in this system. In addition, to generate a set of initial global parameters, each authority does not need any interaction with each other. Subsequently, Sect. 2.5 describes this model in detail. Furthermore, their scheme is based on composite order group and achieves full (adaptive) security under the random oracle model. However, this scheme does not take into account the privacy protection of the user. In order to generate the secret key, the user directly submits his GID to the authority in the key generation phase.

Han et al. [13] proposed a privacy-preserving decentralized key-policy attribute-based encryption (PPDKP-ABE) scheme in 2012. The scheme realized the hiding of user's GID in the interaction between the user and the authority through an anonymous key distribution protocol. It is noteworthy that it is based on standard complexity assumption (DBDH assumption). Unfortunately, in 2013, Ge et al. [14] proposed a new collusion attack for their scheme and successfully took the user's collusion attack in the light of the linear relationship between the private keys. In 2013, Qian et al. [15] presented a decentralized CP-ABE scheme with fully hidden access structure. The access structure used in this scheme supports AND, OR gates on multi-valued attributes. Meanwhile, they adopted an anonymous key distribution protocol to hide user's global identity GID. However, as in scheme [13], users in these schemes must submit their own attribute information when interacting with authority and thus the authority can collect the user's partial attribute information.

In 2016, Rahulamathavan et al. [16] proposed a privacy-preserving decentralized KP-ABE scheme to reduce the known security vulnerability of user collusion. They improved the key generation such that the linear relationship between the keys does not hold, thereby resisting the collusion attack mentioned in scheme [14]. The security of this scheme is based on standard DBDH complexity assumption. Han et al. [17] proposed a privacy-preserving decentralized CP-ABE scheme, in which each authority can dynamically join or leave the system. To resist the collusion attacks, the secret keys of a user are tied to his GID and simultaneously the user's attribute information is hidden in this scenario. Therefore, the proposed PPDCP-ABE scheme can provide stronger privacy protection compared to the previous PPMA-ABE schemes while eliminating the central authority. Moreover, the security of this scheme depends on the q-PBDH assumption.

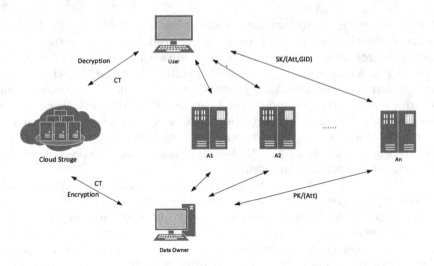

Fig. 1. Decentralized ABE scheme

In 2016, Wang et al. [18] pointed out the security weaknesses of scheme [17], and proposed a method of collusion attack based on the decentralized CP-ABE scheme. By pairing operations of the attribute public key and the known attribute information, the attribute information can be effectively detected, and then the privacy of attributes cannot be effectively provided.

In 2018, Zhang et al. [19] analyzed the scheme [16] and discovered its collusion attack vulnerability. Based on the security of the original scheme, a new privacy-preserving decentralized KP-ABE is proposed.

Contributions. At present, though decentralized ABE is widely used in cloud storage [22,23], the fully privacy-preserving decentralized ABE (When the key exchange is generated, it protects the privacy of the user's global identity GID as well as the user's attribute information from being leaked to the authority, and hides access policies under the access structure LSSS.) has not yet been resolved. Motivated the above, based on Lewko and Waters's scheme, a decentralized attribute-based encryption with preserving the privacy of the identifies and attributes in access structure is proposed in this paper. The presented scheme keeps the security of the original one and removes the random oracle. In the original scheme, the Hash function is used to map the GID to a random element in the group G, and $H(GID)^{y_i}$ is used to bind the user's identity and attributes together to resist user collusion. In the security analysis, they use H as a random oracle. We generate a concrete general function $H = g_1^{\frac{y_i}{\beta_j + u}} h^{uz_i}$ in the anonymous interaction protocol, which also binds the user's identity and attributes, thus removing the random oracle. The Lewko and Waters's scheme can resist collusion attack efficiently. And our scheme maintains this feature. In addition, the proposed scheme avoids the linear attack at present and others attack methods such as the attacks mentioned in the scheme [14,19].

2 Preliminaries

2.1 Composite Order Bilinear Maps

Let $\mathcal{G}$ be an algorithm that takes input a security parameter λ and outputs a tuple $(p_1, p_2, p_3, G, G_T, e)$, where p_1, p_2, p_3 are distinct primes, G and G_T are cyclic groups of order $N = p_1 p_2 p_3$, and $e : G \times G \to G_T$ is a map such that:
1. (Bilinear) $\forall g, h \in G$, $a, b \in Z_N$, $e(g^a, h^b) = e(g, h)^{ab}$;
2. (Non-degenerate) $\exists g \in G$ such that $e(g, g)$ has order N in G_T.
3. (Computable): Group operation $e(g, h)$ is efficiently computable, where $g, h \in G$

2.2 Access Structure

A secret sharing scheme $\prod$ over a set of parties P is called linear (over Z_N) if the following properties can be satisfied:

- The shares for each party form a vector over Z_N.
- For $\prod$, there exists a matrix M with l rows and n columns called the share-generating matrix. For $i = 1, 2, \cdots, l$, the ith row is labeled with a party $\rho(i)$ where $\rho : \{1, 2, \cdots, l\} \to Z_N$. To share a secret $s \in Z_N$, a vector $\overrightarrow{v} = (s, v_2, \cdots, v_n)$ is selected, where $v_2, \cdots, v_n$ are randomly selected from Z_N. $M\overrightarrow{v}$ is the vector of the l shares according to $\prod$. The share $M_i \overrightarrow{v}$ belongs to the party $\rho(i)$, where M_i is the ith row of M.

Linear Reconstruction Property: Let S be an authorized set and $I = \{i|\rho(i) \in S\}$. Then, there exists a set of constants $\{\omega_i \in Z_N\}_{i \in I}$ such that, for any valid shares λ_i according to $\prod$, $\sum_{i \in I} \omega_i \lambda_i = s$. $\{\omega_i\}_{i \in I}$ can be computed in polynomial time with the size of share-generating matrix M.

2.3 Zero Knowledge Proof

A zero-knowledge proof is an interactive protocol for a prover to prove some knowledge without revealing the knowledge. The zero-knowledge proof scheme involved in our construction is introduced by Camenisch and Stadler. By $PoK\{(\alpha, \beta, \gamma) : y = g^\alpha h^\beta \bigwedge \widetilde{y} = \widetilde{g}^\alpha \widetilde{h}^\gamma\}$, we denote a zero knowledge proof of knowledge of integers α, β and γ such that $y = g^\alpha h^\beta$ and $\widetilde{y} = \widetilde{g}^\alpha \widetilde{h}^\gamma$ hold on the group $G = <g> = <h>$ and $\widetilde{G} = <\widetilde{g}> = <\widetilde{h}>$, respectively. Conventionally, the values in the parenthesis denote the knowledge that is being proven, while the rest of the values are known by the verifier. Notably, there exists an efficient extractor that can be used to rewind the knowledge from the successful prover.

2.4   Our Assumptions

Assumption 1 (*Subgroup decision problem for* 3 *primes*). Given a group generator $\mathcal{G}$, we define the following distribution:

$$\mathbf{G} = (N = p_1 p_2 p_3, G, G_T, e) \leftarrow_R \mathcal{G}$$

$$g_1 \leftarrow_{R_1} G_{p_1},$$
$$D = (\mathbf{G}, g_1),$$
$$T_1 \leftarrow_R G, \; T_2 \leftarrow_R G_{p_1}.$$

We define the advantage of an algorithm $\mathcal{A}$ in breaking Assumption 1 to be:

$$Adv1_{\mathcal{G},\mathcal{A}}(\lambda) := |Pr[\mathcal{A}(D, T_1) = 1] - Pr[\mathcal{A}(D, T_2) = 1]|.$$

Definition 1. We say that $\mathcal{G}$ satisfies Assumption 1 if $Adv1_{\mathcal{G},\mathcal{A}(\lambda)}$ is a negligible function of λ for any polynomial time algorithm $\mathcal{A}$.

Assumption 2. Given a group generator $\mathcal{G}$, we define the following distribution:

$$\mathbf{G} = (N = p_1 p_2 p_3, G, G_T, e) \leftarrow_R \mathcal{G},$$
$$g_1, X_1 \leftarrow_R G_{p_1}, X_2 \leftarrow_R G_{p_2}, g_3 \leftarrow_R G_{p_3},$$
$$D = (\mathbf{G}, g_1, g_3, X_1 X_2),$$
$$T_1 \leftarrow_R G_{p_1}, T_2 \leftarrow_R G_{p_1 p_2}$$

We define the advantage of an algorithm $\mathcal{A}$ in breaking Assumption 2 to be:

$$Adv2_{\mathcal{G},\mathcal{A}} := |Pr[\mathcal{A}(D, T_1) = 1] - Pr[\mathcal{A}(D, T_2) = 1]|.$$

Definition 2. We say that $\mathcal{G}$ satisfies Assumption 2 if $Adv2_{\mathcal{G},\mathcal{A}(\lambda)}$ is a negligible function of λ for any polynomial time algorithm $\mathcal{A}$.

Assumption 3. Given a group generator $\mathcal{G}$, we define the following distribution:

$$\mathbf{G} = (N = p_1 p_2 p_3, G, G_T, e) \leftarrow_R \mathcal{G}$$
$$g_1, X_1 \leftarrow_R G_{p_1}, Y_2 \leftarrow_R G_{p_2}, X_3, Y_3 \leftarrow_R G_{p_3},$$
$$D = (\mathbf{G}, g_1, X_1 X_3, Y_2 Y_3)$$
$$T_1 \leftarrow_R G_{p_1 p_2}, T_2 \leftarrow_R G_{p_1 p_3}.$$

We define the advantage of an algorithm $\mathcal{A}$ in breaking Assumption 3 to be:

$$Adv3_{\mathcal{G},\mathcal{A}}(\lambda) := |Pr[\mathcal{A}(D, T_1) = 1] - Pr[\mathcal{A}(D, T_2) = 1]|.$$

Definition 3. We say that $\mathcal{G}$ satisfies Assumption 3 if $Adv3_{\mathcal{G},\mathcal{A}(\lambda)}$ is a negligible function of λ for any polynomial time algorithm $\mathcal{A}$.

Assumption 4. Given a group generator $\mathcal{G}$, we define the following distribution:

$$\mathbf{G} = (N = p_1 p_2 p_3, G, G_T, e) \leftarrow_R \mathcal{G},$$

$$g_1 \leftarrow_R G_{p_1}, g_2 \leftarrow_R G_{p_2}, g_3 \leftarrow_R G_{p_3}, a, b, c, d \leftarrow_R Z_N,$$

$$D = (\mathbf{G}, g_1, g_2, g_3, g_1^a, g_1^b g_3^b, g_1^c, g_1^{ac} g_3^d),$$

$$T_1 = e(g_1, g_1)^{abc}, T_2 \leftarrow_R G_T.$$

We define the advantage of an algorithm $\mathcal{A}$ in breaking Assumption 4 to be:

$$Adv4_{\mathcal{G},\mathcal{A}}(\lambda) := |Pr[\mathcal{A}(D, T_1) = 1] - Pr[\mathcal{A}(D, T_2) = 1]|.$$

Definition 4. We say that $\mathcal{G}$ satisfies Assumption 4 if $Adv4_{\mathcal{G},\mathcal{A}(\lambda)}$ is a negligible function of λ for any polynomial time algorithm $\mathcal{A}$.

2.5   Outline of This Scheme

A decentralized CP-ABE scheme consists of the following five algorithms.

Global Setup: This algorithm takes a security parameter λ as input and returns the system parameters GP.

Authority Setup: The authority runs this algorithm and takes GP as input. Each authority A_k generates his secret key SK_k, public keys PK_k for system.

Key Gen: Each authority A_k takes as input his secret key sk_k, a global identifier $u(GID)$ and a set of attributes $\tilde{A}_u^k$, the key generation algorithm outputs a secret key SK_u^k for U.

Encryption: This algorithm takes as input the system parameters GP, a message M, an access matrix (A, ρ) and the public key for relevant authorities. It outputs the ciphertext CT.

Decryption: The decryption algorithm takes the secret keys SK_u^k, the public parameter, the user's global identifier GID and the ciphertext CT as input. Then, the decryption will be successful if and only if the user's attributes satisfy the access structure.

2.6   Security Model

The security game between the adversary and challenger is given as follows:

Setup: The global setup algorithm is run. The adversary $\mathcal{A}$ gives the challenge access structure (A^*, ρ^*). Then $\mathcal{A}$ submits a set $S' \subseteq S$ of corrupt authorities and a set of good authorities $S - S'$. The challenger obtains public key and secret key by running setup algorithm. The challenger sends the public key to adversary $\mathcal{A}$.

Phase 1: The adversary $\mathcal{A}$ can query secret key by submitting pair (i, GID) to challenger. But it cannot make key queries on any set I_j which satisfies the access structure (A^*, ρ^*). The challenger returns the secret key $K_{i,GID}$.

Challenge: The adversary submits two equal length messages m_0 and m_1 and an access structure (A^*, ρ^*) to the challenger where any attribute set I_j does not satisfy the access structure (A^*, ρ^*) and belong to the corrupted authority set S'. The challenger selects $v \in \{0, 1\}$ and encrypts M_v to get ciphertext CT. Finally, the challenger sends CT to $\mathcal{A}$.

Phase 2: The adversary makes more key queries (i, GID) as long as the attributes set I_j do not satisfies the challenge matrix (A^*, ρ^*).

Guess: The adversary outputs a guess of v. The advantage of adversary is $|Pr[v' = v] - \frac{1}{2}|$.

3   Decentralized CP-ABE Scheme

Global Setup: $(\lambda) \rightarrow (GP)$. G is a group of order $N = p_1 p_2 p_3$. Let g_1 be a generator of the group G_{p_1} and $e : G \times G \rightarrow G_T$ be a bilinear map. We set $h = g_1^\tau$. There are N attribute authorities which are denoted as $A_1, \cdots, A_k$. A_j monitors a set of attributes $i \in \widetilde{A}_j$. Now we select a strong collusion resistant hash function $H : \{0, 1\}^* \rightarrow G$. It used to map the user's GID to an element of G, where $H(GID) \rightarrow u$.

Authority Setup: $(GP) \rightarrow (SK, PK)$. For each attribute i belonging to the authority A_j, A_j selects three random exponents $\alpha_i, y_i, z_i \in Z_N$. Each authority A_j that monitors an attribute set $\widetilde{A}_j$ chooses a random value $\beta_j \in Z_N$ and computes the public key $PK_j = \{e(g_1, g_1)^{\alpha_i}, g_1^{y_i}, g_1^{z_i}, g_1^{\beta_j}\}_{\forall i \in \widetilde{A}_j}$. Then, it calculates the master secret key $SK_j = \{\beta_j, (\alpha_i, y_i, z_i)\}_{\forall i \in I_j}$

Encryption: $(M, (A, \rho), GP, PK) \rightarrow CT$. This algorithm takes as input the global parameter GP, a message M, an $n \times l$ access matrix A with ρ mapping its rows to attributes and the public keys of the relevant authorities. The data owner selects a random exponent $d \in Z_N$ and computes $\gamma_i = e((g_1^{\beta_j})^d, H(i))$, where $i \in \widetilde{A}_m$ denotes a attribute in the access policy and $\widetilde{A}_m$ is the set of attributes in message M. Then the owner uses γ_i to replace the attribute i in the LSSS access matrix (A, ρ). This algorithm chooses a random $s \in Z_N$ and a random vector $v \in Z_N^l$ with s as its first entry. Let $\lambda_x = A_x \vec{v}$, where A_x denoted the x−th row of A. Then, it randomly picks a vector $\vec{w} \in Z_N^l$ with 0 as its first entry. For each row A_x of A, setting $A_x \vec{w}$ as ω_x, it selects a random $r_x \in Z_N$. The ciphertext is computed as follows:

$$C_0 = Me(g_1, g_1)^s, C_{1,x} = e(g_1, g_1)^{\lambda_x} e(g_1, g_1)^{\alpha_{\rho(x)} r_x}$$

$$C_{2,x} = g_1^{r_x}, C_{3,x} = g_1^{y_{\rho(x)} r_x} g_1^{\omega_x}, C_{4,x} = g_1^{r_x z_x}, C_5 = g_1^d$$

Key Gen: $(GID, i, PK, GP) \rightarrow SK$. Attribute authority A_j cooperates with the user to run anonymous key issuing protocol to generate the secret key for the user. Then, the user can obtain the secret key SK_j as follows:

$$SK_j = \{K_1 = g_1^{\alpha_i} g_1^{\frac{y_i}{\beta_j + u}} h^{u z_i}, K_2 = g_1^{\frac{1}{\beta_j + u}}, K_3 = H(i)^{\beta_j}\},$$

where the secret key K_3 is used to hide the attributes.

Decryption: $(CT, SK, GP, PK) \rightarrow M$. The user computes $\lambda_i = e(C_5, K_3) = e(g^d, H(i)^{\beta_j})$ for his attributes set $\tilde{A}_u$. We let $I_u = \{\lambda_i : i \in \tilde{A}_u\}$. For the access policy (A, ρ), the user can gain the set $R' = \{x : \rho_x\}$. Finally, the user chooses constants $c_x \in Z_N$ such as $\sum_{x \in R'} c_x A_x = (1, 0, \cdots, 0)$. This algorithm is executed to decrypt the ciphertext CT under the access structure (A, ρ). If the decryptor has the secret keys SK for a set of each row of A. Then, the decryption process proceeds as follows:

$$\frac{C_{1,x} e(K_2, C_{3,x}) e(h^u, C_{4,x})}{e(K_1, C_{2,x})}$$

$$= \frac{e(g_1, g_1)^{\lambda_x} e(g_1, g_1)^{\alpha_{\rho(x)} r_x} e(g_1^{\frac{1}{\beta_j + u}}, g_1^{y_{\rho(x)} r_x} g_1^{\omega_x}) e(h^u, g_1^{z_x r_x})}{e(g_1^{\alpha_i} g_1^{\frac{y_i}{\beta_j + u}} h^{u z_i}, g_1^{r_x})}$$

$$= e(g_1, g_1)^{\lambda_x} e(g_1^{\frac{1}{\beta_j + u}}, g_1)^{\omega_x}$$

The decryptor uses constants $c_x \in Z_N$, where $\sum_x c_x A_x = (1, 0, \cdots, 0)$.

$$\prod_x (e(g_1, g_1)^{\lambda_x} e(g_1^{\frac{1}{\beta_j + u}}, g_1)^{\omega_x})^{c_x} = e(g_1, g_1)^s$$

$$M = \frac{C_0}{e(g_1, g_1)^s}$$

4 Security Analysis

We apply the dual system encryption technique to prove security of the proposed scheme. Similar to Lewko and Waters' scheme, secret key and ciphertext can either be normal or semi-functional in the dual system encryption. The first game, $Game_{Real}$, is the real security game. We next define $Game'_{Real}$, which is like the real security game, except that the random oracle maps identities GID to random element of G_{p_1} instand of G.

Normal keys can decrypt semi-functional ciphertexts, and semi-functional keys can decrypt normal ciphertexts. But semi-functional keys cannot decrypt semi-functional ciphertext. To more describe the semi-functional ciphertext and keys, we first fix random value $z_i', t_i' \in Z_N$ for each attribute i which will be common to semi-functional ciphertext and keys.

Semi – functional Ciphertexts: In order to generate the semi-functional ciphertext, we have to run the generation algorithm to generate the normal ciphertext like Lewko and Waters' scheme:

$$C_0', C_{1,x}' = e(g_1, g_1)^{\lambda_x} e(g_1, g_1)^{\alpha \rho(x) r_x}, C_{2,x}' = g_1^{r_x}$$

$$C_{3,x}' = g_1^{y_{\rho(x)} r_x} g_1^{\omega_x}, C_{4,x} = g_1^{r_x z_x}, \forall x$$

Then we set $g_2 \in G_{p_2}$, $g_3 \in G_{p_3}$ and select two vectors $u_2, u_3 \in Z_N^l$ randomly. Let $\delta_x = A_x u_2$, $\sigma_x = A_x u_3$, where A_x denotes xth row of the access matrix A. We let $\overline{B}$ be the subset of good authorities and B denote the subset of corrupted authorities. We also choose random exponents $\gamma_x, \psi_x, q_x \in Z_N$. The semi-functional ciphertext is as follows:

$$C_0 = C_0', C_{1,x} = C_{1,x}', C_{2,x} = C_{2,x}' g_2^{\gamma_x} g_3^{\psi_x}$$

$$C_{3,x} = C_{3,x}' g_2^{\delta_x + \gamma_x z_{\rho(x)}'} g_3^{\sigma_x + \psi_x t_{\rho(x)}'}, C_{4,x} = C_{2,x}'^{q_x} g_2^{\gamma_x} g_3^{\psi_x}, A_x \in \overline{B}$$

And for each x that satisfies $A_x \in B$, the semi-ciphertext is as follows:

$$C_{1,x} = C_{1,x}', C_{2,x} = C_{2,x}', C_{3,x} = C_{3,x}' g_2^{\delta_x} g_3^{\sigma_x}, C_{4,x} = C_{2,x}'^{q_x}$$

We say a ciphertext is nominally semi-functional when the values δ_x are share of 0.

Semi – functional Keys: $K_{i,u}$ denotes the key for identity $GID(u)$. We let $H(u)$ be a random element of G and we choose a random exponent $c \in Z_N$. The semi-functional key of Type 1 is as follows:

$$H(u) = (g_1^{\frac{1}{\beta_j + u}}) g_2^c, K_1 = g_1^{\alpha_i} H(u)^{y_i} g_2^{cz_i'} h^{u z_i} = K_{i,GID}' g_2^{cz_i'}$$

The semi-functional key of Type 2 is as follows:

$$H(u) = (g_1^{\frac{1}{\beta_j + u}}) g_2^c, K_1 = g_1^{\alpha_i} H(u)^{y_i} g_3^{ct_i'} h^{u z_i} = K_{i,GID}' g_3^{ct_i'},$$

where $K_{i,GID}' = g_1^{\alpha_i} g_1^{\frac{y_i}{\beta_j + u}} h^{u z_i}$ When a semi-functional key of Type 1 is used to decrypt a semi-functional ciphertext, the additional terms $e(g_2, g_2)^{cz_x' \delta_x}$ prevent decryption from succeeding, except when the values δ_x are shares of 0. When a semi-functional key of Type 2 is used to decryption a semi-functional ciphertext, the additional terms $e(g_3, g_3)^{ct_x' \delta_x}$ prevent successful decryption.

Then we define $Game_0$, which is like $Game_{Real}'$ except that the ciphertext given to $\mathcal{A}$ is semi-functional. We let q be the number of key queries. Then we define $Game_{j,1}$ and $Game_{j,2}$ for each j from 1 to q as follows:

$Game_{j,1}$: $Game_{j,1}$ is like $Game_0$ except that for the first $j-1$ queried identities, the received keys are semi-functional of Type 2, and the received key for the jth queried identity is semi-functional of Type 1. The remaining keys are normal.

$Game_{j,2}$: This is like $Game_0$, except that for the first j queried identities, the received keys are semi-functional of Type 2. The remaining keys are normal. We note that in $Game_{q,2}$, all keys are semi-functional of Type 2.

$Game_{Final}$: In this game, all keys are semi-functional of Type 2, and the ciphertext is semi-functional encryption of a random message. We note that the $\mathcal{A}$ has advantage 0 in this game.

Subsequently, we show these games are indistinguishable in the following lemmas. We just give the proof of lemma 3 as follows:

Lemma 1. *Suppose there exists a polynomial time algorithm $\mathcal{A}$ such that $Game_{Real}Adv_{\mathcal{A}} - Game_{Real'}Adv_{\mathcal{A}} = \epsilon$. Then we can construct a polynomial time algorithm $\mathcal{B}$ with advantage ϵ in breaking Assumption 1.*

Lemma 2. *Suppose there exists a polynomial time algorithm $\mathcal{A}$ such that $Game_{Real'}Adv_{\mathcal{A}} - Game_0 Adv_{\mathcal{A}} = \epsilon$. Then we cam construct a polynomial time algorithm $\mathcal{B}$ with advantage negligibly close to ϵ in breaking Assumption 1.*

Lemma 3. *Suppose there exists a polynomial time algorithm $\mathcal{A}$ such that $Game_{j-1,2}Adv_{\mathcal{A}} - Game_{j,1}Adv_{\mathcal{A}} = \epsilon$. Then we can construct a polynomial time algorithm $\mathcal{B}$ with advantage negligibly close to ϵ in breaking Assumption 2.*

Lemma 4. *Suppose there exists a polynomial time algorithm $\mathcal{A}$ such that $Game_{j,1}Adv_{\mathcal{A}} - Game_{j,2}Adv_{\mathcal{A}} = \epsilon$. Then we can construct a polynomial time algorithm $\mathcal{B}$ with advantage ϵ in breaking Assumption 3.*

Lemma 5. *Suppose there exists a polynomial time algorithm $\mathcal{A}$ such that $Game_{q,2}Adv_{\mathcal{A}} - Game_{Final}Adv_{\mathcal{A}} = \epsilon$. Then we can construct a polynomial time algorithm $\mathcal{B}$ with advantage ϵ in breaking Assumption 4.*

Proof (Lemma 3).
Firstly, $\mathcal{B}$ receives the tuple of Assumption $2(g_1, g_3, X_1X_2, T)$. Now, $\mathcal{B}$ will simulate $Game_{j-1,2}$ or $Game_{j,1}$ with $\mathcal{A}$, depending on the value of T. g_1 is the public generator of G_{p_1} and N is the group order of G. $\mathcal{A}$ submits a corrupted authority set $S' \subseteq S$, where S is the set of all authorities. For attribute $i \in S - S'$, $\mathcal{B}$ chooses $\alpha_i, y_i, z_i, \beta_j \in Z_N$ and gives $\mathcal{A}$ the parameters $e(g_1, g_1)^{\alpha_i}, g_1^{y_i}, g_1^{z_i}, g_1^{\beta_j}, h = g_1^\tau$. We let GID_k denote the kth identity queried by $\mathcal{A}$. $\mathcal{A}$ makes a key query (i, GID_k). $\mathcal{B}$ responds as follows:

If $k > j$, $H(GID_k) = H(u) = g_1^{\frac{1}{\beta_j + u}}$.

$$K'_{i,GID_k} = K_{i,GID_k} = g_1^{\alpha_i} H(u)^{y_i} h^{uz_i},$$

where K'_{i,GID_k} is normal key.

If $k < j$, $H(GID_k) = H(u) = (g_1 g_3)^{\frac{1}{\beta_j + u}}$. The K'_{i,GID_k} is semi-functional key of Type 2.

$$K'_{i,GID_k} = g_1^{\alpha_i} g_1^{\frac{y_i}{\beta_j + u}} h^{uz_i} g_3^{\frac{y_i}{\beta_j + u}} = K_{i,GID_k} g_3^{c\kappa_i},$$

where $c = \frac{1}{\beta_j + u}$, $\kappa_i = y_i$

when $k = j$, we let $T = g_1^{\theta_1}$ if $T \in G_{p_1}$, then $H(u) = T^{\frac{1}{\beta_j + u}}$. Now, $K'_{i,GID} = g_1^{\alpha_i} g_1^{\frac{\theta_1 y_i}{\beta_j + u}} h^{u z_i}$ is the normal key. If $T \in G_{p_1 p_2}$, we let $T = g_1^{\theta_2} g_2^{\theta_3}$. Then $H(u) = T^{\frac{1}{\beta_j + u}} = g_1^{\frac{\theta_2}{\beta_j + u}} g_2^{\frac{\theta_3}{\beta_j + u}}$. Now, $K'_{i,GID} = g_1^{\alpha_i} g_1^{\frac{\theta_2 y_i}{\beta_j + u}} h^{u z_i} g_2^{\frac{\theta_3 y_i}{\beta_j + u}} = K_{i,GID} g_2^{\frac{\theta_3 y_i}{\beta_j + u}} = K_{i,GID} g_2^{c \varepsilon_i}$, where $K'_{i,GID}$ is a semi-functional key of Type 1 and $\varepsilon_i = \theta_3 y_i$, $c = \frac{1}{\beta_j + u}$.

Then $\mathcal{A}$ submits two equal length messages M_0, M_1 and an access matrix (A, ρ) to $\mathcal{B}$. $\mathcal{B}$ flips a random coin $\beta \in \{0, 1\}$ and encrypts M_β as follows: $\mathcal{B}$ chooses a random $s \in Z_N$ and sets $C_0 = e(g_1, g_1)^s$. Then it selects three vectors $\vec{v} = (s, v_2, \cdots, v_l)$, $\vec{w} = (0, w_2, \cdots, w_l)$ and $\vec{u} = (u_1, \cdots, u_l)$. where $v_2, \cdots, v_l, w_2, \cdots, w_l, u_1, \cdots, u_l \in_R Z_N$. We let $\lambda_x = A_x \vec{v}$, $w_x = A_x \vec{w}$ and $\sigma_x = A_x \vec{u}$.

Let B be the subset of rows of A whose corresponding attributes $i \in S'$ and $\overline{B}$ be the subset of rows of A whose corresponding attributes $i \in S - S'$. For $\rho(A_x) \in B$, $\mathcal{B}$ chooses a value $r_x \in Z_N$ randomly. For $\rho(A_x) \in \overline{B}$, $\mathcal{B}$ chooses random values $\psi_x, r'_x, \omega'_x \in Z_N$, and will implicitly set $r_x = r r'_x, \omega_x = r \omega'_x$, where g_1^r is X_1.

For attribute $x \in B$, the ciphertext is set as follows:

$$C_{1,x} = C'_{1,x}, C_{2,x} = C'_{2,x}, C_{4,x} = C_{2,x}^{z_x}$$

$$C_{3,x} = (g_1^{y_{\rho(x)}})^{r_x} (X_1 X_2)^{w_x} g_3^{\sigma_x} = (g_1^{y_{\rho(x)}})^{r_x} g_1^{w_x} (X_2)^{w_x} g_3^{\sigma_x} = C'_{3,x} (X_2)^{w_x} g_3^{\sigma_x}$$

For attribute $x \in \overline{B}$, the ciphertext is given as follows:

$$C_{1,x} = C'_{1,x}, C_{2,x} = (X_1 X_2)^{r'_x} g_3^{\psi_x} = g_1^{r_x} (X_2)^{r'_x} g_3^{\psi_x} = C'_{2,x} (X_2)^{r'_x} g_3^{\psi_x}, C_{4,x} = C_{2,x}^{z_x}.$$

$$C_{3,x} = (X_1 X_2)^{y_{\rho(x)} r'_x} g_3^{y_{\rho(x)} \psi_x} (X_1 X_2)^{w'_x} g_3^{\sigma_x} = g_1^{y_{\rho(x)} r_x} g_1^{w_x} (X_2)^{y_{\rho(x)} r'_x + w'_x} g_3^{y_{\rho(x)} \psi_x + \sigma_x}$$

In summary, when $T \in G_{p_1}$, $\mathcal{B}$ properly simulates $Game_{j-1,2}$. When $T \in G_{p_1 p_2}$, $\mathcal{B}$ properly simulates $Game_{j,1}$ with probability negligibly close to 1. Hence, $\mathcal{B}$ can use $\mathcal{A}$ to obtain advantage negligibly close to ϵ in breaking Assumption 2. Same to scheme [20,21], we introduce the secret key $K_3 = H(i)^{\beta_j}$ and the ciphertext $C_5 = g_1^d$ which are used to hide the attributes in access structure. So we ignored the proofs of the security of K_3 and C_5 in this scheme.

5   Anonymous Key Issuing Protocol

The detail of protocol in the Table 1 is as follows.

(1) The user u chooses $z, z_1, z_2, z_3, \rho_1 \in Z_N$ and computes $T = g_1^z h^u, P_1 = g_1^{\rho_1}, T'_1 = g_1^{z_1} h^{z_2}, P'_1 = g_1^{z_3}$. The user sends (T, T', P_1, P'_1) to AA.

(2) AA chooses $c \leftarrow_R Z_N$ and sends c to user u.

(3) The user computes $s = z_1 - cz_1, s_2 = z_2 - cu, s_3 = z_3 - c\rho_1$, then sends s_1, s_2, s_3 to AA.

(4) AA checks $T' \stackrel{?}{=} g_1^{s_1} h^{s_2} T^c, P' \stackrel{?}{=} g_1^{s_3} P_1^c$. If they are correctly verified, then AA continues; otherwise, it aborts.

Then AA needs to prove that he knows $(\alpha_i, y_i, z_i, \beta_j)$ in zero knowledge to the user. AA chooses $\rho_2 \in Z_N$ randomly and generates $\eta = \rho_1 \rho_2 (\beta_j + u)$ by two-party secure computation.

(1) AA randomly generates $b_1, b_2, b_3, b_4, b_5, b_6$ and computes $P_2 = g_1^{\rho_2}, P_2' = g_1^{b_1}, P_3 = g_1^{\beta_j}, P_3' = g_1^{b_5}, K_1' = g_1^{\alpha_i} P_1^{\frac{\rho_2 y_i}{\eta}} T^{z_i}, K_1'' = g_1^{b_2} P_1^{\frac{b_3}{\eta}} T^{b_4}, K_2' = P_2^{\frac{y_i}{\eta}},$
$K_2'' = P_2^{\frac{b_6}{\eta}}$. Then it sends $(P_2, P_2', K_1', K_1'', K_2', K_2'')$ to the user.

(2) The user chooses $c_1 \in_R Z_N$, and sends it to AA.

(3) AA calculates $b_1' = b_1 - c_1 \rho_1, b_2' = b_2 - c_1 \alpha_i, b_3' = b_3 - c_1 \frac{y_i \rho_2}{\eta}, b_4' = b_4 - c_1 z_i, b_5' = b_5 - c_1 \beta_j, b_6' = b_6 - c_1 \frac{y_i}{\eta}$ and sends them to the user.

(4) The user verifies $K_1'' \stackrel{?}{=} g_1^{b_2'} P_1^{b_3'} T^{b_4'} K_1'^{c_1}, K_2'' \stackrel{?}{=} K_2'^{c_1} g_1^{b_6'}$; otherwise, it aborts.

(5) Finally, the user generates $K_1 = \frac{K_1'}{(g_1^{z_i})^z}, K_2 = (K_2')^{\rho_1}$.

Table 1. Anonymous key issuing protocol

User	AA
1. Selects $\rho_1, z \leftarrow_R Z_p$ and computes $T = h^u g_1^z$ $P_1 = g_1^{\rho_1}, Pok\{(u, \rho_1, z) : T \wedge P_1\}$ and sends T, P_1 to AA.	
$\overrightarrow{2PC}$	
	2. Randomly selects $\rho_2, \eta = \rho_1 \rho_2 (\beta_j + u)$, Then computes $P_2 = g_2^{\rho_2}, K_1' = g_1^{\alpha_i} P_1^{\frac{\rho_2 y_i}{\eta}} T^{z_i}, K_2' = P_2^{\frac{y_i}{\eta}}$ $PoK\{(\alpha_i, y_i, z_i, \rho_2) : K_1' \wedge K_2' \wedge P_2\}$
$\overleftarrow{PoK \sum}$	
3. $K_1 = \frac{K_1'}{(g_1^{z_i})^z}, K_2 = (K_2')^{\rho_1}$	

6 Performance Analysis

In this section, we will give some comparisons of the proposed scheme with scheme [22] and [23]. As shown in Tables 2 and 3, K is the number of AAs and N denotes the number of attributes. $|G|$ and $|G_T|$ denote the number of bits for

Table 2. Performance analysis

Scheme	Hidden policy	Resist collusion	Hidden GID
[23]	✓	✓	✗
[22]	✗	✓	✓
Our scheme	✓	✓	✓

Table 3. Performance analysis

Scheme	Key size	Ciphertext size	Decryption cost
[23]	$(N + K)|G|$	$(1 + N)|G_T| + (2N + 1)|G|$	$3NP + NE$
[22]	$(N + K + 1)|G|$	$(N + 2)|G| + |G_T|$	$(K + 1 + N)P + NE$
Our scheme	$(N + 2K)|G|$	$(1 + N)|G_T| + (3N + 1)|G|$	$4NP + NE$

the representation of element of G and G_T. By contrast, our scheme has a slight increase in key size, ciphertext size, and decryption cost. But it achieves better privacy protection. This scheme preserves the user's GID privacy and hides the access policy in the ciphertext.

7   Conclusion

Based on the proposals of Lewko and Waters, a novel DABE is proposed. In the presented scheme, we remove the need of a random oracle and replace it with a concrete function H mapping identities to group elements. In addition, this scheme can resist collusion attack same to Lewko and Waters's scheme. It not only realizes the user's identity privacy preservation but also hides the attribute in the access policy. Additionally, the proposed scheme has the same security as the Lewko and Waters's scheme based on dual system encryption. Unfortunately, the new construction relied on the composite order group. How to construct a DABE in a prime order group but keep the same efficiency and security is a challenge problem. We leave it as an open problem.

Acknowledgment. This work was supported in part by the National Cryptography Development Fund of China under Grant MMJJ20180209.

References

1. Bethencourt, J, Sahai, A, Waters, B.: Ciphertext-policy attribute-based encryption. In: IEEE Symposium on Security and Privacy, pp. 321–334 (2007)
2. Goyal, V., Pandey, O., Sahai, A., et al.: Attribute-based encryption for fine-grained access control of encrypted data. In: ACM Conference on Computer and Communications Security, pp. 89–98. ACM (2006)

3. Ostrovksy, R., Sahai, A., Waters, B.: Attribute based encryption with non monotonic access structures. In: ACM Conference on Computer and Communications Security, pp. 195–203. ACM (2007)
4. Goyal, V., Jain, A., Pandey, O., Sahai, A.: Bounded ciphertext policy attribute based encryption. In: Aceto, L., Damgård, I., Goldberg, L.A., Halldórsson, M.M., Ingólfsdóttir, A., Walukiewicz, I. (eds.) ICALP 2008. LNCS, vol. 5126, pp. 579–591. Springer, Heidelberg (2008). https://doi.org/10.1007/978-3-540-70583-3_47
5. Ling, C., Newport, C.: Provably secure ciphertext policy ABE. In: ACM Conference on Computer and Communications Security, pp. 456–465. ACM (2007)
6. Chase, M.: Multi-authority attribute based encryption. In: Vadhan, S.P. (ed.) TCC 2007. LNCS, vol. 4392, pp. 515–534. Springer, Heidelberg (2007). https://doi.org/10.1007/978-3-540-70936-7_28
7. Chase, M., Chow, S.S.M.: Improving privacy and security in multi-authority attribute-based encryption. In: ACM Conference on Computer and Communications Security, pp. 121–130. ACM (2009)
8. Waters, B.: Ciphertext-policy attribute-based encryption: an expressive, efficient, and provably secure realization. In: Catalano, D., Fazio, N., Gennaro, R., Nicolosi, A. (eds.) PKC 2011. LNCS, vol. 6571, pp. 53–70. Springer, Heidelberg (2011). https://doi.org/10.1007/978-3-642-19379-8_4
9. Lewko, A., Okamoto, T., Sahai, A., Takashima, K., Waters, B.: Fully secure functional encryption: attribute-based encryption and (hierarchical) inner product encryption. In: Gilbert, H. (ed.) EUROCRYPT 2010. LNCS, vol. 6110, pp. 62–91. Springer, Heidelberg (2010). https://doi.org/10.1007/978-3-642-13190-5_4
10. Sahai, A., Waters, B.: Fuzzy identity-based encryption. In: Cramer, R. (ed.) EURO-CRYPT 2005. LNCS, vol. 3494, pp. 457–473. Springer, Heidelberg (2005). https://doi.org/10.1007/11426639_27
11. Li, J., Huang, Q., Chen, X., et al.: Multi-authority ciphertext-policy attribute-based encryption with accountability. In: ACM Symposium on Information, Computer and Communications Security, ASIACCS 2011, pp. 386–390. ACM, Hong Kong (2011)
12. Lewko, A., Waters, B.: Decentralizing attribute-based encryption. In: Paterson, K.G. (ed.) EUROCRYPT 2011. LNCS, vol. 6632, pp. 568–588. Springer, Heidelberg (2011). https://doi.org/10.1007/978-3-642-20465-4_31
13. Han, J., Susilo, W., Mu, Y., et al.: Privacy-preserving decentralized key-policy attribute-based encryption. IEEE Trans. Parallel Distrib. Syst. 23(11), 2150–2162 (2012)
14. Ge, A., Zhang, J., Zhang, R., et al.: Security analysis of a privacy-preserving decentralized key-policy attribute-based encryption scheme. IEEE Trans. Parallel Distrib. Syst. 24(11), 2319–2321 (2013)
15. Qian, H., Li, J., Zhang, Y.: Privacy-preserving decentralized ciphertext-policy attribute-based encryption with fully hidden access structure. In: Qing, S., Zhou, J., Liu, D. (eds.) ICICS 2013. LNCS, vol. 8233, pp. 363–372. Springer, Cham (2013). https://doi.org/10.1007/978-3-319-02726-5_26
16. Rahulamathavan, Y., Veluru, S., Han, J., et al.: User collusion avoidance scheme for privacy-preserving decentralized key-policy attribute-based encryption. IEEE Trans. Comput. 65(9), 2939–2946 (2016)
17. Han, J., Susilo, W., Mu, Y., Zhou, J., Au, M.H.: PPDCP-ABE: privacy-preserving decentralized ciphertext-policy attribute-based encryption. In: Kutyłowski, M., Vaidya, J. (eds.) ESORICS 2014. LNCS, vol. 8713, pp. 73–90. Springer, Cham (2014). https://doi.org/10.1007/978-3-319-11212-1_5

18. Wang, M., Zhang, Z., Chen, C.: Security analysis of a privacy-preserving decentralized ciphertext-policy attribute-based encryption scheme. Concurrency Comput.: Practice Exp. **28**(4), 1237–1245 (2016)
19. Zhang, L., Liang, P., Mu, Y.: Improving privacy-preserving and security for decentralized key-policy attributed-based encryption. IEEE Access **6**, 12736–12745 (2018)
20. Zhong, H., Zhu, W., Xu, Y., et al.: Multi-authority attribute-based encryption access control scheme with policy hidden for cloud storage. Soft Comput. **22**(1), 1–9 (2016)
21. Shao, J., Zhu, Y., Ji, Q.: Privacy-preserving online/offline and outsourced multi-authority attribute-based encryption. In: International Conference on Computer and Information Science, pp. 285–291. IEEE (2017)
22. Li, Q., Ma, J., Li, R., et al.: Large universe decentralized key-policy attribute-based encryption. Secur. Commun. Netw. **8**(3), 501–509 (2015)
23. Li, Q., Ma, J., Li, R., et al.: Secure, efficient and revocable multi-authority access control system in cloud storage. Comput. Secur. **59**(C), 45–59 (2016)

Post-quantum Cryptography

Efficient Lattice FIBS for Identities in a Small Universe

Yanhua Zhang[1]([⊠]), Yong Gan[2], Yifeng Yin[1], Huiwen Jia[3],
and Mingming Jiang[4]

[1] Zhengzhou University of Light Industry, Zhengzhou 450002, China
{yhzhang,yinyifeng}@zzuli.edu.cn
[2] Zhengzhou Institute of Technology, Zhengzhou 450044, China
yongg@zzuli.edu.cn
[3] Guangzhou University, Guangzhou 510006, China
hwjia@gzhu.edu.cn
[4] Huaibei Normal University, Huaibei 235000, China
jiangmm3806586@126.com

Abstract. Fuzzy identity-based signature (FIBS) is exactly like a traditional identity-based signature except that the signature issued under an identity id can be verified under any identity id$'$ that is "close enough" to id. This property allows FIBS having an efficient application in biometric authentication and only three schemes over lattices exist, among which two constructions are existentially unforgetable against adaptively chosen identity and message attacks (EU-aID-CMA) in the random model, the only exception proved to be strongly unforgetable against selectively chosen identity and message attacks (SU-sID-CMA) is constructed in the standard model. In this work, we propose a new FIBS from the hardness of lattice problems for identities living in a small universe, i.e., $\{0,1\}^{\ell}$, the new construction is proved to be SU-sID-CMA in the standard model. In particular, compared with the existing lattice FIBS schemes, the new construction enjoys a smaller communication cost, and the faster signing and verifying operations, thus, it is more practical.

Keywords: FIBS · Small universe · Lattice · Standard model

1 Introduction

Identity-based cryptosystem was put forward by Shamir [12] to reduce the complexity of managing the public key infrastructure. In this cryptosystem, including identity-based encryption (IBE), identity-based signature (IBS) and identity-based key agreement (IBKA), the identity is regarded as the public key, and the private key generator can generate a private key corresponding to that identity information. Fuzzy identity-based encryption (FIBE) was first proposed by Sahai and Waters [11]. In such a system, identities are regarded as a set of biometric attributes (e.g., fingerprints and irises) instead of an arbitrary string like an

© Springer Nature Singapore Pte Ltd. 2018
F. Li et al. (Eds.): FCS 2018, CCIS 879, pp. 83–95, 2018.
https://doi.org/10.1007/978-981-13-3095-7_7

email address in previous system. Soon afterwards, a novel cryptographic primitive called fuzzy identity-based signature (FIBS) was introduced by Yang, Cao and Dong [16]. In a FIBS scheme, a signature issued by a signer with identity id can be validly verified by identity id′ if and only if id and id′ are "close enough" and within certain distance. Then, a large number of FIBS schemes based on the hardness of number-theoretic cryptographic problems (e.g., integer factorization and discrete logarithm) were proposed [14,15,17,20]. However, none of those constructions are secure in the future with large-scale quantum computers [13].

Lattice-based cryptography, as one of the most promising candidates for postquantum cryptography, has attracted significant interest in recent years, due to several potential benefits: asymptotic efficiency, worst-case hardness assumptions and security against quantum computers. To design secure and efficient latticebased cryptographic schemes are interesting and challenging.

RELATED WORK. The first lattice-based FIBS scheme was constructed by Yao and Li [19], and their construction is existentially unforgeable against adaptively chosen identity and message attacks (EU-aID-CMA) in the random oracle model. A construction without random oracle (i.e., in the standard model) was proposed by Yang et al. [18], moreover, it achieves a strong unforgeability under selectively chosen identity and message attacks (SU-sID-CMA). Recently, using the lattice basis delegation technique to keep the lattice dimension invariant, another FIBS scheme in the random oracle model was given [21]. However, all constructions can only support identities in a small universe, namely, only considering identities as bit-vectors in $\{0,1\}^{\ell}$, where ℓ is the identities size.

OUR CONTRIBUTIONS. In order to have a more practical and secure construction for FIBS, in this work, we present a new lattice FIBS scheme for a small universe, i.e., $\{0,1\}^{\ell}$. The new scheme is also proved to be SU-sID-CMA in the standard model. Moreover, compared with the existing schemes, the new construction has a competitive advantage of signature size, the time cost for signer and verifier, thus, our construction has a smaller communication cost and faster signing and verifying operations, meanwhile, keeping the same size of master key and signer's private key.

ORGANIZATION. The rest of this work is organized as follows. In Sect. 2, we recall several useful knowledge on lattices. Then, Sect. 3 turns to the definition and security requirements of FIBS. Finally, a new FIBS construction, the security and efficiency analysis are presented in Sect. 4.

2   Preliminaries

2.1   Notations

Vectors are in column form and denoted by bold lower-case letters (e.g., $\mathbf{e}$), and matrix is viewed as the set of its column vectors and denoted by bold upper-case letters (e.g., $\mathbf{A}$). The Euclidean norm of $\mathbf{e}$ is denoted as $\|\mathbf{e}\|$, and define the norm of $\mathbf{A}$ as the norm of its longest column (i.e., $\|\mathbf{A}\| = \max_i \|\mathbf{a}_i\|$). $\mathcal{O}$ and ω are used to classify the growth of functions, and all logarithms are of base 2. Let poly(n) denote an function $f(n) = \mathcal{O}(n^c)$ for $c > 0$. If $f(n) = \mathcal{O}(g(n) \cdot \log^c n)$, it is denoted as $f(n) = \widetilde{\mathcal{O}}(g(n))$. negl($n$) denotes a negligible function $f(n) = \mathcal{O}(n^{-c})$ for all $c > 0$, and a probability is called overwhelming if it is $1 - \text{negl}(n)$.

2.2 Lattices

Definition 1. *For integer n, m, prime $q \geq 2$ and matrix $\mathbf{A} \in \mathbb{Z}_q^{n \times m}$, define:*

$$\Lambda_q^{\perp}(\mathbf{A}) = \{\mathbf{e} \in \mathbb{Z}^m \ s.t. \ \mathbf{A} \cdot \mathbf{e} = \mathbf{0} \bmod q\}.$$

Given $\mathbf{u} \in \mathbb{Z}_q^n$, define a coset, $\Lambda_q^{\mathbf{u}}(\mathbf{A}) = \{\mathbf{e} \in \mathbb{Z}^m \ s.t. \mathbf{A} \cdot \mathbf{e} = \mathbf{u} \bmod q\}$.
For $s > 0$, define the Gaussian function on $\mathbb{R}^m$ with center $\mathbf{c}$:

$$\forall \mathbf{e} \in \mathbb{R}^m, \ \rho_{s,\mathbf{c}}(\mathbf{e}) = exp(-\pi \|\mathbf{e} - \mathbf{c}\|^2 / s^2).$$

For $\mathbf{c} \in \mathbb{R}^m$, real $s > 0$, define the discrete Gaussian distribution over Λ as:

$$\forall \mathbf{e} \in \Lambda, \ \mathcal{D}_{\Lambda,s,\mathbf{c}}(\mathbf{e}) = \rho_{s,\mathbf{c}}(\mathbf{e}) / \rho_{s,\mathbf{c}}(\Lambda).$$

For convenience, we denote $\mathcal{D}_{\Lambda,s,\mathbf{c}}$ as $\mathcal{D}_{\Lambda,s}$ if $\mathbf{c} = \mathbf{0}$.

The smoothing parameter is a new lattice quantity put forward by Micciancio and Regev [10].

Definition 2. *For lattice Λ and real $\epsilon > 0$, the smoothing parameter η_ϵ is the smallest real $s > 0$ such that $\rho_{1/s}(\Lambda^* \setminus \{0\}) \leq \epsilon$, where Λ^* is the dual of Λ.*

Lemma 1. *Assume that the columns of $\mathbf{A} \in \mathbb{Z}_q^{n \times m}$ generate $\mathbb{Z}_q^n$, let $\epsilon \in (0, 1/2)$, $s \geq \eta_\epsilon(\Lambda^{\perp}(\mathbf{A}))$. For $\mathbf{e} \leftarrow D_{\mathbb{Z}^m,s}$, the distribution of syndrome $\mathbf{u} = \mathbf{A} \cdot \mathbf{e} \bmod q$ is within statistical distance 2ϵ of uniform over $\mathbb{Z}_q^n$.*

Ajtai [3] firstly introduced how to obtain a uniform random matrix $\mathbf{A} \in \mathbb{Z}_q^{n \times m}$ together with a low Gram-Schmidt norm basis $\mathbf{T_A}$ for $\Lambda_q^{\perp}(\mathbf{A})$, then two improved algorithms investigated by [4,9].

Lemma 2. *Let $n \geq 1$, $q \geq 2$ and $m = \lceil 2n\log q \rceil$. There exists a PPT algorithm* TrapGen(q, n, m) *that outputs $\mathbf{A}$ and $\mathbf{T_A}$, such that $\mathbf{A}$ is statistically close to a uniform matrix in $\mathbb{Z}_q^{n \times m}$ and $\mathbf{T_A} \in \mathbb{Z}^{m \times m}$ is a short basis for $\Lambda_q^{\perp}(\mathbf{A})$, satisfying $\|\widetilde{\mathbf{T}}_{\mathbf{A}}\| \leq \mathcal{O}(\sqrt{n\log q})$ with all but a negligible probability in n.*

Given a short basis of $\Lambda_q^{\perp}(\mathbf{A})$, Gentry et al. [7] showed how to sample from a discrete Gaussian distribution over lattices.

Lemma 3. *Let $q \geq 2$, $\mathbf{A} \in \mathbb{Z}_q^{n \times m}$, and real $0 < \epsilon < 1$. Let $\mathbf{T_A}$ be a short basis for $\Lambda_q^{\perp}(\mathbf{A})$, parameter $s \geq \|\widetilde{\mathbf{T}}_{\mathbf{A}}\| \cdot \omega(\sqrt{\log m})$. Then, for $\mathbf{c} \in \mathbb{R}^m$ and $\mathbf{u} \in \mathbb{Z}_q^n$:*

1. $\Pr_{\mathbf{e} \leftarrow \mathcal{D}_{\Lambda,s,\mathbf{c}}}[\|\mathbf{e} - \mathbf{c}\| > s\sqrt{m}] \leq \frac{1+\epsilon}{1-\epsilon} \cdot 2^{-m}$.
2. *There exists a PPT algorithm* SampleGau($\mathbf{A}, \mathbf{T_A}, s, \mathbf{c}$) *returns a short vector $\mathbf{e} \in \Lambda_q^{\perp}(\mathbf{A})$ drawn from a distribution statistically close to $\mathcal{D}_{\Lambda_q^{\perp}(\mathbf{A}),s,\mathbf{c}}$.*
3. *There exists a PPT algorithm* SamplePre($\mathbf{A}, \mathbf{T_A}, \mathbf{u}, s$) *returns a short vector $\mathbf{e} \in \Lambda_q^{\mathbf{u}}(\mathbf{A})$ sampled from a distribution statistically close to $\mathcal{D}_{\Lambda_q^{\mathbf{u}}(\mathbf{A}),s}$.*

2.3 Some Facts

We recall several useful facts on lattices in literatures.

The first two lemmas put forward by Cash *et al.* [6] are main techniques for a cultivation of bonsai trees.

Lemma 4. *On input* $\mathbf{A} \in \mathbb{Z}_q^{n \times m}$, *whose columns generate the entire group* $\mathbb{Z}_q^n$ *and an arbitrary* $\mathbf{A}' \in \mathbb{Z}_q^{n \times m'}$. *Given a basis* $\mathbf{T_A}$ *of* $\Lambda_q^{\perp}(\mathbf{A})$, *there is a deterministic polynomial-time algorithm* ExtBasis$(\mathbf{T_A}, \hat{\mathbf{A}} = [\mathbf{A}|\mathbf{A}'])$ *that outputs a basis* $\mathbf{T_{\hat{A}}}$ *for* $\Lambda_q^{\perp}(\hat{\mathbf{A}}) \subseteq \mathbb{Z}^{m+m'}$ *such that* $\|\widetilde{\mathbf{T_{\hat{A}}}}\| = \|\widetilde{\mathbf{T_A}}\|$. *Moreover, this statement holds even for any given permutation of the columns of* $\hat{\mathbf{A}}$.

Lemma 5. *On input* $\mathbf{A} \in \mathbb{Z}_q^{n \times m}$, *real* $s \geq \|\widetilde{\mathbf{T_A}}\| \cdot \omega(\sqrt{\log n})$. *Given a basis* $\mathbf{T_A}$ *of* $\Lambda_q^{\perp}(\mathbf{A})$, *there is a PPT algorithm* RandBasis$(\mathbf{A}, \mathbf{T_A}, s)$ *that outputs a short basis* $\mathbf{T'_A} \in \mathbb{Z}^{m \times m}$ *for* $\Lambda_q^{\perp}(\mathbf{A})$ *such that* $\|\mathbf{T'_A}\| \leq s\sqrt{m}$ *and no information specific to* $\mathbf{T_A}$ *is leaked.*

The followings are two basic facts and a new sampling algorithm proposed by Agrawal *et al.* [1].

Lemma 6. *Let* $n \geq 1$, *suppose that* $m > (n+1)\log q + \omega(\log n)$ *and* q *is a prime. Let* $\mathbf{A}$ *and* $\mathbf{B}$ *be two matrices chosen uniformly in* $\mathbb{Z}_q^{n \times m}$, *and* $\mathbf{R}$ *is an* $m \times m$-*matrix chosen uniformly in* $\{-1,1\}^{m \times m}$. *Then, for all* $\mathbf{w} \in \mathbb{Z}_q^m$, *the distribution* $(\mathbf{A}, \mathbf{A}\mathbf{R}, \mathbf{R}^{\top}\mathbf{w})$ *is statistically close to* $(\mathbf{A}, \mathbf{B}, \mathbf{R}^{\top}\mathbf{w})$.

Lemma 7. *Let* $\mathbf{R}$ *be an* $m \times m$-*matrix chosen at random from* $\{-1,1\}^{m \times m}$. *For vectors* $\mathbf{e} \in \mathbb{R}^m$, $\Pr\left[\|\mathbf{R} \cdot \mathbf{e}\| > \|\mathbf{e}\| \cdot \sqrt{m} \cdot \omega(\sqrt{\log m})\right] < \text{negl}(m)$.

Lemma 8. *Let prime* $q \geq 3$, *integer* n, *and* $m > n$, $\mathbf{A}, \mathbf{B} \in \mathbb{Z}_q^{n \times m}$ *and a real* $s \geq \|\widetilde{\mathbf{T_B}}\| \cdot \sqrt{m} \cdot \omega(\log m)$. *There is a PPT algorithm* SampleRight$(\mathbf{A}, \mathbf{B}, \mathbf{R}, \mathbf{T_B}, \mathbf{u}, s)$ *that given a short basis* $\mathbf{T_B}$ *for* $\Lambda_q^{\perp}(\mathbf{B})$, *a low norm matrix* $\mathbf{R} \in \{-1,1\}^{m \times m}$ *and a vector* $\mathbf{u} \in \mathbb{Z}_q^n$, *outputs a vector* $\mathbf{e} \in \mathbb{Z}^{2m}$ *distributed statistically close to* $\mathcal{D}_{\Lambda_q^{\mathbf{u}}(\mathbf{F}),s}$, *where* $\mathbf{F} = [\mathbf{A}|\mathbf{A}\mathbf{R} + \mathbf{B}]$.

2.4 The SIS Problem

We now give the definition of small integer solution (SIS) problem.

Definition 3. *The* SIS *problem in the Euclidean norm is that given a integer* q, *a matrix* $\mathbf{A} \in \mathbb{Z}_q^{n \times m}$ *and a real* β, *to find a non-zero vector* $\mathbf{e} \in \mathbb{Z}^m$ *satisfying* $\mathbf{A} \cdot \mathbf{e} = \mathbf{0} \mod q$, *and* $\|\mathbf{e}\| \leq \beta$.

The SIS$_{q,n,m,\beta}$ problem was first shown to be hard as the worst-case lattice problems by Ajtai [3], then by Micciancio and Regev [10] and Gentry *et al.* [7].

Lemma 9. *For poly-bounded* m, $\beta = \text{poly}(n)$ *and prime* $q \geq \beta \cdot \omega(\sqrt{n \log n})$, *the average-case* SIS$_{q,n,m,\beta}$ *problem is as hard as approximating the shortest independent vector problem* SIVP$_{\gamma}$ *to within certain* $\gamma = \beta \cdot \widetilde{\mathcal{O}}(\sqrt{n})$ *factor.*

3 Fuzzy Identity-Based Signature

We now formalize the definition and security model of FIBS.

A fuzzy identity-based signature is described as follows:

FIBS.Setup(1^n): A PPT algorithm that takes as input the security parameter n, and outputs a public parameters PP that contains an error tolerance parameter k and a master key MK.

FIBS.Extract(PP, MK, id): A PPT algorithm that takes as input the parameters PP, the master key MK, and an identity id, and outputs a private key associate with id, denoted by SK_{id}.

FIBS.Sign(PP, SK_{id}, m): A PPT algorithm that takes as input the public parameters PP, a private key SK_{id} associated with an identity id, and a message $m \in \{0,1\}^*$, and outputs a signature $\sigma_{id,m}$ for identity id with m.

FIBS.Verify(PP, id', m, $\sigma_{id,m}$): A deterministic algorithm that takes as input the public parameters PP, an identity id' such that $|id \cap id'| \geq k$, a message m and the corresponding signature $\sigma_{id,m}$, and outputs 1 if the signature is valid or 0, otherwise.

The correctness is that for a fixed identity id, and any id' such that $|id \cap id'| \geq k$, for (PP, MK, Sk_{id}) outputted by algorithms FIBS.Setup and FIBS.Extract and a message $m \in \{0,1\}^*$, the following holds,

$$FIBS.Verify(PP, id', m, FIBS.Sign(PP, SK_{id}, m)) = 1.$$

Let $\mathcal{A}$ be any PPT adversary, and $\mathcal{C}$ be a challenger assumed to be a probabilistic Turing machine taking as input the security parameter n. In this work, we consider the security model of FIBS as strongly unforgeable against selectively chosen identity and message attacks (SU-sID-CMA). In SU-sID-CMA, the adversary $\mathcal{A}$ is not only allowed to forge a signature for a fresh message $m^* \neq m_i$, but allowed to forge a fresh signature for m_i, where the signature of m_i was known by $\mathcal{A}$.

Consider the following game between $\mathcal{A}$ and $\mathcal{C}$:

Initialization: $\mathcal{A}$ declares a target identity id^*.

Setup: $\mathcal{C}$ runs FIBS.Setup and provides $\mathcal{A}$ the public parameters PP.

Queries: $\mathcal{A}$ is allowed to make poly-bounded queries as follows:

- Extract query: $\mathcal{A}$ can issue private key queries for any identities id_i, where $|id_i \cap id^*| < k$.
- Signing query: $\mathcal{A}$ can issue sign queries for any identities id_i on any message $m_i \in \{0,1\}^*$ adaptively.

Forgery: Finally, $\mathcal{A}$ outputs (id*, m*, σ^*_{id,m^*}), and $\mathcal{A}$ is considered to be succeed if the following conditions hold:

1. FIBS.Verify(PP, id*, m*, σ^*_{id,m^*}) = 1.

2. For any $(\mathsf{id}, \mathsf{m}, \sigma_{\mathsf{id},\mathsf{m}})$ that is generated in Signing query, we have
   a. $|\mathsf{id} \cap \mathsf{id}^*| \geq k$, $(\mathsf{m}, \sigma_{\mathsf{id},\mathsf{m}}) \neq (\mathsf{m}^*, \sigma^*_{\mathsf{id},\mathsf{m}^*})$; or
   b. $|\mathsf{id} \cap \mathsf{id}^*| < k$.

Thus, we define the advantage of $\mathcal{A}$ by

$$\mathsf{Adv}_{\mathcal{A}}(n) = \Pr[\mathsf{FIBS}.\mathsf{Verify}(\mathsf{PP}, \mathsf{id}^*, \mathsf{m}^*, \sigma^*_{\mathsf{id},\mathsf{m}^*}) = 1].$$

Definition 4. *A FIBS scheme is said to be SU-sID-CMA if* $\mathsf{Adv}_{\mathcal{A}}(n)$ *is negligible in the security parameter* n *for any PPT* $\mathcal{A}$.

Furthermore, adopting a family of chameleon hash functions (CHF), there is a generic construction of a stronger security model, strongly unforgeable against adaptively chosen identity and message attacks (SU-aID-CMA) from any SU-sID-CMA [8].

4   Lattice FIBS for Identities in a Small Universe

Inspired by the efficient IBE scheme [1] and a lattice-based mixing and vanishing trapdoor scheme [5], we now construct a FIBS scheme with a shorter signature size and provably SU-sID-CMA secure in the standard model for identities in a small universe, i.e., $\{0, 1\}^{\ell}$.

4.1   Our Construction

The main steps are provided as follows:

FIBS.Setup(1^n): Take as input the security parameter n and set the parameters $\ell, k, k', q, m, s_1, s_2$ as specified in the next subsection, where ℓ (ℓ depends on n) is the identity size, k ($k < \ell$) is an error tolerance parameter, k' denotes the length of a message. Then, do the steps as follows:
   1. For $i = 1, 2, \ldots, \ell, b \in \{0, 1\}$, run TrapGen($q, n, m$) to generate a uniformly random $n \times m$-matrix $\mathbf{A}_{i,b} \in \mathbb{Z}_q^{n \times m}$ together with a short basis $\mathbf{T}_{\mathbf{A}_{i,b}}$ for $\Lambda_q^{\perp}(\mathbf{A}_{i,b})$.
   2. For $i = 1, 2, \ldots, \ell, b \in \{0, 1\}$, select two uniformly random $n \times m$-matrices $\mathbf{C}_{i,b}$ and $\mathbf{B}_i$ in $\mathbb{Z}_q^{n \times m}$.
   3. Select k' vectors $\mathbf{v}_1, \mathbf{v}_2, \ldots, \mathbf{v}_{k'} \in \mathbb{Z}_q^n$ at random.
   4. Let $\mathcal{H} : \mathbb{Z}_q^n \to \mathbb{Z}_q^{n \times n}$ be a full rank differences map as [1].
   5. Output the public parameters PP and the master key MK,
      PP $= (\{\mathbf{A}_{i,b}, \mathbf{C}_{i,b}, \mathbf{B}_i\}_{i=1,2,\ldots,\ell, b \in \{0,1\}}, \{\mathbf{v}_i\}_{i=1,2,\ldots,k'}, \mathcal{H})$,
      MK $= (\{\mathbf{T}_{\mathbf{A}_{i,b}}\}_{i=1,2,\ldots,\ell, b \in \{0,1\}})$.
FIBS.Extract(PP, MK, id): Take as input the public parameters PP, the master key MK, and an identity $\mathsf{id} = (id_1, id_2, \ldots, id_{\ell}) \in \{0, 1\}^{\ell}$, then do the steps as follows:

1. For id_i, $i = 1, 2, \ldots, \ell$, construct an $n \times 2m$-matrix,
$$\mathbf{A}'_{i,id_i} = [\mathbf{A}_{i,id_i} | \mathbf{C}_{i,id_i} + \mathcal{H}(\mathsf{id}, id_i, i) \cdot \mathbf{B}_i].$$

2. For id_i, $i = 1, 2, \ldots, \ell$, compute a matrix $\mathbf{T}_{\mathbf{A}'_{i,id_i}} \in \mathbb{Z}^{2m \times 2m}$ using algorithm RandBasis(ExtBasis($\mathbf{T}_{\mathbf{A}_{i,id_i}}, \mathbf{A}'_{i,id_i}$), $\mathbf{A}'_{i,id_i}, s_1$).

3. Output $\mathsf{SK}_{\mathsf{id}} = (\mathbf{T}_{\mathbf{A}'_{1,id_1}}, \mathbf{T}_{\mathbf{A}'_{2,id_2}}, \ldots, \mathbf{T}_{\mathbf{A}'_{\ell,id_\ell}})$.

FIBS.Sign(PP, $\mathsf{SK}_{\mathsf{id}}$, m): Take as input the public parameters PP, the private key $\mathsf{SK}_{\mathsf{id}}$ associated with an identity $\mathsf{id} = (id_1, \ldots, id_\ell) \in \{0,1\}^\ell$ and a message $\mathsf{m} = (m_1, m_2, \cdots, m_{k'}) \in \{0,1\}^{k'}$, then do the steps as follows:

1. Set vector $\mathbf{v} = \sum_{i=1}^{k'} (-1)^{m_i} \mathbf{v}_i \bmod q$.

2. Construct ℓ shares of $\mathbf{v} = (v_1, \ldots, v_n) \in \mathbb{Z}_q^n$ using a Shamir Secret-Sharing scheme applied to each coordinate of $\mathbf{v}$ independently. Namely, for each $j = 1, 2, \ldots, n$, choose a uniformly random polynomial $p_j \in \mathbb{Z}_q[x]$ of degree $k - 1$ such that $p_j(0) = v_j$.

3. Construct the j-th share vector, $\hat{\mathbf{v}}_j = (p_1(j), p_2(j), \ldots, p_n(j)) \in \mathbb{Z}_q^n$. Thus for all $J \subseteq \{1, 2, \ldots, \ell\}$ satisfying $|J| \geq k$, there are fractional Lagrangian coefficients $L_j \in \mathbb{Z}_q$ such that $\mathbf{v} = \sum_{j \in J} L_j \cdot \hat{\mathbf{v}}_j \bmod q$.

4. For id_i, $i = 1, 2, \ldots, \ell$, compute a $2m$-dimensional vector $\mathbf{e}_i \in \mathbb{Z}^{2m}$ using SamplePre($\mathbf{A}'_{i,id_i}, \mathbf{T}_{\mathbf{A}'_{i,id_i}}, q\hat{\mathbf{v}}_i, s_2$).

5. Output the signature $\sigma_{\mathsf{id},\mathsf{m}} = (\mathsf{m}, \mathsf{id}, \mathbf{e}_1, \ldots, \mathbf{e}_\ell)$.

FIBS.Verify(PP, id', m, $\sigma_{\mathsf{id},\mathsf{m}}$): Take as input the public parameters PP, identity $\mathsf{id}' = (id'_1, \ldots, id'_\ell) \in \{0,1\}^\ell$, message $\mathsf{m} \in \{0,1\}^{k'}$, and a signature $\sigma_{\mathsf{id},\mathsf{m}}$, then do the steps as follows:

1. Let $J \subseteq \{1, \ldots, \ell\}$ denote the set of matching elements in id and id'. If $|J| < k$, then output $\bot$. Otherwise, for $j \in J$, compute $\mathbf{A}'_{j,id_j} = [\mathbf{A}_{j,id_j} | \mathbf{C}_{j,id_j} + \mathcal{H}(\mathsf{id}, id_j, j) \cdot \mathbf{B}_j]$.

2. Set $\mathbf{v} = \sum_{i=1}^{k'} (-1)^{m_i} \mathbf{v}_i$.

3. If $\|\mathbf{e}_i\| \leq s_2\sqrt{2m}$ and $\sum_{j \in J} L_j \cdot \mathbf{A}'_{j,id_j} \mathbf{e}_j = q\mathbf{v}$, where $L_j = \prod_{j \in J, i \neq j} \frac{i}{i-j}$ is the Lagrangian coefficient, then output 1. Otherwise, 0.

4.2   Parameters

The above construction depends on several parameters $\ell, k, k', q, m, s_1, s_2$, which are set so that all algorithms are implemented in a polynomial time correctly and the security properties hold. The security parameter is n and all other parameters are determined as follows:

- For TrapGen(q, n, m) in Lemma 2, we need $m = 2n\lceil \log q \rceil$.
- To ensure that the $\mathsf{SIS}_{q,n,m,\beta}$ problem has a worst-case lattice reduction, then according to Lemma 9, we set $q \geq \beta \cdot \omega(\sqrt{n \log n})$. The parameter β is set in the next subsection.
- The identity size $\ell = n^\epsilon$ for some constant $\epsilon \in (0, 1)$ and the error tolerance parameter $k < \ell$.
- Due to Lemma 4, we set $s_1 = \mathcal{O}(\sqrt{n \log q}) \cdot \omega(\sqrt{\log n})$.
- Due to Lemmas 5 and 3, $\|\widetilde{\mathbf{T}_{\mathbf{A}'_{i,id_i}}}\| \leq \|\mathbf{T}_{\mathbf{A}'_{i,id_i}}\| \leq \mathcal{O}(\sqrt{n \log q}) \cdot \sqrt{2m} \cdot \omega(\sqrt{\log n})$, $s_2 \geq \|\widetilde{\mathbf{T}_{\mathbf{A}'_{i,id_i}}}\| \cdot \omega(\sqrt{\log 2m})$, we set $s_2 = s_1 \cdot \sqrt{2m} \cdot \omega(\sqrt{\log 2m})$.

4.3 Correctness

Let $\sigma_{id,m} = (m, id, e_1, \ldots, e_\ell)$ be a valid signature. To check the correctness, it is only need to consider the case $|J| \geq k$, where $J \subseteq \{1, 2, \ldots, \ell\}$ denotes the set of matching elements in id and id'. According to Lemma 3, for $i = 1, 2, \ldots, \ell$, $e_i \in \mathbb{Z}^{2m}$ satisfies $\mathbf{A}'_{i,id_i} e_i = q\hat{v}_i$ and it is drawn from a distribution statistically close to $\mathcal{D}_{\Lambda_q^{q\hat{v}_i}(\mathbf{A}'_{i,id_i}),s_2}$. Thus, $\|e_i\| \leq s_2\sqrt{2m}$ and $\sum_{j \in J} L_j \cdot \mathbf{A}'_{j,id_j} e_j = \sum_{j \in J} L_j \cdot q\hat{v}_j = qv = q \sum_{i=1}^{k'} (-1)^{m_i} v_i$.

4.4 Proof of Security

The theorem below reduces the SIS problem to the SU-sID-CMA of our construction. The proof involves a forger $\mathcal{A}$ and a solver $\mathcal{B}$.

Theorem 1. *For a prime modulus $q = \text{poly}(n)$, if there is a PPT forger $\mathcal{A}$ that outputs an existential signature forgery with probability ε, in time τ, then there exists a PPT algorithm $\mathcal{B}$ that solves the $\text{SIS}_{q,n,m\ell,\beta}$ problem in time $\tau' \approx \tau$, and with a probability $\varepsilon' \geq (1 - 3^{-k}) \cdot \varepsilon$, for $\beta = (\ell!)^3 \cdot (1 + \sqrt{m} \cdot \omega(\sqrt{\log m})) \cdot 2s_2\sqrt{2m\ell}$.*

Proof. Given a random instance of the $\text{SIS}_{q,n,m\ell,\beta}$ problem, $\mathcal{B}$ is asked to return an admissible solution.

- $\mathcal{B}$ is given an $n \times m\ell$-matrix $\mathbf{A} \in \mathbb{Z}_q^{n \times m\ell}$ from the uniform distribution.
- $\mathcal{B}$ is requested any $e \in \mathbb{Z}^{m\ell}$ such that $\mathbf{A} \cdot e = \mathbf{0} \bmod q$ and $0 \neq \|e\| \leq \beta$.

The operations performed by $\mathcal{B}$ are as follows:

Initialization: $\mathcal{A}$ declares the target identity $id^* = (id_1^*, \ldots, id_\ell^*) \in \{0, 1\}^\ell$.
Setup: $\mathcal{B}$ gives $\mathcal{A}$ the public parameters as follows:
  1. Parse $\mathbf{A}$ as $\mathbf{A} = [\mathbf{A}_1, \mathbf{A}_2, \ldots, \mathbf{A}_\ell]$, where $\mathbf{A}_i \in \mathbb{Z}_q^{n \times m}$ for $i = 1, 2, \ldots, \ell$.
  2. For $i = 1, 2, \ldots, \ell$, pick a uniformly random $n \times m$-matrix $\mathbf{A}'_i \in \mathbb{Z}_q^{n \times m}$.
  3. For $i = 1, 2, \ldots, \ell$, let $\mathbf{A}_{i,id_i^*} = \mathbf{A}_i$, $\mathbf{A}_{i,1-id_i^*} = \mathbf{A}'_i$.
  4. For $i = 1, 2, \ldots, \ell$, run algorithm $\text{TrapGen}(q, n, m)$ to obtain a uniformly random $n \times m$-matrix $\mathbf{B}_i \in \mathbb{Z}_q^{n \times m}$ together with a short basis $\mathbf{T}_{\mathbf{B}_i} \in \mathbb{Z}^{m \times m}$ for $\Lambda_q^{\perp}(\mathbf{B}_i)$.
  5. Choose a full rank differences map $\mathcal{H} : \mathbb{Z}_q^n \to \mathbb{Z}_q^{n \times n}$.
  6. For $i = 1, 2, \ldots, \ell$, select an $m \times m$-matrix $\mathbf{R}_i \in \{-1, 1\}^{m \times m}$ at random, and compute $\mathbf{C}_{i,id_i} = \mathbf{A}_{i,id_i}\mathbf{R}_i - \mathcal{H}(id^*, id_i^*, i)\mathbf{B}_i \in \mathbb{Z}_q^{n \times m}$. So, according to Lemma 6, $\mathbf{C}_{i,id_i}$ is indistinguishable from that in the real scheme.
  7. Select k' vectors $v_1, \ldots, v_{k'} \in \mathbb{Z}_q^n$ at random.
  8. Output the public parameters,
     $\text{PP} = (\{\mathbf{A}_{i,b}, \mathbf{C}_{i,b}, \mathbf{B}_i\}_{i=1,\ldots,\ell,b \in \{0,1\}}, \{v_i\}_{i=1,\ldots,k'}, \mathcal{H})$.
Extract query. For a request of private key for id, $\mathcal{B}$ constructs a private key for id, where $|id \cap id^*| < k$ (id^* is the target identity) as follows:
  1. For $i = 1, 2, \ldots, \ell$, $\mathcal{B}$ computes $\mathbf{A}'_{i,id_i} = [\mathbf{A}_{i,id_i} | \mathbf{A}_{i,id_i}\mathbf{R}_i + (\mathcal{H}(id, id_i, i) - \mathcal{H}(id^*, id_i^*, i))\mathbf{B}_i]$ and generate a basis $\mathbf{T}_{\mathbf{A}'_{i,id_i}}$ for $\Lambda_q^{\perp}(\mathbf{A}'_{i,id_i})$ by using $\mathbf{T}_{\mathbf{B}_i}$. (For $|id \cap id^*| < k$, $\mathcal{H}(id, id_i, i) - \mathcal{H}(id^*, id_i^*, i)$ is non-singular, thus, $\mathbf{T}_{\mathbf{B}_i}$ is also a trapdoor for $\Lambda_q^{\perp}(\mathbf{B}'_i)$, where $\mathbf{B}'_i = (\mathcal{H}(id, id_i, i) - \mathcal{H}(id^*, id_i^*, i)) \cdot \mathbf{B}_i$).

2. $\mathcal{B}$ returns $(\mathbf{T}_{\mathbf{A}'_{1,id_1}}, \ldots, \mathbf{T}_{\mathbf{A}'_{\ell,id_\ell}})$.

Signing query. For $\mathcal{A}$'s requests of id, $\mathbf{m} = (m_1, m_2, \cdots, m_{k'}) \in \{0,1\}^{k'}$, $\mathcal{B}$ does as follows:

1. Compute $\mathbf{v} = \sum_{i=1}^{k'}(-1)^{m_i}\mathbf{v}_i$.
2. Construct ℓ shares of $\mathbf{v} = (v_1, \ldots, v_n) \in \mathbb{Z}_q^n$ by using a Shamir Secret-Sharing scheme applied to each coordinate of $\mathbf{v}$ independently. Namely, for each $j = 1, 2, \ldots, n$, choose a uniformly random polynomial $p_j \in \mathbb{Z}_q[x]$ of degree $k - 1$ such that $p_j(0) = v_j$.
3. Construct the j-th share vector, $\hat{\mathbf{v}}_j = (p_1(j), p_2(j), \ldots, p_n(j)) \in \mathbb{Z}_q^n$. Thus for all $J \subseteq \{1, 2, \ldots, \ell\}$ satisfying $|J| \geq k$, there are fractional Lagrangian coefficients $L_j \in \mathbb{Z}_q$ such that $\mathbf{v} = \sum_{j \in J} L_j \cdot \hat{\mathbf{v}}_j \bmod q$.
4. For id_i, $i = 1, 2, \ldots, \ell$, compute a $2m$-dimensional vector $\mathbf{e}_i \in \mathbb{Z}^{2m}$ using SampleRight$(\mathbf{A}_{i,id_i}, \mathbf{B}_i, \mathbf{R}_i, \mathbf{T}_{\mathbf{B}_i}, q\hat{\mathbf{v}}_i, s_2)$, then return $(\mathbf{m}, id, \mathbf{e}_1, \ldots, \mathbf{e}_\ell)$.

Forgery: $\mathcal{A}$ outputs a valid forgery $(id^*, \mathbf{m}^*, \mathbf{e}_1^*, \ldots, \mathbf{e}_\ell^*)$, and the followings hold:

1. For $i = 1, 2, \ldots, \ell$, $\|\mathbf{e}_i^*\| \leq s_2\sqrt{2m}$.
2. There is a set $J \subseteq \{1, 2, \ldots, \ell\}$ and $|J| \geq k$ satisfying that $\sum_{j \in J} L_j \cdot \mathbf{A}'_{j,id_j^*} \cdot \mathbf{e}_j^* = q\sum_{i=1}^{k'}(-1)^{m_i}\mathbf{v}_i$ where $\mathbf{A}'_{j,id_j^*} = [\mathbf{A}_{j,id_j^*}|\mathbf{C}_{j,id_j^*} + \mathcal{H}(id^*, id_j^*, j)\mathbf{B}_j]$.

Let scalar $D = (\ell!)^2$, for $j \in \{1, 2, \ldots, k\}$, $\mathcal{B}$ does as follows:

1. Parse $\mathbf{e}_j^* = (\mathbf{e}_{j,0}^*, \mathbf{e}_{j,1}^*)^\top$, where $\mathbf{e}_{j,0}^*, \mathbf{e}_{j,1}^* \in \mathbb{Z}^m$.
2. If message $\mathbf{m}^* \in \{0,1\}^{k'}$ has been queried in Signing query, the signature is $(\mathbf{m}^*, id^*, \mathbf{e}_1', \ldots, \mathbf{e}_\ell')$. For $i = 1, 2, \ldots, \ell$, let $\widehat{\mathbf{e}_{i,0}} = \mathbf{e}_{i,0}^* - \mathbf{e}_{i,0}'$, $\widehat{\mathbf{e}_{i,1}} = \mathbf{e}_{i,1}^* - \mathbf{e}_{i,1}'$, and return $\mathbf{e}^* = (D \cdot L_1(\widehat{\mathbf{e}_{1,0}} + \mathbf{R}_1\widehat{\mathbf{e}_{1,1}}), D \cdot L_2(\widehat{\mathbf{e}_{2,0}} + \mathbf{R}_2\widehat{\mathbf{e}_{2,1}}), \ldots, D \cdot L_k(\widehat{\mathbf{e}_{k,0}} + \mathbf{R}_k\widehat{\mathbf{e}_{k,1}}), \mathbf{0}, \ldots, \mathbf{0})$ as a solution to the $\text{SIS}_{q,n,m\ell,\beta}$ problem.
3. If message $\mathbf{m}^* \in \{0,1\}^{k'}$ was not queried in Signing query, then return $\mathbf{e}^* = (D \cdot L_1(\mathbf{e}_{1,0}^* + \mathbf{R}_1\mathbf{e}_{1,1}^*), D \cdot L_2(\mathbf{e}_{2,0}^* + \mathbf{R}_2\mathbf{e}_{2,1}^*), \ldots, D \cdot L_k(\mathbf{e}_{k,0}^* + \mathbf{R}_k\mathbf{e}_{k,1}^*), \mathbf{0}, \ldots, \mathbf{0})$ as a solution to the $\text{SIS}_{q,n,m\ell,\beta}$ problem.

The detail analysis is as follows:

i. If $\mathbf{m}^*$ was queried, the signature is $(\mathbf{m}^*, id^*, \mathbf{e}_1', \ldots, \mathbf{e}_\ell')$, and id^* is the target identity, for $j = 1, 2, \ldots, k$, $\mathbf{A}'_{j,id_j^*} = [\mathbf{A}_{j,id_j^*}|\mathbf{A}_{j,id_j^*}\mathbf{R}_j]$. So $\sum_{j \in J} L_j \cdot \mathbf{A}'_{j,id_j^*}\mathbf{e}_j^* = q\mathbf{v} = \sum_{j \in J} L_j \cdot \mathbf{A}'_{j,id_j^*}\mathbf{e}_j'$, that is to say,

$$(\mathbf{A}_{1,id_1^*}|\mathbf{A}_{1,id_1^*}\mathbf{R}_1, \ldots, \mathbf{A}_{\ell,id_\ell^*}|\mathbf{A}_{\ell,id_\ell^*}\mathbf{R}_\ell) \cdot (L_1\mathbf{e}_1^*, \ldots, L_k\mathbf{e}_k^*, \mathbf{0}, \ldots, \mathbf{0})^\top =$$
$$(\mathbf{A}_{1,id_1^*}|\mathbf{A}_{1,id_1^*}\mathbf{R}_1, \ldots, \mathbf{A}_{\ell,id_\ell^*}|\mathbf{A}_{\ell,id_\ell^*}\mathbf{R}_\ell) \cdot (L_1\mathbf{e}_1', \ldots, L_k\mathbf{e}_k', \mathbf{0}, \ldots, \mathbf{0})^\top \bmod q.$$

Thus, we have
$$(\mathbf{A}_{1,id_1^*}, \ldots, \mathbf{A}_{\ell,id_\ell^*}) \cdot (L_1(\widehat{\mathbf{e}_{1,0}} + \mathbf{R}_1\widehat{\mathbf{e}_{1,1}}), \ldots, L_k(\widehat{\mathbf{e}_{k,0}} + \mathbf{R}_k\widehat{\mathbf{e}_{k,1}}), \mathbf{0}, \ldots, \mathbf{0})^\top =$$
$$(\mathbf{A}_1, \ldots, \mathbf{A}_\ell) \cdot (L_1(\widehat{\mathbf{e}_{1,0}} + \mathbf{R}_1\widehat{\mathbf{e}_{1,1}}), \ldots, L_k(\widehat{\mathbf{e}_{k,0}} + \mathbf{R}_k\widehat{\mathbf{e}_{k,1}}), \mathbf{0}, \ldots, \mathbf{0})^\top = \mathbf{0} \bmod q.$$

We use the conclusion that for $i = 1, 2, \ldots, \ell$, $D \cdot L_i \in \mathbb{Z}$ and $|D \cdot L_i| \leq (\ell!)^3$ [2] to clear the denominators of L_i, thus,

$$\mathbf{A} \cdot \underbrace{(D \cdot L_1(\widehat{\mathbf{e}_{1,0}} + \mathbf{R}_1\widehat{\mathbf{e}_{1,1}}), \ldots, D \cdot L_k(\widehat{\mathbf{e}_{k,0}} + \mathbf{R}_k\widehat{\mathbf{e}_{k,1}}), \mathbf{0}, \ldots, \mathbf{0})^\top}_{(\mathbf{e}^*)^\top} = \mathbf{0} \bmod q.$$

Next, we show that $\mathbf{e}^*$ is with high probability a short non-zero preimage of $\mathbf{0}$ under $\mathbf{A}$.

$\mathbf{R}_i$ is a low-norm matrix with coefficients ± 1, according to Lemma 7, $\Pr[\|\mathbf{R}_i\| > \sqrt{m} \cdot \omega(\sqrt{\log m})] < \mathrm{negl}(m)$, and for $i = 1, 2, \ldots, \ell$, $\|\mathbf{e}_i^*\|$, $\|\mathbf{e}_i'\| \leq s_2\sqrt{2m}$, thus, with overwhelming probability $\|\mathbf{e}^*\| \leq \beta$ for $\beta = (\ell!)^3 \cdot (1 + \sqrt{m} \cdot \omega(\sqrt{\log m})) \cdot 2s_2 \cdot \sqrt{2m\ell}$.

Finally, to show $\mathbf{e}_{i,i}^* = D \cdot L_i(\widehat{\mathbf{e}_{i,0}} + \mathbf{R}_i\widehat{\mathbf{e}_{i,1}}) \neq \mathbf{0}$. For an easy case, suppose that $\mathbf{e}_{i,1}^* = \mathbf{e}_{i,1}'$, for a valid forgery, we must have $\mathbf{e}_{i,0}^* \neq \mathbf{e}_{i,0}'$ and $D \cdot L_i\mathbf{R}_i\widehat{\mathbf{e}_{i,0}} \ll q$, thus $\mathbf{e}_{i,i}^* \neq \mathbf{0} \bmod q$. On the contrary, $\mathbf{e}_{i,1}^* \neq \mathbf{e}_{i,1}'$, in this case, $0 \neq \|\widehat{\mathbf{e}_{i,1}}\| = \|\mathbf{e}_{i,1}^* - \mathbf{e}_{i,1}'\| \leq 2s_2\sqrt{2m}$ and there must be at least one coordinate of $\widehat{\mathbf{e}_{i,1}}$ that is non-zero modulo q. We use the same method as in Sect. 4.4, let this coordinate be the last one in $\widehat{\mathbf{e}_{i,1}}$, and call it $\widehat{g}$. Let $\mathbf{r}_i$ be the last column of $\mathbf{e}_i$ and $\mathbf{g}_i = \widehat{g}\mathbf{r}_i$. Vector $\mathbf{e}_{i,i}^*$ can be rewritten as $\mathbf{e}_{i,i}^* = \mathbf{g}_i + \mathbf{g}_i'$, where $\mathbf{g}_i'$ does not depends on $\mathbf{r}_i$. The only information about $\mathbf{r}_i$ available to $\mathcal{A}$ is just contained in the last column of $\mathbf{C}_{i,id_i} = \mathbf{A}_{i,id_i}\mathbf{R}_i - \mathcal{H}(id^*, id_i^*, i)\mathbf{B}_i$. $\mathcal{A}$ cannot know the value of $\mathbf{g}_i$ with probability exceeding $1/3$ and at most one such value can result in a cancelation of $\widehat{\mathbf{e}_{i,1}}$, for if some $\mathbf{g}_i$ caused all coordinates of $\widehat{\mathbf{e}_{i,1}}$ to cancel, then every other $\mathbf{g}_i$ would fail to do so. Thus, $\mathbf{e}^*$ is with high probability $\varepsilon_1 \geq (1 - 3^{-k}) \cdot \varepsilon$ a short non-zero preimage of $\mathbf{0}$ under $\mathbf{A}$, and $0 \neq \|\mathbf{e}^*\| \leq \beta$ for $\beta = (\ell!)^3 \cdot (1 + \sqrt{m} \cdot \omega(\sqrt{\log m})) \cdot 2s_2\sqrt{2m\ell}$.

ii. If m^* was not queried in Signing query, the analysis is same as above just for that $\sum_{j \in J} L_j \cdot \mathbf{A}_{j,id_j}'\mathbf{e}_j^* = q\mathbf{v} = \mathbf{0} \bmod q$. Thus, $\mathbf{e}^*$ is also with probability $\varepsilon_2 \geq (1 - 3^{-k}) \cdot \varepsilon$ a short non-zero preimage of $\mathbf{0}$ under $\mathbf{A}$, and $0 \neq \|\mathbf{e}^*\| \leq \beta$ for $\beta = (\ell!)^3 \cdot (1 + \sqrt{m} \cdot \omega(\sqrt{\log m})) \cdot s_2\sqrt{2m\ell}$.

Therefore, we can deduce that vector $\mathbf{e}^*$ is with high probability $\varepsilon' = \varepsilon_1/2 + \varepsilon_2/2 \geq (1 - 3^{-k}) \cdot \varepsilon$ a short non-zero preimage of $\mathbf{0}$ under $\mathbf{A}$, i.e., $\mathbf{Ae}^* = \mathbf{0} \bmod q$ and $0 \neq \|\mathbf{e}^*\| \leq \beta$ for $\beta = (\ell!)^3 \cdot (1 + \sqrt{m} \cdot \omega(\sqrt{\log m})) \cdot 2s_2\sqrt{2m\ell}$.

4.5   Efficiency Analysis

The comparison with related lattice FIBS schemes in terms of public parameters size $\|PP\|$, master key size $\|MK\|$, private key size for id, $\|SK_{id}\|$, signature size $\|\sigma_{id,m}\|$, private key extraction cost (Ext-Cost), signing cost (Sig-Cost) and verification cost (Ver-Cost) are shown in Table 1. Here, ℓ is the identity size, $k < \ell$ is the error tolerance parameter and k' is the message size.

For simplicity, we set,

- T_1' denotes the time cost of RandBasis(ExtBasis) with module pq, T_1 denotes it with q and T_1'' denotes the cost of fixed dimension lattice basis delegation with q;
- T_2 denotes the cost of Shamir Secret-Sharing operation;
- T_3 denotes the cost of SampleGau;
- T_4' denotes the cost of SamplePre with module pq, T_4 denotes it with q;
- T_5' denotes the cost of inner product in $\mathbb{Z}_{pq}^{2m}$, T_5 denotes it in $\mathbb{Z}_q^m$;
- T_6' denotes the cost of scalar multiplication in $\mathbb{Z}_{pq}^{2n}$, T_6 denotes it in $\mathbb{Z}_q^{2n}$.

Table 1. Comparison of lattice FIBS schemes

Schemes	[18]	[19]	[21]	This work
$\|PP\|$	$((4\ell + k' + 1)m + 1)n\log q$	$2\ell nm\log pq$	$2\ell nm\log q$	$(5\ell m + k')n\log q$
$\|MK\|$	$2\ell m^2\log q$	$2\ell m^2\log pq$	$\ell m^2\log q$	$2\ell m^2\log q$
$\|SK_{id}\|$	$4\ell m^2\log q$	$4\ell m^2\log pq$	$4\ell m^2\log q$	$4\ell m^2\log q$
$\|\sigma_{id,m}\|$	$3\ell m\log q$	$2\ell m\log pq$	$\ell m\log q$	$2\ell m\log q$
Ext-Cost	ℓT_1	$\ell T_1'$	$\ell T_1''$	ℓT_1
Sig-Cost	$nT_2 + \ell(T_3 + T_4 + nT_5)$	$nT_2 + \ell T_4'$	$mT_2 + \ell T_4 + n\ell T_5$	$nT_2 + \ell T_4$
Ver-Cost	$k(3nT_5 + T_6)$	$k(nT_5' + T_6')$	$(k+1)nT_5 + kT_6$	$k(nT_5 + T_6)$
Universe	$\{0,1\}^\ell$	$\{0,1\}^\ell$	$\{0,1\}^\ell$	$\{0,1\}^\ell$
Security	SU-sID-CMA	EU-aID-CMA	EU-aID-CMA	SU-sID-CMA
Model	Standard	ROM	ROM	Standard

The results in Table 1 show that in the standard model (Standard), [18] has a slight advantage of $\|PP\|$, while in the random model (ROM), [21] has a slight advantage of $\|PP\|$, $\|SK_{id}\|$, $\|\sigma_{id,m}\|$ and Ver-Cost.

The results also show that in the standard model, our construction enjoys the competitive advantages of $\|\sigma_{id,m}\|$, Sig-Cost and Ver-Cost, namely, our scheme has a smaller communication cost and the faster signing and verifying operations, meanwhile, keeping the same size of $\|MK\|$, $\|SK_{id}\|$, and the time cost in Ext-Cost as [18].

For security, our construction and [18] are proved to be SU-sID-CMA, thus, enjoying a strong security compared with [19,21].

5 Conclusions

A new efficient FIBS scheme based on the SIS problems over lattices are proposed in this paper. The new construction is proved to be SU-sID-CMA in the standard model for identities living in a small universe. Compared with the existing lattice FIBS schemes, the new construction has made a great improvement on enhancing the efficiency and the signature size, namely, a smaller communication cost and a faster signing and verifying operations, thus, the new scheme is more practical. To construct an efficient lattice FIBS in the standard model for identities living in a large universe will be our future work.

Acknowledgments. We thank the anonymous referees for their helpful comments and the research of authors is supported by the National Natural Science Foundation of China (No. 61572445) and the Anhui Provincial Natural Science Foundation of China (No. 1708085QF154).

References

1. Agrawal, S., Boneh, D., Boyen, X.: Efficient lattice (H)IBE in the standard model. In: Gilbert, H. (ed.) EUROCRYPT 2010. LNCS, vol. 6110, pp. 553–572. Springer, Heidelberg (2010). https://doi.org/10.1007/978-3-642-13190-5_28
2. Agrawal, S., Boyen, X., Vaikuntanathan, V., Voulgaris, P., Wee, H.: Functional encryption for threshold functions (or fuzzy IBE) from lattices. In: Fischlin, M., Buchmann, J., Manulis, M. (eds.) PKC 2012. LNCS, vol. 7293, pp. 280–297. Springer, Heidelberg (2012). https://doi.org/10.1007/978-3-642-30057-8_17
3. Ajtai, M.: Generating hard instances of lattice problems (extended abstract). In: STOC, pp. 99–108 (1996)
4. Alwen, J., Peikert, C.: Generating shorter bases for hard random lattices. In: STACS, pp. 75–86 (2009)
5. Boyen, X.: Lattice mixing and vanishing trapdoors: a framework for fully secure short signatures and more. In: Nguyen, P.Q., Pointcheval, D. (eds.) PKC 2010. LNCS, vol. 6056, pp. 499–517. Springer, Heidelberg (2010). https://doi.org/10.1007/978-3-642-13013-7_29
6. Cash, D., Hofheinz, D., Kiltz, E., Peikert, C.: Bonsai trees, or how to delegate a lattice basis. In: Gilbert, H. (ed.) EUROCRYPT 2010. LNCS, vol. 6110, pp. 523–552. Springer, Heidelberg (2010). https://doi.org/10.1007/978-3-642-13190-5_27
7. Gentry, C., Peikert, C., Vaikuntanathan, V.: How to use a short basis: trapdoors for hard lattices and new cryptographic constructions. In: STOC, pp. 197–206 (2008)
8. Krawczyk, H., Rabin, T.: Chameleon signatures. In: NDSS, pp. 143–154 (2000)
9. Micciancio, D., Peikert, C.: Trapdoors for lattices: simpler, tighter, faster, smaller. In: Pointcheval, D., Johansson, T. (eds.) EUROCRYPT 2012. LNCS, vol. 7237, pp. 700–718. Springer, Heidelberg (2012). https://doi.org/10.1007/978-3-642-29011-4_41
10. Micciancio, D., Regev, O.: Worst-case to average-case reductions based on gaussian measures. SIAM J. Comput. $37(1)$, 267–302 (2007)
11. Sahai, A., Waters, B.: Fuzzy identity-based encryption. In: Cramer, R. (ed.) EUROCRYPT 2005. LNCS, vol. 3494, pp. 457–473. Springer, Heidelberg (2005). https://doi.org/10.1007/11426639_27
12. Shamir, A.: Identity-based cryptosystems and signature schemes. In: Blakley, G.R., Chaum, D. (eds.) CRYPTO 1984. LNCS, vol. 196, pp. 47–53. Springer, Heidelberg (1985). https://doi.org/10.1007/3-540-39568-7_5
13. Shor, P.W.: Polynomial-time algorithms for prime factorization and discrete logarithms on a quantum computer. SIAM J. Comput. $26(5)$, 1484–1509 (1997)
14. Wang, C.J.: A provable secure fuzzy identity based signature scheme. Sci. China Inf. Sci. $55(9)$, 2139–2148 (2012)
15. Wang, C.J., Kim, J.H.: Two constructions of fuzzy identity based signature. In: BMEI, pp. 1–5. IEEE Press, New York (2009)
16. Yang, P.Y., Cao, Z.F., Dong, X.L.: Fuzzy identity based signature. IACR Cryptology ePrint Archive 2008/002 (2008)
17. Yang, P.Y., Cao, Z.F., Dong, X.L.: Fuzzy identity based signature with applications to biometric authentication. Comput. Electr. Eng. $37(4)$, 532–540 (2011)
18. Yang, C.L., Zheng, S.H., Wang, L.C., Tian, M.M., Gu, L.Z., Yang, Y.X.: A fuzzy identity-based signature scheme from lattices in the standard model. Math. Prob. Eng. $2014(8)$, 1–10 (2014)
19. Yao, Y.Q., Li, Z.J.: A novel fuzzy identity based signature scheme based on the short integer solution problem. Comput. Electr. Eng. $40(6)$, 1930–1939 (2014)

20. Zhang, L.Y., Wu, Q., Hu, Y.P.: Fuzzy biometric identity-based signature in the standard model. App. Mech. Mater. **44**(4), 3350–3354 (2011)
21. Zhang, X.J., Xu, C.X., Zhang, Y.: Fuzzy identity-based signature scheme from lattice and its application in biometric authentication. TIIS **11**(5), 2762–2777 (2017)

Efficient KEA-Style Lattice-Based Authenticated Key Exchange

Zilong Wang[✉] and Honggang Hu[✉]

Key Laboratory of Electromagnetic Space Information,
Chinese Academy of Sciences, School of Information Science and Technology,
University of Science and Technology of China, Hefei 230027, China
wzl0830@mail.ustc.edu.cn, hghu2005@ustc.edu.cn

Abstract. Lattice-based cryptographic primitives are believed to have the property against attacks by quantum computers. In this work, we present a KEA-style authenticated key exchange protocol based on the ring learning with errors problem whose security is proven in the BR model with weak perfect forward secrecy. With properties of KEA such as implicit key authentication and simplicity, our protocol also enjoys many properties of lattice-based cryptography, namely asymptotic efficiency, conceptual simplicity, worst-case hardness assumption, and resistance to attacks by quantum computers. Our lattice-based authenticated key exchange protocol is more efficient than the protocol of Zhang et al. (EUROCRYPT 2015) with more concise structure, smaller key size and lower bandwidth. Also, our protocol enjoys the advantage of optimal online efficiency and we improve our protocol with pre-computation.

Keywords: Lattice-based cryptography · Authenticated key exchange
Post-quantum cryptography · Ring-LWE

1 Introduction

1.1 KE and AKE

Key exchange (KE) is one of the most fundamental cryptographic primitives. In practice, a common secret key (session key) generated by their personal keys (static key) should be shared with KE before the session starts, as the network is considered to be insecure. The communication data will later be transmitted on a trusted channel established with the session key. An authenticated key exchange (AKE) is quite similar to KE while AKE provides authentication which can avoid man-in-the-middle attack.

AKE can be divided into explicit AKE and implicit AKE according to the technique that achieves authentication. Explicit AKE always needs extra cryptographic primitives such as signatures, message authentication codes, or hash functions to provide authentication, which brings additional computation and communication overhead and makes the protocol more complicated. The IKE

© Springer Nature Singapore Pte Ltd. 2018
F. Li et al. (Eds.): FCS 2018, CCIS 879, pp. 96–109, 2018.
https://doi.org/10.1007/978-981-13-3095-7_8

[22], SIGMA [24], SSL [16], TLS [13], JFK [2] are all explicit AKEs. Implicit AKE achieves authentication by ingenious design of the algebraic structure. The KEA [33], OPACITY [32], MQV [29], HMQV [23] and OAKE [35] are families of implicitly AKE.

Intuitively, an AKE is secure if no probabilistic polynomial time (PPT) adversary is able to extract any useful information from the data exchanged during the session. Formally, the widely used security models for AKE include the BR model [4,36], the CK model [10] and the ACCE model [20]. The BR model, which is introduced by Bellare and Rogaway, is an indistinguishability-based security model. The CK model, which accounts for scenarios in which the adversary can obtain information about a party's static secret key or a session state, inherits from Krawczyk's SIGMA family of protocols. The ACCE model is a variant of the BR model which has separated properties for entity authentication and channel security.

Another property of AKE protocols is perfect forward secrecy (PFS). PFS requires that an adversary who corrupts one of the parties can not destroy the security of previous sessions. However, Krawzcyk [23] showed that no 2-pass implicit AKE protocol can achieve PFS. Alternatively, he presented a notion of weak perfect forward secrecy (wPFS) which says that the session key of an honest session remains secure if the static keys are compromised after the session is finished.

1.2 Lattice-Based Cryptosystems

It is important to construct protocols based on lattice problems as lattice-based cryptography is believed to resist quantum computers attacks. For instance, a post-quantum cryptography competition is held by NIST to advance the process of post-quantum cryptography standard.

The most widely used lattice problem to construct lattice-based cryptography is the learning with errors (LWE) problem which was first proposed by Regev [31] as an extension of learning parity with noise (LPN) problem [5]. Later in [28], Lyubashevsky et al. introduced the ring-LWE which is the ring -based analogue of LWE, and proved the hardness of ring-LWE. (ring-)LWE has attracted a lot of attention in theories and applications due to its good asymptotical efficiency, strong security, and exquisite construction. LWE has been used to construct public-key encryption [19,26,31], identity-based encryption [1,11], key exchange [3,7,14,21,36], and fully homomorphic encryption [8,9], etc.

1.3 Techniques and Relation to KEA

The key idea behind our protocol, which was firstly proposed by Linder et al. [26], is that the two parties share a common secret: $I(\boldsymbol{x}, \boldsymbol{y}) = \boldsymbol{x}A\boldsymbol{y}$, where $\boldsymbol{x}$ and $\boldsymbol{y} \in \mathbb{Z}_q^n$ are the static keys of two parties, and A is randomly chosen from $\mathbb{R}_q^{n \times n}$. When it comes to ring-LWE, the form is simpler: $I(x, y) = xay$, where x and $y \in \mathbb{R}$ are the static keys of two parties, and a is randomly chosen from $\mathbb{R}$.

The definition of ring-LWE indicates that it will bring some small errors during the session. These small errors may be beneficial in security, but they make the protocol incorrect. A common method to deal with these errors is reconciliation mechanism which was first proposed by Ding et al. [14] and soon improved with a more bandwidth-efficient and unbiased one presented by Peikert [30]. In [3], Erdem et al. proposed a more efficient reconciliation mechanism based on a varying error distribution at the expense of security. In [21], Jin et al. formalized reconciliation mechanism as a black-box called key consensus (KC) and gave the upper bound on parameters for any KC. What's more, they designed a KC called OKCN which can achieve the upper bound.

Our AKE protocol is inspired by KEA which was designed by the NSA and later standardized by the NIST. However, they are very different in the underlying algebraic structures. In the original KEA protocol, the shared key is $H_K(A^y \oplus X^b)$. Later in [25], Lauter et al. improved the original KEA with a provably secure version KEA$^+$. Throughout our work, we simply refer KEA to the provably secure version KEA$^+$. Formally, let G be a cyclic group with generator $g \in G$ and $|G| = n$. Randomly choose s_i, $s_j \in \{1, ..., n\}$ as the static keys of Party i and Party j. The specification of KEA is given in Fig. 1, where H is a hash function.

Party i	Party j
PK: $P_i = g^{s_i} \in G$	PK: $P_j = g^{s_j} \in G$
SK: $s_i \in \{1, ..., n\}$	SK: $s_j \in \{1, ..., n\}$
$X = g^x$	
x randomly chosen from $\{1, ..., n\}$ $\xrightarrow{i, X}$	$Y = g^y$
$\xleftarrow{j, Y}$	y randomly chosen from $\{1, ..., n\}$
$K_i = H(Y^{s_i}, P_j^x, i, j)$	$K_j = H(P_i^y, X^{s_j}, i, j)$

Fig. 1. Specification of KEA

As shown in [35], KEA enjoys the advantage of optimal online efficiency. The separation of two exponentiations, which allow off-line pre-computation, makes KEA much more desirable for deployments on low-power devices, such as smart cards and phones over wireless setting. Take Party i as an example, Party i pre-computes X and P_j^x before session starts, where j is one of the potential parties which Party i may communicate with.

Thanks to the simplicity of KEA, there is no complicated computation for each party to compute a closed value for reconciliation mechanism. Compared to the protocol in [36], the error of these two values is smaller. Consequently, a smaller q is sufficient for ensuring the correctness of reconciliation mechanism, which has two advantages: (1) A smaller q can reduce the bit length of public keys and the bandwidth as they are proportional to $log\,q$; (2) For any fixed error rate α, higher security level can be achieved with a smaller q as the security of (ring-)LWE is partially dependent on the ratio of q and α.

In KEA, the $X^{s_j} = g^{xs_j}$ do not reveal any information about s_j even x is chosen by adversary. However, it is well-known that the Regev's encryption [31] is not chosen-ciphertext attack (CCA) secure. This vulnerability was utilized by Ding et al. [15] who show an attack depends on the leakage of signal function [14]. The adversary can extract the static key of target party after $2q$ queries. But this type of attack is inefficient to our protocol for two reasons: (1) Similar as PKI, the public keys of parties will be updated periodically, and there are no enough queries for adversary to extract the static keys; (2) The signal function in our protocol is probabilistic polynomial time algorithm. It is more difficult for adversary to decide the period of the signal value during the attack.

1.4   Related Works and Our Contributions

The raise of attention to post-quantum cryptography stimulates more constructions of lattice-based AKE protocols in the last few years. A passive-secure KE protocol based on (ring-)LWE, which was proposed by Ding et al. is translated from standard Diffie-Hellman protocol [14]. The most significant contribution of Ding' work is that they proposed the concept of reconciliation mechanism to deal with the errors. Fujioka et al. [17] proposed a generic construction of AKE from CCA secure KEMs, which can be proven secure in the CK^+ model. However, their construction was just of theoretic interest. In [18], Fujioka et al. gave a more practical AKE protocol which can be constructed from any one-way CCA secure KEM in the random oracle model. In [30], Peikert presented an efficient key encapsulation mechanism (KEM) based on ring-LWE, and then translated it into an AKE protocol using the SIGMA-style structure. After that, Bos et al. [7] utilized Peikerts KEM as a DH-like KE protocol, and integrated it into the TLS protocol. Strictly speaking, their protocol is not a lattice-based AKE protocol because classical signatures were employed to provide explicit authentication. Alkim et al. [3] then improved the performance of Peikert's KEM to make the AKE protocol more practical, and their new protocol that called NewHope was applied to the Google's browser Chrome. It is the first post-quantum AKE protocol adopted by real world. Zhang et al. [36] proposed the first lattice-based implicit AKE whose structure is similar as HMQV. In [21], Jin et al. introduced the notion of key consensus (KC) as a tool and presented generic constructions of KE based on KC.

A rough comparison of lattice-based AKEs is given in Table 1. A more detailed comparison between our protocols and the protocol in [36] is showed in Table 2 as they are very similar and are all implicit AKE protocols.

1.5   Organization

Section 2 presents some basic notations and facts. The AKE protocol based on ring-LWE problem is given in Sect. 3 and the analysis of the protocol is also given in Sect. 3. In Sect. 4, a new protocol which is more efficient for the Internet is considered. In the last section, we analyze the concrete choices of parameters along with the consideration of their security.

Table 1. Comparison of lattice-based AKEs.

Protocols	KEM/PKE	Signature	Message-pass	Security	Num. of rings
Fujioka [17]	CCA	-	2-pass	CK$^+$	$\gg 7$
Fujioka [18]	OW-CCA	-	2-pass	CK$^+$	7
Peikert [30]	CPA	EUF-CMA	3-pass	SK-security	$> 2^{(a)}$
Bos [7]	CPA	EUF-CMA	4-pass	ACCE	2
Alkim [3]	CPA	EUF-CMA	4-pass	-	$2 + x^{(b)}$
Zhang [36]	-	Implicit	2-pass	BR with wPFS	2
Ours	-	Implicit	2-pass	BR with wPFS	2

[a] 2 ring elements for KEM and more for the concrete lattice-based signatures.
[b] The actual number of ring elements depends on the signature, and it can be a traditional signature, so $x \geq 0$

Table 2. Comparison between ours and Zhang's protocol [36] with 80 bits security. mult. refers to the total number of multiplications over rings.

Protocols	n	α	log q	mult.	pk	sk	init. msg	resp. msg
Zhang [36]	1024	3.397	45	4	5.625 KB	1.5 KB	5.625 KB	5.75 KB
Section 3	1024	3.192	30	3	3.75 KB	0.75 KB	3.75 KB	4 KB
Section 4	1024	3.192	30	1	3.75 KB	0.75 KB	3.75 KB	4 KB

2 Preliminaries

2.1 Notation

Let κ be the security parameter. Bold capital letters denote matrices. Bold lowercase letters denote vectors. For any integer q, let $\mathbb{Z}_q$ denote the quotient ring $\mathbb{Z}/q\mathbb{Z}$. We use $a \leftarrow_r B$ to denote that a is an element randomly chosen from B, where B is a distribution or a finite set. When we say that a function $f(x)$ is negligible, we mean that for every $c > 0$, there exists a X satisfies: $f(x) < 1/x^c$ for all $x > X$. The statistical distance between two distributions, X and Y, over some finite set S is defined as:

$$\Delta(X, Y) = \frac{1}{2} \sum_{s \in S} |Pr(X = s) - Pr(Y = s)| .$$

If $\Delta(X, Y)$ is negligible, we say that X and Y are statistically indistinguishable.

2.2 Lattice and Gaussian Distributions

A lattice always connects to a matrix $\boldsymbol{B}$, and it is finitely generated as the integer linear combinations of the column vectors of $\boldsymbol{B} = \{\boldsymbol{b}_1, ..., \boldsymbol{b}_k\}$:

$$\mathcal{L} = \mathcal{L}(\boldsymbol{B}) = \{\sum_{i=1}^{n} z_i \boldsymbol{b}_i : z_i \in \mathbb{Z}\} .$$

The integer n is called the rank of the basis, and it is an invariant of the lattice. For any positive integer n and real $s > 0$, define the Gaussian function of parameter s as:

$$\rho_s(\boldsymbol{x}) = exp(-\pi\|\boldsymbol{x}\|/s^2) \,.$$

We define a Gaussian distribution over lattice $\mathcal{L}$ as:

$$D_s(\boldsymbol{x}) = \rho_s(\boldsymbol{x})/\rho_s(\mathcal{L}) \,.$$

where $\rho_s(\mathcal{L}) = \sum_{\boldsymbol{x}\in\mathcal{L}} \rho_s(\boldsymbol{x})$.

Fact 1. *Let χ denote the Gaussian distribution with standard deviation σ and mean zero. Then, for all $C > 0$, it holds that:*

$$Pr(e \leftarrow_r \chi : |e| > C \cdot \sigma) \leq \frac{2}{C\sqrt{2\pi}} exp(-C^2/2) \,.$$

This fact shows that the probability that the samples from χ are not around the mean is small. Specially, for $C = 10$, the probability is less than 2^{-70}.

Fact 2. *Let $x, y \in R$ be two polynomials whose coefficients are distributed according to a discrete Gaussian distribution with standard deviation σ and τ, respectively. The individual coefficient of the $x \cdot y$ is then normally distributed with standard deviation $\sigma\tau\sqrt{n}$, where n is the degree of the polynomial.*

Let the integer n be a power of 2. For any positive integer, we define the ring $R = \mathbb{Z}[x]/(x^n + 1)$, and $R_q = \mathbb{Z}_q[x]/(x^n + 1)$. Obviously, the discrete Gaussian distribution over the ring R can be naturally defined as the distribution of ring elements whose coefficients are distributed according to the discrete Gaussian distribution over $\mathbb{Z}^n$. Consequently, for any $x \in R_q$, we define $x \leftarrow_r \chi_\alpha$ that we sample x whose coefficients are distributed according to χ_α.

Define R_q as above. For any $s \in R_q$, the ring-LWE distribution $A_{s,\chi}$ over $R_q \times R_q$ is sampled by choosing $a \leftarrow_r R_q$ at random, choosing $e \leftarrow_r \chi$ and e is independent of a, and outputting $(a, b = s \cdot a + e \bmod q)$.

Definition 1. *Let $A_{s,\chi}$ be defined as above. Given m independent samples $(a_i, b_i) \in R_q \times R_q$ where every sample is distributed according to either: (1) $A_{s,\chi}$ for a uniformly random $s \leftarrow_r R_q$ (fixed for all samples), or (2) the uniform distribution, no PPT algorithm can distinguish, with non-negligible probability, which distribution they are chosen from.*

The ring-LWE assumption can be reduced to some hard lattice problems such as the Shortest Independent Vectors Problem (SIVP) over ideal lattices [28]:

Lemma 1 *(Hardness of the Ring-LWE Assumption). Let n be a power of 2 and α be a real number in $(0, 1)$. Let q and R_q be defined as above. Then there exists a polynomial time quantum reduction from $O(\sqrt{n}/\alpha) - SIVP$ in the worst case to average-case ring-LWE$_{q,\beta}$, where $\beta = \alpha q \cdot (n\ell = \log(n\ell))^{1/4}$.*

In [28], Lyubashevsky et al. showed that the ring-LWE assumption still holds even if s is chosen according to the error distribution χ_β rather than uniformly.

2.3   Reconciliation Mechanism

Reconciliation mechanism was first proposed by Ding et al. [14] and later be reconstructed by a series of works [3,21,30]. It enables two parties to extract identical information from two "almost" same elements σ_1 and $\sigma_2 \in \mathbb{Z}_q$. In our protocol, the reconciliation mechanism OKCN [21] is adopted, and a brief description of OKCN is given as follows.

The OKCN consists of two algorithms (Con, Rec) which have parameters q (dominating security and efficiency), m (parameterizing range of consensus key), g (parameterizing bandwidth), and d (parameterizing error rate). Define $params = (q, m, g, d, aux)$ where $aux = (q' = lcm(q, m), \alpha = q'/q, \beta = q'/m)$. The probabilistic polynomial time algorithm Con takes a security parameter $(\sigma_1, params = (q, m, g, d))$ as input and outputs (k_1, ω) where $k_1 \in \mathbb{Z}_m$ is the shared value and $\omega \in \mathbb{Z}_g$ is the signal that will be publicly delivered to the communicating peer. The deterministic algorithm Rec, on input $(\sigma_2, \omega, params)$, outputs k_2 which is identical to k_1 with overwhelming probability. The details of OKCN are presented in Algorithm 1.

Algorithm 1. Reconciliation Mechanism: OKCN

1: **function** $\text{CON}(\sigma_1, params)$
2:     $e \leftarrow [-\lfloor(\alpha - 1)/2\rfloor, \lfloor\alpha/2\rfloor]$
3:     $\sigma_A = (\alpha\sigma_1 + e) \bmod q'$
4:     $k_1 = \lfloor\sigma_A/\beta\rfloor$
5:     $\omega = \lfloor(\sigma_A \bmod \beta)g/\beta\rfloor \in \mathbb{Z}_g$
6:     **return** (k_1, ω)
7: **end function**
8: **function** $\text{REC}(\sigma_2, \omega, params)$
9:     $k_2 = \lfloor\alpha\sigma_2/\beta - (\omega + 1/2)/g\rceil \bmod m$
10:     **return** k_2
11: **end function**

Lemma 2. *For OKCN: (1) k_1 and ω are independent, and k_1 is uniformly distributed over $\mathbb{Z}_m$, whenever $\sigma_1 \leftarrow \mathbb{Z}_q$; (2) If the system parameters satisfy $(2d + 1)m < q(1 - 1/g)$ where $m \geq 2$ and $g \geq 2$, then the OKCN is correct $(k_1 = k_2)$.*

2.4   Security Model

The BR security model, which is one of the most common models for KE protocol, is usually strong enough for many practical applications. It was first proposed by Bellare and Rogaway in [4], and later in [6], the BR model was extended to adapt to the public-key setting.

A protocol is a pair of functions $P = (\Pi, \mathcal{G})$, where Π specifies how parties behave and $\mathcal{G}$ generates keys for each party. For an AKE protocol, define N to be the maximum number of parties in the AKE protocol. Each party is identified by an integer $i \in \{1, 2, 3, ..., N\}$. A single run of the protocol is called a session. A session starts with message (ID, I, i, j) or (ID, R, j, i, X_i), where ID is the identification of the protocol, and I and R stand for the party's roles. We define session identifier for the session activated by message (ID, I, i, j) as $sid = (ID, I, i, j, X_i, Y_j)$ and session identifier for the session activated by message (ID, R, j, i, X_i) as $sid = (ID, R, j, i, X_i, Y_j)$. A session is said to be completed when its owner successfully computes a session key. The matching session of $sid = (ID, I, i, j, X_i, Y_j)$ is the session with identifier $\widetilde{sid} = (ID, R, j, i, X_i, Y_j)$.

We adopt the technique in [36] to describe the adversarial capabilities: an adversary, $\mathcal{A}$, is a PPT Turing Machine taking the security parameter 1^k as input. We allow $\mathcal{A}$ to make six types of queries to simulate the capabilities of $\mathcal{A}$ in the real world.

- $\boldsymbol{Send_0}(ID, I, i, j)$: $\mathcal{A}$ activates Party i as an initiator. The oracle returns a message X_i intended for Party j.
- $\boldsymbol{Send_1}(ID, R, j, i, X_i)$: $\mathcal{A}$ activates Party j as a responder using message X_i. The oracle returns a message Y_j intended for Party i.
- $\boldsymbol{Send_2}(ID, R, i, j, X_i, Y_j)$: $\mathcal{A}$ sends Party i the message Y_j to complete a session previously activated by a $\boldsymbol{Send_0}(ID, I, i, j)$ query that returned X_i.
- $\boldsymbol{SessionKeyReveal}(sid)$: The oracle returns the session key in the session sid if it has been generated.
- $\boldsymbol{Corrupt}(i)$: The oracle returns the static secret key of Party i. A party whose key is given to $\mathcal{A}$ in this way is called dishonest; a party who does not compromise in this way is called honest.
- $\boldsymbol{Test}(sid^*)$: The oracle chooses a bit $b \leftarrow_r \{0, 1\}$. If $b = 0$, it returns a key chosen uniformly at random; if $b = 1$, it returns the session key associated with sid^*. We only allow $\mathcal{A}$ to query this oracle once, and only on a **fresh** session sid^*.

Definition 2. *(Freshness): Let* $sid^* = (ID, I, i^*, j^*, X_i, Y_j)$ *or* $(ID, R, j^*, i^*, X_i, Y_j)$ *be a completed session with initiator Party* i^* *and responder Party* j^*. *We say that* sid^* *is fresh under the following conditions:*

*(1) $\mathcal{A}$ has not made a **SessionKeyReveal** query on sid^*.*
*(2) $\mathcal{A}$ has not made a **SessionKeyReveal** query on sid^*'s matching session.*
(3) Neither Party i^* nor Party j^* is dishonest if sid^*'s matching session does not exist.

Security Definition: The adversary $\mathcal{A}$ can make any sequence of queries to the first five oracles above. After that $\mathcal{A}$ can make a query to $\boldsymbol{test}$ on a fresh session. Then $\mathcal{A}$ outputs a guess b' for b. We define the advantage of $\mathcal{A}$:

$$\boldsymbol{Adv}_{\mathcal{A}}^{ID} = |Pr(b' = b) - 1/2| .$$

Definition 3. *(Security): An AKE protocol ID is secure under the following conditions:*

(1) Two honest parties get the same session key with overwhelming probability.
(2) For any PPT adversary $\mathcal{A}$, $\boldsymbol{Adv}_{ID, \mathcal{A}}$ is negligible.

3   The KEA-Style Authenticated Key Exchange

In this section, we describe our protocol in details. Let n be a power of 2. Define ring $R_q = Z_q[x]/(x^n + 1)$. Let $H : \{0,1\}^* \rightarrow \{0,1\}^\kappa$ be a hash function to derive session keys, where κ is the length of the session key. In our protocol, this hash function is simulated by a random oracle. Let χ_α be a discrete Gaussian distribution with parameter $\alpha \in R^+$. Let $a \in R_q$ be the public parameter uniformly chosen from R_q. Suppose Party i is the initiator, and Party j is the responder. Let $s_i \leftarrow_r \chi_\alpha$ be the static secret key of Party i, and $p_i = as_i + e_i$ is the public key of Party i, where $e_i \leftarrow_r \chi_\alpha$. Similarly, $s_j \leftarrow_r \chi_\alpha$ is the static secret key of Party j, and Party j's public key is $p_j = as_j + e_j$, where $e_j \leftarrow_r \chi_\alpha$.

Initiation: Initiator i proceeds as follows to activate the session:

a. Sample $r_i, f_i \leftarrow_r \chi_\alpha$, and compute $x_i = ar_i + f_i$;
b. Send x_i to Party j.

Response: After receiving x_i from Party i, Party j proceeds as follows:

1. Sample $r_j, f_j \leftarrow_r \chi_\alpha$, and compute $y_j = ar_j + f_j$;
2. Sample $g_{j1}, g_{j2} \leftarrow_r \chi_\alpha$, and compute $k_{j1} = p_i \cdot r_j + g_{j1}$ and $k_{j2} = x_i \cdot s_j + g_{j2}$;
3. Compute $(\sigma_{j1}, \omega_{j1}) \leftarrow Con(k_{j1}, params)$ and $(\sigma_{j2}, \omega_{j2}) \leftarrow Con(k_{j2}, params)$;
4. Party j derives his session key $sk_j = H(\sigma_{j1}, \sigma_{j2}, i, j, x_i, y_j, \omega_{j1}, \omega_{j2})$;
5. Send $y_j, \omega_{j1}, \omega_{j2}$ to Party i.

Finish: After receiving $y_j, \omega_{j1}, \omega_{j2}$ from Party j, Party i proceeds as follows:

c. Sample $g_{i1}, g_{i2} \leftarrow_r \chi_\alpha$, and compute $k_{i1} = p_j \cdot r_i + g_{i1}$, $k_{i2} = y_j \cdot s_i + g_{i2}$;
d. Compute $\sigma_{i1} = Rec(k_{i1}, \omega_{j2}, params)$ and $\sigma_{i2} = Rec(k_{i2}, \omega_{j1}, params)$, then Party i derives his session key $sk_i = H(\sigma_{i2}, \sigma_{i1}, i, j, x_i, y_j, \omega_{j1}, \omega_{j2})$ (Fig. 2);

3.1   Analysis of the Protocol

Theorem 1 *(Correctness). For appropriately chosen parameters, both parties compute the same session key with overwhelming probability, which means $sk_i = sk_j$.*

Proof. To show $sk_i = sk_j$, it is sufficient to show that $\sigma_{i1} = \sigma_{j2}$ and $\sigma_{i2} = \sigma_{j1}$ according to the way the session keys are computed. We just need to show that k_{i1} is closed to k_{j2} and k_{i2} is closed to k_{j1}. Due to the symmetry, we only estimate the size of $\|k_{i2} - k_{j1}\|$.

$$k_{i2} - k_{j1} = ((ar_j + f_j)s_i + g_{i2}) - ((as_i + e_i)r_j + g_{j1})$$
$$= (f_j s_i - e_i r_j) + (g_{i2} - g_{j1}) . \tag{1}$$

According to Lemma 2, if $\|k_{i2} - k_{j1}\| < \frac{(g-1)q-gm}{2gm}$, we have $\sigma_{i2} = \sigma_{j1}$. Similarly, we have $\sigma_{i1} = \sigma_{j2}$. Here we just need to know if q is big enough, then the inequality can be satisfied. The concrete parameters will be considered in Sect. 5. ∎

Party i		Party j
PK: $p_i = as_i + e_i \in R_q$		PK: $p_j = as_j + e_j \in R_q$
SK: $s_i \leftarrow_r \chi_\alpha$		SK: $s_j \leftarrow_r \chi_\alpha$
$x_i = ar_i + f_i \in R_q$		
where $r_i, f_i \leftarrow_r \chi_\alpha$	$\xrightarrow{\ x_i\ }$	$y_j = ar_j + f_j \in R_q$
		where $r_j, f_j \leftarrow_r \chi_\alpha$
		$k_{j1} = p_i \cdot r_j + g_{j1}$
		$k_{j2} = x_i \cdot s_j + g_{j2}$
		where $g_{j1}, g_{j2} \leftarrow_r \chi_\alpha$
		$(\sigma_{j1}, \omega_{j1}) \leftarrow Con(k_{j1}, params)$
$k_{i1} = p_j \cdot r_i + g_{i1}$	$\xleftarrow{y_j, \omega_{j1}, \omega_{j2}}$	$(\sigma_{j2}, \omega_{j2}) \leftarrow Con(k_{j2}, params)$
$k_{i2} = y_j \cdot s_i + g_{i2}$		
where $g_{i1}, g_{i2} \leftarrow_r \chi_\alpha$		
$\sigma_{i1} = Rec(k_{i1}, \omega_{j2}, params)$		
$\sigma_{i2} = Rec(k_{i2}, \omega_{j1}, params)$		
$sk_i = H(\sigma_{i2}, \sigma_{i1}, i, j, x_i, y_j, \omega_{j1}, \omega_{j2})$		$sk_j = H(\sigma_{j1}, \sigma_{j2}, i, j, x_i, y_j, \omega_{j1}, \omega_{j2})$

Fig. 2. Our AKE protocol from ring-LWE

Theorem 2 *(Security). Let n, q, α be defined as above. Let H be a random oracle. If ring-$LWE_{q,\alpha}$ is hard, then the proposed AKE is secure.*

The complete proof of Theorem 2 appears in the full version of this paper [34], and a proof sketch is given as follows.

Proof (sketch). The proof proceeds by a sequence of games. In each game, a simulator $\mathcal{S}$ answers the queries of $\mathcal{A}$. We show that the output of $\mathcal{S}$ in the first game is computationally indistinguishable with the output in the last game, and $\mathbf{Adv}_\mathcal{A}^{ID}$ of last game is negligible. Here are the basic ideas.

a. (P_i, a) (with secret s_i) and (P_j, a) (with secret s_j) are ring-LWE pairs. Given P_i and P_j, $\mathcal{A}$ cannot get any information about s_i and s_j.
b. (x_i, a) (with secret r_i) and (y_j, a) (with secret r_j) are ring-LWE pairs. Given x_i and y_j, $\mathcal{A}$ cannot get any information about r_i and r_j.
c. Due to the nice properties of ring-LWE, k_{j1}, k_{j2}, k_{i1}, k_{i2} are randomly distributed in R_q.
d. The distribution of ω_{j1} and ω_{j2} reveals no information about k_{j1} and k_{j2}.

These together indicate that the shared session key is secure. That is to say, the session key is uniformly random and independent of the messages exchanged during the session. ∎

4   Efficient AKE with Pre-computing

In this section, we consider the pre-computation to make our AKE protocol more efficient for the Internet. As we see, the most inefficient operation in our protocol is the multiplication over a ring. Inspired by KEA, we show that it is possible to pre-compute something off-line in our protocol, which can reduce the number of multiplication over a ring on-line. Define N is the maximum number of parties, and $[N] := \{0, ..., N-1\}$. Let $s_i \leftarrow_r \chi_\alpha$ be the static secret key of Party i, and $p_i = as_i + e_i$ is the public key of Party i, where $e_i \leftarrow_r \chi_\alpha$. Similarly, $s_j \leftarrow_r \chi_\alpha$ is the static secret key of Party j, and Party j's public key is $p_j = as_j + e_j$, where $e_j \leftarrow_r \chi_\alpha$. We give the description of our pre-computing version AKE protocol:

Off-line: Take Party i as an example. Party i chooses $r_i, f_i \leftarrow_r \chi_\alpha$ and $g_{i1} \leftarrow_r \chi_\alpha$, and computes $x_i = ar_i + f_i$ and $k_{i1}^j = p_j \cdot r_i + g_{i1}$ for every $j \in [N]/i$. Party i holds the Table T_i which stores the N values (x_i and k_{i1}^j for $j \in [N]/i$) computed above. Similarly, for $j \in N/i$, Party j executes the same as Party i, and holds its Table T_j.

On-line: Suppose Party i is a initiator and Party j is a responder.

Initiation: Party i proceeds as follows to activate the session:

a. Look up the Table T_i for x_i.
b. Send x_i to Party j.

Response: After receiving x_i from Party i, Party j proceeds as follows:

1. Look up the table T_j for y_j;
2. Sample $g_{j1}, g_{j2} \leftarrow_r \chi_\alpha$, and compute $k_{j2} = x_i \cdot s_j + g_{j2}$. Look up the Table T_j for $k_{j1} = k_{j1}^i$;
3. Compute $(\sigma_{j1}, \omega_{j1}) \leftarrow Con(k_{j1}, params)$ and $(\sigma_{j2}, \omega_{j2}) \leftarrow Con(k_{j2}, params)$;
4. Party j derives his session key $sk_j = H(\sigma_{j1}, \sigma_{j2}, i, j, x_i, y_j, \omega_{j1}, \omega_{j2})$;
5. Send $y_j, \omega_{j1}, \omega_{j2}$ to Party i.

Finish: After receiving $y_j, \omega_{j1}, \omega_{j2}$ from Party j, Party i proceeds as follows:

c. Sample $g_{i1}, g_{i2} \leftarrow_r \chi_\alpha$, and compute $k_{i2} = y_j \cdot s_i + g_{i2}$. Look up the Table T_i for $k_{i1} = k_{i1}^j$;
d. Compute $\sigma_{i1} = Rec(k_{i1}, \omega_{j1}, params)$ and $\sigma_{i2} = Rec(k_{i2}, \omega_{j2}, params)$, then Party i derives his session key $sk_i = H(\sigma_{i2}, \sigma_{i1}, i, j, x_i, y_j, \omega_{j1}, \omega_{j2})$;

In practice, the number N is not very big. Therefore, the size of Table T_i is N ring elements, which is small. Table lookups have advantages in efficiency over multiplication over rings. There is only 1 multiplication in our protocol compared with 3 multiplications in the protocol from Sects. 3 and 4 multiplications in the protocol from [36].

5   Parameters and Concrete Security

To maintain the property of correctness, according to the conclusion of Theorem 1, $\|k_{i2} - k_{j1}\| < \frac{(g-1)q - gm}{2gm}$ must be satisfied, that is to say:

$$(f_j s_i - e_i r_j) + (g_{i1} - g_{j1}) < \frac{(g-1)q - gm}{2gm} . \tag{2}$$

Combine the Fact 1 and Fact 2, with high probability, we have:

$$(f_j s_i - e_i r_j) + (g_{i1} - g_{j1}) \leq (\|f_j s_i\| + \|e_i r_j\| + \|g_{i1}\| + \|g_{j1}\|)$$
$$\leq (6\alpha^2 \sqrt{n} + 6\alpha^2 \sqrt{n} + 6\alpha + 6\alpha)$$
$$= 12(\alpha^2 \sqrt{n} + \alpha) .$$

So we have the inequality:

$$q > \frac{24gm(\alpha^2 \sqrt{n} + \alpha)}{g - 1} . \tag{3}$$

As recommended in [26,31], it is necessary to set the Gaussian parameter α as:

$$\alpha \geq 8/\sqrt{2\pi} . \tag{4}$$

To estimate the concrete security of our protocol, we consider the approach of [12], which investigates the two most efficient ways to solve the underlying (ring-)LWE problem, namely the embedding attack and the decoding attack. The embedding attack is more efficient than the decoding attack when the adversary only has access to a few samples. In our protocol, the decoding attack is more efficient as m is close to the optimal dimension $\sqrt{nlg(q)/lg(\delta)}$. Thus we concentrate on the decoding attack.

The decoding attack was introduced by Lindner et al. [26], which is inherently from nearest-plane algorithm. It is further improved by Liu et al. [27] with pruned enumeration approach. For a instance of (ring-)LWE, the decoding attack first uses a lattice reduction algorithm, and then applies a decoding algorithm from [26] or [27]. The output is a set of vectors closed to the target vector. There is a continuous correspondence between the success probability of returning the actual closest vector and the Hermite factor. In our analysis, we follow the approach proposed by Lindner et al. [26] to predict this success probability, and the runtime of lattice reduction algorithm is predicted by $T(\delta) = 1.8/lg(\delta) - 110$.

Above all, the candidates of our parameters are given in Table 3. The size of sk is the value of expectation computed using Fact 1 ($sk \in (-10\alpha, 10\alpha)$ with high probability).

Table 3. Candidates of our parameters.

n	m	g	α	$\log q$	Security	pk	sk	init. msg	resp. msg	$|K|$
1024	2^4	2^1	3.192	32	80	4 KB	0.75 KB	4 KB	4.25KB	2KB
1024	2^2	2^1	3.192	24	132	3 KB	0.75 KB	3 KB	3.25 KB	0.5KB
1024	2^1	2^1	3.192	18	190	2.25 KB	0.75 KB	2.25 KB	2.5 KB	0.125KB

References

1. Agrawal, S., Boneh, D., Boyen, X.: Efficient lattice (H)IBE in the standard model. In: Gilbert, H. (ed.) EUROCRYPT 2010. LNCS, vol. 6110, pp. 553–572. Springer, Heidelberg (2010). https://doi.org/10.1007/978-3-642-13190-5_28
2. Aiello, W., et al.: Just fast keying: key agreement in a hostile internet. ACM Trans. Inf. Syst. Secur. **7**(2), 242–273 (2004)
3. Alkim, E., Ducas, L., Poppelmann, T., Schwabe, P.: Post-quantum key exchange-a new hope. In: USENIX Security Symposium, pp. 327–343 (2016)
4. Bellare, M., Rogaway, P.: Entity authentication and key distribution. In: Stinson, D.R. (ed.) CRYPTO 1993. LNCS, vol. 773, pp. 232–249. Springer, Heidelberg (1994). https://doi.org/10.1007/3-540-48329-2_21
5. Berlekamp, E., McEliece, R.J., Van Tilborg, H.: On the inherent intractability of certain coding problems. IEEE Trans. Inf. Theory **24**(3), 384–386 (1978)
6. Blake-Wilson, S., Johnson, D., Menezes, A.: Key agreement protocols and their security analysis. In: Darnell, M. (ed.) Cryptography and Coding 1997. LNCS, vol. 1355, pp. 30–45. Springer, Heidelberg (1997). https://doi.org/10.1007/BFb0024447
7. Bos, J., Costello, C., Naehrig, M., Stebila, D.: Post-quantum key exchange for the TLS protocol from the ring learning with errors problem. In: IEEE Symposium on Security and Privacy, pp. 553–570 (2015)
8. Brakerski, Z., Vaikuntanathan, V.: Efficient fully homomorphic encryption from (standard) LWE. SIAM J. Comput. **43**(2), 831–871 (2014)
9. Brakerski, Z., Vaikuntanathan, V.: Fully homomorphic encryption from ring-LWE and security for key dependent messages. In: Rogaway, P. (ed.) CRYPTO 2011. LNCS, vol. 6841, pp. 505–524. Springer, Heidelberg (2011). https://doi.org/10.1007/978-3-642-22792-9_29
10. Canetti, R., Krawczyk, H.: Analysis of key-exchange protocols and their use for building secure channels. In: Pfitzmann, B. (ed.) EUROCRYPT 2001. LNCS, vol. 2045, pp. 453–474. Springer, Heidelberg (2001). https://doi.org/10.1007/3-540-44987-6_28
11. Cash, D., Hofheinz, D., Kiltz, E., Peikert, C.: Bonsai trees, or how to delegate a lattice basis. J. Cryptol. **25**(4), 601–639 (2012)
12. Dagdelen, Ö., et al.: High-speed signatures from standard lattices. In: Aranha, D.F., Menezes, A. (eds.) LATINCRYPT 2014. LNCS, vol. 8895, pp. 84–103. Springer, Cham (2015). https://doi.org/10.1007/978-3-319-16295-9_5
13. Dierks, T., Allen, C.: The TLS protocol version 1.0 (1999)
14. Ding, J., Xie, X., Lin, X.: A simple provably secure key exchange scheme based on the learning with errors problem. http://eprint.iacr.org/2012/688
15. Ding, J., Alsayigh, S., Saraswathy, R.V., Fluhrer, S., Lin, X.: Leakage of signal function with reused keys in RLWE key exchange. In: 2017 IEEE International Conference Communications (ICC). IEEE (2017)
16. Freier, A., Karlton, P., Kocher, P.: The secure sockets layer (SSL) protocol version 3.0 (2011)
17. Fujioka, A., Suzuki, K., Xagawa, K., Yoneyama, K.: Strongly secure authenticated key exchange from factoring, codes, and lattices. In: Fischlin, M., Buchmann, J., Manulis, M. (eds.) PKC 2012. LNCS, vol. 7293, pp. 467–484. Springer, Heidelberg (2012). https://doi.org/10.1007/978-3-642-30057-8_28
18. Fujioka, A., Suzuki, K., Xagawa, K., Yoneyama, K.: Practical and post-quantum authenticated key exchange from one-way secure key encapsulation mechanism. In: ASIACCS 2013, pp. 83–94 (2013)

19. Gentry, C., Peikert, C., Vaikuntanathan, V.: Trapdoors for hard lattices and new cryptographic constructions. In: Proceedings of the Fortieth Annual ACM Symposium on Theory of Computing (STOC 2008), pp. 197–206. ACM, New York (2008)
20. Jager, T., Kohlar, F., Schäge, S., Schwenk, J.: On the security of TLS-DHE in the standard model. In: Safavi-Naini, R., Canetti, R. (eds.) CRYPTO 2012. LNCS, vol. 7417, pp. 273–293. Springer, Heidelberg (2012). https://doi.org/10.1007/978-3-642-32009-5_17
21. Jin, Z., Zhao, Y.: Optimal key consensus in presence of noise. http://eprint.iacr.org/2017/1058
22. Kaufman, C.: Internet key exchange (IKEv2) protocol (2005)
23. Krawczyk, H.: HMQV: a high-performance secure Diffie-Hellman protocol. In: Shoup, V. (ed.) CRYPTO 2005. LNCS, vol. 3621, pp. 546–566. Springer, Heidelberg (2005). https://doi.org/10.1007/11535218_33
24. Krawczyk, H.: SIGMA: the 'SIGn-and-MAc' approach to authenticated Diffie-Hellman and Its use in the IKE protocols. In: Boneh, D. (ed.) CRYPTO 2003. LNCS, vol. 2729, pp. 400–425. Springer, Heidelberg (2003). https://doi.org/10.1007/978-3-540-45146-4_24
25. Lauter, K., Mityagin, A.: Security analysis of KEA authenticated key exchange protocol. In: Yung, M., Dodis, Y., Kiayias, A., Malkin, T. (eds.) PKC 2006. LNCS, vol. 3958, pp. 378–394. Springer, Heidelberg (2006). https://doi.org/10.1007/11745853_25
26. Lindner, R., Peikert, C.: Better key sizes (and attacks) for LWE-based encryption. In: Kiayias, A. (ed.) CT-RSA 2011. LNCS, vol. 6558, pp. 319–339. Springer, Heidelberg (2011). https://doi.org/10.1007/978-3-642-19074-2_21
27. Liu, M., Nguyen, P.Q.: Solving BDD by enumeration: an update. In: Dawson, E. (ed.) CT-RSA 2013. LNCS, vol. 7779, pp. 293–309. Springer, Heidelberg (2013). https://doi.org/10.1007/978-3-642-36095-4_19
28. Lyubashevsky, V., Peikert, C., Regev, O.: On ideal lattices and learning with errors over rings. J. ACM **60**(6), 1–35 (2013)
29. Menezes, A., Qu, M., Vanstone, S.: Some new key agreement protocols providing mutual implicit authentication. In: SecondWorkshop on Selected Areas in Cryptography (1995)
30. Peikert, C.: Lattice cryptography for the internet. In: Mosca, M. (ed.) PQCrypto 2014. LNCS, vol. 8772, pp. 197–219. Springer, Cham (2014). https://doi.org/10.1007/978-3-319-11659-4_12
31. Regev, O.: On lattices, learning with errors, random linear codes, and cryptography. J. ACM **56**(6), 34 (2009)
32. Saint, E.L., Fedronic, D., Liu, S.: Open protocol for access control identification and ticketing with privacy. OPACITY protocol specification (2011)
33. Skipjack, N.: KEA algorithm specifications (1998)
34. Wang, Z., Hu, H.: Efficient KEA-style lattice-based authenticated key exchange. http://eprint.iacr.org/2018/690
35. Yao, A.C.C., Zhao, Y.: OAKE: a new family of implicitly authenticated Diffie-Hellman protocols. In: Proceedings of the 2013 ACM SIGSAC Conference on Computer and Communications Security (CCS 2013), pp. 1113–1128. ACM, New York (2013)
36. Zhang, J., Zhang, Z., Ding, J., Snook, M., Dagdelen, Ö.: Authenticated key exchange from ideal lattices. In: Oswald, E., Fischlin, M. (eds.) EUROCRYPT 2015. LNCS, vol. 9057, pp. 719–751. Springer, Heidelberg (2015). https://doi.org/10.1007/978-3-662-46803-6_24

Identity-Based Multi-bit Proxy Re-encryption Over Lattice in the Standard Model

Jinqiu Hou, Mingming Jiang[⊠], Yuyan Guo, and Wangan Song

School of Computer Science and Technology, Huaibei Normal University,
Huaibei 235000, Anhui, China
jiangmm3806586@126.com

Abstract. Proxy re-encryption (PRE) allows a semi-trusted proxy to turn Alice's ciphertexts into Bob's ciphertexts, however, the proxy cannot get the corresponding plaintexts. Because of the special property, PRE achieves good reliability and secrecy. Nevertheless, most of the proposed proxy re-encryption schemes are based on the number theoretic problem and their security are proved in the random oracle. Therefore, this paper constructs an efficient and novel identity-based multi-bit PRE scheme based on the learning with errors (LWE) assumption and can resist to quantum attack. What's more, it is proved to be CPA secure in the standard model and has the properties of multi-use and bidirectional.

Keywords: Proxy re-encryption · Lattice cryptography · Gaussian sampling
LWE

1 Introduction

In a proxy re-encryption model, there are three participants are involved, respectively, the proxy, the delegator and the delegatee. The delegator produces a secret information as the proxy's private key. And then the proxy uses the key to transform the delegator's ciphertexts into the delegatee's ciphertexts, but the proxy cannot obtain any information of the plaintext during the process. Identity based proxy re-encryption (IB-PRE) [1] is an identity based encryption (IBE) mechanism that is introduced into a PRE system. The public key can be an arbitrary identity, such as address, telephone number, or e-mail address. IBPRE can effectively avoid the difficulty of key distribution and reduce the burden of key management center, so it can be a flexible tool in many dynamic environments and it has a more abundant practical scene, such as [2, 3] and [4]. Therefore, the study of IBPRE is very meaningful.

1.1 Related Works

In 1998, Blaze et al. [5] put forward the first bidirectional PRE scheme. Moreover, it is proved adaptive chosen-message attack secure. Then PRE was widely studied. With the development of quantum computers, it is very necessary to design PRE schemes which are capable of resisting quantum computer attacks. In recent years, lattice-based cryptography has been become a research hotspot by many cryptographers in the

© Springer Nature Singapore Pte Ltd. 2018
F. Li et al. (Eds.): FCS 2018, CCIS 879, pp. 110–118, 2018.
https://doi.org/10.1007/978-981-13-3095-7_9

quantum era because of its simple computation, resistance to quantum attacks and high efficiency. The first PRE scheme was constructed by using the LWE hard assumption in 2010 [6], which is bidirectional and interactive. And in 2013, Aono et al. [7] proposed a PRE scheme based on lattice. On the IB-PRE scheme with lattices, based on the method of [7]. Later, [8] used the trap generation function to produce the private key, and proved that the scheme can reach the indistinguishability of ciphertexts under an adaptive-identity chosen plaintext attack (IND-pID-CPA). Although more and more PRE schemes based on lattice are proposed, identity-based encryption schemes are rare and mostly cannot resist quantum attack. Therefore, our goal is to construct an efficient identity-based proxy re-encryption over lattice in the standard model.

2 Preliminaries

2.1 Notations

In this paper, we set the following notations. We use $\mathbb{Z}$ and $\mathbb{R}$ to denote the sets of the integers and the real numbers. And denote by $\| \mathbf{A} \|$ or $\| \mathbf{a} \|$ the l_2-norm of a matrix $\mathbf{A}$ or a vector $\mathbf{a}$. For a matrix $\mathbf{A} \in \mathbb{R}^{n \times m}$, We use $\mathbf{A}^{\mathrm{T}}$ to remark its transposed matrix. Let n be the security parameter, other quantities are determined by n. We use big-O to describe the growth of functions. We always use shorted words to express algorithms, such as ReKeyGen is a re-key generation algorithm.

2.2 Lattice

Definition 1. Let a basis $\mathbf{B} = [\mathbf{b_1}, \mathbf{b_2}, \ldots, \mathbf{b_m}] \in \mathbb{R}^{m \times m}$ be an $m \times m$ matrix with linearly independent columns $\mathbf{b_1}, \mathbf{b_2}, \ldots, \mathbf{b_m} \in \mathbb{R}^m$. The lattice Λ generated by the basis $\mathbf{B}$ and its dual Λ^* are defined as (both are m-dimensional):

$$\Lambda = L(\mathbf{B}) = \left\{ \mathbf{y} \in \mathbb{R}^m, \ s.t. \ \exists \mathbf{s} \in \mathbb{R}^m, \ \mathbf{y} = \mathbf{B}\mathbf{S} = \sum_{i=1}^{m} s_i \mathbf{b_i} \right\} \tag{1}$$

$$\Lambda^* = \left\{ \mathbf{z} \in \mathbb{R}^m \ s.t. \ \exists \mathbf{y} \in \Lambda, \ \mathbf{z}^{\mathrm{T}}\mathbf{y} = \langle \mathbf{z}, \mathbf{y} \rangle \in \mathbb{Z} \right\} \tag{2}$$

Definition 2. Let q be a prime and a matrix $\mathbf{A} \in \mathbb{Z}_q^{n \times m}$, define two m-dimensional full-rank integer lattices [9]:

$$\Lambda^{\perp}(\mathbf{A}) = \left\{ \mathbf{e} \in \mathbb{Z}^m \ s.t. \ \mathbf{A}\mathbf{e} = 0 (\mathrm{mod} \, q) \right\} \tag{3}$$

$$\Lambda(\mathbf{A}) = \left\{ \mathbf{y} \in \mathbb{Z}^m \ s.t. \ \exists \mathbf{s} \in \mathbb{Z}^m, \ \mathbf{A}^{\mathrm{T}}\mathbf{s} = \mathbf{y} \ (\mathrm{mod} \, q) \right\} \tag{4}$$

Observe that they are dual when properly scaled, as $\Lambda^{\perp}(\mathbf{A}) = q\Lambda(\mathbf{A})^*$ and $\Lambda(\mathbf{A}) = q\Lambda(\mathbf{A})^*$.

Lemma 1 [10].(*TrapGen*(q, n)) Let q be odd, and $q \geq 3, m = \lceil 6n \log q \rceil$. Then there is a probability polynomial time (PPT) algorithm that output a random matrix $\mathbf{A} \in \mathbb{Z}_q^{n \times m}$ and a group of basis $\mathbf{T} \in \mathbb{Z}_q^{m \times m}$ on a lattice $\Lambda_q^{\perp}(\mathbf{A})$ satisfying:

$$\|\tilde{\mathbf{T}}\| \leq O(\sqrt{n \log q})$$
$$\|\mathbf{T}\| \leq O(n \log q) \tag{5}$$

2.3   Discrete Gaussian Distributions

Definition 3 (Gaussian distribution function [11]). For any positive parameter $\sigma > 0$, centered at $\mathbf{c}$, define the Gaussian distribution function on $\mathbb{R}^n$:

$$\forall \mathbf{x} \in \mathbb{R}^n, \rho_{\sigma, \mathbf{c}} = \exp\left(\frac{-\pi \|\mathbf{x} - \mathbf{c}\|^2}{\sigma^2}\right) \tag{6}$$

Definition 4. For any $\sigma > 0, \mathbf{c} \in \mathbb{R}^n, m$-dimensional lattice Λ, define the discrete Gaussian distribution function over Λ as flowing:

$$D_{\Lambda, \sigma, \mathbf{c}}(x) = \frac{\rho_{\sigma, \mathbf{c}}(\mathbf{x})}{\rho_{\sigma, \mathbf{c}}(\Lambda)} = \frac{\rho_{\sigma, \mathbf{c}}(\mathbf{x})}{\sum_{\mathbf{x} \in \Lambda} \rho_{\sigma, \mathbf{c}}(\mathbf{x})}, \forall \mathbf{x} \in \mathbb{R}^n \tag{7}$$

Lemma 2 (*SampleGaussian*). There is a probabilistic polynomial time algorithm (PPT), input a lattice Λ and an arbitrary basis $\mathbf{B} = \{\mathbf{b}_1, \mathbf{b}_2, \ldots, \mathbf{b}_n\}$ of the lattice Λ. Then input the desired parameters $\sigma > 0, \mathbf{c} \in \mathbb{R}^n$. The output of the algorithm is a lattice vector distributed according to $D_{\Lambda, \sigma, \mathbf{c}}$.

Lemma 3 [10]. Let $q > 2$ and a matrix $\mathbf{A} \in \mathbb{Z}_q^{n \times m}$, $\mathbf{T}_{\mathbf{A}}$ is a basis of $\Lambda_q^{\perp}(\mathbf{A}), \sigma \geq \|\tilde{\mathbf{T}}_{\mathbf{A}}\| \cdot \omega(\sqrt{\log m}), \mathbf{c} \in \mathbb{Z}^m, \mathbf{u} \in \mathbb{Z}_q^n$. Then do:

(1) $\Pr\left[\mathbf{x} \leftarrow D_{\Lambda_q^{\perp}(\mathbf{A}), \sigma} : \|\mathbf{x}\| > \sigma\sqrt{m}\right] \leq negl(n);$

(2) There is a *SampleGaussian*$(\mathbf{A}, \mathbf{T}_{\mathbf{A}}, \mathbf{u}, \sigma)$ in a PPT algorithm, return $\mathbf{x} \in \Lambda_q^{\perp}(\mathbf{A})$ and it is not distinguishable from the discrete Gaussian distribution $D_{\Lambda, \sigma, \mathbf{c}}$;

(3) There is a PPT algorithm $\mathrm{Sample}\,\mathrm{Pr}\,e(\mathbf{A}, \mathbf{T}_{\mathbf{A}}, u, \sigma)$ that makes $\mathbf{x} \in \Lambda_q^{\mathbf{u}}(\mathbf{A})$ statistically close to $D_{\Lambda_q^{\mathbf{u}}(\mathbf{A}), \sigma, \mathbf{c}}$.

Lemma 4 [10]. Set n, q as positive integers and q is a prime number, let $m \geq 2n \log_2 q$. If $\mathbf{A} \in \mathbb{Z}_q^{n \times m}, \sigma \geq \omega(\sqrt{\log_2 m}), \mathbf{e} \in D_{\mathbb{Z}^m, \sigma}$, so the distribution statistics of $\mathbf{u} = \mathbf{A}\mathbf{e} \bmod q$ is close to the uniform distribution on $\mathbb{Z}_q^n$.

2.4   The Learning with Errors (LWE) Problem

Definition 5 [12]**.** For $n, m, q \in \mathbb{Z}$, let χ be a distribution on $\mathbb{Z}_q$. The $\text{LWE}_{q,\chi}$ problem is to distinguish (with non-negligible probability) the distribution $A_{s,\chi}$ and the uniform distribution on $\mathbb{Z}_q^n \times \mathbb{Z}_q$ for some uniform $s \leftarrow \mathbb{Z}_q^n$, where s is a secret. $A_{s,\chi}$ is defined as the distribution on $\mathbb{Z}_q^n \times \mathbb{Z}_q$ and the variable is $(a, a^T s + x)$, where $a \leftarrow \mathbb{Z}_q^n$ is uniform and $x \leftarrow \chi$ are independent.

3   Our Scheme

3.1   Construction

Setup (1^n)**:** Input security parameters 1^n and run the algorithm $TrapGen(q, n)$ to produce a random matrix $\mathbf{A} \in \mathbb{Z}_q^{n \times m}$ and a small norm matrix $\mathbf{T} \in \mathbb{Z}^{m \times m}$ as the trapdoor basis for $\Lambda_q^{\perp}(\mathbf{A})$. And it satisfies $\|\tilde{\mathbf{T}}\| \leq O(\sqrt{n \log q})$. The trapdoor function is $f_{\mathbf{A}}(\mathbf{x}) = \mathbf{A}\mathbf{x} \bmod q$ $(f : \mathbb{Z}^m \to \mathbb{Z}_q^n)$. Choose $m + 1$ matrix $\mathbf{U}_0, \mathbf{U}_1, \cdots, \mathbf{U}_m \in \mathbb{Z}_q^{n \times m}$ randomly. The master public key is $mpk = (\mathbf{A}, \mathbf{U}_0, \mathbf{U}_1, \cdots, \mathbf{U}_m)$, and the master private key is $msk = \mathbf{T}$.

Extract (mpk, msk, id)**:** Input the master public key $mpk = \mathbf{A}$, the master private key $msk = \mathbf{T}$ and the user's identity $id = (id_1, id_2, \ldots, id_m) \in \{0, 1\}^m$. Let $\mathbf{U}_{id} = \mathbf{U}_0 + \sum_{i=1}^{m} id_i \mathbf{U}_i = (\mathbf{u}_1, \mathbf{u}_2, \cdots, \mathbf{u}_m)$, use the algorithm $SamplePre$ to sample a vector $\mathbf{e}_i$ so that $\mathbf{u}_i = \mathbf{A}\mathbf{e}_i \bmod q$, $\|\mathbf{e}_i\| \leq \sigma \sqrt{m}$, where $\mathbf{u}_i \in \mathbb{Z}_q^n$, $\mathbf{e}_i \in \mathbb{Z}_q^m$. Let $\mathbf{E}_{id} = (\mathbf{e}_1, \mathbf{e}_2, \ldots, \mathbf{e}_m)$, then $\mathbf{A}\mathbf{E}_{id} = \mathbf{U}_{id} \bmod q$. The private key is $sk = \mathbf{E}_{id}$.

ReKeyGen $(\mathbf{E}_1, \mathbf{E}_2)$**:** For the user 1 and the user 2, the corresponding private keys are respectively $\mathbf{E}_1$ and $\mathbf{E}_2$, then calculate $rk_{1 \leftrightarrow 2} = \mathbf{E}_1 - \mathbf{E}_2$.

Enc $(mpk, id, \mathbf{b})$**:** Input $mpk = \mathbf{A}$, do:

(1) Choose a random vector $\mathbf{s} \leftarrow \mathbb{Z}_q^n$, a vector $\mathbf{b} \in \{0, 1\}^m$ and an error vector $\mathbf{x} \leftarrow \chi^m$;
(2) Compute $\mathbf{y} = \mathbf{A}^T \mathbf{s} + 2\mathbf{x}$;
(3) Compute $\mathbf{c} = \mathbf{U}_{id}^T \mathbf{s} + 2\mathbf{x} + \mathbf{b}$;
(4) Input the ciphertext $(\mathbf{y}, \mathbf{c})$.

ReEnc $(rk_{1 \leftrightarrow 2}, \mathbf{y}, \mathbf{c})$**:** Input the re-encryption key $rk_{1 \leftrightarrow 2} = \mathbf{E}_1 - \mathbf{E}_2$ and one of the user 1's ciphertexts $\mathbf{c}_1$. The proxy calculates $\mathbf{c}_2 = \mathbf{c}_1 - rk_{1 \leftrightarrow 2}^T \mathbf{y}$. Finally output the ciphertext $(\mathbf{y}, \mathbf{c}_2)$.

Dec $(sk, \mathbf{y}, \mathbf{c})$**:** Input the private key $sk = \mathbf{E}$ and a ciphertext $(\mathbf{y}, \mathbf{c})$. It calculates $\mathbf{b} = \mathbf{c} - \mathbf{E}^T \mathbf{y} \bmod 2$.

3.2 Correctness and Parameters

For the ciphertext $(\mathbf{y}, \mathbf{c})$, the decryption is shown as follows:

$$
\begin{aligned}
\mathbf{c} - \mathbf{E}^{\mathsf{T}}\mathbf{y} \\
&= \mathbf{U}^{\mathsf{T}}\mathbf{s} + 2\mathbf{x} + \mathbf{b} - \mathbf{E}^{\mathsf{T}}(\mathbf{A}^{\mathsf{T}}\mathbf{s} + 2\mathbf{x}) \bmod 2 \\
&= \mathbf{U}^{\mathsf{T}}\mathbf{s} + 2\mathbf{x} + \mathbf{b} - (\mathbf{A}\mathbf{E})^{\mathsf{T}}\mathbf{s} - 2\mathbf{E}^{\mathsf{T}}\mathbf{x} \bmod 2 \\
&= 2\mathbf{x} - 2\mathbf{E}^{\mathsf{T}}\mathbf{x} + \mathbf{b} \bmod 2 \\
&= \mathbf{b} \bmod 2 \\
&= \mathbf{b}
\end{aligned}
\tag{8}
$$

For the re-encryption ciphertext $(\mathbf{y}, \mathbf{c}_2)$, we need to compute:

$$
\begin{aligned}
\mathbf{c}_2 - \mathbf{E}_2^{\mathsf{T}}\mathbf{y} \\
&= \mathbf{c}_1 - rk_{1 \leftarrow 2}^{\mathsf{T}}\mathbf{y} - \mathbf{E}_2^{\mathsf{T}}(\mathbf{A}^{\mathsf{T}}\mathbf{s} + 2\mathbf{x}) \bmod 2 \\
&= \mathbf{U}_1^{\mathsf{T}}\mathbf{s} + 2\mathbf{x} + \mathbf{b} - (\mathbf{E}_1 - \mathbf{E}_2)^{\mathsf{T}}(\mathbf{A}^{\mathsf{T}}\mathbf{s} + 2\mathbf{x}) - \mathbf{E}_2^{\mathsf{T}}(\mathbf{A}^{\mathsf{T}}\mathbf{s} + 2\mathbf{x}) \bmod 2 \\
&= \mathbf{U}_1^{\mathsf{T}}\mathbf{s} + 2\mathbf{x} + \mathbf{b} - \mathbf{U}_1^{\mathsf{T}}\mathbf{s} - 2\mathbf{E}_1^{\mathsf{T}}\mathbf{x} + \mathbf{U}_2^{\mathsf{T}}\mathbf{s} + 2\mathbf{E}_2^{\mathsf{T}}\mathbf{x} - \mathbf{U}_2^{\mathsf{T}}\mathbf{s} - 2\mathbf{E}_2^{\mathsf{T}}\mathbf{x} \bmod 2 \\
&= 2\mathbf{x} - 2\mathbf{E}_1^{\mathsf{T}}\mathbf{x} + \mathbf{b} \bmod 2 \\
&= \mathbf{b} \bmod 2 \\
&= \mathbf{b}
\end{aligned}
\tag{9}
$$

In order to ensure the correctness of the scheme, it needs to satisfy the following conditions:

(1) The algorithm *TrapGen* requires $m > 6n \log q$, $\| \mathbf{T} \| \leq O(n \log q)$ and $q = ploy(n)$;
(2) The algorithm Extract requires $\sigma \geq \|\tilde{\mathbf{T}}\| \cdot \omega(\sqrt{\log n})$;
(3) In order to satisfy the requirement of the correctness of the Dual Encryption algorithm and the requirement of reduction, it requires $q > 5\sigma(m+1)$ and $\alpha < 1/\sigma\sqrt{m}\omega(\log m)$, $\chi = \bar{\Psi}_\alpha$.

In summary, we set the following parameters:
$m = 6n\lceil \log q \rceil$, $q = n^3$, $\sigma = m \cdot \omega(\log n)$, $\alpha = 1/(l+1)\sigma m\omega(\log m)$, Where $l < n$ is the length of users' identity.

Theorem 1 (Multi-use). Let m, q, σ, α be as aforementioned, our scheme satisfies the multi-use.

Proof: For the users $1, 2, \ldots, k$, we suppose that $(\mathbf{y}, \mathbf{c}_1)$ is the ciphertext of the user 1. The re-encryption procedure is performed from 1 to k through 2 to $k - 1$. The re-encryption procedures are as follows:

$$\begin{aligned}
\mathbf{c}_k &= \mathbf{c}_{k-1} - rk_{k-1\leftrightarrow k}^{\mathsf{T}}\mathbf{y}\\
&= \mathbf{c}_{k-2} - rk_{k-2\leftrightarrow k-1}^{\mathsf{T}}\mathbf{y} - rk_{k-1\leftrightarrow k}^{\mathsf{T}}\mathbf{y}\\
&\quad\cdots\cdots\\
&= \mathbf{c}_1 - \sum_{i=1}^{k-1} rk_{i\leftrightarrow i+1}^{\mathsf{T}}\mathbf{y}\\
&= \mathbf{c}_1 - \sum_{i=1}^{k-1}\left(\mathbf{E}_i^{\mathsf{T}} - \mathbf{E}_{i+1}^{\mathsf{T}}\right)\mathbf{y}\\
&= \mathbf{c}_1 - \mathbf{E}_1^{\mathsf{T}}\mathbf{y} + \mathbf{E}_k^{\mathsf{T}}\mathbf{y}\\
&= \mathbf{U}_1^{\mathsf{T}}s + 2\mathbf{x} + \mathbf{b} - \mathbf{E}_1^{\mathsf{T}}(\mathbf{A}^{\mathsf{T}}s + 2\mathbf{x}) + \mathbf{E}_k^{\mathsf{T}}(\mathbf{A}^{\mathsf{T}}s + 2\mathbf{x})\\
&= \mathbf{U}_k^{\mathsf{T}}s + 2(\mathbf{x} - \mathbf{E}_1^{\mathsf{T}}\mathbf{x} + \mathbf{E}_k^{\mathsf{T}}\mathbf{x}) + \mathbf{b}\\
&= \mathbf{U}_k^{\mathsf{T}}s + 2\mathbf{x}' + \mathbf{b}
\end{aligned} \tag{10}$$

Where $\mathbf{x}' = \mathbf{x} - \mathbf{E}_1^{\mathsf{T}}\mathbf{x} + \mathbf{E}_k^{\mathsf{T}}\mathbf{x}$, obviously, $(\mathbf{y}, \mathbf{c}_k)$ is the ciphertext of the user k. It can be decrypted correctly.

3.3 Security Analysis

Theorem 2. If m, q, σ, α be as in the aforementioned and assume that the $\text{LWE}_{q,\chi}$ is hard, then our PRE scheme described is IND - CPA secure in the standard model.

Proof: In the process of proof, we need to use a series of games to prove that the advantage of a polynomial time adversary attack is negligible.

Game 0: This is the original IND - CPA game. When the C receives (i, m_0, m_1) at the challenge phase, it will choose a random $\mathbf{b} \in \{0, 1\}$, and then it will compute the ciphertext of the challenger $\mathcal{C}$: $\mathbf{c}^* = \mathbf{U}^{\mathsf{T}}s + 2\mathbf{x} + \mathbf{b}$. Next sends $\mathbf{c}^*$ to $\mathcal{A}$. At last, $\mathcal{A}$ outputs a guess $\mathbf{b}'$, $\mathcal{C}$ outputs 1 when $\mathbf{b}' = \mathbf{b}$, if not so, outputs 0.

Game 1: The difference between Game 0 and Game 1 is only the generation of the matrix $\mathbf{A}$. In Game 0, the master public key $\mathbf{A}$ is generated by the algorithm $TrapGen(q, n)$. Well, it is random. But in Game 1, we change the method of generating master public key $\mathbf{A}$. We choose $\mathbf{A} \leftarrow \mathbb{Z}_q^{n\times m}$ uniformly at random, obviously, it is not distinguishable from Game 0.

Game 2: In the previous game, $\mathbf{U}_0, \mathbf{U}_1, \cdots, \mathbf{U}_m \in \mathbb{Z}_q^{n\times m}$ are randomly selected. Yet, we just change the generating method of matrix $\mathbf{U}_0, \mathbf{U}_1, \cdots, \mathbf{U}_m$ in this game as follows:

(1) First, the challenger randomly select $m+1$ matrix $\mathbf{E}_0, \mathbf{E}_1, \cdots, \mathbf{E}_m$ according to Gauss distribution $D_{\sigma/(m+1),0}$;
(2) Next, the challenger compute $\mathbf{A}\mathbf{E}_{id} = \mathbf{U}_{id} \bmod q$;
(3) Finally, check whether $\mathbf{U}_{id}$ is linearly independent, if not, repeat steps (1).

Because $\mathbf{E}_{id}$ is selected from the Gauss distribution, and $\mathbf{A}$ is a random matrix, so we know that the distribution of $\mathbf{A}\mathbf{E}_{id} = \mathbf{U}_{id} \bmod q$ is not distinguishable from the uniform distribution via Lemma 2. In the synthesis the factor, the Game1 and Game 2 are not distinguishable.

In this phase, the adversary $\mathcal{A}$ can do extract key queries and re-encryption key queries.

(1) Extract key queries: The adversary $\mathcal{A}$ sends id_i to the challenger $\mathcal{C}$, then $\mathcal{C}$ computes $\mathbf{E}_{id} = \mathbf{E}_0 + \sum_{i=1}^{m} id_i \mathbf{E}_i$. Because of $\mathbf{AE}_{id} = \mathbf{U}_{id} \bmod q$, so $\mathbf{AE}_{id} = \mathbf{U}_{id} = \mathbf{U}_0 + \sum_{i=1}^{m} id_i \mathbf{U}_i \pmod{q}$. At last, $\mathcal{C}$ sends $\mathbf{E}_{id} = \mathbf{E}_0 + \sum_{i=1}^{m} id_i \mathbf{E}_i$ to $\mathcal{A}$ as the private key of the user's identity id_i.

(2) Re-encryption key queries: The adversary $\mathcal{A}$ sends (id_i, id_j) to the challenge $\mathcal{C}$, then $\mathcal{C}$ uses the above method to compute $\mathbf{E}_{id_i}$ and $\mathbf{E}_{id_j}$. Next, the challenger $\mathcal{C}$ returns $rk_{id_i \leftrightarrow id_j} = \mathbf{E}_{id_i} - \mathbf{E}_{id_j}$ to the adversary $\mathcal{A}$.

Game 3: The method produced by the ciphertext of $\mathcal{C}$ is different from the Game 2. We choose a random vector in $\mathbb{Z}_q^m$ as the challenge ciphertext $\mathbf{c}^*$ in game 3.

We will illustrate that for a PPT adversary $\mathcal{A}$, Game 3 and Game 2 are computationally indistinguishable, and then we reduce the problem to the LWE problem.

Reduction from LWE: We suppose that the adversary $\mathcal{A}$ has non-negligible advantage ε to distinguish Game 1 and Game 2. And we construct an algorithm to solve the LWE problem.

The algorithm $\mathcal{B}$ has received m pairs random instances $(\mathbf{a}_i, v_i) \in \mathbb{Z}_q^n \times \mathbb{Z}_q$ of the LWE problem, where $v_i = \langle \mathbf{a}_i, \mathbf{s} \rangle + x_i$. We let $\mathbf{A} = (\mathbf{a}_1, \mathbf{a}_2, \ldots, \mathbf{a}_m)$, $\mathbf{v} = (v_1, v_2, \ldots, v_m)$. Then we do:

(1) We let $\mathbf{c}' = \mathbf{E}^{\mathrm{T}} \mathbf{v}'$;
(2) Let $\mathbf{y}^* = 2\mathbf{v}'$;
(3) Compute:

$$
\begin{aligned}
\mathbf{c}^* &= 2\mathbf{c}' + \mathbf{b} \\
&= \mathbf{E}^{\mathrm{T}} \cdot 2\mathbf{v}' + \mathbf{b} \\
&= \mathbf{E}^{\mathrm{T}} \mathbf{A}^{\mathrm{T}} \cdot 2\mathbf{s}' + 2\mathbf{x}' + \mathbf{b} \\
&= \mathbf{U}^{\mathrm{T}} \cdot 2\mathbf{s}' + 2\mathbf{x}' + \mathbf{b} \\
&= \mathbf{U}^{\mathrm{T}} \cdot \mathbf{s} + 2\mathbf{x}' + \mathbf{b}
\end{aligned}
\tag{11}
$$

Where $\mathbf{s} = 2\mathbf{s}'$, obviously, $(\mathbf{y}^*, \mathbf{c}^*)$ is the ciphertext of the challenger.
(4) If the adversary $\mathcal{A}$ guesses the right $\mathbf{b}$, then $\mathcal{B}$ outputs 1, if not, outputs 0.

If v is a uniformly random vector, then $\mathbf{c}^*$ is also uniformly random. So, $\mathcal{B}$ outputs 1 with probability at most $1/2$; If v is produced by this algorithm $\mathbf{v} = \mathbf{A}^{\mathrm{T}}\mathbf{s} + \mathbf{x} \bmod q$, $\mathbf{c}^*$ is also uniformly distributed. This is the same as the ciphertext distribution obtained by the encryption algorithm Enc $(mpk, id, \mathbf{b})$. And $\mathcal{A}$ guesses the right $\mathbf{b}$ by the probability of $(1 + \varepsilon)/2$ in the case. Therefore, the probability that $\mathcal{B}$ outputs 1 is also $(1 + \varepsilon)/2$. In other words, $\mathcal{B}$ can solve the LWE problem with the advantage of $(1 + \varepsilon)/2$.

3.4   Comparison

In this section, we compare the private key size, directionality, security model and bit encryption with related schemes [13, 8]. The results of the comparison are shown in Table 1 as below.

Table 1. Comparison to related works.

Cryptosystem	Private key size	Directionality	Security model	Bit encryption
[13]	$O(2mlogq)$	Unidirectional	Random oracle model	Single-bit
[8]	$O(mlogq)$	Bidirectional	Random oracle model	Multi-bit
Our scheme	$O(mlogq)$	Bidirectional	Standard model	Multi-bit

4   Conclusion

In this paper, we review the development of proxy re-encryption and construct a novel bidirectional PRE scheme which combined with a simple BGN-Type Cryptosystem of Gentry [14] based on the hardness of LWE problem. Our scheme has many good properties, such as multi-use, bidirectional, and can resist collusion attacks. It can also be proved to be CPA secure in the standard model.

Acknowledgement. We really acknowledge the financial support the Nature Science Foundation of Anhui Higher Education Institutions No. KJ2016A027, No. KJ2017ZD032, No. KJ2018A0398, Anhui Provincial Natural Science Foundation of China, No. 1708085QF154.

References

1. Green, M., Ateniese, G.: Identity-based proxy re-encryption. In: Katz, J., Yung, M. (eds.) ACNS 2007. LNCS, vol. 4521, pp. 288–306. Springer, Heidelberg (2007). https://doi.org/10.1007/978-3-540-72738-5_19
2. Xu, P., Jiao, T., Wu, Q., et al.: Conditional identity-based broadcast proxy re-encryption and its application to cloud email. IEEE Trans. Comput. **65**(1), 66–79 (2016)
3. Zhou, Y., Deng, H., Wu, Q., et al.: Identity-based proxy re-encryption version 2: making mobile access easy in cloud. Future Gener. Comput. Syst. **62**, 128–139 (2016)
4. Ming-Fu, L.I., Chen, L.W.: A secure cloud data sharing scheme from identity-based proxy re-encryption. Nat. Sci. J. Xiangtan Univ. **39**(03), 75–79 (2017)
5. Blaze, M., Bleumer, G., Strauss, M.: Divertible protocols and atomic proxy cryptography. In: Nyberg, K. (ed.) EUROCRYPT 1998. LNCS, vol. 1403, pp. 127–144. Springer, Heidelberg (1998). https://doi.org/10.1007/BFb0054122
6. Xagawa K.: Cryptography with lattices. Department of Mathematical and Computing Sciences, Tokyo Institute of Technology, Tokyo (2010)
7. Aono, Y., Boyen, X., Le, T.P., et al.: Key-private proxy re-encryption under LWE (2013)
8. Singh, K., Rangan, C.P., Banerjee, A.K.: Lattice based identity based unidirectional proxy re-encryption scheme. In: Chakraborty, R.S., Matyas, V., Schaumont, P. (eds.) SPACE 2014. LNCS, vol. 8804, pp. 76–91. Springer, Cham (2014). https://doi.org/10.1007/978-3-319-12060-7_6

9. Yin, W., Wen, Q., Li, W., et al.: Identity based proxy re-encryption scheme under LWE. KSII Trans. Internet Inf. Syst. **11**(12), 6116–6132 (2017)

10. Gentry, C., Peikert, C., Vaikuntanathan, V.: How to use a short basis: trapdoors for hard lattices and new cryptographic constructions. In: STOC 2008, vol. 14, no. 133, pp. 197–206. ACM (2010). https://doi.org/10.1145/1374376.1374407

11. Howe, J., Khalid, A., Rafferty, C., et al.: On practical discrete gaussian samplers for lattice-based cryptography. IEEE Trans. Comput. **PP**(99), 322–334 (2018)

12. Albrecht, M.R.: On dual lattice attacks against small-secret LWE and parameter choices in HElib and SEAL. In: Coron, J.-S., Nielsen, J.B. (eds.) EUROCRYPT 2017. LNCS, vol. 10211, pp. 103–129. Springer, Cham (2017). https://doi.org/10.1007/978-3-319-56614-6_4

13. Jiang, M.M., Hu, Y.P., Wang, B.C., et al.: Lattice-based unidirectional proxy re-encryption. Secur. Commun. Netw. **8**(18), 3796–3803 (2016)

14. Gentry, C., Halevi, S., Vaikuntanathan, V.: A simple BGN-type cryptosystem from LWE. In: Gilbert, H. (ed.) EUROCRYPT 2010. LNCS, vol. 6110, pp. 506–522. Springer, Heidelberg (2010). https://doi.org/10.1007/978-3-642-13190-5_26

Cloud Security and Data Deduplication

Analysis and Improvement of an Efficient and Secure Identity-Based Public Auditing for Dynamic Outsourced Data with Proxy

Jining Zhao[1], Chunxiang Xu[1(✉)], and Kefei Chen[2]

[1] Center for Cyber Security, School of Computer Science and Engineering, University of Electronic Science and Technology of China, Chengdu 610051, China
`kevinchao86@gmail.com, chxxu@uestc.edu.cn`
[2] Hangzhou Key Laboratory of Cryptography and Network Security, Hangzhou Normal University, Hangzhou 311121, China
`kfchen@hznu.edu.cn`

Abstract. In big data age, flexible cloud service greatly enhances productivity for enterprises and individuals in different applications. When cloud access is restricted, data owner could authorize a proxy to process the data, and upload them to enjoy the powerful cloud storage service. Meanwhile, outsourced data integrity breach becomes a serious security issue for cloud storage. Identity Based Provable Data Possession (PDP) as a critical technology, could enable each data owner to efficiently verify cloud data integrity, without downloading entire copy and complicated public key certificate management issue. But it remains a great challenge for multiple data owners to efficiently and securely perform batch data integrity checking on huge data on different storage clouds, with proxy processing. Yu et al. recently proposed an Identity-Based Public Auditing for Dynamic Outsourced Data with Proxy Processing (https://doi.org/10.3837/tiis.2017.10.019), which tried to address this problem. In this article, we first demonstrate that this scheme is insecure since malicious clouds could pass integrity auditing without original data. Additionally, malicious clouds are able to recover the proxys private key and thus impersonate proxy to arbitrarily forge tags for any modified data. Secondly, in order to repair these security flaws, we propose an improved scheme to enable secure identity based batch public auditing with proxy processing. Thirdly, the security of our improved scheme is proved under CDH hard problem in the random oracle model. The complexity analysis of its performance shows better efficiency over identity-based proxy-oriented data uploading and remote data integrity checking in public cloud on single owner effort on a single cloud, which will benefit big data storage if it is extrapolated in real application.

Keywords: Cloud storage · Provable data possession
Identity-based cryptography · Provable security

© Springer Nature Singapore Pte Ltd. 2018
F. Li et al. (Eds.): FCS 2018, CCIS 879, pp. 121–137, 2018.
https://doi.org/10.1007/978-981-13-3095-7_10

1   Introduction

In the age of Big Data with critical Data that is big, powerful cloud storage increasingly contributes to individuals life and enterprises business, by offering flexible and accessible data management services. From IDG report, 127 billion USD is spent globally on public cloud in 2017, with data storage size swelling to trillion gigabytes in 2025 [1]. For infrastructure, application and business processing service, cloud technology increasingly makes critical contribution, shifting to approximately 28% of the total market revenue in 2021 [2]. By managing huge data on different storage clouds, a great number of data owners enjoy customized applications for their business or utilities. When the access to cloud is restricted or owners' mobile devices are of limited computation capacity, a proxy with authorizations could perform data processing tasks before outsourcing them to remote cloud. With some protections from privacy preserving technologies [3], data owners still have to confront with security risks of outsourcing data integrity, due to system failures and external attacks. Meanwhile, cloud storage providers might have the incentives to delete cloud data and keep the accident news off their owners, for the sake of cost and reputations. Therefore, it is imperative to enable secure and efficient remote integrity checking for multiple owners, especially for cloud data which is originally processed by owners authorized proxy in the access restricted scenario.

Provable Data Possession (PDP) [4] as a critical technology, which is proposed by Ateniese et al., could allow efficient data integrity checking without having to download the entire data copy. Meanwhile, Shacham et al. designed proof of retrievability [5] to allow polynomial time data recovering and integrity checking. Based on Public Key Infrastructure (PKI), Wang et al. enabled cloud data integrity public auditing [6] with third party auditor, by performing PDP for single data owner in a privacy preserving manner. In [7,8], PDP is extended to support integrity auditing for data with dynamic update. For scalability of integrity checking tasks, Zhu et al. designed cooperative PDP for distributed cloud data integrity [9], and Yang et al. made further effort of enabling the multiple clouds' data integrity auditing for the multiple data owners [10]. Some works were designed to support data auditing with special features, such as multiple data storage replica [11] and group user data share [12] and revocation. For recent years, continuous progress has been made on data auditing in [13–15]. However, these famous works were all built on PKI, where each owner's public key certificate is required to be transferred and verified.

To eliminate the complicated management issue of public key certificates, Zhao et al. proposed the first identity-based public auditing scheme [16], to enable PDP primi-tive with identity based cryptography [17], where the efficiency is optimized from cryptosystem level. In 2015, Wang et al. designed the identity based distributed PDP to support multi-cloud storage for single owner [20]. In 2016, Liu et al. considered generic identity-based PDP construction [19] by combining PKI based PDP and Identity Based Signature [18]. Later, Yu et al. enabled zero knowledge privacy integrity checking for identity based PDP in [21]. In the setting of restricted cloud access, Wang et al. for the first time proposed an identity based PDP scheme, called Identity-based proxy-oriented data uploading and remote data integrity checking in public cloud (ID-PUIC), to support single owners authorized proxy to process data for single cloud [22]. Spontaneously, security flaws were found in some classic designs but luckily were repaired in [18,19,23]. So the challenging problem still remained to be unsolved, i.e., how to efficiently perform multiple clouds data integrity checking for multiple data owners with proxy processing data.

In 2017, Yu et al. designed an identity based batch public auditing scheme [25], to facilitate secure data integrity checking on multiple clouds for multiple owners, and support proxy data processing, without public key certificate managing issue. Unfortunately, after careful analysis, this work is not able to address the challenging problem of better efficiency and security simultaneously, when coming across malicious behaviors.

Contributions: Firstly, we demonstrate that this work [25] is vulnerable to data loss attack and proxy private key recovering attack. Especially, malicious clouds are able to use masked data rather than original data to pass integrity checking, and arbitrary two pairs of data and tags are sufficient to recover private key of the authorized proxy. Secondly, we propose an improved scheme, which could perform integrity checking and resist these above security flaws. Thirdly, we prove security of our scheme in random oracle under CDH assumption. In the end, our improved scheme illustrates better efficiency of complexity over identity-based proxy-oriented data uploading and remote data integrity checking scheme in public cloud [22] on single owner effort on single cloud, which will benefit big data storage if extrapolated to real application.

Paper Organization: The rest of the paper starts with notations and reviews of definition of identity-based batch public auditing with proxy processing scheme (ID-BPAP) along with its system and security model in Sect. 2. After revisiting of ID-BPAP scheme in Sect. 3, two security flaws are demonstrated in Sect. 4. We present our improved scheme in Sect. 5, and formally prove its security in Subsect. 5.1 under random oracle model. In Sect. 6, we compare our improved scheme with Wang et al.s ID-PUIC, in the context of overheads based on complexity analysis, to study the trend of efficiency for computation and communication. Section 7 concludes our paper.

2 Preliminary

2.1 Notations and Computational Assumption

- G_1 and G_2 are two cyclic groups of same large prime order q, additive and multiplicative groups respectively. e is a bilinear pairing mapping $e : G_1 \times G_1 \to G_2$.
- (mpk, msk) are the Private Key Generator (PKG)'s master public and private keys pair. sk_i is ith data owner's corresponding identity-based private key.

- There are n_o data owners, outsourcing N blocks on n_J clouds. $\tilde{F}_{ijk}$ is i-th owner's k-th block on cloud CS_j, with proxy tag σ_{ijk} from its masked F_{ijk} or encrypted $\hat{F}_{ijk}$.
- f is a pseudo random function (PRF) $f : Z_q \times \{1, \cdots, N\} \to Z_q$; π is a pseudo random permutation $\pi : Z_q \times \{1, \cdots, N\} \to \{1, \cdots, N\}$.
- $chal$ is challenge token generated by third party auditor (TPA). $chal_j$ is the specific challenge token for CS_j. c_{ij} is challenged number of blocks for ith owner and $a_{ij} \in [1, c_{ij}]$ further specifies index of each block as $k = \pi_{v_{ij,1}}(a_{ij})$.
- C is the index set of challenged data picked by TPA. O is the index set of data owner's identities upon challenged blocks, and J is the index set of challenged clouds, where $|O| = n_1$ and $|J| = n_2$. P_j is the proof of storage generated by CS_j.

CDH Problem on G_1: Given $g, g^a, g^b \in G_1$, to compute g^{ab} with a probabilistic polynomial time (PPT) algorithm, without knowing random $a, b \in Z_q$.

2.2   Definition of ID-BPAP

In this section, we will present the definition of Identity-Based Batch Public Auditing scheme with Proxy Processing (ID-BPAP) from the original paper [25], in the seven algorithms below.

1. Setup(1^k)$\to$ ($params, mpk, msk$) is initialized by PKG with security parameter k. It outputs the public parameters $params$, master key pairs (mpk, msk).
2. Extract($params, msk, ID_i$)$\to$ sk_i is executed by PKG with as input $params$, master private key msk and data owner's identity ID_i, it outputs the private key sk_i for the owner. It also extracts private key sk_p for proxy of ID_p.
3. ProxyKeyGen($params, ID_i, sk_i, ID_p, sk_p$)$\to$ u_{pi} is run by proxy ID_p with interaction of data owner ID_i. With input of parameters $params$ and its private key sk_i, data owner generates warrant and corresponding signature to send to proxy. Then proxy outputs the proxy secret key u_{pi} with its private key sk_p.
4. TagGen($params, ID_i, sk_p, u_{pi}, mpk, \{\tilde{F}_{ijk}\}$)$\to$ $\{\sigma_{ijk}\}$ is run by proxy. It takes as input parameters $params$, owner's identity ID_i, its individual private key sk_p, corresponding secret key u_{pi}, master public key mpk and owners' blocks $\{\tilde{F}_{ijk}\}$ to be outsourced. Then proxy tags $\{\sigma_{ijk}\}$ of above blocks could be generated.
5. Challenge($\{(i, j, k)\}$)$\to$ ($chal, \{chal_j\}$) is executed by TPA. It takes as input data index set $\{(i, j, k)\}$ and selects some index as challenge token $chal$ for this instance. According to the specified indexes $\{j\}$, the challenge token $chal$ is further divided into a set of tokens $\{chal_j\}$ and only forwarding $chal_j$ to the cloud CS_j.
6. ProofGen($params, chal_j, \{ID_i\}, \{\sigma_{ijk}\}, \{\tilde{F}_{ijk}\}$)$\to$ P_j is run by cloud CS_j. It takes as input the parameters $params$, the challenge token $chal_j$, the specified set of data owners' identities $\{ID_i\}$, the set of tags $\{\sigma_{ijk}\}$, and the blocks $\{\tilde{F}_{ijk}\}$. Then the proof P_j is generated for challenge token $chal_j$, and is sent back to TPA.

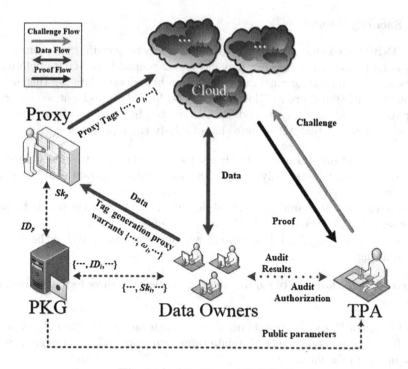

Fig. 1. Architecture of ID-BPAP

7. Verify$(params, chal, \{ID_i\}, \{P_j\}, mpk) \rightarrow \{0, 1\}$ is executed by TPA. It takes as input public parameters $params$, challenge token $chal$, specified set of data owners' identities $\{ID_i\}$, set of proofs $\{P_j\}$ from all challenged clouds, and the master public key mpk. 1 will be output if the proofs are valid, otherwise 0 is output.

2.3   System Model

As it depicts in Fig. 1, there are five kinds of entities in an ID-BPAP scheme, i.e., the *PKG*, data *Owners*, *Proxy*, multiple *Clouds*, and a batch *TPA*. *PKG* initializes the system parameters and extracts private keys for data owners and proxy of their own identities. Data *Owners* delegate *Proxy* to process their massive data before storing them in multiple clouds. *Proxy* of abundant computation and bandwidth resource, helps data owners to generate proxy data tags and upload them to clouds, with data owners' special warrants. Multiple *Clouds* maintain powerful storage and computation resources to provide storage service for data owners. The batch *TPA* is a trusted third party auditor to offer the batch data integrity verification on multiple clouds for the data owners.

2.4 Security Model

In an ID-BPAP scheme, we assume PKG is trusted to execute the scheme, and proxy honestly generates tags but may have management fault of data before tag generation. Meanwhile, original data owners might generate data tag themselves without the delegated proxy. Clouds could also hide data accident for the sake of reputation and saving cost, and TPA is trusted but curious about the data content. A secure ID-BPAP scheme should satisfy three properties:

(1) Proxy-protection: Data owners themselves are not able to masquerade as proxy to generate tags. Only proxy with authorization warrant could generate proxy tags.
(2) Unforgeability: It is infeasible to fabricate valid data storage proofs to pass the auditing of TPA if any cloud data is modified or deleted.
(3) Privacy-preserving: Real data content will not be revealed during the process of auditing.

According to the security requirements, we review the three formal definitions as follows:

1. Definition of **Proxy-Protection:** The scheme is proxy-protected, if any probabilistic polynomial time (PPT) data owner wins proxy Tag-Forge game with negligible probability.
   Setup: Challenger C_1 in the role of PKG and TPA, first generates master public/private key pair and system parameter. It runs Extract to generate private key sk_p for proxy of ID_p and keeps its secret. Those public and not secret parameters could be sent to adversary A_1 as data owner.
   Queries: Besides all hash functions, A_1 could adaptively query Extract for private key sk_i for identity ID_i except ID_p. Denote index set of identities as S_1 ($p \notin S_1$). It could also query proxy tag secret key $u_{p'i}$ for $(ID_{p'}, ID_i)$ except for pair having ID_p. Denote index set of pairs as S_1' ($(p,i) \notin S_1'$). Upon block $\tilde{F}_{ijk}$, A_1 could also adaptively query proxy tag $\sigma_{p'ijk}$ with the same identity requirement. Let us denote tuples set of indexes and corresponding block as S_1'', $(p,i,j,k,\tilde{F}_{ijk}) \notin S_1''$.
   Output: A_1 wins the game if it creates a valid proxy tag $\sigma_{i^*j^*k^*}$ for data block $\tilde{F}_{i^*j^*k^*}$ by itself , for which it has neither extracted private key nor proxy tag secret key for proxy ID_p, i.e., where $p \notin S_1$, $(p,i^*) \notin S_1'$, and $(p,i^*,j^*,k^*,\tilde{F}_{i^*j^*k^*}) \notin S_1''$.

2. Definition of **Unforgeability:** The scheme is unforgeable if any PPT clouds win the Proofs-Forge game below, with negligible probability.
   Setup: Challenger C_2 in the role of PKG and TPA, first generates master public/private key pair and system parameter. It runs Extract to generate private key sk_p for proxy of ID_p and keeps its secret. Those public and not secret parameters could be sent to adversary A_2 as clouds.
   First phase queries: Besides all hash functions, A_2 could adaptively query Extract for private key sk_i for identity ID_i except ID_p. Denote index set

of identities as S_2 ($p \notin S_2$). It could also query proxy tag secret key $u_{p'i}$ for $(ID_{p'}, ID_i)$ except for pair having ID_p. Denote index set of pairs as S_2' $((p,i) \notin S_2')$. Upon block $\tilde{F}_{ijk}$, $\mathcal{A}_2$ could also adaptively query proxy tag $\sigma_{p'ijk}$ with the same identity requirement. Let us denote tuples set of indexes and corresponding block as S_2'', $(p,i,j,k,\tilde{F}_{ijk}) \notin S_2''$.

Challenge: $\mathcal{C}_2$ generates challenge set $chal$ with ordered number set $\{c_{i^*j^*}\}$ to specify every block $\tilde{F}_{i^*j^*k^*}$ on the j^*th cloud for owner of ID_{i^*}, where $\{(p,i^*,j^*,k_n^*)| 1 \leq n \leq c_{i^*j^*}\}$, $i^* \neq p$, $(p,i^*) \notin S_2'$, and $(p,i^*,j^*,k_n^*,\tilde{F}_{i^*j^*k_n^*}) \notin S_2''$. $chal$ will be sent to $\mathcal{A}_2$.

Second phase queries: Similar to First phase queries, denote index set of identities for Extract private keys as S_3, index set of identity pairs for proxy tag secret key queries as S_3', tuple set of index and data for proxy tag queries as S_3''. We require that $p \notin S_2 \cup S_3$, $(p,i) \notin S_2' \cup S_3'$, and $(p,i^*,j^*,k_n^*,\tilde{F}_{i^*j^*k_n^*}) \notin S_2'' \cup S_3''$.

Output: $\mathcal{A}_2$ wins the game if it fabricates valid proofs $\{P_{j^*}\}$ for the same challenge $chal$ on the specified set of blocks.

3. Definition of **Privacy-Preserving:** Proofs are privacy-preserving if TPA cannot retrieve original value about the cloud data during the auditing.

3 Revisiting of ID-BPAP

In this section,we will revisit the ID-BPAP scheme of seven algorithms in [25].

1. Setup: PKG uses this algorithm to generate a bilinear map $e : G_1 \times G_1 \to G_2$ with two groups G_1 and G_2 of the same order $q > 2^k$, where g is the generator of G_1 and k is security parameter. It also selects three cryptographic hash functions $H_1 : \{0,1\}^* \to G_1$, $H_2 : \{0,1\}^* \to Z_q$, $H_3 : Z_q \times \{0,1\}^* \to Z_q$, a pseudo permutation $\pi : Z_q \times \{1, \cdots, N\} \to \{1, \cdots, N\}$ and a pseudo random function $f : Z_q \times \{1, \cdots, n\} \to Z_q$. It picks random $x \in Z_q$ as master private key msk and computes g^x as master public key mpk. The global parameters are $(e, G_1, G_2, g, mpk, H_1, H_2, H_3, \pi, f)$.

2. Extract: Given identity ID_i, PKG extracts the identity-based private key as $sk_i = H_1(ID_i)^x$ and returns to the data owner. For proxy, $sk_p = H_1(ID_p)^x$.

3. ProxyKeyGen: For data owner ID_i, it picks up random $r_i \in Z_q$ and creates its proxy warrant ω_i with its signature $U_i = sk_i^{r_i H_2(\omega_i \| R_i)}$, $\xi_i = g^{r_i}$, where $R_i = H_1(ID_i)^{r_i}$. $(\omega_i, U_i, R_i, \xi_i)$ are sent to proxy, clouds and TPA. Upon the warrant ω_i, TPA and proxy could verify it with signature as $e(U_i, g) = e(R_i^{H_2(\omega_i \| R_i)}, mpk)$, $e(R_i, g) = e(H_1(ID_i), \xi_i)$, and notify the data owner if any equations does not hold. Proxy generates the proxy secret key as $u_{pi} = U_i \cdot sk_p^{r_{pi}} = H_1(ID_i)^{xr_i H_2(\omega_i \| R_i)} \cdot H_1(ID_p)^{xr_{pi}}$ by picking up random $r_{pi} \in Z_q$. It also computes the not secret $R_{pi} = H_1(ID_p)^{r_{pi}}$, which is sent to TPA for future verification.

4. TagGen: Data owner of ID_i first divides original data $\tilde{F}_i$ into blocks $\{\tilde{F}_{ijk}\}$, and computes each $F_{ijk} = \tilde{F}_{ijk} + H_2(\tilde{F}_{ijk})$. Data blocks $\{\tilde{F}_{ijk}\}$ are outsourced

to corresponding clouds while masked $\{F_{ijk}\}$ are sent to proxy. Then proxy generates proxy tag for each data block as

$$\sigma_{ijk} = sk_p^{H_3(i||j||k,name_{ijk}||time_{ijk})} \cdot u_{pi}^{F_{ijk}} \tag{1}$$

where $name_{ijk}$ is the name of block $\tilde{F}_{ijk}$, and $time_{ijk}$ is the time stamp when proxy generates the tag. All the tags $\{\sigma_{ijk}\}$ and not secret R_{pi} will be transferred to corresponding clouds, which will not accept them and inform the owner unless the warrant ω_i and the proxy tag σ_{ijk} could be verified by having the following equations holds as

$$e(R_i, g) = e(H_1(ID_i), \xi_i), e(U_i, g) = e(R_i^{H_2(\omega_i||R_i)}, mpk)$$

$$e(\sigma_{ijk}, g) = e(H_1(ID_p)^{H_3(i||j||k,name_{ijk}||time_{ijk})} \cdot (R_i^{H_2(\omega_i||R_i)} \cdot R_{pi})^{F_{ijk}}, mpk) \tag{2}$$

5. **Challenge:** For data owner of ID_i on jth cloud's data, TPA picks up number of challenged blocks as c_{ij} and random $v_{ij,1}$ and $v_{ij,2} \in Z_q$. Denote O_j as index set of identities for owners having data on jth cloud. It generates the challenge token $chal_j = \{(c_{ij}, v_{ij,1}, v_{ij,2})\}_{i \in O_j}$, and sends it to the cloud.

6. **ProofGen:** According to the challenge token $chal_j = \{(c_{ij}, v_{ij,1}, v_{ij,2})\}_{i \in O_j}$, cloud CS_j first generates index set δ_{ij} of challenged blocks for owner of ID_i where each index $k = \pi_{v_{ij,1}}(a_{ij})$ $(1 \le a_{ij} \le c_{ij})$ with specified challenge number c_{ij} and then the corresponding co-efficient $h_{ijk} = f_{v_{ij,2}}(i, j, k) \in Z_q$. The proof of storage P_j includes aggregate tag T_j' and masked data proof $\{F_{ij}'\}$ for the data owners of identities with index set O_j:

$$T_j' = \prod_{i \in O_j} \prod_{k \in \delta_{ij}} \sigma_{ijk}^{h_{ijk}}, F_{ij}' = \sum_{k \in \delta_{ij}} h_{ijk} \cdot F_{ijk} \tag{3}$$

where $F_{ijk} = \tilde{F}_{ijk} + H_2(\tilde{F}_{ijk})$. $P_j = (T_j', \{F_{ij}'\}_{i \in O_j})$ will be sent to TPA.

7. **Verify:** After receiving all the proofs $\{P_j\}$ from challenged clouds, TPA denotes $O = \cup_{j \in J} O_j$ as identity index set of all the challenged data owners from challenge tokens $\{chal_j = \{(c_{ij}, v_{ij,1}, v_{ij,2})\}_{i \in O_j}\}_{j \in J}$, and computes index set of all challenged blocks by $\{k\} = \{\pi_{v_{ij,1}}(a_{ij}) | 1 \le a_{ij} \le c_{ij}\}$ and co-efficient set $\{h_{ijk}\} = \{f_{v_{ij,2}}(i, j, k)\}$, as in ProofGen. With all valid set of warrant $\{\omega_i\}$ and corresponding signatures $\{(U_i, R_i, \xi_i)\}$ from data owners, together with blocks names and time stamps $\{(name_{ijk}, time_{ijk})\}$, TPA is able to verify data integrity as:

$$e(\prod_{i \in O}(R_i^{H_2(\omega_i||R_i)} \cdot R_{pi})^{\Sigma_{j \in J} F_{ij}'} \cdot H_1(ID_p)^{\Sigma_{i \in O} \Sigma_{j \in J} \Sigma_{k \in \delta_{ij}} h_{ijk} \cdot H_3(i||j||k,name_{ijk}||time_{ijk})}, mpk)$$

$$= e(\prod_{j \in J} T_j', g) \tag{4}$$

It will output 1 (valid) if the above equation holds and 0 (invalid) otherwise.

4   On the Security of ID-BPAP

With security analysis in [25], Yu et al.'s ID-Batch Batch Public Auditing with Proxy Processing (ID-BPAP) should satisfy security properties for data proof with unforge-ability and tag generation with proxy-protection. However, their proposed ID-BPAP in [25], may suffer from two security issues, as the analysis in the following.

4.1   First Issue: Generating Valid Proof Without Original Data

In Yu et al.'s ID-BPAP scheme, the TPA utilizes masked data proof to evaluate the original data integrity on the cloud. This design indeed helps to prevent TPA obtain original data content, but also leaves the room for malicious clouds to launch data attack as follows.

In the ProofGen, for the output $P_j = (T'_j, \{F'_{ij}\}_{i \in O_j})$, honest cloud takes original data $\tilde{F}_{ijk}$ as input to get masked data $F_{ijk} = \tilde{F}_{ijk} + H_2(\tilde{F}_{ijk})$, and do the combination with the fresh challenge co-efficient $\{h_{ijk}\}$, as $F'_{ij} = \sum_{k \in \delta_{ij}} h_{ijk} \cdot F_{ijk}$. That is to say, the data integrity proof, is generated by combining of fresh challenge co-efficient and masked data, rather than directly with the original data itself. Therefore, for malicious clouds, by pre-computing and storing masked data F_{ijk}, it is able to directly generate valid integrity proof $P_j = (T'_j, \{F'_{ij}\}_{i \in O_j})$, without having to store the original data $\tilde{F}_{ijk}$. In this way, malicious clouds could modify original data $\tilde{F}_{ijk}$ as $\tilde{F}^*_{ijk}$ or even delete it, and successfully pass TPAs integrity checking.

4.2   Second Issue: Recovering Private Key of Proxy and Proxy Tag Secret Key

With proxy-protection property, only proxy with authorization could generate the data tags for integrity verification. As analysis below, we could find that it is feasible to recover proxys private key and thus impersonate proxy to generate data tag, for those who could access the data and tags.

In TagGen, for data $\tilde{F}_{ijk}$, tag $\sigma_{ijk} = sk_p^{H_3(i||j||k, name_{ijk}||time_{ijk})} \cdot u_{pi}^{F_{ijk}}$ is generated by proxy, with its individual private key sk_p and proxy tag secret key u_{pi}, and then uploads tag on the cloud. Afterwards, malicious clouds or curious data owner of ID_i, retrieve two arbitrary data blocks $(\tilde{F}_{ijk_1}, \tilde{F}_{ijk_2})$ with corresponding tags $(\sigma_{ijk_1}, \sigma_{ijk_2})$, and do the computation:

$$sk_p = \left(\frac{\sigma_{ijk_1}^{\frac{1}{F_{ijk_1}}}}{\sigma_{ijk_2}^{\frac{1}{F_{ijk_2}}}}\right)^{\frac{F_{ijk_1}F_{ijk_2}}{H_3(i||j||k_1, name_{ijk_1}||time_{ijk_1})F_{ijk_2} - H_3(i||j||k_2, name_{ijk_2}||time_{ijk_2})F_{ijk_1}}}, u_{pi} = \left(\frac{\sigma_{ijk_1}^{\frac{1}{H_3(i||j||k_1, name_{ijk_1}||time_{ijk_1})}}}{\sigma_{ijk_2}^{\frac{1}{H_3(i||j||k_2, name_{ijk_2}||time_{ijk_2})}}}\right)^{Ep}$$

Where $Ep = \frac{H_3(i||j||k_2, name_{ijk_2}||time_{ijk_2})H_3(i||j||k_1, name_{ijk_1}||time_{ijk_1})}{F_{ijk_1}H_3(i||j||k_2, name_{ijk_2}||time_{ijk_2}) - F_{ijk_2}H_3(i||j||k_1, name_{ijk_1}||time_{ijk_1})}$, and masked data $(F_{ijk_1}, F_{ijk_2}) = (\tilde{F}_{ijk_1} + H_2(\tilde{F}_{ijk_1}), \tilde{F}_{ijk_2} + H_2(\tilde{F}_{ijk_2}))$. With the recovered proxy private key sk_p and proxy tag secret key u_{pi}, three kinds of security problems could happen. First, for new block $\tilde{F}_{ijk_3}$, the proxy tag could be fabricated as $\sigma_{ijk_3} = sk_p^{H_3(i||j||k_3, name_{ijk_3}||time_{ijk_3})} \cdot u_{pi}^{F_{ijk_3}}$ by the data owner itself. This valid tag will keep Eqs. (2) (3) hold and finally help data to pass the TPA auditing in Eq. (4). And thus proxy-protection security property cannot be guaranteed. Second, if the original block is modified to $\tilde{F}_{ijk_3}^*$, malicious clouds could generate valid tag as $\sigma_{ijk_3}^* = sk_p^{H_3(i||j||k_3, name_{ijk_3}||time_{ijk_3})} \cdot u_{pi}^{F_{ijk_3}^*}$, where $F_{ijk_3}^* = \tilde{F}_{ijk_3}^* + H_2(\tilde{F}_{ijk_3}^*)$, without awareness of data owner and proxy. Certainly this modified data-tag pair will also keep Eqs. (2) (3) hold and help to generate valid integrity proof in Eq. (4), but unforgeability property cannot be guaranteed for falling to check data modification. Third, the digital property belonging to proxy, will be in great risk of illegal access, due to the recovered proxy individual private key by other entities.

5   Improved Scheme

1. **Setup:** PKG uses this algorithm to generate a bilinear map $e : G_1 \times G_1 \to G_2$ with two groups G_1 and G_2 of the same order $q > 2^k$, where g is the generator of G_1 and k is security parameter. It also selects four cryptographic hash functions $H_1 : \{0,1\}^* \to G_1$, $H_2 : \{0,1\}^* \to Z_q$, $H_3 : Z_q \times \{0,1\}^* \to Z_q$, $H_4 : \{0,1\}^* \to G_1$, a pseudo permutation $\pi : Z_q \times \{1, \cdots, N\} \to \{1, \cdots, N\}$ and a pseudo random function $f : Z_q \times \{1, \cdots, n\} \to Z_q$. It picks random $x \in Z_q$ as master private key msk and computes g^x as master public key mpk. The global parameters are $(e, G_1, G_2, g, mpk, H_1, H_2, H_3, H_4, \pi, f)$.

2. **Extract:** Given identity ID_i, PKG extracts the identity-based private key as $sk_i = H_1(ID_i)^x$ and returns to the data owner. For proxy, $sk_p = H_1(ID_p)^x$.

3. **ProxyKeyGen:** For data owner ID_i, it picks up random $r_i \in Z_q$ and creates its proxy warrant ω_i with its signature $U_i = sk_i^{r_i H_2(\omega_i || R_i)}$, $\xi_i = g^{r_i}$, where $R_i = H_1(ID_i)^{r_i}$. $(\omega_i, U_i, R_i, \xi_i)$ are sent to proxy, clouds and TPA. Upon the warrant ω_i, TPA and proxy could verify it with signature as $e(U_i, g) = e(R_i^{H_2(\omega_i || R_i)}, mpk)$, $e(R_i, g) = e(H_1(ID_i), \xi_i)$, and notify the data owner if any equations does not hold. Proxy generates the proxy secret key as $u_{pi} = U_i \cdot sk_p^{r_{pi}} = H_1(ID_i)^{x r_i H_2(\omega_i || R_i)} \cdot H_1(ID_p)^{x r_{pi}}$ by picking up random $r_{pi} \in Z_q$. It also computes the not secret $R_{pi} = H_1(ID_p)^{r_{pi}}$, $\phi_{pi} = g^{r_{pi}}$, which are sent to TPA for future verification.

4. **TagGen:** Data owner of ID_i first divides original data $\tilde{F}_i$ into blocks $\{\tilde{F}_{ijk}\}$. To ensure the data privacy, each block is converted in to its cipher text $\hat{F}_{ijk} \in Z_q$ by symmetric encryption. Cipher text blocks $\{\hat{F}_{ijk}\}$ are outsourced to corresponding clouds and sent to the proxy. For each data block, proxy generates tag $\sigma_{ijk} = (T_{ijk}, S)$ as

$$T_{ijk} = (sk_p, u_{pi})^{H_3(i||j||k, name_i||time_{ijk}) + \hat{F}_{ijk}} \cdot H_4(i||j||k, name_i||time_{ijk}||S)^\eta, S = g^\eta \tag{4}$$

where $name_i$ is the name of file $\tilde{F}_i$, and $time_{ijk}$ is the time stamp when proxy generates the tag. All the tags $\{\sigma_{ijk}\}$ and not secret R_{pi} will be transferred to corresponding clouds, which will not accept them and inform the owner unless the warrant ω_i and the proxy tag σ_{ijk} could be verified by having the following equations holds as $e(R_i, g) = e(H_1(ID_i), \xi_i)$, $e(R_{pi}, g) = e(H_1(ID_i), \phi_{pi})$, $e(U_i, g) = e(R_i^{H_2(\omega_i \| R_i)}, mpk)$

$$e(T_{ijk}, g) = e((H_1(ID_p) \cdot (R_i^{H_2(\omega_i \| R_i)} \cdot R_{pi}))^{H_3(i\|j\|k, name_i \| time_{ijk}) + \hat{F}_{ijk}}, mpk)$$
$$\cdot e(H_4(i\|j\|k, name_i \| time_{ijk} \| S), S) \tag{5}$$

5. **Challenge:** For data owner of ID_i on jth cloud's data, TPA picks up number of challenged blocks c_{ij} and random $v_{ij,1}$ and $v_{ij,2} \in Z_q$. Denote O_j as index set of identities for owners having data on cloud CS_j. It generates the challenge token $chal_j = \{(c_{ij}, v_{ij,1}, v_{ij,2})\}_{i \in O_j}$, and sends it to the cloud.

6. **ProofGen:** According to the challenge token $chal_j = \{(c_{ij}, v_{ij,1}, v_{ij,2})\}_{i \in O_j}$, cloud CS_j first generates index set δ_{ij} of challenged blocks for owner of ID_i where each index $k = \pi_{v_{ij,1}}(a_{ij})$ ($1 \le a_{ij} \le c_{ij}$) with specified challenge number c_{ij} and then the corresponding co-efficient $h_{ijk} = f_{v_{ij,2}}(i, j, k) \in Z_q$. The proof of storage P_j includes aggregate tag T_j', S' and data proof $\{F_{ij}'\}$ for the data owners of identities with index set O_j:

$$T_j' = \prod_{i \in O_j} \prod_{k \in \delta_{ij}} T_{ijk}^{h_{ijk}}, S' = S, F_{ij}' = \sum_{k \in \delta_{ij}} h_{ijk} \hat{F}_{ijk} \tag{6}$$

$P_j = (T_j', S', \{F_{ij}'\}_{i \in O_j})$ will be sent to TPA.

7. **Verify:** After receiving all the proofs $\{P_j\}$ from challenged clouds, TPA denotes $O = \cup_{j \in J} O_j$ as identity index set of all the challenged data owners from challenge tokens $\{chal_j = \{(c_{ij}, v_{ij,1}, v_{ij,2})\}_{i \in O_j}\}_{j \in J}$, and computes index set of all challenged blocks by $\{k\} = \{\pi_{v_{ij,1}}(a_{ij}) | 1 \le a_{ij} \le c_{ij}\}$ and co-efficient set $\{h_{ijk}\} = \{f_{v_{ij,2}}(i, j, k)\}$, as in ProofGen. With all valid set of warrant $\{\omega_i\}$ and corresponding signatures $\{(U_i, R_i, \xi_i)\}$ from data owners, together with files' names and time stamps $\{(name_i, time_{ijk})\}$, TPA is able to verify data integrity as:

$$e(\prod_{j \in J} T_j', g) = e(\prod_{i \in O} ((H_1(ID_p) \cdot (R_i^{H_2(\omega_i \| R_i)} \cdot R_{pi})))^{L_i}, mpk)$$
$$\cdot e(\prod_{i \in O_j} \prod_{j \in J} \prod_{k \in \delta_{ij}} (H_4(i\|j\|k, name_i \| time_{ijk} \| S'))^{h_{ijk}}, S') \tag{7}$$

where $L_i = \sum_{j \in J} F_{ij}' + \sum_{j \in J} \sum_{k \in \delta_{ij}} h_{ijk} \cdot H_3(i\|j\|k, name_i \| time_{ijk})$. It will output 1 (valid) if the above equation holds and 0 (invalid) otherwise.

5.1   Security Analysis of Improved Scheme

Based on the formal definition of ID-BPAP scheme (Subsect. 2.2) and corresponding system model (Subsect. 2.3) and security model (Subsect. 2.4), in this section, we prove security from proxy-protection of tag generation and unforge-ability of proofs, in our improved scheme Sec-ID-BPAP. With data block out-sourced in cipher text form by symmetric encryption, our Sec-ID-BPAP is privacy-preserving in TPA auditing. Compared with [22]s security analysis, we also utilize Corons random oracle model [24] to define the interactions between adversary of our scheme and challenger.

Theorem 1 *(Proxy-Protection). If there exists Probabilistic Polynomial Time (PPT) adversary $\mathcal{A}_1$ who could generate valid proxy tag without proxy individual private key in our Sec-ID-BPAP, then our scheme is proxy-protective when challenger $\mathcal{C}_1$ could solve CDH problem with non-negligibility within PPT time.*

Proof: There are $\hat{N}$ number of selected identities $\{ID_i\}_{i \in O}$ having the proxy ID_p. The original data block $\{\tilde{F}_{ijk}\}_{i \in O, j \in J, k \in \delta_{ij}}$ will be encrypted into corresponding ciphertext blocks $\{\hat{F}_{ijk}\}$ before being outsourced on clouds $\{CS_j\}_{j \in J}$. Certainly, the integrity of ciphertext block is equivalent to integrity of original block.

1. Setup: Simulator $\mathcal{C}_1$ plays in the role of PKG to choose random $a \in Z_q$, then the master private/public keys pair $(msk, mpk) = (a, g^a)$ upon generator $g \in G_1$. It also picks random $b \in Z_q$. CDH instance is g^a, $g^b \in G_1$, computing g^{ab}. Although $\mathcal{A}_1$ is not allowed to query the target proxy tag secret keys u_{pi}, the R_{pi} could be accessed as $H_1(ID_p)^{r_{pi}}$ by $\mathcal{C}_1$ picking up $r_{pi} \in Z_q$.
2. $\mathcal{C}_1$ answers query by maintaining input and output list for every oracle.
3. Hash function Oracle: H_2 and H_3 work as normal hash functions.
   (a) H_1-oracle: $\mathcal{C}_1$ answers with g^{y_i} for $y_i \in Z_q$ if $i \neq p$, and $y_i = b$ for $i = p$.
   (b) H_4-oracle: $\mathcal{C}_1$ answers with $g^{z_{ijk}}$ for $z_{ijk} \in Z_q$.
4. Extract-oracle: $\mathcal{C}_1$ answers $sk_i = (g^a)^{y_i}$ from H_1, if $i \neq p$; else aborts. Denote index set of identities extracting private keys as $S_1(p \notin S_1)$.
5. ProxyKeygen-oracle: $\mathcal{C}_1$ answers $u_{p'i} = U_i \cdot (g^a)^{y_{p'} r_{p'i}}$ from H_1 and $r_{p'i} \in Z_q$, if $i \neq p$; else aborts. Denote index pair set of identities as $S_1' ((p, i) \notin S_1')$.
6. Tag-oracle: $\mathcal{C}_1$ answers $T_{ijk} = ((g^a)^{y_{p'}} \cdot u_{p'i})^{H_{3,ijk} + \hat{F}_{ijk}} \cdot S_{ijk}^{z_{ijk}}$ with $S_{ijk} \in G_1$ from H_1, H_4, if $p' \neq p$; else aborts. Denote query input as set $S_1'' ((p, i, j, k, \hat{F}_{ijk}) \notin S_1'')$.

Forgery Output: Finally $\mathcal{A}_1$ itself outputs a valid tag $\sigma_{i^*j^*k^*} = (T_{i^*j^*k^*}, S')$ for data ciphertext block $\hat{F}_{i^*j^*k^*}$ generated by proxy ID_p with warrant ω_{i^*} and its signature $(U_{i^*}, R_{i^*}, \xi_{i^*})$. $\mathcal{C}_1$ looks up lists of all oracles. It will not abort and terminate only when none of corresponding records exists, i.e., requiring $ID_{i^*} \neq ID_p$, $(p, i^*) \notin S_1'$, $(p, i^*, j^*, k^*, \hat{F}_{i^*j^*k^*}) \notin S_1''$. If game could proceed, $\mathcal{C}_1$ keeps on checking all hash function oracles and makes queries itself if there is no relative record in their lists. $R_{pi^*} = H_1(ID_p)^{r_{pi^*}}$ in Setup and $U_{i^*} = (g^a)^{y_{i^*} r_{i^*} H_2(\omega_{i^*} || R_{i^*})}$ for validity of warrant ω_{i^*}.

Since $\sigma_{i^*j^*k^*} = (T_{i^*j^*k^*}, S')$ satisfies Eq. (5) as valid tag, we will have a solution of CDH problem after simplification with corresponding records of oracles and properties of bilinear mapping:

$$g^{ab} = (T_{i^*j^*k^*} \cdot S'^{-z_{i^*j^*k^*}} \cdot U_{i^*}^{-H_3(i^*||j^*||k^*, name_{i^*}||time_{i^*j^*k^*}) - \hat{F}_{i^*j^*k^*}})^{\frac{1}{W}} \qquad (8)$$

Where $W = (1 + r_{pi^*})(H_3(i^*||j^*||k^*, name_{i^*}||time_{i^*j^*k^*}) + \hat{F}_{i^*j^*k^*})$.

Due to the limitation of space, we will give detailed analysis for the non-negligible probability and polynomial of time in the full version.

Theorem 2 *(Unforgeability). If there exists PPT time adversary $\mathcal{A}_2$ who could forge valid proof of our Sec-ID-BPAP, then our scheme is unforgeable when challenger $\mathcal{C}_2$ could solve CDH problem with non-negligibility within PPT time.*

Proof: There are $\hat{N}$ number of selected identities $\{ID_i\}_{i \in O}$ having the proxy ID_p. The original data block $\{\tilde{F}_{ijk}\}_{i \in O, j \in J, k \in \delta_{ij}}$ will be encrypted into corresponding ciphertext blocks $\{\hat{F}_{ijk}\}$ before being outsourced on clouds $\{CS_j\}_{j \in J}$. Certainly, the integrity of ciphertext block is equivalent to integrity of original block.

1. Setup: Like Theorem 1, $\mathcal{C}_2$ in the role of PKG, generates master private/public keys pair $(msk, mpk) = (a, g^a)$ upon generator g, and CDH instance is g^a, $g^b \in G_1$, computing g^{ab}. It also allows $\mathcal{A}_2$ to access R_{pi} as $H_1(ID_p)^{r_{pi}}$ where $r_{pi} \in Z_q$.
2. H_1-oracle, H_2-oracle, H_3-oracle,H_4-oracle, Extract-oracle, ProxyKeygen-oracle, TagGen-oracle remain the same as Theorem 1.
3. First phase queries: $\mathcal{A}_2$ could access all the hash oracles. Let us denote index set $\{ID_i\}$ of private key extracting as S_2 ($p \notin S_2$), index pair set of $\{(ID_{p'}, ID_i)\}$ of proxy tag secret key query as S_2' ($(p, i) \notin S_2'$), the tuple set of index and data for proxy tag query as S_2'' ($(p, i, j, k, \hat{F}_{ijk}) \notin S_2''$).
4. Challenge phase: $\mathcal{C}_2$ generates challenge set $chal$ with ordered $\{c_{i^*j^*}\}$ to specify every cipher text block $\hat{F}_{i^*j^*k_n^*}$ on CS_{j^*} for ID_{i^*}, where $\{(p, i^*, j^*, k_n^*)| 1 \le n \le c_{i^*j^*}\}$, and $i^* \ne p$, $(p, i^*) \notin S_2'$, $(p, i^*, j^*, k_n^*, F_{i^*j^*k_n^*}) \notin S_2''$. $chal$ will be sent to TPA.
5. Second phase queries: $\mathcal{A}_2$ makes queries similar to First phase queries. Denote index set of identities for Extract private key queries as S_3, index set of identity pairs for proxy tag secret key queries as S_3', tuple set of index and data for proxy taga queries as S_3''. We requires that $p \notin S_2 \cup S_3$, $(p, i) \notin S_2' \cup S_3'$ and $(p, i, j, k, \hat{F}_{ijk}) \notin S_2'' \cup S_3''$.

Forgery Output: Finally, $\mathcal{A}_2$ itself outputs valid proof $\{P_{j^*}\}_{j^* \in J}$ for data cipher text blocks $\{\hat{F}_{i^*j^*k_n^*}\}_{1 \le n \le c_{i^*j^*}}$ and tags generated by proxy ID_p with warrants $\{\omega_{i^*}\}_{i^* \in O}$ and signatures $\{(U_{i^*}, R_{i^*}, \xi_{i^*})\}_{i^* \in O}$. $\mathcal{C}_2$ looks up lists of all oracles and it will abort and terminate unless none of corresponding records exists. If game could proceed, $\mathcal{C}_2$ keeps on checking all hash function oracles and makes queries itself if there is no relative record in their lists. $R_{pi^*} = H_1(ID_p)^{r_{pi^*}}$ in Setup and $U_{i^*} = (g^a)^{y_{i^*} r_{i^*} H_2(\omega_{i^*}||R_{i^*})}$ for validity of warrant ω_{i^*}.

Since $\{P_{j^*}\}_{j^* \in J} = \{(T'_{j^*}, S', \{F'_{i^* j^*}\}_{i^* \in O_j})\}_{j^* \in J}$ satisfies Eq. (7), the CDH problem solution is obtained after simplification with corresponding records of oracles and properties of bilinear mapping:

$$g^{ab} = (W'_1 \cdot W'_2)^{\frac{1}{\sum_{i^* \in O}(1 + r_{pi^*})E_{i^*}}} \tag{9}$$

where $E_{i^*} = \sum_{j^* \in J} F'_{i^* j^*} + \sum_{j^* \in J} \sum_{n \in [1, c_{i^* j^*}]} h_{i^* j^* k_n^*} \cdot H_3(i^* \| j^* \| k_n^*, name_{i^*} \| time_{i^* j^* k_n^*})$

$$W'_1 = \prod_{j^* \in J} T'_j \cdot S'^{-\sum_{i^* \in O} \sum_{j^* \in J} \sum_{n \in [1, c_{i^* j^*}]} z_{i^* j^* k_n^*} \cdot h_{i^* j^* k_n^*}}$$

$$W'_2 = \prod_{i^* \in O} U_{i^*}^{-\sum_{j^* \in J} (F'_{i^* j^*} + \sum_{n \in [1, c_{i^* j^*}]} h_{i^* j^* k_n^*} \cdot H_3(i^* \| j^* \| k_n^*, name_{i^*} \| time_{i^* j^* k_n^*}))}$$

Due to the limitation of space, we will give detailed analysis for the non-negligible probability and polynomial of time in the full version.

6 Efficiency Analysis

In this section, we compare cost of computation and communication of our improved scheme Sec-ID-BPAP, with Wang et al. 's ID-PUIC [22], summarized in Tables 1, and 2, respectively.

Table 1. Computation cost comparison for multiple owners and multiple clouds

Schemes	TagGen	ProofGen	Verify	Security
ID-PUIC[22]	$2NC_{exp}$	cC_{exp}	$2n_1 n_2 C_e + (c + n_1 n_2)C_{exp}$	Secure
Sec-ID-BPAP	$(2N + n_O)C_{exp}$	cC_{exp}	$3C_e + (c + n_1)C_{exp}$	Secure

Table 2. Communication cost comparison for multiple owners and multiple clouds

Schemes	Challenge	Proof	Security
ID-PUIC[22]	$n_1 n_2 \log_2 N + 2n_1 n_2 \log_2 q$	$n_1 n_2 \mathcal{G}_1 + n_1 n_2 \log_2 q$	Secure
Sec-ID-BPAP	$n_1 n_2 \log_2 N + 2n_1 n_2 \log_2 q$	$2n_2 \mathcal{G}_1 + n_1 n_2 \log_2 q$	Secure

1. Assume there are n_O data owners storing N blocks $\{\hat{F}_{ijk}\}$ on n_J clouds, by only *one-off* TagGen and upload. To audit data integrity, *periodical* Challenge and Verify will be executed between clouds and TPA, upon randomly selected c data blocks and tags of n_1 data owners on n_2 clouds, element size of group G_1 is $\mathcal{G}_1$. The dominant cost of this scheme is mostly contributed by ProofGen and Verify.

2. Among all the operations, bilinear pairings C_e, exponentiation C_{exp} on group G_1, and hash C_h on blocks are most expensive, compared with multiplication on G_1 and G_2, operations on Z_q, and other hash operations, which are efficient or can be done for only once. That is why we do not consider computation cost of Challenge mostly relying on efficient operations. Additionally, since ID-PUIC only offers single owner's auditing on one cloud, we consider repeating $n_1 n_2$ loops of ID-PUIC instances, with $N/n_1 n_2$ outsourced blocks and only challenged $c/n_1 n_2$ blocks per loop.

Analysis for Computation: In order to fully protect tags $\{\sigma_{ijk} = (S_{ijk}, T_{ijk})\}$ from being utilized to recover private keys by adversaries, n_O data owners initially require $(2N + n_O)C_{exp}$ operation in TagGen. Luckily, these could be performed off line for owners as one-off task, although a little bit expensive. In ProofGen, computation is cC_{exp} for all $\{P_j\}$. In Verify, to remedy security flaw, i.e., private key recovery of ID-BPAP, we need 3 bilinear pairing computation to allow batch auditing at one time, which thus achieves enhanced security and still outperforms $2n_1 n_2$ pairings in Wang et al.'s ID-PUIC [22], if applied to the multiple clouds and multiple owners scenario.

Analysis for Communication: Communication for Challenge remains the same as ID-BPAP [25]. The total overhead of transmission is still smaller than Wang et al.s ID-PUIC if applied to the multiple clouds and multiple owners setting. Meanwhile, our improved scheme does not suffer from private key recovery as ID-BPAP.

Above all, the enhanced efficiency will become demonstrative if applied to huge data storage utilities like big data analysis. We will provide the analysis in detail upon extensive simulation in the full version of paper.

7   Conclusions

In this paper, we revisited an identity-based batch public auditing scheme with proxy processing (ID-BPAP) scheme designed by Yu et al. in [25], and demonstrated that any cloud server could generate valid data integrity proof without original data. Meanwhile, it is also feasible to recover Proxys private key and generate valid proxy tags for any modified data without Proxys awareness. Therefore, we propose our solution to repair the security flaws and thus enhance the security, at the expense of reasonable overheads while still enjoying better efficiency over Wang et al.'s scheme [22]. As a future work, we will keep on seeking to improve the efficiency of our proposed scheme of enhanced security and privacy, and evaluate it based on real-world multiple clouds storage system, with sound security for data integrity.

Acknowledgments. This work was supported by the National Key R&D Program of China under Grant 2017YFB0802000 and the National Natural Science Foundation of China under Grant 61872060 and 61370203, State Scholarship Fund Program of China Scholarship Council under Grant 201506070077. We also appreciate valuable comments from anonymous reviewers, which helps to contribute to a paper of good quality.

References

1. IDC.com: Worldwide Public Cloud Services Spending Forecast to Reach $122.5 Billion in 2017, According to IDC. http://www.idc.com/getdoc.jsp?containerId=prUS42321417. Accessed 20 Feb 2017
2. Gartner.com: Gartner Forecasts Worldwide Public Cloud Services Revenue to Reach $260 Billion in 2017. https://www.gartner.com/newsroom/id/3815165. Accessed 12 Oct 2017
3. Fu, Z., Wu, X., Guan, C., Sun, X., Ren, K.: Toward efficient multi-keyword fuzzy search over encrypted outsourced data with accuracy improvement. IEEE Trans. Inf. Forensics Secur. 11(12), 2706–2716 (2016)
4. Ateniese, G., et al.: Provable data possession at untrusted stores. In: Proceedings of ACM CCS 2007, pp. 598–609 (2007)
5. Shacham, H., Waters, B.: Compact proofs of retrievability. In: Pieprzyk, J. (ed.) ASIACRYPT 2008. LNCS, vol. 5350, pp. 90–107. Springer, Heidelberg (2008). https://doi.org/10.1007/978-3-540-89255-7_7
6. Wang, C., Chow, S.S.M., Wang, Q., Ren, K., Lou, W.: Privacy-preserving public auditing for secure cloud storage. IEEE Trans. Comput. 62(2), 362–375 (2013)
7. Wang, Q., Wang, C., Ren, K., Lou, W., Li, J.: Enabling public audibility and data dy-namics for storage security in cloud computing. IEEE Trans. Parallel Distrib. Syst. 22, 847–859 (2011)
8. Erway, C.C., Kp, A., Papamanthou, C., Tamassia, R.: Dynamic provable data possession. ACM Trans. Inf. Syst. Secur. 17(4), 15 (2015)
9. Zhu, Y., Hu, H., Ahn, G.J., Yu, M.: Cooperative provable data possession for integrity verification in MultiCloud storage. IEEE Trans. Parallel Distrib. Syst. 23(12), 2231–2244 (2012)
10. Yang, K., Jia, X.: An efficient and secure dynamic auditing protocol for data storage in cloud computing. IEEE Trans. Parallel Distrib. Syst. 24(9), 1717–1726 (2013)
11. Curtmola, R., Khan, O., Burns, R., Ateniese, G.:MR-PDP: multiple-replica provable data possession. In: Proceedings of the 28th International Conference on Distributed Computing Systems, pp. 411–420 (2008)
12. Wang, B., Li, B., Li, H.: Panda: public auditing for shared data with efficient user revocation in the cloud. IEEE Trans. Serv. Comput. 8(1), 92–106 (2015)
13. Liu, C., Ranjan, R., Yang, C., Zhang, X., Wang, L., Chen, J.: MuRDPA: top-down levelled multi-replica merkle hash tree based secure public auditing for dynamic big data storage on cloud. IEEE Trans. Comput. 64(9), 2609–2622 (2015)
14. Barsoum, A.F., Hasan, M.A.: Provable multicopy dynamic data possession in cloud computing systems. IEEE Trans. Inf. Forensics Secur. 10(3), 485–497 (2015)
15. Wang, J., Chen, X., Huang, X., You, I., Xiang, Y.: Verifiable auditing for outsourced database in cloud computing. IEEE Trans. Comput. 64(11), 3293–3303 (2015)
16. Zhao, J., Xu, C., Li, F., Zhang, W.: Identity-based public verification with privacy preserving for data storage security in cloud computing. IEICE Trans. Fundam. Electron. Commun. Comput. Sci. 96(12), 2709–2716 (2013)
17. Boneh, D., Franklin, M.: Identity-based encryption from the weil pairing. In: Kilian, J. (ed.) CRYPTO 2001. LNCS, vol. 2139, pp. 213–229. Springer, Heidelberg (2001). https://doi.org/10.1007/3-540-44647-8_13
18. Yu, Y., Zhang, Y., Mu, Y., Susilo, W., Liu, H.: Provably secure identity based provable data possession. In: Au, M.-H., Miyaji, A. (eds.) ProvSec 2015. LNCS, vol. 9451, pp. 310–325. Springer, Cham (2015). https://doi.org/10.1007/978-3-319-26059-4_17

19. Liu, H., Mu, Y., Zhao, J., Xu, C., Wang, H., Chen, L.: Identity-based provable data possession revisited: security analysis and generic construction. Comput. Stand. Interfaces **54**(1), 10–19 (2017)
20. Wang, H.: Identity-based distributed provable data possession in multicloud storage. IEEE Trans. Serv. Comput. **8**(2), 328–340 (2015)
21. Yu, Y.: Identity-based remote data integrity checking with perfect data privacy preserving for cloud storage. IEEE Trans. Inf. Forensics Secur. **12**(4), 767–778 (2017)
22. Wang, H., He, D., Tang, S.: Identity-based proxy-oriented data uploading and remote data integrity checking in public cloud. IEEE Trans. Inf. Forensics Secur. **11**(6), 1165–1176 (2016)
23. Peng, S., Zhou, F., Xu, J., Xu, Z.: Comments on identity-based distributed provable data possession in Multicloud storage. IEEE Trans. Serv. Comput. **9**(6), 996–998 (2016)
24. Coron, J.-S.: On the exact security of full domain hash. In: Bellare, M. (ed.) CRYPTO 2000. LNCS, vol. 1880, pp. 229–235. Springer, Heidelberg (2000). https://doi.org/10.1007/3-540-44598-6_14
25. Yu, H., Cai, Y., Kong, S.: Efficient and secure identity-based public auditing for dynamic outsourced data with proxy. KSII Trans. Internet and Inf. Syst. **11**(10), 5039–5061 (2017)

Compressive Sensing Encryption Scheme with Anonymous Traitor Tracing for Cloud Storage Security

Peng Zhang[1], Juntao Gao[1(⊠)], Wenjuan Jia[1], and Xuelian Li[2]

[1] ISN State Key Laboratory China, Xi'an, Shaanxi, China
jtgao@mail.xidian.edu.cn
[2] School of Mathematics and Statistics, Xidian University,
Xi'an, Shaanxi, China

Abstract. The explosive growth of information imposes a huge storage burden on the personal communication terminal and causes serious challenges to the communication bandwidth and security. Therefore, many compressive sensing (CS) encryption schemes are proposed to solve this problem. However, the decryption key in these papers needs to be shared with the users and cannot prevent the receivers from intentionally leaking the key. Once the key is compromised, the cloud system could not find the traitor who reveals the key. To address the problem, we propose the compressive sensing scheme with traitor tracing for cloud storage, which can ensure information security and simultaneously reduce the storage and transmission burden while maintaining low overhead at the user side. The work presented supports anonymous traitor tracking that can track any anonymous traitors who reveal their keys, so guarantee the security of the key. In addition, our scheme handles the ciphertext integrity protection and energy leakage in existing CS encryption schemes. Simulation results show that our scheme improves the overall compression and recovery performance compared to other CS encryption schemes. Our scheme can be used to efficiently encrypt sensitive information in online database, virtual currency, Internet of Things (IoT) and cloud encryption systems.

Keywords: Compressive sensing · Cloud storage security · Online database
Traitor tracing · Security transmission · Energy protection

1 Introduction

Cisco reports that, by the end of 2018, data center traffic will increase to 10.8 ZB per year ($1ZB = 2^{40}$ GB), and cloud system traffic will account for more than 76% of the total data center traffic. By 2020, 92% of the global workload will be handled by cloud data centers, and the market share will reach 38.6 million dollars. The advantage of cloud over the traditional devices with limited storage capacity such as mobile phones and static sensors, is its abundant computing resources and huge storage space. However, the huge volume of information stream imposes heavy burden not only on personal terminal, but also on the cloud system. And if the collected information is not properly handled, the cloud system has to waste a lot of space and resources to process

© Springer Nature Singapore Pte Ltd. 2018
F. Li et al. (Eds.): FCS 2018, CCIS 879, pp. 138–152, 2018.
https://doi.org/10.1007/978-981-13-3095-7_11

these uploaded data. What's more, the transmission of the huge amount of data also brings severe challenge to the bandwidth of communications.

In order to solve this problem, people try to use the traditional data compression technique [23] based on the Nyquist sampling theorem. Although the traditional data compression method can reduce the storage burden, it cannot improve the insufficient communication bandwidth problem. Compressive sensing (CS) [1–3] is a novel theory framework for signal description and processing. CS allows accurately or approximately to reconstruct the original signal with much lower sampling rate than the Nyquist sampling theorem, thus addressing the problem of insufficient bandwidth.

On the other hand, the security requirements of cloud data are also increasing. Gartner pointed out that in 2017, the global cyber security industry reached $98.896 billion, and is expected to increase to $106 billion by the end of 2018. The huge volume of data collected and transmitted to the cloud database often contains sensitive or private information. Once the sensitive information is leaked, it may cause serious property loss. In 2017, more than one million Bitcoin stolen events occurred on bitcoin trading platforms such as Bitfinex and Mt. Gox. The survey results showed that the companies' internal staff may have compromised the wallet's key. The reason for such a serious property loss is the inability to trace the traitor who reveals the key.

The traitor tracking technique [14–19] can be used to trace the traitor who intentionally leaks the key. Therefore, we consider combining traitor tracking with CS encryption schemes. In the actual cloud database system, CS is used to achieve efficient transmission, and traitor tracing is used to track traitor who leaks the key. Thereby, our scheme can improve the security of private data and save storage space for the cloud.

1.1 Related Works

CS itself can provide certain security protection for the transmission and storage of information in online databases [9, 22]. In work [4], the theory of measuring matrix as secret key is proposed. In [5], Rachlin and Baron were the first to formally study measurement matrix in 2008. However, using the same measurement matrix to encrypt multiple different signals might result in severe information leakage. Therefore, it is proposed in [6] and [8] to use the key seed to generate different measurement matrices through LFSR. And Gao in [7] generates the measurement matrix by the pseudo random generator to ensure CS security. Consider the issue of protecting the energy information of the signal. It is pointed out in [9] that the sparse signal should be energy normalized to protect encrypt signal energy. In [10, 11] and [24] CS-processed data are uploaded to the cloud to save resources and ensure security. Xue proposes a cloud encryption scheme based on CS, which supports the functionality of random compression, statistical decryption and accurate decryption [12].

The works mentioned above to some certain extent use CS to achieve the security of encrypted data. However, in these papers, the matrix as the secret key must be shared with the receiving users. This may cause the receiving users to deliberately leak the key. Once the key is compromised, the cloud system could not find the traitor. Moreover, none of these papers takes the issue of ciphertext integrity protection [25] into account, the cloud system could not prevent malicious attackers from tampering the ciphertext. Therefore, it will cause serious security problems in practical.

1.2 Our Contributions

To address the problems above, we design the compressive sensing encryption scheme with anonymous traitor tracing for cloud storage security. The work presented in this paper solves the problems of key security and ciphertext integrity protection while saving storage resources and ensuring efficient transmission. In our scheme, the decryption key that the cloud database sends to the user is generated by the secret key, and the secret key is stored secretly in the cloud database. So the user cannot obtain the secret key. Even if the user leaks the decryption key to other illegal users, the anonymous reverse tracking function can also track the traitor. At the same time, in order to ensure the integrity and security of the ciphertext, we design the CS-based ciphertext authentication and energy protection function to prevent malicious users from tampering with ciphertext. Thus improving the security of ciphertext during transmission and decryption. To summarize, our main contributions are as follows:

- Our scheme firstly combines compressed sensing with traitor tracing. The cloud database can track the anonymous traitor who leaks the key, while achieving the user's anonymous authentication, and improving the security of CS encryption system. The simulation results show that compared with other CS encryption schemes, our encryption scheme has better recovery effect while providing stronger security.
- In this paper, the decryption key that user gets from the cloud database is generated by the secret key, and the secret key is kept secretly by the cloud database. Moreover, the user cannot derive any information about the secret key from the decryption key. Therefore, our scheme can guarantee the security of the secret key in the cloud storage system.
- CS-based ciphertext authentication and energy encryption are designed. According to the characteristics of CS, the ciphertext authentication function is designed to prevent the illegal ones from tampering with the ciphertext. At the same time, energy standardization makes the energy of the encrypted data indistinguishable from the energy of the original data.

The rest of the paper is organized as follows. Section 1 introduces compressive sensing and traitor tracing briefly. We provide the detailed scheme in Section 2, and system analysis in Section 3. Section 4 gives our experimental simulation. Finally, Sect. 5 draws a conclusion remarks.

2 The CS-Based Anonymous Traitor Tracing Scheme

2.1 System Architecture and Process

Figure 1 shows the proposed system framework. First, all users apply for registration in the cloud database system to obtain their corresponding identity secret values. After registration, the cloud database system records the user's identity information, and then the database system broadcasts the ciphertext information encrypted by CS in the group. When a registered user wants to order product information from the cloud database system, the user should verify the integrity of the ciphertext broadcast firstly.

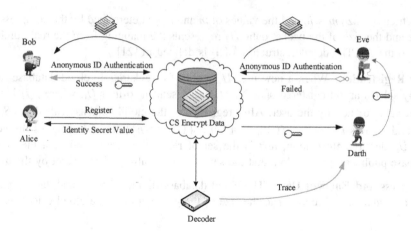

Fig. 1. System workflow and framework. Alice is a legitimate user to be registered. Bob is a registered legal user. Eve is an unregistered malicious user, and Darth is the traitor.

If the encrypted information has not been tampered with, the user performs anonymous identity authentication with the cloud. The cloud database sends session keys and decryption keys to the users who pass the anonymous authentication. Note that the decryption key sent by the cloud database includes the sensing matrix and the secret key is sparse matrix. And the secret key that generates the decryption key is kept secretly in the cloud database. Therefore, even if a traitor leaks the decryption key, the secret key still keeps secure. What's more, the complex CS-based decryption and recovery work are offload to the cloud database with a rich computing resource. The user only needs to use the energy decryption key to recover the original data, thus saving a large amount of computing resources for the user. When a user (traitor) in a group intentionally divulges the decryption key to other illegal users, the cloud database system can trace the identity information of the anonymous traitor through collecting the pirate's decoder. Finally, the cloud database system is allowed to flexibly delete, recover, and add users without changing the keys of other legitimate users.

2.2 Our Scheme

Our design is based on a trusted third party of cloud database, which can compress the encrypted data and track the traitor. The details are described as follows.

System Initialization. The cloud database system first randomly selects two large prime numbers p, q, which satisfy $q|(p-1)$ and $q > n$. n denotes the total number of users in the group, g is a primitive element of $\mathbb{Z}_q$. Then the cloud database randomly chooses a k-degree polynomial $f(x) = a_0 + a_1 x + \ldots + a_k x^k, k > n$ in $\mathbb{Z}_q[x]$. We call the corresponding point $(i, f(i))$ in $f(x)$, $i \in \mathbb{Z}_q \backslash \{0\}, f(i) \neq 0$ as a share, which satisfying $f(i) \neq f(j)$ for any $i \neq j$. Finally, the cloud database chooses a secure hash function H_1, H_2, pseudo-random normal distribution matrix generator Γ, and publishes H_1, H_2 and Γ to the user group. Here hash function $H_1 : A \rightarrow \mathbb{Z}_q^*$, where A denotes a set of matrices of size $m \times n$, and the values of m and n are determined by the compressed value and the size of the packet data. H_2 represents the mapping from the real number field to the $\mathbb{Z}_q^*$. The detailed structure of Γ is defined in [21].

User Registration. When a new user U_i applies for registration, cloud database randomly selects an unregistered share $(i, f(i))$ and send it to user U_i, where $f(i)$ is the secret value owned by the user. After registration, the cloud database calculates $S_i = g^{f(i)}$ and records $text = \{i \parallel f(i) \parallel U_i \parallel S_i | i \in \{1, 2, \ldots, n\}\}$. Here S_i denotes the new user U_i identity information, $text$ is the set of registered users. And then the cloud database publishes $\{g, p\}$. Note that the secret value is always kept secret by the user.

Compress and Encrypt Data. The cloud database divides the original data in parts with an equal size. According to the size of the grouped data, the cloud calculates:

$$\Psi = U\Lambda V^T \tag{3}$$

Where Ψ denotes the sparse matrix that is generated through an over complete learning dictionary which can find the simplest form of a signal. The sparse matrix obtained by this method has better sparseness and can achieve better reconstruction properties when the original signal is reconstructed. Here ^{T} denotes matrix transpose, $\Lambda \in \mathbb{R}^{n \times d}$ contains the singular values in its main diagonal, and $U \in \mathbb{R}^{n \times n}$ and $V^T \in \mathbb{R}^{d \times d}$ are orthonormal matrices. The projection matrix $\Phi = U_m^T$ is constructed by taking the first m columns of the *orthogonal matrix U*. The size of m is equal to the size of the grouped data. For more details about the construction of projection matrices, please refer to [12]. It has been shown in [20] that the measurement matrix constructed by this method has a better performance for reducing the reconstruction error.

The cloud then divides the key *generation parameter K* into two sub-keys K_1 and K_2, where K_1 is the first m bits of K and K_2 is the remaining bits of K. We use K_1 to compute the random perturbation matrix $\rho_i = \Gamma(K_1 + i)$, and use K_2 to compute:

$$c_i = \pi_{K_2}(\parallel \Psi x_i \parallel_2^2) = \pi_{K_2}(\parallel \theta_i \parallel_2^2) = \parallel \theta_i \parallel_2^2 \oplus K_2 \tag{4}$$

where $\rho_i \in \mathbb{R}^{m \times m}$ is the perturbation matrix, and c_i is the energy encryption function, and x_i is the ith group of data. Using the perturbation matrix is to make the cipher texts different even though the original plaintexts are same. The energy encryption function prevents the signal energy leakage and guarantees the signal energy security.

Finally, the cloud database uses the above parameters to encrypt the original data, and then uses the hash function H_1, H_2 to calculate the verification tag therefore:

$$y_i' = \rho_i \Phi \Psi \hat{\theta}_i = \rho_i A \frac{\theta_i}{\parallel \theta_i \parallel_2^2} \tag{5}$$

where y_i' denotes the ith random compress cipher text, and $A = \Phi \Psi$ is the sensing matrix, and $\hat{\theta}_i$ is the sparse data after energy encryption, and $T_1 = H_1(y_i'), T_2 = H_2(c_i)$

are the verification tags of cipher text and energy cipher text. Then the cloud database system packages $(y_i, c_i, T_1, T_2)^T$ and broadcasts to user groups.

Subscribe and Anonymous Authentication. User who wants to subscribe the information products from the cloud database should first calculate $T' = H_1(y_i)$, and then verity whether $T'=T$ or not. If equal, the cloud database authenticates the user's anonymous identity information, otherwise the subscription is terminated. During the anonymous authentication phase, the user firstly selects a random number r, and calculates $g^r, g^{rf(i)}$ and sends $\{g^r \parallel g^{rf(i)}\}$ to cloud database. Note that $r \in \mathbb{Z}_q^*$ and r^{-1} is existed such that $r^{-1} \times r \equiv 1 (\mathrm{mod}\, q - 1)$. After receiving the data sent by the user, the cloud randomly selects s and calculates $D = (g^r)^s$ and $A = (g^{rf(i)})^s$. Then the cloud database keeps D in secret, and sends A to the user. The user calculates $R = (g^{rf(i)s})^{r^{-1}}$ and sends R to the cloud database after receiving the data. Finally, the cloud uses $(g^r)^s$ and user registration identity information S_i to calculate:

$$D' = (g^r)^s + \prod_{i=1}^{n} (R - (S_i)^s) \qquad (6)$$

Then the cloud database verifies whether $D' = D$ or not. If $D' = D$, anonymous authentication is passed, otherwise terminated. Since users do not authenticate with their true identities, but disguised identity information $g^{rf(i)}$. Therefore, the cloud database does not know which user is authenticated, but the cloud knows that the user who passes the anonymous authentication must be a registered legitimate user.

Distribute Decryption Key. The cloud records the session key $k_i = (g^r)^{f(i)}$ for authenticated users. After distributing the session key, the cloud database calculates $y_0 = g^{a_0}, y_1 = g^{a_1}, \ldots, y_k = g^{a_k}$ and publishes public key $pub = \{p, g, y_0, y_1, \ldots, y_k\}$, where $a_0, a_1, \ldots, a_k$ are the coefficients of polynomial $f(x)$. Then the cloud database randomly chooses $\alpha, \lambda \in \mathbb{Z}_q^*$ to construct the filter function $\{C_1(x), C_2\}$:

$$C_1(x) = g^\alpha + \lambda \prod_{i=1}^{n} (x - k_i) \qquad (7)$$

$$C_2 = ((K_1 \parallel K_2 \parallel A)(y_0)^\alpha \times (y_1)^\alpha \times \ldots \times (y_k)^\alpha) \qquad (8)$$

where α^{-1} satisfies that $\alpha^{-1} \times \alpha \equiv 1 (\mathrm{mod}\, q - 1)$. The cloud database broadcasts $\{C_1(x), C_2\}$ in the group. After receiving the broadcast, the user puts $(C_1(x), C_2, k_i, f(i))$ into the decoder and calculates $C_1(k_i) = g^\alpha$. Then obtain the decryption key:

$$\frac{C_2}{C_1(k_i)} = ((K_1 \parallel K_2 \parallel A)(y_0)^\alpha \times (y_1)^{\alpha i} \times \ldots \times (y_k)^{\alpha i^k})/((g^\alpha)^{f(i)}) = (K_1 \parallel K_2 \parallel A)$$

$$\qquad (9)$$

Decryption. When received cipher text data packet $(y_i, c_i, T_1, T_2)^T$ and decryption key $(K_1 \parallel K_2 \parallel A)$, the user first locally calculates the verification tag T_2' for each group of data using system parameters H by $T_2' = H_2(c_i)$. Then the user verifies whether $T_2' = T_2$ or not. If equal, the user calculates the perturbation matrix $\rho_i = \Gamma(K_1 + i)$ and perturbs sensing matrix $A_i' = \rho_i \cdot A$ of each grouped data using the obtained decryption key K_1, A and system parameters Γ, and then sends A_i' to the cloud database. The cloud database uses the CS recovery algorithm $\hat{\theta}_i = rec(y_i, A_i')$ to calculate each set of energy-encrypted sparse data $\hat{\theta}_i$, and gets encrypted data $\hat{x}_i$ by $\hat{x}_i = \Psi\hat{\theta}_i$. Hereafter, the cloud database sends the calculated data $\hat{x}_i$ to user. At last, the user who receives the data calculates the encrypted sparse data θ_i and original data x_i by the obtained energy encryption function c_i and decryption key K_2 as follows:

$$\| \theta_i \|_2^2 = c_i \oplus K_2 \tag{10}$$

$$x_i = \hat{x}_i \times \| \theta_i \|_2^2 \tag{11}$$

Anonymous Traitor Tracing Algorithm. Our anonymous traitor tracing algorithm finds the true identity of the traitor through the private key of the user hidden in the pirate decoder. Assume a pirate decoder hides the traitor's personal information $(f(i), k_i)$. When seized to the traitor decoder, the cloud database selects valid $M, M^{-1} \in \mathbb{Z}_q^*$ such that $M \times M^{-1} \equiv 1 (\mathrm{mod}\, q - 1)$ and calculates:

$$C_1(x) = g^\alpha + \lambda \prod_{i=1}^n (x - k_i) \tag{12}$$

$$C_2 = (M(y_0)^{2\alpha} \times (y_1)^{2\alpha} \times \ldots \times (y_k)^{2\alpha}) \tag{13}$$

Then the cloud database inputs $(C_1(x), C_2)$ into the decoder, the decoder uses the hidden identity information to calculate M':

$$M' = \frac{C_2}{C_1(k_i)} = (M(y_0)^{2\alpha} \times (y_1)^{2\alpha i} \times \ldots \times (y_k)^{2\alpha i^k})/((g^\alpha)^{f(i)}) = Mg^{\alpha f(i)} \tag{14}$$

Finally, the cloud database calculates traitor's identity information S_i' by $S_i' = (M^{-1} \times M')^{\alpha^{-1}} = (M^{-1} \times M(g^{\alpha f(i)}))^{\alpha^{-1}} = g^{f(i)}$. Comparing the calculated identity S_i' with the S_i stored in $text'$, the identity of the traitor user can be determined.

Revocation, Recovery and Add Algorithms. Assuming the set of revoked users is $\Delta = \{U_{i1}, U_{i2}, \ldots, U_{im}\}, 1 \leq m \leq n$, and the set of session keys they hold is $\{k_{i1}, k_{i2}, \ldots, k_{im}\}$. Since the session keys of the registered users are used when distributing the decryption key, the cloud database only needs to remove the uses' session keys from the filter function and re-selecting $\bar{\alpha}, \bar{\lambda} \in \mathbb{Z}_q^*$. Then the cloud database changes and broadcasts the filter functions $(C_1'(x), C_2')$ by $C_1'(x) = g^{\bar{\alpha}} + \lambda \prod_{i=1, U_i \notin \Delta}^n (x - k_i)$ and

$C_2' = ((K_1 \parallel K_2 \parallel A)(y_0)^{\bar{\alpha}} \times (y_1)^{\bar{\alpha}} \times \ldots \times (y_k)^{\bar{\alpha}})$. Note that there exists $\bar{\alpha}^{-1}$ such that $\bar{\alpha}^{-1} \times \bar{\alpha} \equiv 1 (\mathrm{mod}\, q - 1)$. In this case, the users who have not been revoked do not need to update the corresponding session keys, and the plaintext can still be obtained according to the above decryption algorithm. All revoked users will not be able to recover the plain text because the filter function no longer includes their session keys.

To recover some revoked users, the cloud database only needs to modify the filtering function, i.e., the cloud database adds the session keys of the users who need to be recovered to $C_1(x)$. For other users, nothing needs to be done. When a new user makes a registration request, the cloud randomly selects a secret value and sends it to the new user. After the anonymous authentication and the key distribution are completed, the cloud database only needs to add the new user's session key to the filtering function to complete the add algorithm operation, while other users' keys and identity information remain unchanged.

3 System Analysis

3.1 Fully Anonymous Authentication and Tracking

In the anonymous authentication phase, the authentication information received by the cloud database is $\{g^r \parallel g^{rf(i)}\}$, where $r \in \mathbb{Z}_q^*$ is randomly selected by the user. Obviously, the difficulty that the cloud database obtains the user's identity information $g^{f(i)}$ from authentication information $\{g^r \parallel g^{rf(i)}\}$ is equivalent to CDH problem, so it can be ensured that the user's identity authentication process is completely anonymous. At the same time, since the cloud database could not identify the user's identity $g^{f(i)}$, it cannot pretend to be an honest user to commit fraud. Moreover, each time the user randomly selects r in the ordering information phase, the cloud cannot identify the correspondence between orders and users. Therefore, the security of the user's anonymous identity can be guaranteed. Finally, when there is a traitor, the cloud system can track the traitor through a filter function and extract the identity information S_i of the traitor from the anonymous identities hidden in the piracy decoder.

3.2 Key Security

In our scheme, the decryption key sent by the cloud database system includes the sensing matrix A and the secret key is sparse matrix Ψ. And the secret key sparse matrix Ψ generating the sensing matrix A has been kept secretly in the cloud database system. Therefore, even if Eve intercepts the sensing matrix A, he cannot compute any information about the sparse matrix Ψ. Because it is a NP problem to solve the sparse matrix Ψ from the sensing matrix A. And it has been analyzed in [4, 11] that an attacker could not decrypt ciphertext without a sparse matrix Ψ or measurement matrix Φ. On the other hand, suppose a taitor intentionally divulges the decryption key to other users or illegal users, he could only reveal the sensing matrix A. So illegal users also could not get any information about the sparse matrix Ψ. Therefore, the secret key Ψ in our scheme has high security.

3.3   Ciphertext Authentication and Energy Encryption

Compared with the previous CS encryption scheme, we design ciphertext-based authentication according to the characteristics of CS approximate reconstruction. The recovery signal is an approximate estimate of the original signal, if you use MAC-then-CS encryption scheme, it will lead to the failure of ciphertext authentication, and might leak information about the plaintext. Simultaneously, according to *RIP* [13], the CS-encrypted signal has the same energy as the original signal. Our scheme ensures the signal energy is indistinguishable by encrypting the signal energy. Therefore, the integrity and confidentiality of encrypted data can be guaranteed.

3.4   Flexibility and Anti-collusion

Our scheme can be flexible to implement revocation, recovery and add algorithm. As described in chapter III, in the process of add and recovery, the cloud database only needs to add the user's session key to the filter function, and the original legitimate users can still decrypt the broadcast data without changing any key and identity information. In the process of revocation, Assume that the revocation users' private key set is $\{k_{i1}, k_{i2}, \ldots, k_{im}\}, 1 \le m \le n$. Then the cloud database only needs to remove the users' session key from the filter function and then changes the filter parameter α, λ, and other original legitimate users can still decrypt the broadcast data without changing any key and identity information. And the order of polynomials $f(x)$ is greater than the total number of users n. According to the Lagrange interpolation formula, our scheme can completely prevent users' collusion.

4   Experimental Simulation

We conduct a simulation test on the Intel® Core(TM) i3-6100 CPU @ 3.70 GHz in DELL. Simulation test is divided into two main aspects, on the one hand is for personal travel protection, such as personal walking steps per day; on the other hand, the protection of personal daily privacy, such as the need to upload private photos to the cloud. The two simulations illustrate that the proposed CS-based anonymous traitor tracing encryption scheme is secure and feasible.

In the simulation test, we use the cosine function to test the security performance of our scheme. To be more representative, we select four cosine functions with different frequencies and amplitudes for the simulation test. Note that, the tested the signal length is equal to 120 and the compression ratio is 0.5. The four sets of simulation results in Fig. 2 correspond to four different cosine functions. The latter three cosine functions are combinations of cosine functions of different frequencies and amplitudes. The first one on the left represents the original signal figure, the second represents the encrypted signal figure, the third represents the comparison of the original signal with the decrypted signal, and the fourth represents the comparison of the decrypted signal with the undecrypted signal.

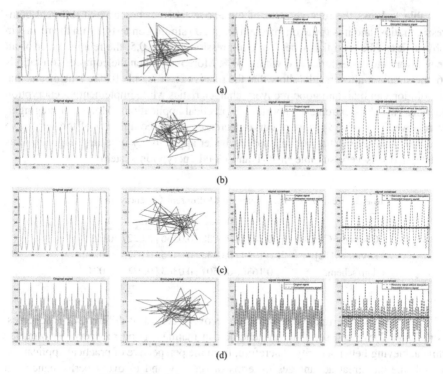

Fig. 2. Simulation comparison of different curves.

By comparing the original signal with the encrypted signal, we can see that the signal after the encryption has been completely distorted. So even if a malicious attacker could get the ciphertext, he cannot find any similarity or association with the plaintext. From the comparison of the original signal and the decrypted signal, we can find that the signal curve recovered basically coincides with the original signal curve. This result shows that our program has very good recovery effect. To further prove the importance of the energy encryption process, we give the final experimental simulation comparison chart which shows the comparison of the recovered decrypted signal and the recovered signal without energy decryption. Obviously, the recovery signal without decryption is completely different from the original signal. Therefore, if the ciphertext is not decrypted, no information of the original data can be obtained. Because after energy normalization, the energy of each signal is protected. If the energy decryption operation is not performed, the recovered signal values are nearly zero. Therefore, our scheme can achieve good data security performance.

Table 1. Relative error of different curves under different compression.

CR	0.2	0.3	0.4	0.5	0.6
(a)	0.2931	0.1798	0.1248	0.0812	0.0727
(b)	0.1636	0.0501	0.0365	0.0311	0.0248
(c)	0.2381	0.0506	0.0344	0.0249	0.0199
(d)	0.1207	0.0377	0.0134	0.0104	0.0038

Table 1 shows the relative error of the above four cosine curve at different compression ratios, and it is the average result from 100 simulation tests. From the results in Table 1, it can be seen that when the compression ratio is 0.5, the relative error of all the recovery curves is controlled within 10%. Moreover, when the compression ratio is 0.6, the simulation test results show that the relative error is only 0.3%. This means that our solution can maintain good recovery characteristics while implementing encryption functions, which is extremely important in practical applications. More encouragingly, the relative error of the recovery curve decreases as the complexity of the test curve increases. This shows that our scheme has better applicability in testing huge amounts of data, and it is very suitable in IOT and cloud encryption system.

Table 2. Relative error comparison of different CS encryption (CSE)

CR	0.2	0.3	0.4	0.5	0.6
Common CSE [7, 8]	0.3494	0.0928	0.0366	0.0227	0.0202
Kryptein [12]	0.1904	0.0533	0.0425	0.0375	0.0272
Our scheme	0.1636	0.0501	0.0365	0.0311	0.0248

Table 2 shows the relative error of the recovery curves of different CSE schemes. From Table 2, we can see that our scheme can maintain good recovery performance while achieving better security. Therefore, from the perspective of practical application, our scheme has great advantages in terms of security and recovery performance. To further illustrate the accuracy and reliability, we extend the continuous curve distribution test to the discrete point distribution test. Here we use the individual walking steps collected from WeChat to test the security of our scheme.

Figure 3 shows the comparison between the original walking data and the decrypt data recovered at a compression ratio of 0.5. It is clear that the recovered motion data are basically the same as the original data, and the test results show that the relative error between the two sets of recovery data is 0.013 and 0.0155, respectively. Therefore, the data recovered by our scheme has a high degree of accuracy. This indicates that our scheme has good recovery characteristics in more sophisticated equipment.

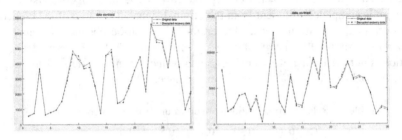

Fig. 3. Comparison of two groups of walking steps (one month) collected from WeChat.

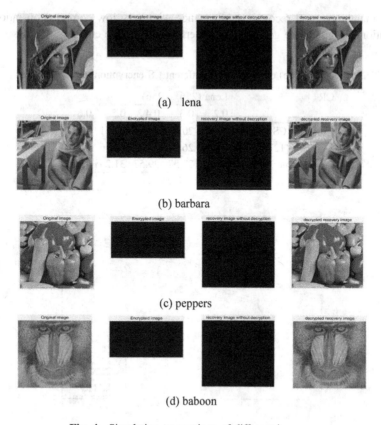

(a) lena

(b) barbara

(c) peppers

(d) baboon

Fig. 4. Simulation comparison of different images.

Figure 4(a)–(d) show the comparison of simulation results for different images of size 256 × 256. Each set of images includes the original image, the encrypted image, the undecrypted restored image, and the decrypted restored image, respectively. It can be seen from the comparison that the restored image has high similarity with the original image, and the simulation results show that the PSNR of the recovered images after decryption of the above four groups of images exceeds 30 db, which indicates that the quality of the recovered images are very high. And it is clear that the encrypted image is completely different from the original image. From the comparison of the recovery image without energy decryption and the recovery image after energy decryption results, we find that the image without energy decryption cannot display any information of the original image at all. This illustrates that our scheme's energy encryption algorithm has good encryption performance for image signals. Therefore, our scheme can also protect the security of media images.

Table 3 shows the PSNR of the recovered image at different compression ratios for different CS encryption schemes. The comparison shows that the recovery effect of our scheme is much better. When the compression ratio exceeds 0.3, the quality of the image recovered by our solution is close to 30 db. Compared with other solutions, our solution maintains good recovery performance with very low compression ratio. So, our solution can guarantee good recovery performance while ensuring image security.

Table 3. PSNR (db) comparison of different CS encryption (CSE) schemes.

CR	Lena (256 × 256)				
	0.2	0.3	0.4	0.5	0.6
Common CSE [7, 8]	15.63	20.40	24.61	27.51	29.11
Kryptein [12]	24.81	26.97	29.62	30.76	31.19
Our scheme	25.34	27.57	29.57	31.25	32.24

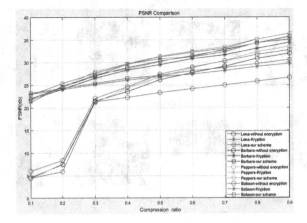

Fig. 5. Comparison of PSNR of the recovered images in different schemes.

Figure 5 gives the PSNR of the recovered images when lena, barbara, peppers and baboon four different images are not encrypted, encrypted with Kryption [11], and encrypted with our scheme. It can be seen from the figure that the recovery effect of our encryption scheme is better than that of no encryption and Kryption. And our encryption scheme still maintains certain recovery characteristics in the case of low compression ratios, while the CS method in non-encryption does not recover any image information at the compression ratio below 0.3.

5 Conclusion

We combine the compressive sensing with traitor tracing for cloud storage, which ensure information security while reducing the burden on storage and transmission. To solve the key security problem caused by shared keys in traditional CS encryption schemes, we provide traitor tracing function which can track the traitor in the group who reveal the key. Meanwhile, our proposed scheme breaks through the traditional CS-based scheme that the decryption key must be in the user's hands, and therefore improves system flexibility. Finally, for the problem of ciphertext security, our paper designs a CS-based ciphertext authentication scheme and energy encryption function to ensure the integrity of ciphertext and greatly improve the security of the system.

The simulation results show that our proposed scheme not only has good compression and encryption effects in data signals but also maintains good security and recovery performance in media image signals. From the comparison, we found that when dealing with huge amount of data and complex images, the proposed scheme achieves better recovery effects. This shows that our scheme has better practicality in processing massive amounts of data. Therefore, it has a wide application range under the framework of virtual currency, internet of things and cloud encryption systems.

Acknowledgments. This work is supported in part by the National Key Research and Development Program of China (No. 2016YFB0800601), the Natural Science Foundation of China (No. 61303217, 61502372), the Natural Science Foundation of Shaanxi province (No. 2013JQ8002, 2014JQ8313).

References

1. Candès, E.J., Romberg, J., Tao, T.: Robust uncertainty principles: exact signal reconstruction from highly incomplete frequency information. IEEE Trans. Inf. Theory **52**(2), 489–509 (2006)
2. Candès, E.J., Tao, T.: Decoding by linear programming. IEEE Trans. Inf. Theory **51**(12), 4203–4215 (2005)
3. Donoho, D.: Compressed sensing. IEEE Trans. Inf. Theory **52**(4), 1289–1306 (2006). Author, F.: Contribution title. In: 9th International Proceedings on Proceedings, pp. 1–2. Publisher, Location (2010)
4. Candès, E.J., Tao, T.: Near-optimal signal recovery from random projections: universal encoding strategies. IEEE Trans. Inf. Theory **52**(12), 5406–5425 (2006)
5. Rachlin, Y., Baron, D.: The secrecy of compressed sensing measurements. In: 46th Annual Allerton Conference on Communication, Control, and Computing, pp. 813–817 (2008)
6. Zhang, M., Kermani, M.M., Raghunathan, A., Jha, N.K.: Energy-efficient and secure sensor data transmission using encompression. In: International Conference on VLSI Design and International Conference on Embedded Systems, pp. 31–36 (2013)
7. Gao, J., Zhang, X., Liang, H., Shen, X.S.: Joint encryption and compressed sensing in smart grid data transmission. In: Global Communications Conference, pp. 662–667 (2014)
8. Pudi, V., Chattopadhyay, A., Lam, K.-Y.: Secure and lightweight compressive sensing using stream cipher. IEEE Trans. Circuits Syst. II Express Briefs 65(3), 371–375
9. Fay, R., Ruland, C.: Compressive sensing encryption modes and their security. In: Internet Technology & Secured Transactions, pp. 119–126 (2017)
10. Wang, C., Zhang, B., Ren, K., Roveda, J.M., Chen, C.W., Xu, Z.: A privacy-aware cloud-assisted healthcare monitoring system via compressive sensing. In: IEEE INFOCOM, pp. 2130–2138 (2014)
11. Hung, T.H., Hsieh, S.H., Lu, C.S.: Privacy-preserving data collection and recovery of compressive sensing. In: IEEE China Summit & International Conference on Signal & Information Processing, pp. 473–477 (2015)

12. Xue, W., Luo, C., Lan, G., Rana, R., Hu, W., Seneviratne, A.: Kryptein: a compressive-sensing-based encryption scheme for the internet of things. In: ACM/IEEE International Conference on Information Processing in Sensor Networks (IPSN 2017), 12p, April 2017
13. Candès, E.: The restricted isometry property and its implications for compressed sensing. Comptes Rendus Mathematique **346**(9), 589–592 (2008)
14. Chor, B., Fiat, A., Naor, M.: Tracing traitors. IEEE Trans. Inf. Theory **6**, 257–270 (1994)
15. Boneh, D., Franklin, M.: An efficient public key traitor tracing scheme. In: Wiener, M. (ed.) CRYPTO 1999. LNCS, vol. 1666, pp. 338–353. Springer, Heidelberg (1999). https://doi.org/10.1007/3-540-48405-1_22
16. Yuji, W., Coichiro, H., Hideki, L.: Efficient public key traitor tracing scheme. In: Proceedings of the CT-RSA 2001, Springer, Berlin (2001)
17. Boneh, D., Sahai, A., Waters, B.: Full collusion resistant traitor tracing with short cipher ciphertext and private keys. In: Proceedings of the 13th ACM Conference on Computer and Communications Security. ACM, New York (2006)
18. Wang, Q.L., Yang, B., Han, Z.: Free conspiracy public key traitor tracking scheme. J. Commun. **12**, 6–9 (2006)
19. Han, L.L., He, S.F., et al.: An anonymous public key traitor tracing scheme. J. ChangSha Univ. **9**(30), 62–65 (2016)
20. Rana, R., Yang, M., Wark, T., Chou, C.T., Hu, W.: SimpleTrack: adaptive trajectory compression with deterministic projection matrix for mobile sensor networks. Sens. J. IEEE **15**(1), 365–373 (2015)
21. Kargupta, H., Data, S., Wang, Q., Sivakumar, K.: On the privacy preserving properties of random data perturbation techniques. In: Proceedings of ICDM, pp. 99–106. IEEE (2003)
22. Agrawal, S., Vishwanath, S.: Secrecy using compressive sensing. In: Information theory workshop (ITW), pp 563–567. IEEE (2011)
23. Landau, H.J.: Sampling, data transmission, and the Nyquist rate. Proc. IEEE **55**(10), 1701–1706 (1967)
24. Qi, J., Hu, X., Ma, Y., Sun, Y.: A hybrid security and compressive sensing-based sensor data gathering scheme. IEEE Access **3**, 718–724 (2015)
25. Fay, R., Ruland, C.: Compressed sampling and authenticated-encryption. In: SCC; International ITG Conference on Systems (2017)

A Hybrid Data Deduplication Approach in Entity Resolution Using Chromatic Correlation Clustering

Charles R. Haruna[1,2]([envelope])[ID], Mengshu Hou[1][ID], Moses J. Eghan[2][ID],
Michael Y. Kpiebaareh[1][ID], and Lawrence Tandoh[1]

[1] University of Electronic Science and Technology of China, Chengdu, China
mshou@uestc.edu.cn, michael.kpiebaareh@sipingsoft.com, 3065550735@qq.com
[2] University of Cape Coast, Cape Coast, Ghana
{charuna,meghan}@ucc.edu.gh

Abstract. Entity resolution (ER) classifies records that refer to the same real-world entity and is fundamental to data cleaning. Identifying approximate but not exact duplicates in database records is a vital task. These duplicates may refer to the same real-world entity due to; 1. data entry errors, 2. differences in the detailed schemas of records from multiple databases, 3. unstandardized abbreviations, among several reasons. Machine-based techniques have been improving in quality, but still are a long way from being perfect. On the other hand, crowdsourcing platforms are widely accepted as a means for resolving tasks that machine-based approaches are not good at. Though they also offer relatively more accurate results, they are expensive and are slow in bringing human perception into the process.

In this paper, we present a machine-based technique for data deduplication which adopts a novel clustering algorithm under a crowd-based environment. We propose a non-trivial technique; 1. To reduce the time the crowd (humans) use in performing deduplication. 2. To reduce the crowdsourcing overheads and 3. For higher accuracy in data deduplication. Comparing with some existing human-machine based approaches; the experiments proved that our proposed approach outperforms some methods by incurring low crowdsourcing cost and offering a high accuracy of deduplication as well as deduplication efficiency.

Keywords: Data deduplication · Clustering · Edge-pivot graphs
Entity resolution · Crowdsourcing

1 Introduction

In database systems, entity resolution also referred to, in other works as entity reconciliation, duplicate detection or deduplication, record linkage and merge/purge, is the process of identifying different records that represent the same real-world entity [1–4]. In data deduplication, records that are identical to

© Springer Nature Singapore Pte Ltd. 2018
F. Li et al. (Eds.): FCS 2018, CCIS 879, pp. 153–167, 2018.
https://doi.org/10.1007/978-981-13-3095-7_12

each other in the real world are clustered into numerous groups. This is a problem because common identifiers may not exist at all or are noisy, thus accurate deduplication of records is a challenge. On the contrary, if the records have a common identifier, this problem is easy to solve. In Table 1 for example, records r_1 and r_2 refer to the same real world entity though they have different texts in the product details.

Numerous algorithms for data deduplication in entity resolution (see [2] for survey) have been proposed. For each pair of records, a basic machine-based approach calculates similarities between them using metrics such as Cosine or Jaccard similarity metrics [30,31]. Pairs of records with their similarity values higher than a given threshold are considered to be of the same real world entity. However, when one is presented with records that look highly similar but have different entities to process, machine-based algorithms often face challenges. Furthermore, machine-based techniques are found to have poor data deduplication accuracy. Human-based techniques are used to improve the accuracy, because in solving complex tasks, humans are way better than machines [14].

Given a record with a number of set, crowdsourcing approach is used for data deduplication by creating all possible pairs of records. Then the crowd is further used to examine each pair of records to determine duplicates. Huge overheads are caused by using this approach because of the vast number of pairs of records to be examined by the crowd. In modern era, due to this problem, a lot of researchers with easily accessible crowdsourcing platforms, have proposed human-machine based (hybrid) techniques, some of which aim to cluster the records relating to the same entity in the real world into several groups [5,6,10].

Table 1. Table of products.

Record ID	Product details	Price
r_1	Huawei P10 16GB Wifi Black	3200Rmb
r_2	Huawei Ten 16GB Wifi Black	5550Rmb
r_3	Huawei Ascend P One 16GB Wifi White	4000Rmb
r_4	Huawei Ascend P1 16GB Wifi White	3200Rmb
r_5	Huawei Ascend Y7 Prime 2GB Waterproof White	3900Rmb

The contributions of this paper are summarized as follows:

1. We use a machine-based technique called Cosine similarity to prune the duplicates records.
2. We generate clusters from the records using a proposed algorithm and the crowd examines the record pairs.
3. We experimentally compare our technique to existing models.

2 Problem Definition

Let $R = (r_1, r_2, ..., r_n)$ and g be the set of records and a function respectively, that map r_i to the real world entity they represent. The function g, is often too difficult to obtain in many cases, thus it is assumed that a similarity value function f: $R \times R \rightarrow [0, 1]$ exists, such that $f(r_i, r_j)$ is equal to the possibility of r_i and r_j representing the same real world entity. Using a machine-based algorithm, such functions can be constructed. The aim of data deduplication is to partition the given set of records R, into a set of clusters $C = \{C1, C2, ..., Ck\}$. So for any edge with pair of records selected $(r_i, r_j) \in R$, if $g(r_i) = g(r_j)$ then r_i and r_j must be in the same cluster, meaning they may be of the same real world entity. Otherwise, they are not put in the same cluster and are thus not similar. Like in existing works [10,32,33], we also adopt in this paper a metric cost $\Lambda(R)$ on machine-based deduplication. Equation 1 states;

$$\Lambda(R) = \sum_{r_i, r_j \in R.i<j} x_{i,j} \cdot (1 - f(r_i, r_j)) + \sum_{r_i, r_j \in R.i<j} (1 - x_{i,j}) \cdot (1 - f(r_i, r_j))$$

$$(1)$$

Table 2. Example of records with similarity scores.

Pairwise records	Similarity score	Pairwise records	Similarity score
(a, b)	0.75	(b, g)	0.60
(b, f)	0.72	(d, e)	0.58
(b, c)	0.70	(e, h)	0.55
(c, h)	0.69	(a, g)	0.49
(a, e)	0.65	(c, d)	0.45
(c, e)	0.63	...	<0.4

If two records pairs r_i and r_j are in the same cluster, then $r_{i,j} = 1$, otherwise $r_{i,j} = 0$. The metric cost $\Lambda(R)$ thus assigns a penalty of $1 - f(r_i, r_j)$ on a pair that are put in the same cluster. In Table 2 for example, assuming we have a set of eight records $R = \{a, b, c, d, e, f, g, h, i\}$, with similarity scores. Records pairs with similarity scores less than the threshold 0.4 are pruned out. Forming triangle of clusters $\langle a, b, f \rangle$ and $\langle d, e, h \rangle$ from the records, we can validate that the metric cost $\Lambda(R)$ is minimized. In works [10,34], trying to minimize the metric cost $\Lambda(R)$ is NP-hard problem. Correlation clustering which was adopted in [10] was assumed to be NP-hard problem. Thus, Chromatic-correlation clustering [34], an instance of correlation clustering is also NP-hard problem too. Quite a number of machine-based algorithms have been proposed to solve the NP-hard problem but they are unable to handle record pairs that have similar representations but differ characteristically. Crowdsourcing on the other hand tends to improve the accuracy thus in this paper we propose a hybrid technique.

3   Contributions of the Work

Our solution presented for the human-machine based deduplication consists of:

1. Firstly, we use a machine-based algorithm [30,31], specifically Cosine similarity with a threshold on the set of records R to obtain a candidate set S. S can be defined as a set containing all pairs of records (r_1, r_2) such that $(r_1, r_2) \geq$ threshold. Cosine similarity is defined as

$$C(x, y) = \frac{\vec{x} \cdot \vec{y}}{||x|| \cdot ||y||} = \frac{\sum_i x_i y_i}{\sqrt{|x|} \cdot \sqrt{|y|}} \qquad (2)$$

2. Secondly, the records pairs in S are clustered into disjoint sets C = $\{C1, C2, ..., Ck\}$. Then based on a proposed algorithm, the crowd examines the clusters and issues their results.
3. We experimentally compared our technique to some existing models. Our results showed that our proposed approach outperforms some works by incurring low crowdsourcing cost and offering a high accuracy of deduplication.

3.1   Solitary Cluster Generation Algorithm

This section introduces and discusses the algorithm used in the cluster generation. Reducing the cost metric is the goal in this section. Crowd confidence [10] is defined as the fraction of humans who inspected a record pair (r_1, r_2) and inferred them to be of the same entity. The crowd-based similarity score is set as $R \times R \rightarrow [0, 1]$, such that the crowd's confidence $f_c(r_1, r_2)$ implies that $r_1 = r_2$. If the record pair was eliminated in the machine-based technique step, $f_c(r_1, r_2) = 0$ is set. Motivated by Bonchi et al. [34] categorical way of clustering in chromatic correlation clustering, where clusters are formed in triangles, we define in this paper another crowd confidence $f_t(r_1, r_2, r_3)$ where $((r_1, r_2), (r_1, r_3), (r_2, r_3)) \in E$ are the set of edges in E, forming a cluster in a form of a triangle. We term this score as the Triangular crowd confidence. The triangular crowd confidence can be defined as the sum of all the $f_c(r_1, r_2)$ in a cluster, divided by the number of total edges in the cluster. If $f_t(r_1, r_2, r_3) \geq$ a set threshold, then the cluster can be formed and inferred that all the records in the triangle belong to the same real world entity, otherwise they are not.

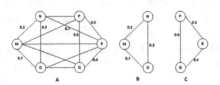

Fig. 1. An undirected graph with examples of crowd's confidence scores.

a. For example if edge (n,o) is chosen as pivot in Fig. 1A and selecting all other objects $x \in R'$ for which there is a triangle $\langle m, n, o \rangle$, it is impossible to form a cluster like in Fig. 1B, because the triangle crowd confidence $f_t(m,n,o)$ gives 0.4 which is less than the triangle crowd confidence threshold 0.5. This implies that the records do not belong to the same entity.

b. Whereas in Fig. 1C a cluster can be formed. For example selecting edge (p,q) as a pivot and all other objects $x \in R'$ for which there is a triangle $\langle p, q, r \rangle$, it is possible to form a cluster. One can notice that the crowd's confidence $f_c(q,r)$ is less than the crowd's confidence threshold 0.5. But calculating the triangle crowd confidence $f_t(p,q,r)$ gives 0.5 which is equal to the triangle crowd confidence threshold 0.5. Hence we assume, though one edge has a crowd's confidence less than its threshold, their triangle crowd confidence is the same or greater than the threshold, thus a cluster can be formed. It is inferred that the records belong to the same real world entity.

$$\Lambda'(R) = \sum_{r_i, r_j \in R. i < j} x_{i,j} \cdot (1 - f_c(r_i, r_j)) + \sum_{r_i, r_j \in R. i < j} (1 - x_{i,j}) \cdot (1 - f_c(r_i, r_j))$$

(3)

In Eq. 3 if two records pairs r_i and r_j are in the same cluster, then $x_{i,j} = 1$, otherwise $x_{i,j} = 0$. Since chromatic-correlation clustering is an instance of correlation clustering, and minimization of metric cost $\Lambda'(R)$ in Eq. 3 is NP-hard under correlation clustering, we conclude that minimization of metric cost $\Lambda'(R)$ in Eq. 3 is NP-hard under chromatic-correlation clustering too. In Fig. 1 for example if all clusters were formed, the solution clusters in Fig. 1B and C formed from Fig. 1A, will have a cost of 7 which is equal to the number of edges eliminated. In this paper, under human-machine-based technique, motivated by the chromatic balls algorithm [34], we adopt an edge as the pivot. This implies that rather than a single record r_i taken as a pivot, a pair of objects (r_i and r_j) is chosen. The adoption of the edge as pivot is non-trivial since they are a categorical algorithm in chromatic balls and clusters are constructed one-by-one and the i-th ($i > 1$) cluster is dependent on the first $i - 1$ clusters. Thus, employing the edge pivot into our algorithm implies that the clusters are to be generated one at a time which is time wasting and presents huge crowd overheads. In this paper, we will present the constructing of multiple clusters, reducing the total time needed to complete the generation of the clusters.

Our human-edge-pivot pseudo code is summarized in Algorithm 1. It is a simple edge as a pivot algorithm adopted from [34]. It takes into account the edges in order to build the clusters. The pivot chosen in each iteration of the algorithm is an edge, a pair of objects, and not a vertex, a single object. The input of the human-edge-pivot includes an undirected graph $G = (V_r$ and $E_s)$, where R contains records of each vertex in V_r and each $(r_i, r_j) \in E_s$ that corresponds to a pair of record in S. Our output is the set of disjoint clusters $C = \{C1, C2, ..., Ck\}$, when put together, they form R. A set R' which is initially equal to R, is initialized to keep all the vertices yet to be assigned to a cluster. At each iteration, an edge (r_i, r_j) is randomly selected as a pivot (line 5). With edge (r_i, r_j) as pivot,

---

Algorithm 1. Human-Edge-Pivot Algorithm

Require: an undirected graph $G = (V_r$ and $E_s)$ where V_r are the records in R and E_s are the edges corresponding to a record pair in the candidate set, S.
Ensure: A set of clusters, C.
 1: **Initialize** an empty set, C.
 2: **Initialize** Cc as an empty set.
 3: $R' \leftarrow R$; $i \leftarrow 1$.
 4: **While** there exists (r_i, r_j) $\epsilon R'$ such that (r_i, r_j) ϵ E do.
 5: **Randomly** pick (r_i, r_j) $\epsilon R'$ as an edge pivot, such that (r_i, r_j) ϵ E.
 6: **Select** all other objects r_k $\epsilon R'$ for which there is a triangle $\langle r_i, r_j, r_k \rangle$.
 7: **Add** (r_i, r_j), (r_i, r_k) and (r_j, r_k) to Cc
 8: **Issue** Cc to the crowd
 9: **For** each edge in Cc do.
10: **Calculate** $f_c(r_i, r_j)$.
11: **If** the crowd decides that $f_t(r_i, r_j, r_k) \geq 0.5$ then
12: **Put** Cc into C.
13: **Remove** all edges and vertices in G.
14: $C(r_k) \leftarrow$ i.
15: $i \leftarrow i{+}1$.
16: **return** C.

---

all other edges $r_k \epsilon R'$ for which a triangle $\langle r_i, r_j, r_k \rangle$ has records belonging to the same real world entity or not, that is (r_i, r_j), (r_i, r_k) and (r_j, r_k) are selected and put in Cc and is issued to the crowd (lines 6–8). Where the crowd then decides which pair of records are equal. In lines 9–11, the algorithm calculates the crowd's confidence $f_c(r_i, r_j)$ for all the edges and further calculates the triangular crowd confidence $f_t(r_i, r_j, r_k)$. If the result $f_t(r_i, r_j, r_k) \geq 0.5$ a cluster is formed around the triangle and all edges and records are removed from G (lines 12 and 13). Otherwise the algorithm recursively selects another edge. In lines 14 and 15, all other edges and objects remaining in R' are made single clusters. Finally, a cluster C containing all disjoint clusters is returned and the algorithm terminates.

Triangle Cluster-Based HIT. In Fig. 2, we show an example of a user interface which we developed for a triangle cluster-based HIT for the crowd. On the interface, we have a four-labelled column; 1. Record pairs column, which shows the edges and ID's of the records. 2. Product details, which has descriptions of the records. 3. Prices of the products. 4. Your choice, which allows the user to check the radio buttons after making their comparisons for each pair. The user checks 'same' for the records being identical or 'not same' if otherwise. Note that the submit button is disabled and has a caption of (2 of 3), which means there is one more choice to be made. The user has not made a choice on the third pair of records, thus they cannot proceed to submit the answers. After all choices have been made the submit button will be active and with a click away, the answers would be submitted.

Computational Complexity. The computational complexities of our algorithm are the pivots selection and building the clusters. Choosing a random edge as a pivot requires $O(m \log n)$ time, where $n = |V|$ and $m = |E|$. With random priorities, selecting a random edge as a pivot can be implemented by

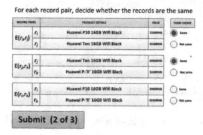

Fig. 2. A triangle cluster-based HIT with three records.

building a priority queue of edges. Whether an edge in the graph is selected as pivot or not, the edge is removed once from the priority queue. Also, a single cluster that is being built, needs to access all of its neighbors of the pivot edge (r_i, r_j). The neighbors of each pivot edge chosen are not considered again because forming the current cluster means removing it from the set of uncovered objects at the end of the iteration. The process of selecting objects into the current cluster involves visiting each edge at most once and it takes $O(m)$ time. Finally, we can infer that the complexity in computing our algorithm is $O(m \log n)$.

3.2 Compound Clustering

In Algorithm 1, it is evident that in each iteration, a set of edges which may form a triangular cluster is issued to the crowd for comparisons to determine in their answers whether the records belong to the same entity. The running time of our algorithm depends solely on the number of iterations. In order to reduce the running time, we reduce the number of iterations by simultaneously creating multiple clusters in each iteration through the selection of only one edge as a pivot.

In Fig. 3A, all the edges have the same probability of being selected as a pivot in Algorithm refAlgorithmsps1. Depending on which edge is selected as pivot, other edges may end up being pruned from the graph and thus not being issued to the crowd. For example, selecting edge (O, Q) in Algorithm 1 as pivot, human-edge-pivot will remove triangle $\langle O, Q, U \rangle$ and submit it to the crowd. Assuming a cluster is formed based on the crowd's results, and then only one cluster will be formed. That is removing vertex Q from the graph also eliminates other edges which any of them would have been a good candidate for a pivot to build multiple clusters around. Implying the problem in executing Algorithm 1 still persists.

Our next algorithm, which is motivated by the lazy chromatic balls algorithm [34], basically tries to minimize the chances of randomly selecting a bad edge as a pivot. Given a vertex $r_i \in R$, let $d(r_i)$ be the number of edges incident to r_i. Also, we denote by $\Delta(r_i) = \max d(r_i)$ and $\lambda(r_i) = \arg \max d(r_i)$. During each iteration, firstly, a vertex r_i is selected with a probability directly proportional to $\Delta(r_i)$. That is a vertex r_i with the highest number of edges to it. Secondly,

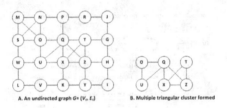

Fig. 3. An example of a compound clustering.

among the neighbors of r_i with probability proportional to $d(r_j, \lambda(r_i))$, another vertex r_j is selected. With the edge pivot (r_i, r_j), the algorithm may form clusters by adding all vertices r_k such that $\langle r_i, r_j, r_k \rangle$ is a triangle. Furthermore, it keeps adding vertices r_k in the cluster as long as they form a triangle $\langle W, X, Z \rangle$, where X is either r_i or r_j, and Z can be any other vertex that belongs to the present cluster. In the Fig. 3, vertices Q and X have the maximum number of edges, with 5 each. We therefore choose one of them as the first pivot vertex with higher probability than the others. Assuming we set $r_i = X$ as first vertex, then among the neighbors of X, we select r_j which has the next higher number of edges with probability proportional to $d(r_j, \lambda(r_i))$. The higher the edges incident to a vertex, the higher the chances of the vertex being chosen. Q would likely be chosen as the second vertex, therefore making (X, Q) the selected edge as pivot. Then, vertices $\{Q, X, Z\}$ forms a triangle and a temporary cluster is formed. Then, vertex U also enters, because it can also form a triangle $\langle O, Q, U \rangle$ with O and Q which is already in the temporary cluster. Vertex T comes in as well because X is also in the cluster and forms another triangle $\langle T, X, Z \rangle$. A temporary cluster demonstrated in Fig. 3B is finally generated. Then the temporary cluster is then issued to the crowd to be examined for similarities between the pairwise records within it, to determine whether the records are of the same real world entity. After the crowd has calculated the crowd's confidence $f_c(r_1, r_2)$ of each edge or pair of records, the triangle crowd confidence $f_t(p, q, r)$ of each single triangle in the big cluster are calculated too. Should triangle crowd confidence $f_t(p, q, r)$ be less than the threshold set, the corresponding triangle is removed from the cluster and added back to the $G = (V_r, E_s)$. The iteration continues until the algorithm terminates. Finally, the remaining triangles are put in a single cluster and passed to the crowd to examine whether the records belong to the same real world entity.

Computational Complexity. Similar to human-edge-pivot, the computational complexity is the running time which is determined by the selection of the edge-pivot and further building of the different clusters. In selecting the edge-pivot, the first vertex to be chosen can be implemented with a priority queue with priorities Δx rnd, where rnd is any random number. For all objects, it needs to calculate for Δ which takes $O(n + m)$. To deal with the queue itself needs $O(n \log n)$, because at each iteration each object is either added to or removed from the queue only once. Having already chosen u as the first vertex,

v is selected as the second vertex by analyzing all neighbors of u which have not been chosen. Throughout the execution of one iteration, for each vertex u, its neighbors are visited only once taking $O(m)$ time. Lastly, to build the clusters requires $O(m)$ time, because accessing each edge during each visit of the graph requires $O(1)$ times. The computational complexity is thus $O(n(\log n) + m)$.

4 Experiments

In this section, we performed experiments and evaluated the results of the proposed hybrid approach against existing works; CrowdEr [5], TransM [6], Transnode [8] and ACD [10], in terms of deduplication accuracy, the number of crowdsourced record pairs, and the number of iterations performed by the crowd.

4.1 Setup of Experiment

Three benchmark datasets in crowd-machine based deduplication literature [5–7]; Paper [35], Product [36] and Restaurant [21] datasets were used. In Table 3 are the number of records and entities in each dataset. In the CrowdEr, the authors did not indicate the algorithm for clustering crowdsourced record pairs. Like in the work of ACD, we also adopt the sorted neighbourhood clustering algorithm [7] on the answers from the crowd to generate clusters. We denote this implementation as $CrowdEr^*$ in the experiments of this work. Firstly, we applied the F-1 measure which was also used in work [6] to scale the deduplication accuracy of all the approaches. Furthermore, we also evaluated the cost of the methods used in the experiment in terms of the number of record pairs incurred in crowdsourcing.

Table 3. Characteristics of datasets and crowd answers.

Datasets	# of records	# of entities	# of candidate pairs S	Rate of errors of crowds (3w)	Rate of errors of crowds (5w)
Paper	997	191	29,581	23%	21%
Product	858	752	4,788	0.8%	0.2%
Restaurant	3,073	1,076	3,154	9%	5%

Similarity-Machine-Based Approach:

In the experiments, we needed to generate a set of candidate pairs S for all the methods. We used the Cosine similarity function to compute the machine-based similarity score for the pairs of records. The threshold value was set at $t = 0.4$. This implies that, only pairs of records with scores greater than 0.4 are classified as candidate set S and have been recorded on each dataset in Table 3.

Crowdsourcing Platform:

We must note that the evaluation method was adopted from previous works such as in CrowdEr [5], TransM [6] and ACD [10]. In this work, we employed as a crowdsourcing platform, the Amazon Mechanical Turk (AMT). All pairs of records in the candidate set S for each dataset were posted to the AMT. For consistency, all the methods compared in this work used the same answers which were stored in a local file (for faster retrieval of record pairs instead of accessing the crowdsourcing platforms several times). We contacted the authors of CrowdEr [5] and ACD [10] to obtain and reuse in the experimental evaluation, the answers they obtained from their experiments. The results were as follows:

1. An HIT is made up of twenty (20) pairs of records each. Each record pair involved inputs from 3 workers (3w), where workers underwent qualification test before they could work on the HITs, if they passed successfully. They were paid 2 cents upon completion of a HIT.
2. To reduce the overheads of the crowd, for each record pair, the involvement of 5 workers (5w) were needed. Each HIT had only 10 pairs of records. In Table 3, from the results given to us by authors from the previous works, we show incorrect answers from the crowd under 5w and 3w settings. It can be seen that the results from the 5w setting effect accurate results but at a higher cost. The error rate from the answers for product and restaurant is below 10% and that of Paper is above 20%. This implies that comparing restaurant and product to paper, they are easier to deduplicate.

4.2   Evaluation with Some Existing Methods

In this subsection of the experiments, we assess and compare some of the existing methods with the proposed method based on;

1. Deduplication accuracy using the F1-measure which was used in other works.
2. Crowdsourcing overheads. That is the cost incurred in terms of crowdsourcing the record pairs.
3. Crowdsourcing efficiency. The efficiency is measured in terms of the number of iterations a crowd examines the record pairs.

Deduplication Accuracy:

In Fig. 4, we showed results of the experiments performed under both 3w and 5w settings, and evaluated the data deduplication accuracy of each method on the three datasets using the F-1 measure, which is the number of crowdsourced pairs of records. On all datasets under both settings, comparatively, $CrowdEr^*$ provided the highest deduplication accuracy, followed by ACD. Our algorithm, provided the third highest accuracy, thus outperforming TransNode and TransM. TransNode provided the least accuracy followed by TransM on all datasets. On paper dataset especially, TransM and TransNode provided very poor accuracy because these works are prone to errors made by the crowd. On product and restaurant datasets, they performed better as a result of errors being reduced

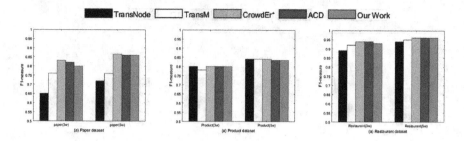

Fig. 4. Comparison of deduplication accuracy.

by the workers. Our algorithm shows the same accuracy as compared to ACD and $CrowdEr^*$, with slight differences in the margins. In conclusion, on product and restaurant, all methods, comparably performed fairly equally which implies that the crowd may have provided accurate results.

Crowdsourcing Cost:
In Fig. 5, though $CrowdEr^*$ provided better accuracy as shown (Fig. 4) and described earlier, it incurs crowdsourcing overheads particularly on paper dataset under both settings. This could be due to issuing all the candidate set S to the crowd. Like in data deduplication accuracy results, the algorithm is almost comparable to ACD when it comes to crowdsourcing cost, though, our technique incurs a little more cost than ACD. On paper and product under both settings, TransNode and TransM incur little cost compared to our technique, ACD and $CrowdEr^*$. However, on restaurant under both settings, TransNode and TransM incur more cost compared to our technique and ACD. This could be due to the fact that during processing of the pairs of records, the crowd made reasonably smaller number of errors.

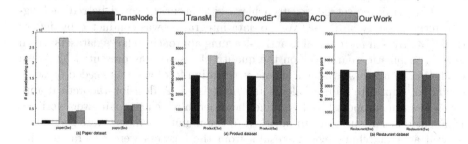

Fig. 5. Comparison of crowdsourcing costs.

Crowdsourcing Efficiency: Figure 6 shows the comparisons of all methods' crowdsourcing efficiency. The graphs illustrate, in each method, the number of

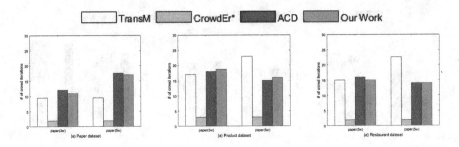

Fig. 6. Comparison of crowdsourcing efficiency.

crowd iterations. *CrowdEr** needs the very least number of iterations, less than 2 iterations, because it issues all the candidate set S in one group. The other methods, as can be seen are all comparable on all datasets under both 3w and 5w settings. Our algorithm's efficiency is superior to TransM and *CrowdEr**. ACD is the only method that has better efficiency compared to our method.

We could summarize, based on the experiments and comparisons, that our algorithm does provide a high data deduplication accuracy incurring relative crowdsourcing cost compared to some works. Also, we can conclude that the crowdsourcing efficiency is on a par with some of the existing works. Our work can therefore be considered good under crowd-based data deduplication.

5   Related Work

Elmagarmid et al. presented a survey [2] on ER deduplication. Other works were presented on how deduplication benefited from human interaction. An ER method using active learning, which allows a user to label a training set interactively, was proposed by Sarawagi et al. [12]. Their method showed that the size of the training set needed to achieve high accuracy could be reduced significantly. A study on pay-as-you-go data integration was conducted by Jeffery et al. [13]. Also, a more scalable active-learning approach to large datasets which gave probabilistic guarantees on the quality of results was presented by Arasu et al. [14]. In all these systems, a user verification feedback was needed on some candidate duplicate pairs of elements that existed. A decision-theoretical approach was thus proposed to determine the order in which the pairs were verified. Different types of questions to be asked to community members were generated, as well as a matching schema results from the answers were generated. This schema matching in online communities was studied by McCann et al. [15].

Significant works have been developed under crowdsourcing under several platforms for various tasks in both industrial and academic communities (a recent survey [16]). Relational database query language SQL was extended to CrowdSQL by enabling crowd-based operators, and developed CrowdDB database, presented by Franklin et al. [17,18]. Parameswaran et al. [19] developed a database system with the help of the crowd, to answer declarative queries posted over relational data and called it Deco. A hybrid crowd-machine data integration system was created by Jeffery et al. [13,20].

A data deduplication method, called Crowd-clustering [9] that identifies records which belongs to the same category was designed. A system, though it provides high precision of data deduplication, but incurs a huge crowdsourcing cost was proposed [5]. Other methods which reduce cost but compromise data deduplication were presented in TransM, GCER and TransNode [6–8]. Finally, for better accuracy of deduplication and incurring moderate crowdsourcing overheads, ACD which adopts a correlation clustering algorithm under a crowd-based setting was proposed [10]. Li et al. [24] presented a mechanism that firstly, uses similarity-based and knowledge-based rules to obtain matching pairs, and developed some algorithms to learn the rules. Verroios et al. [25] proposed an approach that makes a combination of two common interfaces for the crowd to make some key observations. In the work of Altowim et al. [27], ProgressER, a progressive approach to relational ER, was proposed and aimed at producing a result in its highest quality, given a constraint specified by the user on the resolution budget.

Many research works done in record linkage, targeting link records representing the same entity across database using crowdsourcing. Records pairs are pruned based on assumptions. In data deduplication, such assumptions cannot be inferred, thus irrelevant under data deduplication. Using crowds to do record linkage of online pages for large collections was proposed by Demartini et al. [22]. In Gokhale et al. [23], without involving developers, how to do hands-off crowdsourcing record linkage was studied. Human power was used to build up classifiers for the dataset in Arasu et al. [14]. In [5], though human power was used, the technique faced challenges processing the records that presented different entities. Existing algorithms were not compared under the same framework making it hard for practitioners to make the appropriate choice of algorithm. Thus, Zheng et al. [26] presented a survey on existing algorithms, making comparisons and performing comprehensive evaluation. Demartini et al. [28] discussed an overview of the different existing techniques under the scenarios such as natural language processing, semantic web, machine learning, data management, information retrieval, and multimedia for which human-machine systems have already been used.

6   Conclusion

In this work, a hybrid deduplication method has been proposed. The hybrid deduplication method uses cosine similarity and a chromatic correlation clustering which to the best of our knowledge has not been used in entity resolution. We experimentally compared the proposed algorithm with other works. In classifying duplicate, one can clearly see it significantly reduced the errors made by the crowd. Also, compared with some other works, ours improved the deduplication accuracy efficiently. Finally, the algorithm presented, improved the deduplication accuracy incurring minimum crowdsourcing cost compared to some of the work. In future, we can further improve on the clustering, by looking at the output clustering made up of a pre-defined number of K clusters.

Acknowledgment. We thank Anthony Padua Bangdome and Barbie Eghan-Yartel for providing insightful comments that helped improve the paper. We are most grateful.

References

1. Christen, P.: Data Matching: Concepts and Techniques for Record Linkage, Entity Resolution, and Duplicate Detection. Data-Centric Systems and Applications. Springer, Berlin (2012). https://doi.org/10.1007/978-3-642-31164-2
2. Elmagarmid, A.K., Ipeirotis, P.G., Verykios, V.S.: Duplicate record detection: a survey. IEEE Trans. Knowl. Data Eng. **19**(1), 1–16 (2007)
3. Jain, A.K., Murty, M.N., Flynn, P.J.: Data clustering: a review. ACM Comput. Surv. **31**(3), 264–323 (1999)
4. Winkler, W.: Overview of record linkage and current research directions. Technical report, Statistical Research Division, U.S. Bureau of the Census, Washington, DC (2006)
5. Wang, J., Kraska, T., Franklin, M.J., Feng, J.: CrowdER: crowdsourcing entity resolution. Proc. VLDB Endow. **5**(11), 1483–1494 (2012)
6. Wang, J., Li, G., Kraska, T., Franklin, M.J., Feng, J.: Leveraging transitive relations for crowdsourced joins. In: Proceedings of the 2013 International Conference on Management of Data, pp. 229–240. ACM (2013)
7. Whang, S.E., Lofgren, P., Garcia-Molina, H.: Question selection for crowd entity resolution. Proc. VLDB Endow. **6**(6), 349–360 (2013)
8. Vesdapunt, N., Bellare, K., Dalvi, N.: Crowdsourcing algorithms for entity resolution. Proc. VLDB Endow. **7**(12), 1071–1082 (2014)
9. Gomes, R., Welinder, P., Krause, A., Perona, P.: Crowdclustering. In: NIPS, pp. 558–566 (2011)
10. Wang, S., Xiao, X., Lee, C.H.: Crowd-based deduplication: an adaptive approach. In: Proceedings of the 2015 ACM SIGMOD International Conference on Management of Data, pp. 1263–1277. ACM, May 2015
11. Kopcke, H., Thor, A., Rahm, E.: Evaluation of entity resolution approaches on real-world match problems. PVLDB **3**(1), 484–493 (2010)
12. Sarawagi, S., Bhamidipaty, A.: Interactive deduplication using active learning. In: KDD, pp. 269–278 (2002)
13. Jeffery, S.R., Franklin, M.J., Halevy, A.Y.: Pay-as-you-go user feedback for dataspace systems. In: SIGMOD Conference, pp. 847–860 (2008)
14. Arasu, A., Gotz, M., Kaushik, R.: On active learning of record matching packages. In: SIGMOD Conference, pp. 783–794 (2010)
15. McCann, R., Shen, W., Doan, A.: Matching schemas in online communities: a web 2.0 approach. In: ICDE, pp. 110–119 (2008)
16. Doan, A., Ramakrishnan, R., Halevy, A.Y.: Crowdsourcing systems on the world-wide web. Commun. ACM **54**(4), 86–96 (2011)
17. Feng, A., et al.: CrowdDB: query processing with the VLDB crowd. PVLDB **4**(12), 1387–1390 (2011)
18. Franklin, M.J., Kossmann, D., Kraska, T., Ramesh, S., Xin, R.: CrowdDB: answering queries with crowdsourcing. In: SIGMOD, pp. 61–72 (2011)
19. Parameswaran, A., Park, H., Garcia-Molina, H., Polyzotis, N., Widom, J.: Deco: declarative crowdsourcing. Technical report, Stanford University. http://ilpubs. stanford.edu:8090/1015/
20. Jeffery, S.R., Sun, L., DeLand, M., Pendar, N., Barber, R., Galdi, A.: Arnold: declarative crowd-machine data integration. In: CIDR (2013)

21. http://dbs.uni-leipzig.de/Abt-Buy.zip
22. Demartini, G., Difallah, D.E., Cudré-Mauroux, P.: Zencrowd:leveraging probabilistic reasoning and crowdsourcing techniques for large-scale entity linking. In: WWW, pp. 469–478 (2012)
23. Gokhale, C., et al.: Corleone: hands-off crowdsourcing for entity matching. In: Proceedings of the 2014 ACM SIGMOD International Conference on Management of Data (2014)
24. Li, G.: Human-in-the-loop data integration. Proc. VLDB Endow. **10**(12), 2006–2017 (2017)
25. Verroios, V., Garcia-Molina, H., Papakonstantinou, Y.: Waldo: an adaptive human interface for crowd entity resolution. In: Proceedings of the 2017 ACM International Conference on Management of Data, pp. 1133–1148. ACM, May 2017
26. Zheng, Y., Li, G., Li, Y., Shan, C., Cheng, R.: Truth inference in crowdsourcing: is the problem solved? Proc. VLDB Endow. **10**(5), 541–552 (2017)
27. Altowim, Y., Kalashnikov, D.V., Mehrotra, S.: ProgressER: adaptive progressive approach to relational entity resolution. ACM Trans. Knowl. Discov. Data (TKDD) **12**(3), 33 (2018)
28. Demartini, G., Difallah, D.E., Gadiraju, U., Catasta, M.: An introduction to hybrid human-machine information systems. Found. Trends® Web Sci. **7**(1), 1–87 (2017)
29. Xiao, C., Wang, W., Lin, X., Yu, J.X., Wang, G.: Efficient similarity joins for near-duplicate detection. ACM Trans. Database Syst. (TODS) **36**(3), 15 (2011)
30. Bayardo, R.J., Ma, Y., Srikant, R.: Scaling up all pairs similarity search. In: WWW, pp. 131–140 (2007)
31. Chaudhuri, S., Ganti, V., Kaushik, R.: A primitive operator for similarity joins in data cleaning. In: ICDE, p. 5 (2006)
32. Hassanzadeh, O., Chiang, F., Lee, H.C., Miller, R.J.: Framework for evaluating clustering algorithms in duplicate detection. Proc. VLDB Endow. **2**(1), 1282–1293 (2009)
33. Chen, Z., Kalashnikov, D.V., Mehrotra, S.: Exploiting context analysis for combining multiple entity resolution systems. In: Proceedings of the 2009 ACM SIGMOD International Conference on Management of data (2009)
34. Bonchi, F., Gionis, A., Gullo, F., Tsourakakis, C.E., Ukkonen, A.: Chromatic correlation clustering. ACM Trans. Knowl. Discov. Data (TKDD) **9**(4), 34 (2015)
35. http://www.cs.umass.edu/~mccallum/data/cora-refs.tar.gz
36. http://www.cs.utexas.edu/users/ml/riddle/data/restaurant.tar.gz

Secure Data Deduplication with Ownership Management and Sharing in Cloud Storage

Hua Ma, Guohua Tian$^{(\boxtimes)}$, Zhenhua Liu, and Linchao Zhang

School of Mathematics and Statistics, Xidian University, Xi'an 710126, China
gh_tian0621@163.com

Abstract. Recently, some researchers adopt key-encrypting key (KEK) tree to realize efficient ownership management in deduplication scheme. However, none of the existing schemes realize the data sharing based on KEK tree. In this paper, we propose a randomized client-side deduplication scheme that alleviates duplicate-faking attack and uses randomized file tags to resist the offline brute-force attack launched by outside adversary. Besides, we propose a novel data sharing technique based on KEK tree. Security and efficiency analyses show that our scheme achieves the desired security requirements while saving system resource efficiently.

Keywords: Deduplication · Data sharing · Key-encrypting key tree
Ownership management

1 Introduction

The ever-increasing volume of outsourced data challenges the storage capacity of cloud computing, as well as network bandwidth [1]. Therefore, the service providers employ client-side deduplication to minimize service overheads, where the cloud server only requests the users to upload the unduplicated data, and all valid users access the unique data copy through a link. However, various security issues surrounding outsourced data are watched closely.

For the privacy of outsourced data in deduplication, Douceur et al. [2] proposed Convergent Encryption (CE) to realize deduplication over encrypted data, where the data hash value is used as the encryption key to encrypt data. Bellare et al. [3] presented Message-Locked Encryption (MLE) and gave a formalized privacy model and corresponding proof for CE. Subject to the limited keyspace, the MLE-based deduplication schemes are vulnerable to offline brute-force attack (BFA)[4]. For a predictable file, the adversary can acquire the plaintext with some knowledge (eg. a hash value) by constructing a lot of candidate files and verifying them. Bellare et al. [4] try to address this problem by introducing an additional key server (KS) to extend the key space of data. However, Liu et al. [5] argued that the KS is very difficult to meet in commercial cloud services. Thus, how to resist the offline BFA is a challenge that remains to be solved.

© Springer Nature Singapore Pte Ltd. 2018
F. Li et al. (Eds.): FCS 2018, CCIS 879, pp. 168–176, 2018.
https://doi.org/10.1007/978-981-13-3095-7_13

Considering the secure ownership authentication, Halevi et al. [6] presented a novel notion called Proof-of-Ownership (PoW) and gave three concrete constructions based on Merkle Hash tree (MHT). PoW ensures that only the user who actually owns the file can obtain valid ownership without uploading the file itself. Li et al. [7] proposed an efficient version, which supports efficient ownership authentication by challenging multiple data blocks simultaneously. Even so, the malicious user who owns the data may launch a duplicate-faking attack (DFA) by identifying the data and uploads a poison version in the initial upload phase [8]. Then, the subsequent uploader only can access the poison data after uploading the data. Wang et al. [8] proposed a novel deduplication scheme, called TrDup, which can trace the malicious user by incorporating traceable signatures with MLE. Kim et al. [9] presented a novel solution that requires the cloud server to generate the second file tag with encrypted data in the initial upload phase.

In the commercial cloud services, the frequent ownership changes weaken the forward and backward secrecy of the outsourced data. Hur et al. [10] proposed an ownership management technique that requires the cloud server to update encrypted data while the ownership changes and the corresponding updated key is distributed through a key-encrypting key (KEK) tree securely. Jiang et al. [11] presented a lazy update strategy to improve the performance of KEK-tree-based ownership management technique. Many other applications of KEK tree in data deduplication, such as data sharing, are worth exploring.

In this paper, we propose a secure client-side deduplication scheme. Our main contributions are listed as follows:

- We propose a randomized deduplication scheme that alleviates the duplicate-faking attack and adopts randomized file tags to deter the offline BFA launched by outside adversary (Out-offline BFA).
- We present a novel data sharing technique based on the KEK tree [10] while realizing ownership management.

2 Preliminaries

1. **Discrete logarithm problem (DLP):** For a group $\mathbb{G}$ with prime order p and generator g, given $g^a \in \mathbb{G}$, $a \in \mathbb{Z}_p$, there is no polynomial time algorithm can compute a with non-negligible probability.
2. **The lifted ElGamal encryption [12]:**
   - $Gen(1^\lambda)$: Inputs the security parameter 1^λ, the algorithm outputs a secret key $sk = (\mathbb{G}, g, x)$ and public key $pk = (\mathbb{G}, g, h)$, where $\mathbb{G}$ is a cyclic group with prime order p and generator g, $x \in_R \mathbb{Z}_p$, $h = g^x \in \mathbb{G}$.
   - $Enc(pk, m)$: Inputs the public key pk and a plaintext $m \in \mathbb{Z}_p$ the algorithm outputs $c = (c_1, c_2) = (g^y, g^m \cdot h^y)$ where $y \in_R \mathbb{Z}_p$.
   - $Dec(sk, c)$: Inputs secret key sk and (c_1, c_2), outputs $\frac{c_2}{(c_1)^x} = \frac{g^m \cdot h^y}{g^{xy}} = g^m$.
3. **Static KEK tree [10]:** For a four-level KEK tree shown in Fig. 1, each node $n_j (1 \leq j \leq 15)$ holds a KEK value KEK_j. Each valid user $u_t (1 \leq t \leq 8)$ maintains a unique leaf node and a set of path keys.(eg. The path keys of

u_1 is $PK_1 = \{KEK_1, KEK_3, KEK_7, KEK_{15}\}$). Suppose that the ownership group is $G = \{u_1, u_2, u_5, u_6, u_7, u_8\}$, the cloud server will obtain a set of root node value $KEK(G) = \{KEK_3, KEK_{14}\}$ for the minimum cover set of G. The elements of $KEK(G)$ are used as KEKs to encrypt the group key.

3   Problem Formulation

3.1   Cloud Storage System

Fig. 2 shows the descriptive system model for cloud storage:

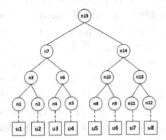

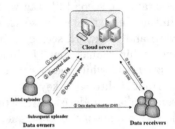

Fig. 1. Static KEK tree.   **Fig. 2.** Cloud storage system.

Cloud Server (CS): CS deduplicates the outsourced data uploaded by users, and stores the deduplicated data locally.

Data Owner: The entity who wants to outsource data to the cloud server. If the data do not exist in CS, the data owner is called the initial uploader, otherwise known as a subsequent uploader. The valid data owners are allowed to share their data with another user through a data sharing identifier (DSI).

Data Receiver: The user who can access the outsourced data with DSI issued by valid data owners.

3.2   Adversarial Model

We consider two adversaries [11] in our adversary model.

Outside Adversary: The outside adversary may learn some knowledge of the outsourced data, and pretends as a common data owner to interact with CS.

Inside Adversary: We regard CS as an honest-but-curious (HBC) inside adversary, which learns as much knowledge of data as possible while executing the assigned tasks honestly. Besides, S does not collude with outside adversaries.

3.3 Security Requirements

1. **Privacy** [10]: Both outside and inside the adversary should be prevented from accessing the plaintext of outsourced data.
2. **Integrity** [10]: The proposed scheme should deter malicious adversary to launch a DFA, and allows data owners to check the tag consistency of data.
3. **Forward and backward secrecy** [10]: The proposed scheme should guarantee the forward and backward secrecy by deterring the revoked users and unauthorized data owners to access the plaintext of the outsourced data.
4. **Out-offline BFA resilience** [5]: The proposed scheme should prevent the outside adversary who obtains the file tag illicitly from acquiring the plaintext by constructing a lot of candidate files and verifying them.

4 The Proposed Scheme

Setup(1^λ): Let $\mathbb{G}$ be a multiplicative group with prime order p and generator g. Let $H : \{0,1\}^* \to \{0,1\}^\lambda$ be a collision-resilient hash function. Besides, CS picks a secret key $x \in_R \mathbb{Z}_p$ and generates the corresponding public key $h = g^x \in \mathbb{G}$.

Data Encryption: When a data owner u_i wants to upload file F_i to CS, u_i computes the encryption key $FK_i = H(F_i)$ and the encrypted data $FC_i = E(FK_i, F_i)$, where E is a encryption algorithm of traditional symmetric encryption scheme. Then, u_i generates the first randomized file tag $FT_{i,1}$ via lifted ElGamal encryption [12] according to Eq. (1).

$$FT_{i,1} = (c_1, c_2) = (g^y, g^{FK_i} \cdot h^y), (y \in_R \mathbb{Z}_p). \tag{1}$$

$$Ft_{i,1} = g^{FK_i} = c_2/(c_1)^x = (g^{FK_i} \cdot h^y)/g^{xy}. \tag{2}$$

Data Upload: Upon receiving a upload request, CS computes the first file tag $Ft_{i,1}$ by Eq. (2), and searches $Ft_{i,1}$ in CS.

1. *Initial upload:* If $Ft_{i,1}$ is not in CS, u_j upload FC_i to CS. CS constructs a MHT based on FC_i and retains the root value R_{FC_i}. Then, CS picks a random access tag FT_i and sends to u_j. u_j retains FK_i and FT_i.
2. *Subsequent upload:* If $Ft_{i,1}$ exists in CS, CS triggers Li et al.'s **PoW** protocol [7] to verify the ownership of u_j. Due to the space limitation, we omit the detail procedures here.
   - If u_j proves to CS that she/he owns the data successfully, CS returns FT_i to u_j. u_j retains FK_i and FT_i.
   - If u_j fails, CS requests FC_i' from u_j, and constructs the corresponding MHT. Then, CS searches the root value $R_{FC_i'}$ of the new MHT in CS. If $R_{FC_i'}$ is not in CS, CS picks and sends a random access tag FT_i' to u_j and remains FC_i'. Otherwise, CS deletes FC_i' and returns FT_i' to u_j.

Ownership Management: When FC_i is uploaded by u_j initially, CS creates an ownership list $L_i = <Ft_{i,1} \| R_{FC_i} \| FT_i \| G_{FC_i}>$ for FC_i, and inserts u_j into the ownership group G_{FC_i}. Then, CS picks a random group key GK to re-encrypt FC_i according to Eq. (3), and stores $FC_{i,1} \| C_{i,1}$ in cloud storage.

1. For backward secrecy, CS inserts u_j into G_{FC_i} after u_j is identified as a subsequent uploader, and obtains an updated ownership group G'_{FC_i}. As is illustrated in Eqs. (4) and (5), CS computes the new re-encrypted data $FC'_{i,1}$ with a random group key GK'. After that, CS updates $FC_{i,1} \| C_{i,1}$ with $FC'_{i,1} \| C'_{i,1}$.
2. For forward secrecy, CS removes u_t ($\in G_{FC_i}$) from G_{FC_i} after u_j deletes FC_i, and obtains a new ownership group G'_{FC_i}. Then, CS computes the updated data based on Eqs. (4) and (5), and updates $FC_{i,1} \| C_{i,1}$ with $FC'_{i,1} \| C'_{i,1}$.

$$FC_{i,1} = E(GK, FC_i), C_{i,1} = E(KEK, GK), (KEK \in KEK(G_{FC_i})). \quad (3)$$

$$FC_i = D(GK, FC_{i,1}), FC'_{i,1} = E(GK', FC_i). \quad (4)$$

$$C'_{i,1} = E(KEK, GK'), (KEK \in KEK(G'_{FC_i})). \quad (5)$$

Data Download: When u_t wants to download the outsourced data, u_j sends $download \| FT_i \| u_t$ to CS. If $u_t \in G_{FC_i}$, CS returns $FC_{i,1} \| C_{i,1}$ to u_j. Then, u_j decrypts data by Eqs. (6) and (7). u_j can check the integrity of data based on whether the equation $FK_i = H(F'_i)$ holds.

$$KEK = KEK(G_{FC_i}) \cap PK_t, GK = D(KEK, C_{i,1}). \quad (6)$$

$$FC_i = D(GK, FC_{i,1}), \ F_i = D(FK_i, FC_i). \quad (7)$$

Data Sharing: In our scheme, the modification of the leaf node value of u_j does not influence the group key distribution of other users. Based on this characteristic, we propose a novel data sharing technique. When u_j wants to share FC_i stored in cloud storage to a receiver who holds a pair of key $k = (w, v)$, where $w \in_R \mathbb{Z}_p, v = g^w \in \mathbb{G}$. u_j requests CS to replace the leaf node value of u_j with v, and generates data sharing identifier $DSI_{i,j} = T_{i,j} \| K_{i,j}$ according to Eqs. (8) and (9).

$$T_{i,j} = (c_1, c_2) = (g^r, (FT_i \| u_j) \cdot h^r), (r \in_R \mathbb{Z}_p). \quad (8)$$

$$K_{i,j} = (c'_1, c'_2) = (g^m, FK_i \cdot v^m), (m \in_R \mathbb{Z}_p). \quad (9)$$

To access the file F_i, the receiver performs the interactive protocol shown in Fig. 3. Bounded by the security of lifted ElGamal encryption algorithm [12], the receiver can only obtain the data encryption key from $DSI_{i,j}$, and CS only acquires the $FT_i \| u_j$ from $DSI_{i,j}$. Besides, when u_j deletes the file F_i or changes the public key of receiver stored in KEK tree, the $DSI_{i,j}$ will be unavailable. Evidently, the proposed data sharing technique is secure.

Receiver	Cloud server

$$DSI_{i,j} \rightarrow T_{i,j} \text{ and } K_{i,j} \quad \xrightarrow{DSI_{i,j}} \quad DSI_{i,j} \rightarrow T_{i,j} \text{ and } K_{i,j}$$

$$FK_i = \frac{c'_2}{(c'_1)^w} = \frac{FK_i \cdot v^m}{(g^m)^w} \qquad FT_i \| u_j = \frac{c_2}{(c_1)^x} = \frac{(FT_i \| u_j) \cdot h^r}{(g^r)^x}$$

$$\text{If } u_j \text{ is valid:}$$

$$GK = \frac{GK \cdot v^l}{(g^l)^w} \qquad \xleftarrow{FC_{i,1}, C'_{i,1}} \qquad C'_{i,1} = (g^l, GK \cdot v^l), (l \in_R \mathbb{Z}_p).$$

$$FC_i = D(GK, FC_{i,1})$$

$$F_i = D(FK_i, FC_i)$$

Fig. 3. Data sharing protocol

5 Security Analysis

5.1 Privacy

Depended on the security of the MLE algorithm [3], our scheme is PRV\$-CDA security if the data is unpredictable. The PRV\$-CDA means that the encryptions of unpredictable data are indistinguishable from a random string of the same length. Furthermore, CS cannot derive FK_i from the first file tag $Ft_{i,1} = g^{FK_i}$ bounded by the DLP. For the malicious outside adversaries, they cannot access the outsourced data without valid ownership since they never own the data.

5.2 Integrity

During the data upload phase, our scheme can guarantee the normal upload operation of valid users even if the outside adversary has launched a duplicate-faking attack on F_i. Specifically, both the valid data and its poison version are stored in CS. In the download phase, the data owners are allowed to check the integrity of outsourced data.

5.3 Forward Secrecy and Backward Secrecy

Due to the KEK-tree-based ownership management technique, our scheme realizes the identical forward and backward secrecy as that of Hur et al.'s [10] scheme. Thus, we omit the detailed analysis here due to space limitation.

5.4 Out-Offline BFA Resilience

To illustrate a stronger security, we assume that the outside adversary has obtained the first randomized file tag $FT_{i,1}$, or the access tag FT_i. Bounded by the security of lifted ElGamal encryption algorithm [12], the outside adversary is unable to derive the file tags $Ft_{i,1}$ from $FT_{i,1}$. In this case, there is no deterministic connection between the plaintext and the eavesdropped tags. Thus, it is computationally infeasible for outside adversary to obtain the plaintext by constructing a lot of candidate files and verifying them.

Table 1. Comparisons of security attributes

	Tag consistency	Duplicate-faking attack	Proof of ownership	Ownership management	Out-offline BFA	Data sharing
MLE [3]	✓	✗	✗	✗	✗	✗
Kim [9]	✓	✓	✓	✗	✗	✗
Hur [10]	✓	✗	✗	✓	✗	✗
Jiang [11]	✓	✗	✓	✓	✗	✗
Ours	✓	✓	✓	✓	✓	✓

6 Efficiency Analysis

6.1 Comparison of Security Attributes

We compare the security attributes of our scheme with some existing schemes in Table 1. Note that we choose the RCE of MLE as a comparison. Evidently, our scheme provides more comprehensive security for data than other schemes.

6.2 Theoretical Analysis

For a convincing theoretical analysis, we let n and m be the volume of KEK tree and ownership group. Let b and $l(\le b)$ be the number of file blocks and challenged blocks during PoW phase. Besides, the $H, E/D(E_K/D_K), Enc/Dec$ are regard as the evaluation of hash function, symmetric encryption algorithm on file (key) and ElGamal algorithm. Finally, we regard S_K, S_F, S_T and S_{Enc} as the size of the key, file F, and file tag, the ciphertext of Enc, respectively.

Table 2. Comparison of computation costs.

	Initial upload	Subsequent upload	Download	Data sharing
MLE [3]	$E + 2H$	$E + 2H$	$D + 2H$	N/A
Kim [9]	$E + 2H$	$E + 3H$	$D + 2H$	N/A
Hur [10]	$2E + E_K + 2H$	$2E + D + E + E_K + 2H$	$2D + D_K + 2H$	N/A
Jiang [11]	$2E + E_K + (2+b)H$	$2E + D + E_K + (2+l)H$	$2D + D_K + 2H$	N/A
Ours	$2E + E_K + H$ $+Enc + Dec$	$2E + D + E_K + Enc + Dec$ $+\sum_{i=1}^{l}(\log b + 2 - i)H$	$2D + D_K + H$	$3(Enc + Dec)$

Computation Costs: Table 2 shows the computation costs of comparison schemes in different phases. Due to the implementation of ownership management, the computation costs of our scheme is similar to that of Hur's scheme, Jiang's scheme. Notably, our scheme invokes additional operations $Enc + Dec$ during data upload phase to generate randomized file tag to resist offline BFA.

Communication Overheads: Table 3 summarizes the communication overheads of comparison schemes in different phases. Both in the initial and subsequent upload, our scheme consumes the least communication overheads. During the download phase, the communication overhead of our scheme is higher than that of MLE and Kim's scheme, but lower than the other two schemes.

Table 3. Comparison of the communication overheads

	Initial upload	Subsequent upload	Download	Data sharing
MLE [3]	$S_F + S_K + S_T$	$S_F + S_K + S_T$	$S_F + S_K$	N/A
Kim [9]	$S_F + S_T$	$2S_T$	S_F	N/A
Hur [10]	$S_F + S_K + S_T$	$S_F + S_K + S_T$	$S_F + ((n-m)\log\frac{n}{n-m} + 1)S_K$	N/A
Jiang [11]	$S_F + S_K + S_T$	$S_K + (l+1)S_T$	$S_F + ((n-m)\log\frac{n}{n-m} + 2)S_K$	N/A
Ours	$S_F + S_{Enc}$	$S_{Enc} + 2lS_T$	$S_F + (n-m)\log\frac{n}{n-m}S_K$	$S_F + 2S_{Enc}$

7   Conclusion

This paper has proposed a randomized client-side deduplication scheme, which not only resists the brute-force attack and duplicate-faking attack, but also realizes the ownership management and data sharing. We also evaluate the practicality of the proposed scheme via security and efficiency analysis.

Acknowledgment. This work is supported by the Fundamental Research Funds for the Central Universities (XJS17053, JBF181501).

References

1. Pooranian, Z., Conti, M.: RARE: defeating side channels based on data deduplication in cloud storage. In: INFOCOM Workshops CCSNA (2018)
2. Douceur, J., Adya, A., Bolosky, W., Simon, D., Theimer, M.: Reclaiming space from duplicate files in a serverless distributed file system. In: Proceedings of the 22nd International Conference on Distributed Computing Systems, pp. 617–624. IEEE, Vienna (2002)
3. Bellare, M., Keelveedhi, S., Ristenpart, T.: Message-locked encryption and secure deduplication. In: Johansson, T., Nguyen, P.Q. (eds.) EUROCRYPT 2013. LNCS, vol. 7881, pp. 296–312. Springer, Heidelberg (2013). https://doi.org/10.1007/978-3-642-38348-9_18
4. Bellare, M., Keelveedhi, S., Ristenpart, T.: DupLESS: server-aided encryption for deduplicated storage. In: SEC 2013 Proceedings of the 22nd USENIX Conference on Security, pp. 179–194. ACM, Washington (2013)
5. Liu, J., Asokan, N., Pinkas, B.: Secure deduplication of encrypted data without additional independent servers. In: Proceedings of the ACM Conference on Computerand Communications Security, pp. 874–885. ACM, Colorado (2015)

6. Halevi, S., Harnik, D., Pinkas, B., Shulman-Peleg, A.: Proofs of ownership in remote storage systems. In: CCS 2011, pp. 491–500. ACM, Chicago (2011)
7. Li, J., Li, J., Xie, D., Cai, Z.: Secure auditing and deduplicating data in cloud. IEEE Trans. Comput. **65**(8), 2386–2396 (2016)
8. Wang, J., Chen, X., Li, J., Kluczniak, K., Kutylowski, M.: A new secure data deduplication approach supporting user traceability. In: 10th International Conference on Broadband and Wireless Computing, Communication and Applications, BWCCA 2015, pp. 120–124. IEEE, Krakow (2015)
9. Kim, K., Youn, T., Jho, N., Chang, K.: Client-side deduplication to enhance security and reduce communication costs. ETRI J. **39**(1), 116–123 (2017)
10. Hur, J., Koo, D., Shin, Y., Kang, K.: Secure data deduplication with dynamic ownership management in cloud storage. IEEE Trans. Knowl. Data Eng. **28**(11), 3113–3125 (2016)
11. Jiang, S., Jiang, T., Wang, L.: Secure and efficient cloud data deduplication with ownership management. IEEE Trans. Serv. Comput., 1–14 (2017). https://ieeexplore.ieee.org/document/8100969
12. ElGamal, T.: A public key cryptosystem and a signature scheme based on discrete logarithms. IEEE Trans. Inf. Theory **31**(4), 469–472 (1985)

Access Control

An SDN-Based Wireless Authentication and Access Control Security Solution

Yanyan Han[1], Guohao Li[1,2]([✉]), and Binbin Feng[1]

[1] Beijing Electronics Science Institute, 7 Fufeng Road, Beijing, China
lghzzz@163.com
[2] Xidian University, 2 Taibai South Road, Xi'an, Shannxi, China

Abstract. Software-defined networking (SDN) is a relatively new app-roach in network management that proposes to separate the network control (Control plane) and the forwarding process (Data plane) to opti-mize the network infrastructure and improve network performance, con-trollability, manageability and flexibility. However, like every emerging technology, SDN has brought its own new challenges in terms of secu-rity. The security of SDN is the premise of its large-scale deployment and implementation. In this paper, we propose a wireless authentication and access control security framework under the SDN architecture which provides an optimal and secure network access with low latency. Consid-ering the ability of SDN to handle authentication and access control in a wireless environment, we installed wireless authentication modules into the Ryu controller. Meanwhile, we added the concept of management unit to the RBAC model to achieve hierarchical authorization in the wireless authentication environment. We have implemented and tested our architecture to show its performance.

Keywords: Software-defined network · RBAC
Wireless authentication · Access control

1 Introduction

SDN has become the focus of computer network. SDN splits data and con-trol plane enabling networking programmability through a standard protocol (e.g.OpenFlow), and manages network devices through a centralized controller. While the advent of SDN has brought new features, it has implicitly brought some new security challenges. For example, the openness of SDN makes it have better application prospect, but it also brings a lot of security risks to the archi-tecture. In the same way, centralized control brings convenience to the architec-ture, as well as problems such as security vulnerabilities, misconfiguration and privacy disclosure. This leads to changes in the security measures of the network architecture. In other words, the SDN architecture can improve the performance

Supported by organization x.

of the network, but it also brings some unprecedented security problems different from traditional network architecture. The security of the SDN is the first problem that SDN continues to develop and large-scale deployment [1].

At present, multiple research papers have been proposed to tackle SDN security issues. For SDN security analysis, in [2] Kreutz et al., analyzed the SDN network security. The conclusion of its work is that SDN networks must introduce a series of new security mechanisms to resist threat because the nature of centralized control and network programmability determines, meanwhile it also proposes a series of security mechanisms for SDN security issues, including network element replication, data diversification and the introduction of security protection components. In Bowman et al., conducted a corresponding analysis of the security issues in the actual trials of ProtoGENI [3]. The authors proposed a series of countermeasures against the malicious messages and flood attacks. Beijing University of Posts and Telecommunications has proposed a SDN-based Portal/Radius authentication method, which enables the wireless authentication. Portal/Radius authentication method ensures that the controller does not overload in the authentication process while performs poor fine-grained authentication for different levels of users. In SDN-based certification research, in [4] Matias et al., proposed the flow based network access control (FlowNAC) which is a Network Access Control solution to perform fine-grained flow-based network access control. FlowNAC allows users to grant access to the network based on the requested target service. Each service defined individually as a set of streams can be independently requested, and can be authorized to multiple services at the same time. However, in wireless network environment, the authentication delays can be longer than those of IEEE 802.1X port-based authentication. In this paper, we proposes an OpenFlow-based SDN wireless authentication and access control network architecture, and builds an experimental platform to test and verify its feasibility. For the purpose, we made changes to the Ryu controller. We added the wireless authentication module to the Ryu controller so that the controller can complete the rights authentication and structural analysis of the accessing user. Meanwhile, we add the concept of management unit to RBAC model to achieve hierarchical authorization in wireless authentication environment.

2   Related Work

2.1   SDN and OpenFlow Protocol

The SDN architecture, as shown in Fig. 1, consists of the application layer, the control layer and the infrastructure layer. The control layer exchanges data with the other two layers through the northbound interface and the southbound interface (such as OpenFlow). The control layer invokes the infrastructure layer implementation function according to the application layer functional requirements. The infrastructure layer performs data forwarding, storing, or uploading according to the instructions issued by the control layer.

OpenFlow [5], as the standard specification for building SDN network, is a centralized control model. The elements include the controller, OVS, connections established via the OpenFlow channel between the controller and OVS, the OVS flow table [6]. In the SDN, the channels build, device configuration, periodic interaction implementations are implemented through the OpenFlow message. OpenFlow supports three types of messages: Controller-to-Switch, Asynchronous and Symmetric. Among them, Symmetric is the controller and data forwarding device that can be independently initiated, Symmetric is a self-initiated controller and data forwarding device, It is generally used for device initialization, and no request or confirmation is required before sending. Before the controller and the data forwarding device are connected, the Hello message and ECHO information used to establish the connection are belonging to Symmetric. Although this type of message is the simplest, it is the most important type of message for channel establishment and maintaining a stable connection. (see Fig. 1).

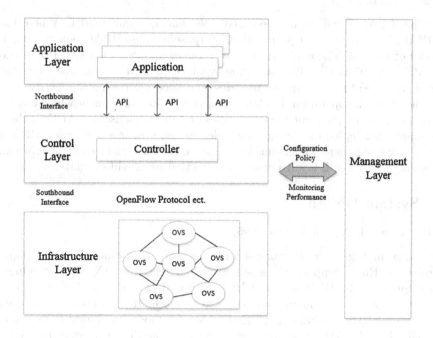

Fig. 1. SDN architecture.

2.2 Role-Based Access Control

Traditional Access Control includes Discretionary Access Control and Mandatory Access Control. Role-based Access Control is an extension of traditional Access Control. In RBAC [7], there is a strong connection between permissions and roles. When the user becomes a certain role, user will get the corresponding authority, which will bring great convenience to the follow-up management authority. RBAC supports three well-known security principles: which will bring great convenience to the follow-up management authority. RBAC supports three well-known security principles: the principle of minimum privilege, separation of responsibilities and data abstraction. The principle of minimum privilege can set roles as a minimum group; Separation of duties allows two mutually incompatible roles to accomplish a single task; the principle of data abstraction abstracts the authority of the role. RBAC believes that granting permissions is actually a matter of Who, What and How. The model's access permission triples are who, what and how, Who operates on what objects?

Who: the owner of the authority (such as Principal, User, Group, Role, Actor, and so on)
What: The object that the authority targets. (Resource, Class)
How: specific permissions (Privilege, forward authorization and negative authorization).

The RBAC97 [8] is a role-based role management model. When the ARBAC97 model was first proposed, its purpose is to use RBAC policy to manage all of its data. The model consists of three components: URA97, PRA9 and RRA97. URA97 is User-Role assignment which plays a crucial role when the user is assigned to a role, or the user does not need a certain role identity after completion of the operation. PRA97 is role-permission assignment which creates a one-to-one correspondence between roles and permissions. In RABC97, there are many roles including management roles and non-management roles, RRA97 is role-role assignment which aims to manage these roles and to avoid confusion. If chaos occurs, it will lead to cross-errors so that work will stagnate.

3   System Design

3.1   Network Architecture Design

As shown in Fig. 2, the network security architecture proposed in this paper consists of Host (supplicant), a legacy switch IEEE 802.1X support, Open-Flow Switches, RADIUS server, DHCP server, database and SDN controller. An OpenFlow network might consist of one or more OF- Switches. In the other part, we have the traditional IEEE 802.1X with OpenFlow-based SDN where the DHCP and RADIUS servers are placed near the SDN controller for better performance and latency reduction purposes.

The authentication access control process is as follows:

(1) In a wireless environment, the user issues a wireless authentication request, and the switch OVS1 captures or injects 802.1X/EAPOL messages from the requester (host) according to the installed rules. Switch OVS3 sends a request to the RADIUS server for user authentication, RADIUS server is compared with the existing definition rules in the database and send the wireless environment certification results to the switch.

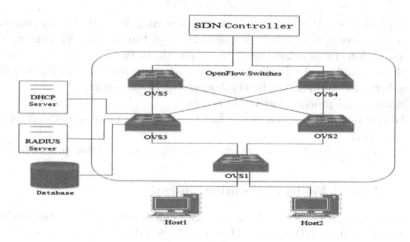

Fig. 2. Proposed architecture.

(2) The other switch sends the authentication result in the wireless environment to the controller. According to the result of the certification under
the infinite environment, the controller instructs the OF switch to deliver
the corresponding flow entry and deploy the corresponding specific rule.

In our architecture, the OpenFlow controller is not invoked in the authentication process, which eliminates the additional workload. We devolved the authentication functionalities to the IEEE 802.1X legacy switch in order to avoid heavy
request load on a SDN controller might result in longer delays. The supplicant
is authenticated only through the legacy switch which is the main entrance door
to SDN. The authentication flow will never reach the SDN.

3.2 Ryu Controller System Design

The Ryu controller side development was done on Ubuntu. The programming
structure of the Ryu controller is object-oriented, each function has a large number of modules, the core components are all present in the ryu folder consist of
app, cmd, services, tests, base, controller, lib, ofproto, topology and contrib.

In order to implement the authentication and access control modules, this
paper adds new modules to the Ryu program framework to ensure the implementation of authentication and access control. The wireless-authentication.py
module is added to the app folder, the wireless authentication module is used to
deal with wireless authentication in the wireless environment and access control
after wireless authentication. The WirelessAuthentication class of this module
inherits from the app-manager. RyuApp class, it has the following main functions:

(1) In the wireless environment, change and handle the switch connection state,
while listening StateChange event.

(2) Depending on the situation and requirements, it sends the appropriate instructions to the switch. At the same time, the switch OVS changes the connection status according to the required functions.

(3) Monitor and handle PacketIn events. The controller will call the function to listen for and handle the event when the event occurs.

(4) Monitor and process PortStatus events.

(5) Add or delete flow table entry functions and perform access control list processing.

(6) Non-mac address type packet and mac address type packet processing.

3.3   ARBAC97 Model Application Design

ARBAC97 [9] still has two problems in rights management. One is the duplication of authorization in the respect of user - role, and the second; the management scope of the management role in ARBAC97 is not clearly defined. To address the issue of rights management, we have improved the ARABC97 model. We add the concept of the Administration Unit to the RBAC model. Essentially, a management unit is a collection of managed objects. Each management unit consists of a user set, a role set, a permission set and a constraint set. The RBAC hierarchy model is used in the management unit to realize the allocation of roles management and permissions. Each management unit contains a basic role. All roles in the unit must inherit the role.

We rationalize users, permissions and constraints in the traditional RBAC model into hierarchical management units. Management work is assigned to each management unit, which helps simplify and smooth management work, meanwhile achieves hierarchical authorization. The theoretical basis for hierarchical authorization is distributed thinking, which will reduce the workload when is used in rights management.

In the RBAC hierarchical authorization management system, the management unit administrator can assign users and permissions to it, and the manner of the assignment can be direct or indirect. This granted user and privilege scope refer only to their own.

The management unit is divided into external operation and internal operation. An external operation is to create or delete a management unit based on requirements, add administrative roles or permissions. An internal operation is to create a role based on requirements, assign a role to it according to a role and assign a specific role to it depends on the level of the visitor.

When creating a new management unit, the new management unit is blank for ease of use. After the management unit is created, the operator will design the corresponding role AR according to the requirements and assign the required permissions to these roles. After a certain operation is completed, the unused management unit will be deleted; the roles and permissions will also be deleted. In addition to deleting or adding the corresponding units, the roles are assigned to the corresponding user and the assignment relationship is revoked, the corresponding user becomes an ordinary user.

In this model, sometimes management confusion arises due to unclear permission settings. So as to avoid this problem, the model stipulates that the indirect manager of the unit can only create its next level of management unit. The same unit is deleted if it is no longer needed, when deleting, it should be noted that only the next level of management unit will be deleted. The deleted user or permission is not discarded directly, but is retrieved by the superior unit so that it can be called directly next time.

4   System Platform Construction and Testing

4.1   Wireless Authentication and Access Control Module Design

In this system, the behavior of the authentication and access control process illustrated in Fig. 3 are described as follows:

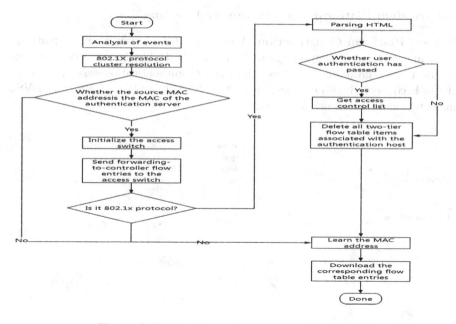

Fig. 3. Authentication and access control process.

In the network for wireless authentication, user authentication requests first, then the request message 802.1 X / EAPOL [10] to be captured in the connected switches to obtain the user's MAC address, the MAC address is stored in the logging data in the table, in the transmission process using MD5 encryption algorithm. The switch sends the captured authentication message to other switches. The switch sends the authentication message to the RADIUS server; RADIUS will acquire the corresponding role when it compares the received user MAC address with the list of user roles already in the original database. ARADIUS needs to obtain the corresponding role access control list from the database, the corresponding sql statement: "select * from user role, role where UserID ="+userID"and user role.RoleID = role.Role ID".

After the success of the user authentication, the RADIUS server sends a successful authentication message to the corresponding switch. The switch encapsulates the message as a packet-in message, which contains the packet information of the OpenFlow protocol header. The Packet-in message is then sent to the Ryu controller for controller analysis, and its forward Action: datapath. Ofproto-parse.OPFActiOnO utput (datapath ofproto. OFPP-CONTROLLER, 0 XFFFF). According to the analytical results, the wireless authentication symbol and the corresponding access control list are obtained, the Ryu controller delivers the corresponding flow entry for the access control list. If the user goes offline, all Layer 2 flow entries related to the host that sends the wireless authentication request are recovered.

4.2   System Platform Construction and Testing

System Platform Construction. We set up the experimental test platform according to the topology diagram shown in Fig. 4. The Switch OVS0 is connected to the database server and the wireless authentication server, the controller is connected with each switch separately. Switch OVS1, OVS2 and OVS3 make up the tree network topology.

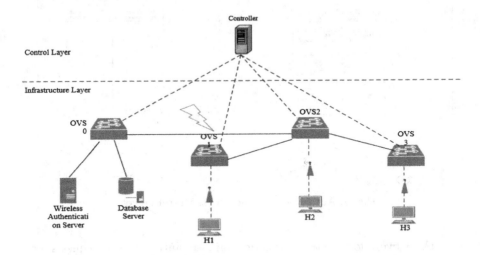

Fig. 4. Experimental test.

The system of the controller, switch, wireless authentication server and database server is Ubuntu. The specific configuration is shown in Table 1. The window7 system is installed on hosts H1, H2 and H3. The OpenFlow switch installation uses the online installation method to install Open vSwitch 1.10.0 on Ubuntu Server 12.04 LTS.

Table 1. System configuration.

Equipment	Configuration	System	Software or serve
Controller	Xeon E5506, 8G	UbuntuDesktop 14.04.2 LTS	Ryu3.16
Switches	Core 2 Q8200,2G	Ubuntu Server 12.04 LTS	OpenvSwitch1.11.0
Wireless authentication server	Xeon E5506,8G	Ubuntu Desktop	Radius7.0.20
Database server	Xeon E5506,8G	Ubuntu Desktop 14.04.2 LTS	Mysql5.5.35

As shown in Table 2, there are four types of users, userA, userB, userC and userD that correspond to four different levels of users. UserA can access all the hosts on the network. userB can only access host H1. userC can only access host H2. userD can only access host H3. The new test of the wireless authentication back-end management system is performed by adding four types of users and ratings.

Table 2. Experimental user rights.

Username	Role introduction
userA	Access to all hosts in the network
userB	Only the host H1 can be accessed
userC	Only the host H2 can be accessed
userD	Only the host H3 can be accessed

Test Process and Result Analysis. This system framework has network bottom layer equipment, end users and various servers. Therefore, the principle to be followed when starting up is to start the basic equipment first, then the server, and finally the end user. The specific steps are as follows:

1. The network devices involved need to be configured on demand.
2. Start four OVS switches.
3. Start the wireless authentication server, including the database server.
4. Start the Ryu controller and run the wireless-authentication.py module.
5. Add four levels and corresponding four different levels of users in the background management system.
6. Compare experiments and analyze the results.

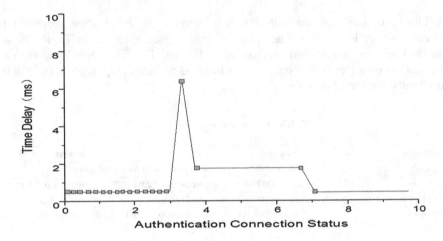

Fig. 5. Connection status before and after user login.

Figure 5 shows the connection state before and after user login. The result of the former is login timeout; The latter is the time delay before returning to normal. Figures 6 and 7 show the comparison between user userA and user userB when they are authenticated, when accessing host H2. The Fig. 6 shows the user userA certification process, the use of network resources, time delay is negative on behalf of the "request timeout", when the time delay is positive on behalf of the "request", on behalf of the user logoff when time delay is zero. When the user is not authenticated, it is displayed as a request timeout; after the 10th "request timeout", the time delay is shown to be positive; After the authentication access is successful, it will be displayed as "0", which means the controller will recycle the network resources immediately. Similarly, Fig. 7 shows the process of authenticating user userB and accessing network resources. Compared to Figs. 6 and 7, it can be seen that users of different levels have different access rights to network resources.

In addition to user userA and userB, the user userC and userD were also compared and tested respectively. By the testing principle, according to the rules, the user userC and userD to host H2 line access, user userC certification after success to be able to access the host H2, before and after the visit of state is the same with the principle of described earlier; In contrast, user userD has a negative time delay in the entire authentication and access control process, which means no access to host H2.

Through authentication and access control tests for different levels of users, it is verified that different levels of users have different access control rights, can access different network resources, and effectively verify wireless authentication and access control.

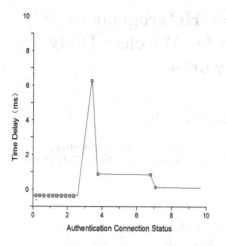

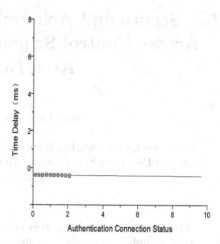

Fig. 6. UserA authentication and access to network resources process.

Fig. 7. UserB authentication and access to network resources process.

5   Summary

Security, although a crucial aspect of networking, has not been extensively studied in the context of SDN. In this paper, we have proposed a wireless authentication and access control security framework under the SDN architecture. By devolving the authentication capabilities to the legacy switch, we can solve the delays and security issues. Moreover, the improvement of the Ryu controller and the design of the RABC model have achieved the expected effect, which realized the hierarchical authorization under the wireless environment system.

References

1. Kreutz, D.: Software defined networking: a comprehensive survey. Proc. IEEE **103**(1), 14–76 (2015)
2. Bowman, A.R.: ProtoGENI[EB]. Accessed 19 Mar 2018. http://www.protogeni.net/trac/protogeni
3. Matias, J.: FlowNAC: flow-based network access control. In: 2014 Third European Workshop (2014)
4. Mckeown, N., Anderson, T., Balakrishnan, H., et al.: OpenFlow:enabling innovation in campus networks. ACM SIGCOMM Comput. Commun. Rev. **38**(2), 69–74 (2008)
5. Feamster, N., Rexford, J., Zegura, E.: The road to SDN. ACM SIGCOMM Comput. Commun. Rev. **44**(2), 87–98 (2014)
6. Sandhu, R.S., Coyne, E.J., Feinstein, H.L., et al.: Role-based access control model. IEEE Comput. **29**, 38–47 (1996)
7. Sandhu, R., Bhamidipati, V., Munawer, Q.: The ABRAC97 model for role-based administration of roles. ACM Trans. Inf. Syst. Secur. **2**, 105–135 (1999)
8. IEEE 802.lx Standard Group Website. http://www.ieee802.org/1x

Secure and Achievable Heterogeneous Access Control Scheme for Wireless Body Area Networks

Zhaoqi Li and Yuyang Zhou[✉]

Center for Cyber Security, School of Computer Science and Engineering,
University of Electronic Science and Technology of China, Chengdu 611731, China
1339256418@qq.com

Abstract. Wireless body area networks (WBANs) play an important role in implementing smart health care. Sensors in WBANs are used to collect and process user-related physiological characteristics data. Only the authorized legal users can access the corresponding resources. So it's important to guarantee the user's personal privacy data. In this paper, we design a heterogeneous signcryption scheme (HGSC). In HGSC, sensors in WBANs belong to the identity-based cryptography (IBC) environment and users who want to get the sensor's data belong to a certificateless cryptography (CLC) environment. According to the HGSC, we propose an access control scheme for WBANs. The scheme is implemented by PBC library, which verifies the heterogeneity of the scheme saves the cryptographic operation time, and has the advantage of computational cost and communication cost compared with the same type of cryptographic scheme.

Keywords: WBANs · Access control · Heterogeneous signcryption

1 Introduction

As the main technology for the realization of smart medical care, WBANs are human-centered and consist of some sensors or controllers that can be worn or implanted in the human body [1]. Sensors can monitor the physical characteristics (e.g., electrocardiogram, EGC, etc.) and activities of the human body in real time. Controllers can collect, analyze and transmit human's privacy data to a remote network server. The monitoring end (e.g., doctors, etc.) can access the data through the server.

Because the data monitored by the sensors is mainly the patient's treatment data and the body's physiological data, these all involve the patient's personal privacy. Any illegal acquisition, loss and malicious tampering of this data will have serious consequences. Currently, most network attacks can intrude or interfere with the normal application of WBANs in reality, such as unauthorized access. Most of the current high-mature, high-security information protection methods cannot be directly applied to the actual deployment of the WBANs. In

© Springer Nature Singapore Pte Ltd. 2018
F. Li et al. (Eds.): FCS 2018, CCIS 879, pp. 190–198, 2018.
https://doi.org/10.1007/978-981-13-3095-7_15

order to ensure that confidential information will not be unauthorized accessed, we need to achieve the confidentiality and integrity of the data; in order to ensure only authorized user can access the specified user data, we need to achieve the authenticity of the data. Therefore, implementing data access control must be solved in the actual deployment of WBANs.

1.1   Related Work

In 2014, Zhao [2] designed an identity-based and efficient anonymous authentication protocol for WBANs. The scheme is based on IBC. The scheme does not require a certificate authority. At the same time, it also provides mutual authentication between the client and the application to ensure the anonymity of the user. The public key/private key of the user in the IBC is generated by the private key generator (PKG). Among them, the user's identity may include personal information such as the user's mailbox communication address, ID number, and computer IP address. PKG is a third party trust agency. The authenticity of the public key is clearly verified without a certificate, so IBC eliminates the issue of the certificate management of the public key infrastructure (PKI), including certificate distribution, storage, verification, and revocation. Lightweight IBC schemes are well suited for use in WBANs. However, because PKG knows the private keys of all users in the IBC, it has key escrow problems. PKG can decrypt any ciphertext in the identity-based encryption (IBE) scheme and can forges the signature of any message in the identity-based signature (IBS) scheme. Therefore, IBC is only suitable for small networks, such as in-body com-munication in WBANs; while for large-scale networks, such as the Internet, IBC is not suitable. In 2016, Li et al. [3] proposed an efficient access control scheme for WBANs. The solution is based on certificateless signcryption (CLSC), which reduces the amount of computation while ensuring confidentiality, reliability, integrity, and other security features. In addition, the program also eliminates the issue of public certificates and key escrow. Signcryption [4] is a cryptographic technique capable of simultaneously acquiring encryption and digital signatures in the same logical steps. Its cost is significantly lower than the traditional "encryption-signature" or "signature-encryption" method.

In order to adapt to the real application environment, some heterogeneous access controls are proposed. In 2010, a PKI-IBC and an IBC-PKI scheme were proposed by Sun et al. [5]. However, Sun et al.'s agreement cannot guarantee the non-repudiation of the message because it is only safe for outsiders. Recently, some heterogeneous access control schemes for the Internet of Things have been proposed, and two online/offline heterogeneous access control schemes have been proposed in [6] and [7] respectively, both of which are based on the IBC-PKI environment.

1.2   Motivation and Contribution

Because the size of the human sensor part in the WBANs is relatively small and the key escrow problem is not serious, in order to save computing time, we have designed a heterogeneous signcryption scheme for WBANs. Here we call it the HGSC scheme. One side is the user A, which belongs to the IBC environment; the other side is the user B, which belongs to a CLC environment. The PKG can only generate partial private key of the user B, so even if the ciphertext sent by the user A is intercepted, the PKG cannot decrypt the ciphertext. At the same time, the PKG cannot falsify the user B to send an illegal signature to the user A for verification by the user B.

1.3 Organization

The rest of the paper is arranged as follows. The network model and security requirements are introduced in Sect. 2. The HGSC scheme is proposed in Sect. 3. The access control scheme for WBANs is given in Sect. 4 and its performance analysis is given in Sect. 5. Finally, the conclusions are given in Sect. 6.

2 Preliminaries

2.1 Network Model

The heterogeneous access control scheme proposed in this paper consists of an IBC and a CLC system. Figure 1 shows a simple network model. In this network model, the heterogeneity of the scheme can be clearly demonstrated. Among them, KMC represents the key management center. It not only acts as the KGC in the CLC system, but also acts as the PKG in the IBC system.

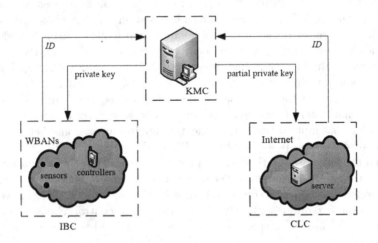

Fig. 1. Heterogeneous network model

2.2   Security Requirements

The secure communication of data in the WBANs needs to meet the following security requirements: (1) confidentiality. Privacy data can only be accessed by authorized users; (2) integrity. Data will not be tampered by illegal attackers; (3) identity authentication. The sending and receiving of data must be legitimate users. The authentication includes the legal authentication of the user and the legal authentication of the device; (4) non-repudiation. Users cannot deny the data they sent or received.

3   A Heterogeneous Signcryption Scheme

In 2016, Li et al. [8] proposed a CLSC scheme. Since the network size of the human sensor part of the WBANs is small and the key escrow problem is not serious. The CLSC scheme in [8] is not very suitable for this circumstance. In order to save the computing time, we have improved this CLSC scheme to design a HGSC scheme applicable for the WBANs. The sender is a sensor node belongs to the IBC environment; the receiver is a controller node and belongs to the CLC environment. The heterogeneous signcryption schemes proposed by us include the establishment of a system (Setup), the extraction of the user's partial private key in a CLC environment (CLC-EPK), the generation of a user's public key in a CLC environment (CLC-UPK), the setting of a user's full private key in a CLC environment (CLC-USK), the extraction of a user's key in the IBC environment (IBC-KG), signcryption (SC), and unsigncryption (USC). Among them, we assume that the sender's identity is IDs and the receiver's identity is IDr. The specific algorithm is described as follows.

- **Setup:** Let k be the safety parameter, G_1 is the cyclic additive group generated by P, the order is p, and G_2 is a cyclic multiplicative group with the same order p, which is a bilinear map. The KMC randomly selects a master key s and calculates $P_{pub} = sP$ and $g = \hat{e}(P, P)$, n is the number of bits used to transmit data. $H_1 : \{0,1\}^* \rightarrow Z_p^*$, $H_2 : G_1 \rightarrow Z_p^*$, $H_3 : G_2 \rightarrow \{0,1\}^n$, $H_4 : \{0,1\}^n \times \{0,1\}^* \times G_2 \rightarrow Z_p^*$ are four secure Hash functions. $\{G_1, G_2, p, \hat{e}, n, P, P_{pub}, g, H_1, H_2, H_3, H_4\}$ are public system parameters. The KMC exposes them and saves s.
- **CLC-EPK:** The receiver submits his identity to KMC. KMC calculates partial private key $D_r = \frac{1}{H_1(ID_r)+s}P$, and return the D_r to the receiver.
- **CLC-UPK:** The receiver selects $x_r \in Z_p^*$ randomly and calculates $PK_r = x_r(H_1(ID_r)P + P_{pub})$ as its own public key.
- **CLC-USK:** The receiver's full private key $S_r = \frac{1}{x_r + H_2(PK_r)}D_r$ is generated by the receiver's partial private key D_r, random secret value x_r, the user's public key PK_r, and the receiver's identity ID_r.
- **IBC-KG:** The sender submits his own ID_s to the KMC. The KMC calculates the sender's private key $S_r = \frac{1}{H_1(ID_s)+s}P$, and returns S_s to the sender.
- **SC:** Determine the sent message $m \in \{0,1\}^n$, the sender's private key S_s and identity ID_s. The receiver's ID_r and his public key PK_r, the algorithm steps are as follows:

1. Randomly select $x \in Z_p^*$.
2. Calculate $r = g^x$, $c = m \oplus H_3(r)$.
3. Calculate $h = H_4(m, ID_s, r)$.
4. Calculate $S = (x + h)S_s$.
5. Calculate $T = x(PK_r + H_2(PK_r)(H_1(ID_r)P + P_{pub}))$.

The ciphertext is $\sigma = (c, S, T)$.

- **USC:** The receiver R has ciphertext σ, the sender's identity ID_s and his own private key S_r. The algorithm steps are as follows:
  1. Calculate $r = \hat{e}(T, S_r)$.
  2. Calculate $m = c \oplus H_3(r)$.
  3. Calculate $h = H_4(m, ID_s, r)$.
  4. If and only if the equation $r = \hat{e}(S, H_1(ID_s)P + P_{pub})g^{-h}$ is established, can receive information m; otherwise the error symbol $\perp$ is output.

The biggest difference between the HGSC scheme and the CLSC scheme in [8] is that our scheme has a heterogeneous nature, which is very suitable for the transmission of WBANs. The HGSC scheme satisfies confidentiality (IND-CCA2) and unforgeability (EUF-CMA). The proof process is similar to the Li et al. [3]. The biggest difference between CLSC and HGSC scheme' security proof is we only need to solve the difficult problem of q-SDH if we want to win a EUF-CMA game in the HGSC scheme. The proof is omitted because of page limitation. The full version is available by contacting the authors.

4   A Secure and Achievable Heterogeneous Access Control Scheme

In this section we design a heterogeneous access control scheme for WBANs based on the HGSC algorithm. KMC can generate the complete private key of the node in the WBANs. But for users (doctors, nurses, etc.), KMC can only generate their partial private keys, so KMC cannot eavesdrop the private information sent by the sensor node to the users. The scheme consists of four parts: initial phase, registration phase, verification and authorization phase, withdrawal phase. Figure 2 summarizes these four phases.

- **Initial phase:** At this phase, the KMC runs **Setup** algorithms to deploy WBANs. The KMC configures an identifier ID_C and a private key S_C for the controller C. The private key S_C can be transmitted online or offline. If the key is transmitted online, the secure socket layer protocol can be used to ensure the confidentiality of the key during transmission.
- **Registration phase:** A user needs to register with KMC to gain access to WBANs. The user U first submits his own ID_U to the KMC, and then KMC detects whether the ID_U is a valid user identity. If the ID_U is not valid, the KMC rejects the user's registration request. Otherwise, the KMC sets an access validity ED for the user U, and then runs the **CLC-PSK** algorithm to generate the user's partial private key $D_U = \frac{1}{H_1(ID_U \| ED) + s} P$ and returns it to the user. Here, $\|$ denotes a connection symbol. After user U receives

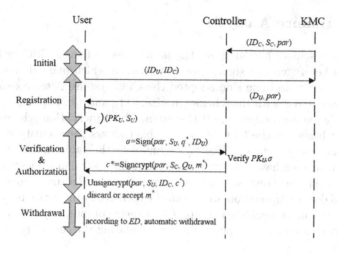

Fig. 2. The proposed access control scheme

the D_U, verifies whether the formula $\hat{e}(D_U, H_1(ID_U \parallel ED)P + P_{pub}) = g$ is equal. If they are equal, the D_U is the valid partial private key of the user U, otherwise the D_U is the invalid for the user U. After receiving the D_U, the user U runs the **CLC-UPK** algorithm to generate the user public key PK_U, and runs the **CLC-USK** algorithm to generate the user full private key S_U. The user exposes PK_U without a certificate.

- **Verification and authorization phase:** When a user U wants to access the data monitored by the sensors in the WBANs, the user U needs to create a query request message q. In order to resist replay attacks and gain anonymity, user U generates a new message $q^* = q \parallel TS \parallel ID_U \parallel PK_U$ using time stamp TS. After C receives the signature, it verifies σ to see if σ is a valid signature. If it is not, it is discarded. Otherwise, the patient data m is processed by $m^* = m \parallel TS \parallel ID_C \parallel PK_C$ according to the user query information q. After that, C runs the **SC** algorithm and output the signing message $\sigma = (c, S, T)$. Finally, the C sends the σ to the user U. After user U receives σ, calculates $r = \hat{e}(T, S_U)$, then uses $m \parallel TS \parallel ID_C \parallel PK_C = C \oplus H_3(r)$ to recover m, and runs a **USC** algorithm. Where, if and only if the equation $r = \hat{e}(S, H_1(ID_s \parallel ED)P + P_{pub})g^{-h}$ is true, the user accepts the sensor information m sent by the C; otherwise outputs $\perp$.

- **Withdrawal phase:** User registration will be automatically revoked due to the expiration of the due date ED. For example, if the deadline is "2018-03-25", then the user can only access the controller before March 25, 2018. After this deadline, the user's partial private key and full private key will automatically expire. If due to some special reasons, the deadline is advanced. Then the KMC will send an identifier to the controller to revoke the user's identity. The controller will create a table to save the identity of these invalid users. At the same time, we can also use the methods of Tsai and Tseng [9] to revoke the power of user access.

5   Performance Analysis

This section discusses and analyzes the performance of the HGSC system. Our scheme is a heterogeneous signcryption system, in which one side adopted the IBC-based system and one side adopted the CLC system. After consulting the data, we compared it with the schemes in [10], [11], and [8]. Paper [10] proposes a signing scheme is based on the IBC system. The signcryption schemes in [11] and [8] are based on the CLC system. Table 1 shows the security comparison of each signcryption scheme. The "$\checkmark$" symbol in the table indicates that this signcryption scheme has security features, and the "$\times$" sign indicates that this signcryption scheme does not have security features. Because exponentiation, pairing, and dot multiplication are the most expensive in the entire project, other computations can be neglected compared to their computations. Therefore, we use these three as the basic operations for calculating the cost of the solution in this section.

Table 1. Comparison of scheme's security

Scheme	Confidentiality	Authenticity Integrity Non-repudiation	Key escrow	Environment
[8]	$\checkmark$	$\checkmark$	$\checkmark$	CLC
[10]	$\checkmark$	$\checkmark$	$\times$	IBC
[11]	$\times$	$\checkmark$	$\checkmark$	CLC
Ours	$\checkmark$	$\checkmark$	$\checkmark$	IBC+CLC

Table 2 shows the comparison of the calculation costs and communication costs of these schemes. Here, we use PM to denote the dot multiplication operation in the group G_1, use Exp to denote the exponent operation in the group G_2, and use P to denote the pairing operation on the bilinear map. For communication costs, we use $|m|$ to denote the number of bits of message m, $|G_1|$ indicates the number of bits of an element in group G_1, $|G_2|$ indicates the number of bits of an element in group G_2, $|Z_p^*|$ indicates the number of bits of an element in the ring, $|ID|$ indicates the number of bits of the group. From Table 2, we can see that our solution is less demanding in the computational cost of the controller than the solutions in [11] and [8]. Here, we take the experimental results in [9], and its experimental environment is equipped with an ATMerga128 clocked at 7.3728 MHz on the MICA2, an 8-bit processor, 4 KB of RAM, and 128 KB of ROM. In [9], we know that the pairing computation time on the bilinear map is 1.9 s, and the exponent computation time in group G_2 is 0.9 s. Therefore, for computation costs, our plan is also smaller than [10]. And the scheme in [10] completely adopts the IBC and has obvious key escrow problem. In terms of communication cost, we set $|m|=160$ bits, $|ID|=80$ bits, and use a curve with groups G_1 and G_2 whose prime order length is 252 bits on the binary domain. Among them, the [9] points out that $|G_1| = 542$ bits, $|G2| = 1084$ bits, $|Z_p^*| = 32$ bits.

Table 2. Comparison of scheme's performance

Scheme	Computation cost		Communication cost
	User	Controller	
[8]	4PM+Exp	2PM+Exp+2P	$3|G_1| + |m| + |ID|$
[10]	3PM+P	PM+3P	$2|G_1|+|m|+|ID|$
[11]	4PM+Exp	PM+2Exp+3P	$4|G_1|+2|Z_p^*|+|m|+|ID|$
Ours	4PM+Exp	PM+Exp+2P	$3|G_1|+|m|+|ID|$

Figure 3(a) shows the communication costs of these schemes. It can be seen from the figure that the scheme communication cost in [10] is the smallest, followed by scheme [8] and our scheme, and the scheme communication cost is the largest in [11]. Although the demand for communication cost is greater than that in [10], our solution is still in an acceptable range, and our solution is not based on a single basis. Key escrow problems are not as serious as those in the [10]. Therefore, the proposed HGSC heterogeneous signcryption scheme is suitable for application in WBANs.

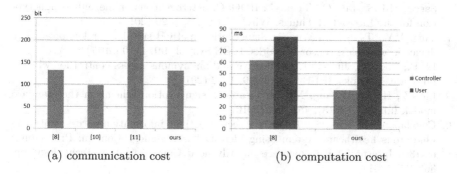

(a) communication cost   (b) computation cost

Fig. 3. Comparison of schemes

Also, we use the PBC library to implement the HGSC scheme and the CLSC signcryption scheme in [8]. In order to make the experimental values more representative, we cycled the entire schemes 100 times to get the average time. Figure 3(b) shows the comparison of computation cost between the HGSC scheme and the CLSC scheme. From Fig. 3(b), it can be seen that our HGSC scheme has clear advantages over the CLSC scheme in terms of computational costs.

6   Conclusions

In this paper, we designed a heterogeneous access control scheme for WBANs. The scheme adopted the heterogeneous signcryption scheme we proposed, in which the sender in the IBC environment, and the receiver in the CLC environment. So it prevented the key escrow problem in the receiving part. We used the PBC library to implement our proposed scheme and other signcryption schemes, and showed our proposed scheme have smaller computation cost and communication cost.

References

1. He, D., Chan, S., Tang, S.: A novel and lightweight system to secure wireless medical sensor networks. IEEE J. Biomed. Health Inform. **18**(1), 316–326 (2014)
2. Zhao, Z.: An efficient anonymous authentication scheme for wireless body area networks using elliptic curve cryptosystem. J. Med. Syst. **38**(2), 1–7 (2014)
3. Li, F., Hong, J.: Efficient certificateless access control for wireless body area networks. IEEE Sens. J. **16**(13), 5389–5396 (2016)
4. Zheng, Y.: Digital signcryption or how to achieve cost(signature & encryption) $\ll$ cost(signature) + cost(encryption). In: Kaliski, B.S. (ed.) Advances in Cryptology – CRYPTO 1997. LNCS, vol. 1294, pp. 165–179. Springer, Heidelberg (1997). https://doi.org/10.1007/BFb0052234
5. Sun, Y., Li, H.: Efficient signcryption between TPKC and IDPKC and its multireceiver construction. Sci. China Inf. Sci. **53**(3), 557–566 (2010)
6. Saeed, M.E.S., Liu, Q., Tian, G.: HOOSC: heterogeneous online/offline signcryption for the Internet of Things. Wirel. Netw. **15**, 1–20 (2017)
7. Ting, P.Y., Tsai, J.L., Wu, T.: Signcryption method suitable for low-power IoT device in a wireless sensor networks. IEEE Syst. J. **99**, 1–10 (2017)
8. Li, F., Han, Y., Jin, C.: Cost-effective and anonymous access control for wireless body area netwoks. IEEE Syst. J. **99**, 1–12 (2016)
9. Liu, Z., Hu, Y., Zhang, X.: Certificateless signcryption scheme in the standard model. Inf. Sci. **180**(3), 452–464 (2010)
10. Cagalaban, G., Kim, S.: Towards a secure patient information access control in ubiquitous healthcare system using identity-based signcryption. In: Proceedings of 13th International Conference on Advanced Communication Technology, pp. 863–867 (2011)
11. Shim, K.A., Lee, Y.R., Park, C.M.: EIBAS: an efficient identity-based broadcast authentication scheme in wireless sensor networks. Ad Hoc Netw. **11**(1), 182–189 (2013)

Attack and Behavior Detection

Intelligent Vehicle Knowledge Representation and Anomaly Detection Using Neural Knowledge DNA

Juan Wang$^{(\boxtimes)}$, Haoxi Zhang, Fei Li, Zuli Wang, and Jun Zhao

School of Cybersecurity, Chengdu University of Information Technology,
Chengdu, China
{wangjuan,haoxi,lifei,wangzuli,zhaojun}@cuit.edu.cn

Abstract. The anomaly detection and its knowledge expression of the intelligent vehicle are studied. includes Detection rules are divided into simple rules based on features or statistical characteristics and complex sequence rules based on neural networks. The former can effectively detect the specific CAN command and flooding, replay attacks, the latter uses neural networks to learn the characteristics of CAN commands, which can effectively detect the complex attacks. The simple detection rules are standardized by SOEKS knowledge expression and the complex detection rules storage in Neural Knowledge DNA framework. With this unified knowledge expression, the detection rules can be shared and inherited easily. A secure gateway for intelligent vehicle is also designed. The gateway is placed between the external network and the vehicle bus network and it prevent all suspicious external data. The simulations of real car data prove the feasibility of the methods.

Keywords: Vehicle system security · CAN bus security · Anomaly detection
Neural network · SOEKS

1 Introduction

Movie 'Fast & Furious 8' described a terrible scene for us: attackers hacked in intelligent vehicles and remotely controlled these vehicles to surround and attack targets. With the improvement of vehicle intelligence, similar scene may come true soon. So, the security technology of intelligent vehicles receives more and more attentions in recent years. Research hotspots in the field can be roughly divided into the following categories:

(1) **Driving behavior analysis.** The researchers studied driving behavior for two main purposes: (1) predicting driving behavior and conducting traffic control [1, 2]; (2) To distinguish drivers by driving behavior characteristic [3, 4].

(2) **Threat and defense technology of vehicular ad hoc network (VANET).** VANET is a special ad hoc network that lacking infrastructure and communicating entities move with various accelerations. Accordingly, it is hard to establish reliable end-to-end communication paths and having efficient data transfer [5]. Thus, VANETs have more severe security challenges than other wireless networks, such as the high mobility make VANET nodes requires the less execution time of security protocols,

© Springer Nature Singapore Pte Ltd. 2018
F. Li et al. (Eds.): FCS 2018, CCIS 879, pp. 201–215, 2018.
https://doi.org/10.1007/978-981-13-3095-7_16

and VANET nodes lack enough compute capacity to execute complexity security algorithms [6]. Up to now, security study of VANETs are focus on secure routing algorithm design, secure message transmission design, low complexity encryption algorithm design [5–8], attack taxonomy of VANET [9] and so on.

(3) **Security technology of In-Vehicle Network.** In-vehicle network refers to an intranet that is connected by the CAN (Controller Area Network) bus through each ECU (Electronic Control Units) within the vehicle. For vehicle itself security, new security architecture and authentication protocol of in-vehicle network have been proposed [10–12]. In Vehicle, all commands need ECU to receive/sent and execute, however, under the current architecture, it is impossible to know which ECU sent the command. So, ECUs Identification methods also have been studied [13, 14] which is part of Intrusion Detection study. And various Intrusion Detection System (IDS) have been proposed to discover abnormal action that compromised ECUs [15, 16].

Once attacks compromise in-vehicle ECUs, attackers can control the vehicle maneuver and force vehicle do danger actions without driver's permission! In severe cases, the driver's life may be endangered. Attacks from out of vehicle whether through Internet via VANET should compromise ECUs before it can control the whole vehicle. So, in-vehicle security is more important than outside ones, but little attention has been devoted to in-vehicle security. The existing research payed attention to the algorithm itself, and ignored the knowledge representation, which leads to the difficult sharing and inheritance of the existing experience. In this paper, we studied on in-vehicle anomaly detection method and the knowledge representation of security experience which can easily share and inherit security knowledge.

2 The Neural Knowledge DNA

The NK-DNA uses four essential elements, namely, States, Actions, Experiences, and Networks, as Fig. 1 shows.

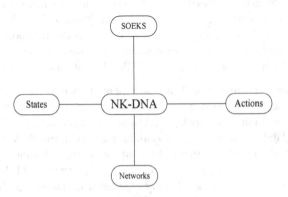

Fig. 1. Conceptual structure of the NK-DNA

To store and represent knowledge captured in intelligent systems that use neural networks. The core of the model is networks in which store details of neural networks used for training, such as the network structure, weights, bias [17]. Actions are used to store the domain's decisions set; and the Experiences, which are described by the Set of Experience Knowledge Structure (SOEKS) [18, 19], contain domain's historical operation segments with feedbacks from the outcomes. The last component—the States are situations in which a decision can be performed.

Each state (represented as $S_1, S_2, \ldots S_n$) can have connections with a set of actions (represented as $a_1, a_2, \ldots a_n$). The connection between a state and an action means the action is an available option in that state. To a specific state, there are multiple actions can be selected, and which one is the best choice is stored in trained neural network. Finally, series selections and their feedbacks of outcomes constitute experience which describe as *SOEKS* structure. The *SOEKS* is the combination of four components that characterize decision making actions (see Fig. 2) [20]:

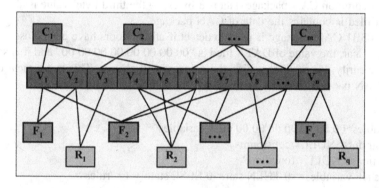

Fig. 2. Set of experience knowledge structure

Variables (represented as $V_1, V_2 \ldots V_n$) are the source of the other components, and use an attribute-value language (i.e. by a vector of variables and values) to represent knowledge;

Functions (represented as $F_1, F_2 \ldots F_r$) describe associations between a dependent variable and a set of input variables;

Constraints (represented as $C_1, C_2 \ldots Cm$) are the limitation of variables;

Rules (represented as $C_1, C_2 \ldots C_m$) are suitable for representing inferences, or for associating actions with conditions. They are relationships between a condition and a consequence connected by the statements IF-THEN-ELSE.

3 Intelligent Vehicle Knowledge Representation Based on NK-DNA

In-vehicle security technologies usually take the CAN bus data as data source. And many experiences of CAN bus data have already been discovered [13–16, 21]. We also found some experience of CAN data. In this section, we use NK-DNA to describe those experiences so that experiences can be easily shared and inherited. The CAN packages used for examples are collected from the real car-2010 Ford Escape [21].

Experience can be divided into simple experience and complex experience. The former one can simply be described as one SOEKS record, and the latter one need Networks, SOEKS even Actions and States to describe.

3.1   Simple Experience Representation

1. The experience of single CAN package

One of the most common and simple experiences is about specific single CAN package. Here is an example, one CAN package as follow:

ID: 03B1 Len:08 DATA: 00 00 00 00 00 00 00 00

A CAN package of 2010 Ford Escape usually has 11 bytes. The first two bytes are the ID of CAN package, and the third byte tells the length of DATA filed. For the length of common CAN package data is 8 bytes, so the third byte' value is always 08. The last filed is contains the data of CAN package.

The 03B1 CAN package is used to detect if all the doors have been closed. When no door is ajar, the value of DATA filed is "00 00 00 00 00 00 00 00" and it is safe for vehicle security. If any door is ajar, the value of will change. This is a typical rule of single CAN package and can be described by SOEKS structure as:

```
<03B1>
  <variables>00 00 00 00 00 00 00 00 </variables >
  <constraints>NULL</constraints >
  <functions> NULL</functions >
  <rules>IF variables==0 THEN state=0 ELSE state = 1 </rules >
</03B1>
```

The value '0' of state represents that this CAN package is safe for vehicle security, and '1' represents that this CAN package is unsafe for vehicle security.

This kind of experiences are abstracted as follows:

```
<CAN ID>
  <variables > Values </variables >
  <constraints> Constraints </constraints >
  <functions> Functions </functions >
  <rules> Rules</rules >
</CAN ID>
```

2. The experience of CAN ID count

The second simple experience is about the count of CAN ID. In normal driving, the count of each CAN ID shows obviously regularity that the count limit to a certain range. If the count over range, there are likely flood attacks.

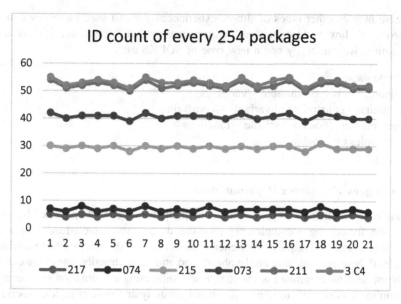

Fig. 3. ID count range

We also took 2010 Ford Escape for example. Reference [21] offered kinds of normal driving data, and we got ID count from every 254 CAN packages for packages lack of timestamp and about 254 CAN packages produced in 1 s. Some ID count shown in Fig. 3.

We can easily see every ID'count limitation: ID:0217 ∈ [4, 5], ID:0215 ∈ [22, 23], ID:211 ∈ [11,12], ID:03C4 ∈ [22, 23]. And the count limitation can be described as following SOEKS:

```
<COUNT>
  <variables>CAN ID</variables >
  <constraints>count limit to [min, max]</constraints >
  <functions> NULL</functions >
  <rules>IF count>=min and count<=max THEN state=0 ELSE state =1 </rules >
</COUNT>
```

Taking 0215 for example, its count is from 22 to 23, and can be described as

```
<COUNT>
  <variables>0215 </variables >
  <constraints>count limit to [22,23]</constraints >
  <functions> NULL</functions >
  <rules>IF count>=22 and count<=23 THEN state=0 ELSE state =1 </rules >
</COUNT>
```

There may be other types of simple experiences, we just used these tow common ones to explain how to describe simple experiences by SOEKS structure. If there is new type joining, we can easily add a new type of SOEKS as:

<new type name>
  <variables> new type variable </variables >
  <constraints> constraints of variable </constraints >
  <functions> functions of variable </functions >
  <rules> rules of variable </rules >
</ new type name >

3.2   Complex Experience Representation

In many case, whether CAN packages are anomaly or not, cannot be judged by simple experience, for driving is complex behavior that need driver-vehicle-road cooperation. Kinds of attack need complex experience to detect. Using the steering command as an example: if there is no turning on the ahead road and no obstruction ahead the car, then the abrupt steering command is unusual. For similar complex situation need complex detection mechanism. We used neural network to study and store complex experiences follow the NK-DNA framework in order to unify the simple experience together.

For efficiency reasons, we designed a neural network with only three layers: input layer, hidden layer and Output layer (see Fig. 5):

The output layer: the simplest layer, only has two neurons, that '0' neuron represents vehicle is safe, and '1' neuron represents vehicle is unsafe.

The hidden layer: neuron number of hidden layer depending on situation.

The input layer is the most important layer, and its neurons are divided into two parts: the CAN package neurons and surrounding neurons. The former ones represent the condition of the vehicle itself and the latter ones take surrounding information into assessment, includes weather condition, road condition and surrounding vehicle condition, etc. As mentioned in Sect. 2.1.1, there are 11 bytes in CAN package, and each byte has specific meaning, such as the first two bytes is the CAN ID. We used 11 neurons represent each byte respectively. Similarly, the weather condition (e.g. sunny, raining, cloudy…) is described in one neuron. Other complex condition, like road condition, need several neurons to represent whether there is obstruction or not, there is turning on the ahead road or not, and so no. In a word, the neuron number of input layer according to the purpose of the study. Different neural network structures represent different complex experiences which are the Networks of NK-DNA framework (Fig. 4).

3.3   Experience Reusing and Sharing

By using NK-DNA framework to describe vehicle security experience formally, we can easily reuse and share these experiences. We only defined experiences of 2010 Ford Escape, and these experiences can be used by other Ford Escape series for them have the similar vehicle architecture. Maybe some special single CAN package rules need

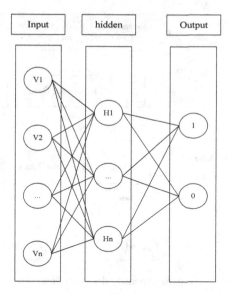

Fig. 4. Complex experience stored in neural network structure

update, and most of simple experiences can be reused directly. Neural network of complex experiences also can be reused after re-training weights and biases with the same layer architecture.

To different series, even different car brand, the types and architectures of experiences can be reused and shared, at least. For example, the 0215 ID count in 2010 Ford Escape is limited from 22 to 23 which was described in SOEKS record, see Sect. 2.1. And in Toyota Prius, the CAN ID count also exist, just the ID and limitation value are different. So, we can describe Toyota Prius' ID count experience in a similar way, using ID 0825 as an example:

```
<COUNT>
  <variables>0825 </variables >
  <constraints>count limit to [14,18]</constraints >
  <functions> NULL</functions >
  <rules>IF count>=14 and count<=18 THEN state=0 ELSE state =1 </rules >
</COUNT>
```

By using unified describe structure, we can use the same detection method by only updating some variable. That is what we said sharing and inheritance.

4   Intelligent Vehicle Anomaly Detection Based on NK-DNA

This section gives an anomaly detection algorithm based on NK-DNA using both simple experience and complex experience as the Fig. 5 shows.

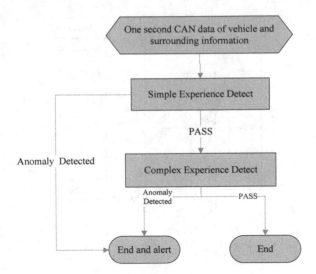

Fig. 5. Anomaly detection flow

Collecting data from both in-vehicle and out-vehicle and checking those data every second by simple experience firstly. IF any CAN package cannot pass simple experience detect, it will be aborted and an alert will be sent. Then the rest of CAN packages which pass the simple experience detect and surrounding information will be detected by complex experience. Similarly, any abnormal CAN package will be abort and trigger an alert, and normal CAN packages will be sent to CAN bus.

This anomaly detection process executed in a gateway that add to the CAN bus inside the vehicle as the Fig. 6 shows. In fact, there are many kinds of bus in the vehicle, and the CAN buses are divided into high-speed CAN and low-speed CAN. The entertainment information system is connected with the high-speed CAN bus. However, this paper focuses on abnormal detection of the data from outside the vehicle, so we simplifying the internal structure of vehicles.

All ECUs can send and receive commands from CAN bus for no gateway in vehicle system. Entertainment information system is the weak point of the system for it directly connect to the CAN bus and connect to Internet by WIFI or 4G. Then hack can intrusion into vehicle system by Internet through entertainment information system. Another way to hack into vehicle is through Vehicular Adhoc Network (VANET) by RFID or Bluetooth Communications Protocol. The gateway detect abnormal packages before them injected into CAN bus. All suspected messages are blocked outside the CAN bus by the gateway, especially messages related to drive.

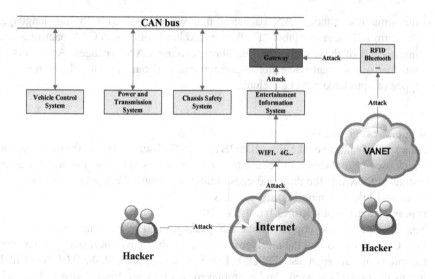

Fig. 6. Gateway to prevent outside attack

5 Simulations and Analysis

The simulation data include two categories:

(1) the driving CAN packages were captured over 22 min from real car- the Ford Escape on the high speed CAN bus with tools KvaserCAN Leaf Light V2 and BusMaster, and included starting and stopping the engine, driving, braking, etc. [21]. To distinguish these normal data from attack data, we added a flag named label to each package and set it to 0 as the Fig. 7 shows. The IDH represents the ID's higher byte and IDL is the ID's lower byte. The 1-8 represent the 8 bytes data.

```
       attack.csv ✕   drive.csv ✕
  1    IDH,IDL,1,2,3,4,5,6,7,8,label
  2    0,128,128,76,45,77,3,1,195,188,0
  3    0,115,115,28,39,23,87,23,89,28,0
  4    0,145,145,89,47,127,118,127,9,168,0
  5    2,17,17,255,254,0,100,0,74,0,0
  6    2,21,21,39,16,39,16,39,16,39,0
  7    4,23,23,0,0,0,0,0,0,0,0
  8    2,48,48,221,0,0,0,0,0,62,0
  9    0,65,65,0,97,0,0,0,0,0,0
 10    0,129,129,76,36,1,0,0,0,0,0
 11    0,128,128,76,45,77,3,1,195,189,0
 12    0,71,71,0,96,0,0,0,0,0,0
 13    2,0,0,39,11,39,88,39,88,1,0
 14    2,1,1,16,45,0,0,39,16,0,0
 15    2,21,21,39,16,39,16,39,16,39,0
 16    2,22,22,254,249,241,236,170,0,0,0
```

Fig. 7. Driving CAN packages with label

(2) the simulated attack CAN packages that we created with Python language, pycharm IDE have the label "1". We created kinds of attacks CAN packages and injected all of them randomly into above driving CAN packages. And checked whether our anomaly detection algorithm can find out these attacks or not. The types of simulated attacks include:

1. **single package attack:**
   Attack CAN package like this: ID:03B1, Len:08, Data:**8**0 00 00 00 00 00 00 00 which used to fool driver to believe the driver's door is ajar, if so the driver may be distracted to switch the door and cause traffic accidents. We repeated the attack 10 times and injected them into normal driving traffic.

2. **replay attack: replay times from 1 to 10**
   This attack is simply cope normal CAN packages and re-transmits them into real-time CAN traffic to fool the receiver into thinking they have successfully completed the protocol run such as: ID:0200, Len:8, DTA:0,39,13,39,88,39,01,1D, which means the brake is pressed. And we replayed this package from 1 time to 10 times.

3. **flood attack: flood package number from 100–1000**
   Flood attack, also named DoS attack (denial-of-service attack) is to inject too many CAN packages into CAN bus and make the receiving ECUs run out of computing resources and fail to accept new commands. For the lower the ID value, the higher the priority of CAN package, the 0000 ID packages have the highest priority to be received by all ECUs. We created 100 to 10000 packages which ID is 0000 to see if our algorithm can detect this flood attack or not.

4. **complex series order attack:**
   This kind of attack need several commands work together, like pedaling, slow down and turning. We made some fake acceleration which had no relation to other commands, and label them with "1".

All the data include normal and attack data were cut to 80% and 20% parts, and former ones used to train and latter ones used to test. We checked the detection rate for those situations which means how many attack packages can be find out of all attack packages. The detection rates as the Table 1 shows, and inside the parenthesis is the class name of the rules:

Table 1. Detection rates

Attack type	Detection rate	Experience type
Single package attack	100%	Simple experience (VALUE)
Replay attack	80%	Simple experience (COUNT)
Flood attack	>97%	Simple experience (COUNT)
Series order attack	98.2%	Complex experience (relu)

The simulation results show the single package attack and flood attack can be easily find out by simple experience which SOEKS class name are value and count. Value rules check CAN value filed gave 100% detection rate. And if the replay times less than 3 the count experience cannot detect the replay attack, so the detection rate of replay is only 80%. Similar to this situation, the flood packages less than certain amount are considered normal. The experiments reveal that COUNT rules can find out mess abnormal packages but can do nothing with few abnormal packages which can only be detected by complex experience.

We took one byte as one input neuron, and the complex experience which using neural networks structure and it detection rates are varies according to different activation function.

We choose three commonly used activation functions, relu, sigmoid, tanh, to find which one is fit for detection anomaly in vehicle. Their accuracy and loss as following figures show, the X axis is learning steps number (Figs. 8 and 9):

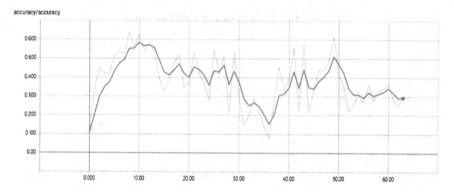

Fig. 8. The accuracy of sigmoid function

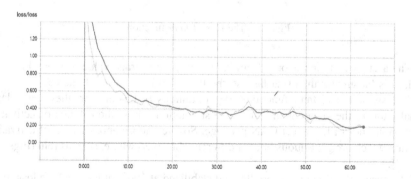

Fig. 9. The loss of sigmoid function

The accuracy of sigmoid is only from 8%–63%, the average value is about 30%, and the loss is far greater than 0 at last, obviously the sigmoid is not a good choice (Figs. 10 and 11).

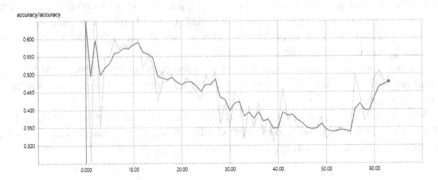

Fig. 10. The accuracy of tanh function

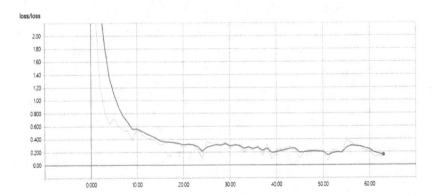

Fig. 11. The loss of tanh function

The accuracy of tanh is only from 25%–75%, the average value is about 44%, and the loss is far greater than 0 at last, so the tanh also is not a good choice.

The sigmoid and tanh functions are continuous and nonlinear, they make large signal gain on the center than sides. The simulations show these kinds of activation function are not fit for detect CAN package. So, we choose another kind of activation function which are continuous but not differentiable everywhere, such as relu (Figs. 12, and 13).

The accuracy of relu rises rapidly, and stabilized at 100% at last, and the loss drops to 0 quickly which proved that Neural Network Architecture with relu activation function can detect complex attack in vehicle. The average detection rate of this neural network is 98.2%.

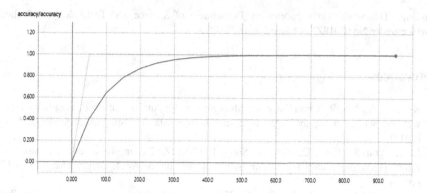

Fig. 12. The accuracy of relu function

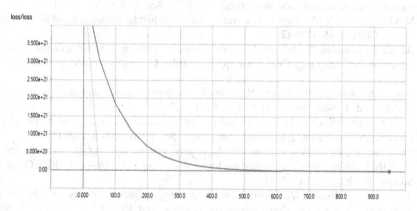

Fig. 13. The loss of relu function

6 Conclusions and Future Work

This paper we discussed the knowledge representation of vehicle security experience and how to detect attacks on CAN bus in vehicle based on various experience, simple or complex. By formally describing the experience as NK-DNA framework, new experiences can be easily added into this framework and can also be easily migrated to another type of vehicle. Then an anomaly detection algorithm based on NK-DNA was proposed which detect in-vehicle anomaly by simple experiences firstly. After removing detected abnormal CAN packages, the remaining CAN packages and surrounding information were checked by complex experience which stored in neural network structure. And the neural network structure can be adjusted according to different demands. Simulations show that our approach has high detection rate and can deal with various attacks. However, in-vehicle anomaly detection based on NK-DNA is at its early research stage, we plan to improve its efficiency and study and model more surrounding information and incorporate them into the complex experiences.

Funding. This work was supported by Department of Science and Technology of Sichuan Province under No. 2018ZR0067 and 2018ZR0220.

References

1. Kusuma, A., Liu, R., Choudhury, C., Montgomery, F.: Analysis of the driving behaviour at weaving section using multiple traffic surveillance data. Transp. Res. Procedia **3**, 51–59 (2014)
2. Li, L., You, S., Yang, C., Yan, B., Song, J., Chen, Z.: Driving-behavior-aware stochastic model predictive control for plug-in hybrid electric buses. Appl. Energy **162**(1), 868–879 (2016)
3. Enev, M., Takakuwa, A., Koscher, K., Kohno, T.: Automobile driver fingerprinting. Proc. Priv. Enhancing Technol. **2016**(1), 34–50 (2016)
4. Abut, H., et al.: Data collection with "uyanik": too much pain; but gains are coming (2007). https://www.researchgate.net/publication/237728452. Accessed 30 May 2014
5. Mokhtar, B., Azab, M.: Survey on security issues in vehicular ad hoc networks. Alexandria Eng. J. **54**(4), 1115–1126 (2015)
6. Bariah, L., Shehada, D., Salahat, E., et al.: Recent advances in VANET security: a survey. In: Vehicular Technology Conference, pp. 1–7. IEEE Computer Society, Washington, DC (2016)
7. Raw, R.S., Kumar, M., Singh, N.: Security challenges, issues and their solutions for VANET. Int. J. Netw. Secur. Appl. **5**(5), 95–105 (2013)
8. Sari, A., Onursal, O., Akkaya, M.: Review of the security issues in vehicular ad hoc networks (VANET). Int. J. Commun. Netw. Syst. Sci. **8**(13), 552–566 (2015)
9. Thing, V.L.L., Wu, J.: Autonomous vehicle security: a taxonomy of attacks and defences. In: 2016 IEEE International Conference on Internet of Things, pp. 164–170. IEEE Computer Society, Washington, DC (2017)
10. Schweppe, H., Roudier, Y.: Security and privacy for in-vehicle networks. In: International Workshop on Vehicular Communications, Sensing, and Computing. pp. 12–17. IEEE Computer Society, Washington, DC (2012)
11. Oguma, H., Yoshioka, A., Nishikawa, M., et al.: New attestation based security architecture for in-vehicle communication. In: Global Telecommunications Conference, pp. 1–6. IEEE Computer Society, Washington, DC (2008)
12. Woo, S., Jo, H.J., Kim, I.S., et al.: A practical security architecture for in-vehicle CAN-FD. IEEE Trans. Intell. Transp. Syst. **17**(8), 2248–2261 (2016)
13. Cho, K.-T., Shin, K.G.: Fingerprinting electronic control units for vehicle intrusion detection. In: Proceedings of the 25th USENIX Security Symposium, pp. 911–927. USENIX Association, Berkeley (2016)
14. Jaynes, M., Dantu, R., Varriale, R., et al.: Automating ECU identification for vehicle security. In: IEEE International Conference on Machine Learning and Applications, pp. 632–635. IEEE Computer Society, Washington, DC (2017)
15. Kang, M.J., Kang, J.W.: Intrusion detection system using deep neural network for in-vehicle network security. PLoS One **1**(6), e0155781 (2016)
16. Kang, M.J., Kang, J.W.: A novel intrusion detection method using deep neural network for in-vehicle network security. In: Vehicular Technology Conference. pp. 1–5, IEEE Computer Society, Washington, DC (2016)
17. Zhang, H., Li, F., Wang, J., et al.: Adding intelligence to cars using the neural knowledge DNA. Cybern. Syst. **48**(3), 267–273 (2017)

18. Sanín, C., Szczerbicki, E.: Using set of experience in the process of transforming information into knowledge. Int. J. Enterp. Inf. Syst. **2**(2), 45–62 (2006)

19. Sanín, C., Szczerbicki, E.: Towards the construction of decisional DNA: a set of experience knowledge structure java class within an ontology system. Cybern. Syst. **38**, 859–878 (2007)

20. Zhang, H., Li, F., Wang, J., et al.: Experience-oriented intelligence for Internet of Things. Cybern. Syst. **3**, 162–181 (2017)

21. Valasek, C., Miller, C.: Adventures in automotive networks and control units. Technical White Paper, 99 (2013). http://www.ioactive.com/pdfs/IOActive_Adventures_in_Automotive_Networks_and_Control_Units.pdf

A Violent Behavior Detection Algorithm Combining Streakline Model with Variational Model

Xiaofei Wang[1,2], Longcheng Yang[1], Jun Hu[1(✉)], and Hao Dai[1]

[1] College of Computer Science, Chengdu Normal University, Chengdu, China
cdnu_xfwang@163.com, 371760788@qq.com,
21165404@qq.com, 809866758@qq.com
[2] School of Electronic Engineering,
University of Electronic Science and Technology of China, Chengdu, China

Abstract. Violent behavior detection has become a hot topic within computer vision. The problems such as diversity of monitoring scene, different crowd density and mutual occlusion among crowds etc. result in a low recognition rate for violent behavior detection. In order to solve these problems, this work proposes an improved method to detect violence sequences. Features which are obtained by combining a streakline model with a variational model are used to discriminate fight and non-fight sequences. Finally, the validity and accuracy of the algorithm are verified via a large amount of challenging real-world surveillance videos.

Keywords: Streakline · Streak flow · Violent behavior detection
Support vector machine

1 Introduction

With the development of social economy, density of population in the city is higher and higher. The occurrence of violent behavior will pose a hazard to social public security. Therefore, violent behavior detection becomes a topic in video monitoring with great value for study. However, it is difficult to detect abnormal crowd behavior owing to following factors: low resolution, camera jitter, large numbers of crowd targets, different velocity of crowd objects, occlusion among objects, obvious variances in different crowd objects, etc.

At present, scholars at home and abroad have made many achievements on violent behavior detection. Some approaches based on hidden Markov model [1, 2], Lagrangian coherent structures [3], social force model [4], Markov random field [5], chaotic invariants [6] and kinematic features [7] have been proposed to detect the abnormal behavior in crowded scenes and can provide excellent performance on some benchmarks [4, 6]. Therefore, understanding the crowd behaviors in whole scene, without knowing the actions of individuals, is often advantageous. However, in the situations when the videos (such as VIF database [8]) have very low resolution, camera jitter, or the speed of objects in the video is too fast or too slow, etc., they may fail to detect the abnormal behavior in crowded scenes.

© Springer Nature Singapore Pte Ltd. 2018
F. Li et al. (Eds.): FCS 2018, CCIS 879, pp. 216–224, 2018.
https://doi.org/10.1007/978-981-13-3095-7_17

Recently, the Violent Flows (ViF) method was proposed by Hassner et al. [9] to identify violent crowds in densely populated areas (VIF database) using changes in optical flow magnitude. Gao et al. [10] introduced a variant of the ViF descriptor (OViF) that utilizes both orientation and magnitude of optical flow to detect violent behavior. It was shown that ViF offers greater classification ability on crowded data when compared to OViF, but when combined they achieve greater accuracy. However, the recognition accuracy of violent behavior detection using these two methods needs to be enhanced because of the poor ability of the optical flow computation methods used in these two algorithms in obtaining spatial and temporal changes of flow in crowded scenes.

Comparing with the optical flow computation method, the streakline model proposed by Mehran et al. [11] can represent spatial and temporal changes of flow in crowded scenes more accurately. With the rapid development of crowd behavior analysis, this model has drawn a great deal of attention recently [12–19]. However, the streakline model is based on the traditional Lucas Kanade method to compute the optical flow information between frames which will bring serious deviations in some scenes because of the poor anti-interference ability of Lucas Kanade method.

The high accurate variational model and motion evaluation system proposed by Brox et al. [20, 21] could enhance the accuracy of optical flow field and had strong anti-interference ability. This variational model estimated the motion flow field using a continuous function, and it was convenient to the analysis of global and local flow field.

The aim of this work is to devise a violent behavior detection algorithm that can perform well in challenging real-world surveillance videos with high crowd density. For the sake of accomplishment of this goal, we firstly modify the streakline model with the variational model to obtain the motion features, and then combine the features with the ViF. Finally, we propose an improved method to detect the violent behaviors in crowded scenes. The remainder of this paper is organized as follows. Sections 2 and 3 describe the variational model and streakline model respectively. In Sect. 4, we present the process of our improved violent behavior detection algorithm. Experimental results and analysis are provided in Sects. 5 and 6 concludes this paper.

2 The Variational Model

Let $I_1, I_2 : (\Omega \subset \mathbb{R}^3) \to \mathbb{R}$ be the first and the second frame to be aligned. $\mathbf{x}: = (x, y, t)^T$ denotes a point in the image domain Ω and $\mathbf{w}: = (u, v, 1)^T$ is the searched displacement vector between an image at time t and another image at time $t + 1$. A common assumption is that corresponding points should have the same gray value. This can be expressed by the energy

$$E_{\text{gray}}(u, v) = \int_{\Omega} \psi(|I_2(\mathbf{x} + \mathbf{w}) - I_1(\mathbf{x})|^2) d\mathbf{x}, \tag{1}$$

which penalizes deviations from this assumption. The robust function $\psi(s^2) = \sqrt{s^2 + \varepsilon^2}$, $\varepsilon = 0.001$, can be used to deal with occlusions and other non-Gaussian deviations of the matching criterion. It corresponds to a Laplace distribution which has longer tails than the Gaussian distribution. The advantage of the Laplace distribution is that the corresponding penalizer is still convex, simplifying the optimization.

Due to illumination effects, matching the gray value is not always reliable. Therefore, it has been suggested to supplement the constraint in (1) by a constraint on the gradient of the image grey value, which can be assumed not to vary due to the displacement. This can be expressed by the energy

$$E_{\text{gradient}}(u, v) = \int_{\Omega} \psi(|\nabla I_2(x + w) - \nabla I_1(x)|^2) dx, \qquad (2)$$

where $\nabla = (\partial_x, \partial_y)^T$ denotes the spatial gradient.

Both (1) and (2) enforce the matching of only weakly descriptive features. Just optimizing the sum of these two energies would result in many ambiguous solutions. Hence, this underlines the importance of introducing a smoothness constraint to describe the model assumption of a piecewise smooth flow field. This is achieved by penalizing the total variation of the flow field, which can be expressed as

$$E_{\text{smooth}}(u, v) = \int_{\Omega} \psi(|\nabla_3 u|^2 + |\nabla_3 v|^2) dx, \qquad (3)$$

where $\nabla_3 := (\partial_x \partial_y \partial_t)^T$ denotes the spatio-temporal gradient.

The total energy is the weighted sum of all of these constraint

$$E(u, v) = E_{\text{gray}}(u, v) + \gamma E_{\text{gradient}}(u, v) + \alpha E_{\text{smooth}}(u, v) \qquad (4)$$

where γ and α are tuning parameters which steer the importance of gradient constancy and smoothness. These parameters can be determined manually according to qualitative evidence on a large variety of videos, or be estimated automatically from truth data [22].

The final goal is to find the parameters of u and v to minimize energy function in (4). This energy is non-convex and can only be optimized locally. According to the calculus of variations, corresponding Euler-Lagrange equations are used to fulfill the minimizer of (4). More implementation details are available in [20].

3   Streakline Model

In fluid mechanics and flow visualization, streakline is well known as a tool for measurement and analysis of the flow. A streakline is the collection of all particles which are initialized at a particular pixel. To explain how streaklines are calculated, let $(x_i^p(t), y_i^p(t))$ be a particle position at time t, initialized at point p and frame i for i, $t = 0, 1, 2, \ldots, T$. The position of particle through point p at any time instant t is computed as described in Ref. [11].

$$x_i^p(t+1) = x_i^p(t) + u(x_i^p(t), y_i^p(t), t)$$
$$y_i^p(t+1) = y_i^p(t) + v(x_i^p(t), y_i^p(t), t), \qquad (5)$$

where u and v are optical flow field. This brings a family of curves, all starting at point p and tracing the path of the flow from that point in frame i.

As invented for visualization purposes, streaklines in fluids transport a color material along the flow, meaning they propagate changes in the flow along their path. Similarly, we allow streaklines to propagate velocities, given by the instantaneous optical flow $\Omega = (u, v)^T$ at the time of initialization, along the flow like a material. To this end, we define an extended particle i as a set of position and initial velocity

$$P_i = \{x_i(t), y_i(t), u_i, v_i\}, \qquad (6)$$

where $u_i = u(x_i^p(i), y_i^p(i), i)$ and $v_i = v(x_i^p(i), y_i^p(i), i)$. In the whole scene, we consider only streaklines comprising extended particles.

To represent the flow more completely in whole scene, a new motion field, named as streak flow $(\Omega_s = (u_s, v_s)^T)$, is constructed based on streaklines. Streak flow can provide motion information of the flow for a period of time and capture crowd motions better in a dynamically changing flow. The computation of u_s is described as follows, and the computation of v_s is similar. Given data in the vector

$$U = [u_i], \qquad (7)$$

where $u_i \in P_i, \forall i, p$, the streak flow in the x direction at each pixel is computed.

Equation (5) implies that each particle P_i has three neighboring pixels (nearest neighbors). It is reasonable to consider u_i being the linear interpolation of the three neighboring pixels. Hence, the definition of u_i is as follows

$$u_i = a_1 u_s(k_1) + a_2 u_s(k_2) + a_3 u_s(k_3), \qquad (8)$$

where k_j is the index of a neighboring pixel, and a_j is the known basis function of the triangulation of the domain for the j-th neighboring pixel. Each $u_s(k_i)$ is computed using a triangular interpolation formula. For all the data points in U, a linear system of equations is formed using (8)

$$Au_s = U, \qquad (9)$$

where a_i are entries of the matrix A, and u_s is the least square solution of (9). More details can be found in Ref. [11].

4   Improved Violent Behavior Detection Algorithm

In this paper, we substitute the Lucas Kanade method with this variational model to compute the optical flow field between frames in the streakline framework. The obtained streaklines and streak flow $(u'_{s_{x,y,t}}, v'_{s_{x,y,t}})$ also have strong anti-interference performance and can provide a better way to recognize flow spatio-temporal changes more accurately in the scene. Figure 1 shows two successive frames in one of UMN datasets [23]. Figure 2 shows the comparison of two optical flow methods. Figure 2(a) represents the optical flow field of these two successive frames obtained by Lucas Kanade method. Figure 2(b) is the corresponding result obtained by the variational model. From the comparison, we note that the latter can provide more dynamic motion information completely and accurately in the scene.

Fig. 1. Two consecutive frames

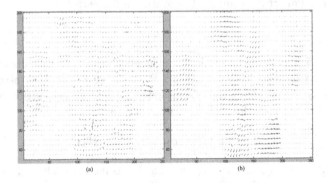

Fig. 2. Comparison of two optical flow methods. (a) The optical flow field obtained by Lucas Kanade method. (b) The optical flow field obtained by high accurate variational model.

In Ref. [9], for a given sequence of video frames $Seq = \{f_1, f_2, \cdots, f_T\}$, the optical flow between consecutive frames is firstly calculated. Compared with the single optical flow, the streak flow combing with the variational model is better able to describe information of the whole scene accurately. Therefore, in our algorithm, we substitute the optical flow vector in the original with the streak flow vector $(u'_{s_{x,y,t}}, v'_{s_{x,y,t}})$ so as to describe the motion information of the whole scene. x, y, t respectively represent location and coordinate of pixel $p_{x,y,t}$ as well as subscript of the video frame, $u'_{s_{x,y,t}}$ denotes the value of streak flow at $p_{x,y,t}$ in x direction and $v'_{s_{x,y,t}}$ denotes the value of streak flow at $p_{x,y,t}$ in y direction. Refer to Ref. [9], the magnitudes of these vectors are considered

$$m'_{x,y,t} = \sqrt{(u'^2_{s_{x,y,t}} + v'^2_{s_{x,y,t}})} \tag{10}$$

Although flow vectors encode meaningful temporal information, their magnitudes are arbitrary quantities. In order to describe the scene information better, the similarities of flow-magnitudes are considered. For each pixel, we obtain a binary indicator $B'_{x,y,t}$, reflecting the significance of the change of magnitude between frames:

$$B'_{x,y,t} = \begin{cases} 1 & \text{if } \left| m'_{x,y,t} - m'_{x,y,t-1} \right| \geq thr \\ 0 & \text{otherwise} \end{cases} \tag{11}$$

where thr is mean of the magnitude variations of the streak flow between frames, shown as follows

$$thr = \frac{\sum\limits_{x=0,y=0}^{x=rows,y=cols} \left(\left| m'_{x,y,t} - m'_{x,y,t-1} \right| \right)}{rows \times cols} \tag{12}$$

where $rows$ and $cols$ respectively indicates the number of rows and columns.

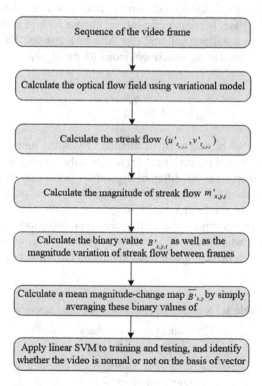

Fig. 3. The architecture of our improved method

Equation (11) provides us with a binary, magnitude-change, significance map for each frame. For each pixel, a mean magnitude-change map by simply averaging these binary values is computed as follows

$$\overline{B}'_{x,y} = \frac{1}{T}\sum_t B'_{x,y,t}.$$ (13)

For a given sequence of frames *Seq*, our improved descriptor is a vector of frequencies of quantized values $\overline{B}'_{x,y}$. Each such vector is then classified as representing an either abnormal or normal video using support vector machines (SVM). In order to understand the detection process better, the architecture of our method is illustrated in Fig. 3. Detailed experimental results and the accuracy comparison will be discussed in Sect. 5.

5 Experiments and Discussions

Some experiments are done to verify the validity and accuracy of our improved method for violent behavior detection by comparing with ViF and OViF algorithm. The VIF database is used, in which video is artificially divided into video clips including normal behaviors and abnormal behaviors. For the accomplishment of target proposed in Sect. 1, 120 video clips including 60 normal videos and 60 abnormal videos are selected from the database. In the experiment, we choose 30% of normal and abnormal videos respectively as a training set, and rest 70% as a test set. The mean prediction accuracy (ACC) is adopted as an assessment index for the algorithm, according to ROC curve theory,

$$ACC = \frac{TP + TN}{P + N}.$$ (14)

where *TP* is the number of true positive samples, *TN* is the number of true negative samples, *P* is the number of positive samples and *N* is the number of negative samples.

The accuracy comparison of different algorithms according to (14) is shown in Table 1. From this table, it is shown that the algorithm in our paper can get a higher accuracy on violent behavior detection. Recognition results of partial normal videos obtained by using our algorithm for detecting abnormal behaviors are shown in Fig. 4, marked as "Normal", while recognition results of partial abnormal videos acquired by using our algorithm for detecting abnormal behaviors are shown in Fig. 5, marked as "Abnormal".

Table 1. Accuracy comparison of different algorithms

Method	Accuracy
ViF [9]	77.4%
OViF [10]	80.9%
Our method	92.8%

Fig. 4. Recognition results of partial normal videos

Fig. 5. Recognition results of partial abnormal videos

6 Conclusion

In order to improve the accuracy of violent behavior detection, an improved algorithm combining the streakline model based on variational model with ViF method is proposed in our paper. The algorithm adopts magnitude variation of the streak flow to describe the crowd behavior in the scene, and combines with SVM to detect and identify violent behavior. Finally, many challenging real-world videos are used to validate our improved algorithm. Experimental results show that our method can performs better in the accuracy of violent behavior detection.

Acknowledgments. This work is supported by the Scientific Research Fund of Sichuan Provincial Education Department of China under Grant no. 2016JY0199, the Open Fund of the Key Laboratory of Pattern Recognition and Intelligent Information Processing of Chengdu University in Sichuan Province under Grant no. MSSB-2016-7, and the College Students' Innovation and Entrepreneurship Training Program under Grant no. 201714389088.

References

1. Andrade, E.L., Blunsden, S., Fisher, R.B.: Hidden markov models for optical flow analysis in crowds. In: 18th International Conference on Pattern Recognition, pp. 460–463. IEEE, Hong Kong (2006)
2. Andrade, E.L., Blunsden, S., Fisher, R.B.: Modeling crowd scenes for event detection. In: 18th International Conference on Pattern Recognition, pp. 175–178. IEEE, Hong Kong (2006)

3. Ali, S., Shah, M.: A lagrangian particle dynamics approach for crowd flow segmentation and stability analysis. In: 2007 IEEE Conference on Computer Vision and Pattern Recognition, pp. 1–6. IEEE, Minneapolis (2007)

4. Mehran, R., Oyama, A., Shah, M.: Violent behavior detection using social force model. In: IEEE Computer Society Conference on Computer Vision and Pattern Recognition, pp. 935–942. IEEE, Miami (2009)

5. Kim, J., Grauman, K.: Observe locally, infer globally: a space-time MRF for detecting abnormal activities with incremental updates. In: IEEE Computer Society Conference on Computer Vision and Pattern Recognition, pp. 2921–2928. IEEE, Miami (2009)

6. Wu, S., Moore, B.E., Shah, M.: Chaotic invariants of lagrangian particle trajectories for anomaly detection in crowded scenes. In: IEEE International Conference on Computer Vision and Pattern Recognition, pp. 2054–2060. IEEE, San Francisco (2010)

7. Ali, S., Shah, M.: Human action recognition in videos using kinematic features and multiple instance learning. IEEE Trans. Pattern Anal. Mach. Intell. **32**(2), 288–303 (2010)

8. Dataset Homepage. http://www.openu.ac.il/home/hassner/data/violentflows/index.html

9. Hassner, T., Itcher, Y., Kliper-Gross, O.: Violent flows: real-time detection of violent crowd behavior. In: 2012 IEEE Computer Society Conference on Computer Vision and Pattern Recognition Workshops, pp. 1–6. IEEE, Providence (2012)

10. Gao, Y., Liu, H., Sun, X., et al.: Violence detection using oriented violent flows. Image Vision Comput. **48**, 37–41 (2015)

11. Mehran, R., Moore, Brian E., Shah, M.: A streakline representation of flow in crowded scenes. In: Daniilidis, K., Maragos, P., Paragios, N. (eds.) ECCV 2010. LNCS, vol. 6313, pp. 439–452. Springer, Heidelberg (2010). https://doi.org/10.1007/978-3-642-15558-1_32

12. Wu, S., Wong, H.S.: Joint segmentation of collectively moving objects using a bag-of-words model and level set evolution. Pattern Recogn. **45**(9), 3389–3401 (2012)

13. Nayak, N.M., Zhu, Y.Y., Roy-Chowdhury, A.K.: Vector field analysis for multi-object behavior modeling. Image Vis. Comput. **31**(6), 460–472 (2013)

14. Hu, Y., Zhang, Y., Davis, L.S.: Unsupervised abnormal crowd activity detection using semiparametric scan statistic. In: IEEE Computer Society Conference on Computer Vision and Pattern Recognition Workshops, pp. 767–774. IEEE, Portland (2013)

15. Wang, X.F., Yang, X.M., He, X.H., et al.: A high accuracy flow segmentation method in crowded scenes based on streakline. Optik **125**(3), 924–929 (2014)

16. Zhou, B., Tang, X., Zhang, H., et al.: Measuring crowd collectiveness. IEEE Trans. Pattern Anal. Mach. Intell. **36**(8), 1586–1599 (2014)

17. Yuan, Y., Fang, J., Wang, Q.: Online anomaly detection in crowd scenes via structure analysis. IEEE Trans. Cybern. **45**(3), 562 (2015)

18. Mohammadi, S., Perina, A., Kiani, H., Murino, V.: Angry crowds: detecting violent events in videos. In: Leibe, B., Matas, J., Sebe, N., Welling, M. (eds.) ECCV 2016. LNCS, vol. 9911, pp. 3–18. Springer, Cham (2016). https://doi.org/10.1007/978-3-319-46478-7_1

19. Wu, S., Yang, H., Zheng, S.: Crowd behavior analysis via curl and divergence of motion trajectories. Int. J. Comput. Vision **123**(3), 499–519 (2017)

20. Brox, T., Bruhn, A., Papenberg, N., Weickert, J.: High accuracy optical flow estimation based on a theory for warping. In: Pajdla, T., Matas, J. (eds.) ECCV 2004. LNCS, vol. 3024, pp. 25–36. Springer, Heidelberg (2004). https://doi.org/10.1007/978-3-540-24673-2_3

21. Brox, T., Malik, J.: Large displacement optical flow: descriptor matching in variational motion estimation. IEEE Trans. Pattern Anal. Mach. Intell. **33**(3), 500–513 (2011)

22. Sun, D., Roth, S., Lewis, J.P., Black, M.J.: Learning optical flow. In: Forsyth, D., Torr, P., Zisserman, A. (eds.) ECCV 2008. LNCS, vol. 5304, pp. 83–97. Springer, Heidelberg (2008). https://doi.org/10.1007/978-3-540-88690-7_7

23. Dataset Homepage. http://mha.cs.umn.edu/Movies/Crowd-Activity-All.avi/

System and Network Security

A Novel Digital Rights Management in P2P Networks Based on Bitcoin System

Danni Wang[1], Juntao Gao[1($\boxtimes$)], Haiyong Yu[1], and Xuelian Li[2]

[1] ISN State Key Laboratory China, Xi'an, Shaanxi, China
jtgao@mail.xidian.edu.cn
[2] School of Mathematics and Statistics, Xidian University,
Xi'an, Shaanxi, China

Abstract. In recent years, digital rights management (DRM) in Peer to Peer (P2P) network becomes more and more important. We propose a novel DRM scheme based on P2P to protect valuable digital content. The digital content is firstly encrypted with a symmetric cryptographic algorithm, and then the symmetric key is encrypted by the RSA scheme such that any unpaid user cannot access the digital content. The symmetric key is only held by the content provider for avoiding the risk of the server leaking the symmetric key. By exploiting Bitcoin system, the content provider and the user have the ability to make a direct payment without relying on the server. Moreover, the payment is a timely payment, that is, when the user's payment is completed, he/she will obtain the private key of RSA immediately. In our scheme, users can download ciphertext of the digital content from any peer who owns the digital content early. In addition, a payment voucher is used to verify users who have paid for the digital content, which can also against the collusion attack. We anonymize the authentication process for protecting the users' privacy. The security analysis shows that our scheme can provide message confidentiality, anonymity of users, and can resist poisoning attack and collusion attack. The simulation shows that our scheme is efficient and practical.

Keywords: Digital rights management · Bitcoin system · Peer to peer (P2P)
Transaction

1 Introduction

With the development of Internet, the valuable digital contents, such as music data, picture data and video data, are very easy to be pirated due to the easy replication. Digital rights management (DRM) can ensure legal consumption of digital contents through some methods such as encryption and licensing, which permit authorized users to access these digital contents. Early DRM is based on a client-server model [3, 4, 8]. The digital content is encrypted by a dedicated server. In addition, the server is responsible for managing and authenticating all users in the system [20]. It also distributes the key that can decrypt a ciphertext of the digital content to the authorized users. However, it is vulnerable to a single point of attack, and the more users, the heavier the load on the server, which will increase the burden of communication and

© Springer Nature Singapore Pte Ltd. 2018
F. Li et al. (Eds.): FCS 2018, CCIS 879, pp. 227–240, 2018.
https://doi.org/10.1007/978-981-13-3095-7_18

decrease the efficiency of the system. Especially when transferring large amount of digital content, the efficiency drops significantly [1, 21, 22]. Peer to Peer (P2P) network is a distributed architecture that can transmit large amount of digital content in high speed. Moreover, it is not affected by the number of users. Researchers have combined P2P network and DRM scheme for addressing the problem of heavy load on server and achieving efficient transmission in various degrees. Generally speaking, P2P based DRM schemes are divided into three categories. i.e., centralized P2P based DRM scheme [6, 7, 23], semi-distributed P2P based DRM scheme [2, 5] and distributed P2P based DRM scheme [13]. We will give a brief summary on these related works.

Centralized P2P Based DRM Scheme. This method is very similar to the traditional client-server architecture. Compared with client-server architecture, the only difference is that encrypted digital content can be downloaded not only from the server but also from any user, namely a peer, who owns the digital content. However, there are some problems that if the server is attacked, information stored on the server will be leaked, including digital content. What is more, the server could be a bottleneck when the number of peers becomes large.

Semi-distributed P2P Based DRM Scheme. This scheme allows users to download an encrypted digital content from the content provider. But the content provider has to communicate with the server for verifying users and getting the decryption key. And then, users can access the digital content after paying. Since only the content provider interacts with the server, the load on server is significantly reduced. However, it is hard for the server to detect a user's status and revoke illegal users.

Distributed P2P Based DRM Scheme. In distributed P2P based DRM architecture, there is no server to manage users' authentication. When the content provider intends to publish a digital content, he broadcasts the information about the digital content. A user who is authenticated by the server or the content provider can download the digital content, and then obtain the decryption key from the content provider. The distributed method makes the service load very low. But the disadvantage of the scheme is that no one can see the income situation about the digital content.

1.1 Our Contributions

To address the problems above, we propose a novel DRM scheme based on P2P. We focus on the security of the digital content, so the symmetric key is only held by the content provider. We anonymize the authentication process by removing the requirement to submit real identities. Regarding billing, we use Bitcoin system [9] to implement peer to peer and transparent transactions between users and the content provider. To summarize, our main contributions are as follows:

- Our scheme combines DRM and Bitcoin system [10, 11]. The Bitcoin system can create an open and transparent transaction. Based on the programmability of Bitcoin scripts, we exploit a special script for secure transmission of the private key.
- A RSA encryption [25] is used to protect the digital content. The content provider encrypts the digital content with a symmetric key firstly, and then encrypts information of the symmetric key with the RSA.

- A payment voucher is used to authenticate a user in an anonymous way. We guarantee the anonymity of users while preventing illegal users who are unpaid from accessing the digital content. In addition, we implement revocation of malicious users through a list maintained by the server.

The rest of the paper is organized as follows. We give our system model in Sect. 2. Section 3 is a detailed description about the DRM scheme. Section 4 shows security, performance and efficiency of the scheme. Finally, Sect. 5 concludes our work.

2 System Model

2.1 Symbols

The following notations shown in Table 1 will be used in this paper:

2.2 The Model

As shown in Fig. 1, the DRM system model based on P2P involves three types of entities: the proxy server (PS), the peers, which are users, and the content provider (CP).

Peers: The peers are users in P2P network who can download the encrypted digital content from the CP. These users who already obtain the content can also share encrypted digital content to others.

Content Provider (CP): The content provider offers digital content. The digital content is encrypted by CP and stored locally. CP can obtain money through selling the content.

Proxy Server (PS): The proxy server is a semi-trusted entity who publishes content information. Moreover, PS manages all users who have downloaded the digital content, supervises these users and deletes malicious users.

As we have described above, our DRM scheme includes three phases: content publish, content purchase and content access.

(1) **Content publish**

The content publish stage mainly finishes encrypting the digital content and issuing a message about the digital content.

(2) **Content purchase**

The content purchase phase mainly realizes that a peer, namely a user, downloads the encrypted digital content and completes the payment for it to get private key.

(3) **Content access**

The content access is mainly to complete the user's online decryption of the encrypted digital content and to deny service to unpaid users.

Table 1. The symbols

m	The digital content
$h(\cdot)$	The collision-resistance one-way hash function [12], where $h: \{0,1\}^* \rightarrow \{0,1\}^\mu$
des_m	The description of m
T_{PU}	The Bitcoin transaction of the user, which is unexpended
pk_{rsacp}, sk_{rsacp}	RSA private and public keys of the content provider which is used to encrypt a message
$pk_{rsacp'}, sk_{rsacp'}$	RSA private and public keys of the content provider which is used to sign a message
pk_{rsaps}, sk_{rsaps}	RSA private and public keys of the proxy server which is used to encrypt a message
pk_B, sk_B	Elliptic curve private and public keys of the user which is used to sign a message [16]
$AE(\cdot), AD(\cdot)$	RSA encryption and decryption algorithms
$SE(\cdot), SD(\cdot)$	Symmetric encryption and decryption functions such as AES-128
$sig(\cdot), ver(\cdot)$	RSA message signature and verification algorithms
$sig_{ecdsa}(\cdot), ver_{ecdsa}(\cdot)$	Elliptic curve signature and verification algorithms

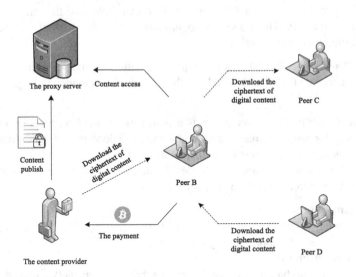

Fig. 1. System model of the DRM scheme.

2.3 Introduction About Security Requirements

In our scheme, we show that the encryption of symmetric key K provides IND-CCA2 secure. Our scheme can provides message confidentiality because of the encryption of symmetric key K is IND-CCA2 secure. And the proxy server (PS) cannot get any information about the digital content of CP. Our scheme can resist the poisoning attack by comparing the hash of ciphertext from other peer with that from CP. Our scheme can avoid collusion attack by verifying the payment. We anonymize the authentication process by removing the requirement to submit real identities.

We will provide detailed proof of these security requirements in Sect. 4.3.

3 The DRM Scheme Based on P2P

3.1 Content Publish

System Setup. The algorithm takes a security parameter λ as input, and generates RSA key pairs for CP and PS. All public keys are certified by Certificate Authority (CA) and known by all participants.

Digital Content Encryption. After CP gets a RSA key pair, he can process digital content m. Specific steps are as follows:

(1) The CP needs to generate a symmetric key K and a random number r such that $K = (k_a||k_b)$ and $|k_a| = |k_b| = |r| = \frac{\mu}{2}$, $||$ is a concatenation operation.
(2) Compute $b = (k_b||r)$ and $a = (k_a||1^{\mu/2}) \oplus h(b)$, where a and b are used to hide the symmetric key K and restore the symmetric key K under certain conditions.
(3) Compute three values. Once a user gets $sk_{rsacp'}$, he/she can calculate the symmetric key K with these:

$$u = h(a) \oplus b \tag{1}$$

$$v = AE(pk_{rsacp}, \sigma) \tag{2}$$

$$w = h(u) \oplus a \tag{3}$$

Where $\sigma = sig(sk_{rsacp'}, u)$.

(4) The CP encrypts the digital content m as follow:

$$C = SE(K, m) \tag{4}$$

(5) The CP provides the digital content identification information CID as follows:

$$CID = \{des_m||l_m||w||v||price||C\} \tag{5}$$

$$\sigma_{CID} = sig(sk_{rsacp'}, CID||T_m) \tag{6}$$

Where l_m is the length of the digital content file, T_m is a time stamp.

6) The CP sends $\{CID||\sigma_{CID}\}$ to the PS.

Information Issuance. When the PS receives the message $\{CID||\sigma_{CID}\}$, he verifies the correctness of the signature σ_{CID} and checks whether T_m is valid. If these operations are successful, PS broadcasts $\{des_m, l_m, price\}$ to all peers in P2P network. At the same time, PS saves $\{v, w, C\}$. Otherwise, PS refuses to provide service.

3.2 Content Purchase

Digital Content Download. In P2P network, the user can download the encrypted digital content C from any peer who has the content. The whole steps of digital content download are described as follows:

(1) The user, as shown in Fig. 1, peer B wants to download the encrypted digital content C. He chooses a random number n_B such that $|n_B| = \mu$ and computes:

$$req = AE(pk_{rsaps}, n_B||des_m||T_{req}) \tag{7}$$

$$\sigma_{req} = sig_{ecdsa}(sk_B, req) \tag{8}$$

And he sends $\{req||\sigma_{req}||pk_B\}$ to the PS.

(2) By the ECDSA signature σ_{req}, PS can be aware of whether the user has enough bitcoins or not. If the signature is correct, PS decrypts req as follow, Otherwise, PS will terminate the download step.

$$AD(sk_{rsaps}, req) = n_B||des_m||T_{req} \tag{9}$$

(3) PS chooses a number s such that $|s| = \mu$, then he computes an identification code Tag_B of the user as follows:

$$Tag_B = h(n_B||s) \tag{10}$$

(4) Assume that some peers have already downloaded the encrypted digital content C, and PS maintains a peers list L that includes these peers. PS encrypts the list L and sends CL to the user.

$$CL = SE(n_B, L) \tag{11}$$

(5) The user decrypts the CL using n_B.

$$L = SD(n_B, CL) \tag{12}$$

(6) The user randomly selects a peer from the list L to download the ciphertext C, the list contains the hash of identification code $h(Tag_i)$. The user sends $h(Tag_i)$ to PS. Note that the user may choose the CP or other peers. Since other peers may be malicious that it is possible to provide false ciphertext, but CP is not. So there are two situations to be discussed. (1) If the CP is selected, the user asks the CP for the ciphertext C directly; (2) If another peer, namely peer D,is selected, PS sends $\{h(C)||h(Tag_D)\}$ to the user. Then, the user obtains ciphertext C from peer D.

Payment. Once the encrypted digital content, namely ciphertext C, is downloaded, the user can initiate a payment request to the CP in order to get the symmetric key K. The user needs to obtain sk_{rsacp} firstly. Assume the price of digital content is d bitcoins, the user needs to build a payment transaction that contains d bitcoins. When the user completes the payment, CP will provide the private key sk_{rsacp} immediately [24].

(1) The user and CP exchange a blind factor y such that $|y| = \log_2^N$ by Diffie-Hellman key exchange protocol.

(2) CP computes $h(x) = h(sk_{rsacp} \oplus y)$ and sends $s = h(x)$ to the user.

(3) The user creates a payment transaction using s. As shown in Fig. 2, the payment transaction T_{pay} redeems the transaction T_{PU}. The input script is a signature for the body of T_{pay}. The output script shows the condition how the payment transaction can be redeemed. Next, the user creates a new transaction called T_{refund} by interacting with CP, the transaction redeems T_{pay} and the user publishes the transaction T_{refund} shown in Fig. 3. When the lock time t is reached, T_{refund} will be added to the ledger only if the transaction T_{pay} has not been redeemed through other condition.

(4) When the payment transaction T_{pay} is confirmed on the ledger, CP receives d bitcoins as his profit. Then CP transfers the private key sk_{rsacp} by creating a new disclosure transaction T_{tf} shown in Fig. 3 that redeems the payment transaction T_{pay} before time t and posts it to the ledger. When the transaction T_{tf} is public, the user can obtain x from input script of T_{tf}. He computes $sk_{rsacp} = x \oplus y$.

(5) If step (4) is not executed when the lock time t is reached, the transaction T_{refund} will be posted to the ledger, the user gets his money back.

The payment transactions can be built by Bitcoin scripts language, the specific output script implementation process is shown in Fig. 4.

3.3   Content Access

Data Decryption. After the user gets the private key sk_{rsacp} from CP, he can send a decryption request to PS. The steps of data decryption are as follows:

$$
\begin{array}{|l|}
\hline
\qquad\qquad\qquad\qquad T_{pay} \\[4pt]
in : T_{PU} \\[4pt]
in-script : \sigma_B = sig_{ecdsa}(sk_B, [T_{pay}]) \\[4pt]
out-script(x, \sigma_{cp}, \sigma_{B'}, \sigma_{cp'}) : \\[4pt]
[(ver_{ecdsa}(pk_{cp}, \sigma_{cp}) \wedge h(x) = s) \vee (ver_{ecdsa}(pk_{B'}, \sigma_{B'}) \wedge ver_{ecdsa}(pk_{cp'}, \sigma_{cp'}))] \\[4pt]
value : d\text{\textBitcoin} \\[4pt]
\hline
\end{array}
$$

Fig. 2. The structure of the payment transaction T_{pay}

$$T_{refund}(in:T_{pay})$$
$$in-script:\sigma_{B'}=sig_{ecdsa}(sk_{B'},[T_{refund}])$$
$$\sigma_{cp'}=sig_{ecdsa}(sk_{cp},[T_{refund}])$$
$$out-script(\sigma_{B'}):ver_{ecdsa}(pk_{B'},\sigma_{B'})$$
$$value:d\text{\Bitcoin}$$
$$time-lock:t$$

$$T_{tf}(in:T_{pay})$$
$$in-script:\sigma_{cp}=sig_{ecdsa}(sk_{cp},[T_{tf}]),x$$
$$out-script(\sigma):ver_{ecdsa}(pk,\sigma)$$
$$value:d\text{\Bitcoin}$$

Fig. 3. The structure of the disclosure transaction and refund transaction

ScriptPubKey:
OP_IF
    OP_SHA256 $<s>$ OP_EQUAL
    <CP publicKey> OP_CHECKSIG
OP_ElSE
    <expiring time> OP_CHECKLOCKTIMEVERIFY
    OP_DROP <user PublicKey> OP_CHECKSIG
    OP_DROP <CP PublicKey> OP_CHECKSIG
OP_ENDIF

Fig. 4. The constructed output script of the payment transaction

(1) The user computes payment voucher and sends it to PS. The payment voucher is:

$$C_{dec} = SE(n_B, \sigma_{dec}||pk_B) \tag{13}$$

Where $\sigma_{dec} = sig_{ecdsa}(sk_B, n_B||T_{dec}||des_m)$.

(2) PS firstly decrypts the ciphertext C_{dec} using n_B and then verifies the signature σ_{dec} using pk_B. The time stamp T_{dec} also needs to be checked. The detail is:

$$\sigma_{dec} = SD(n_B, C_{dec}) \tag{14}$$

$$ver_{ecdsa}(pk_B, \sigma_{dec}) = 1 \tag{15}$$

(3) Finally, PS accesses the public ledger to check the payment record for pk_B. If step (2) fails, PS sends $\perp$ to the user which means PS terminates service. Otherwise, PS sends symmetric key information $\{v.w\}$ to the user.

(4) The user needs to recover the symmetric key K from the $\{v, w\}$.
    (4-1) The user obtains $\sigma = AD(sk_{rsacp}, v)$ and recovers $u = ver(pk_{rsacp'}, \sigma)$.
    (4-2) Computes three values $a = h(u) \oplus w$, $b = h(a) \oplus u$, $\varepsilon = a \oplus h(b)$.
    (4-3) if the rightmost $\mu/2$ bits of ε are "1", the left $\mu/2$ bits are k_a. Otherwise the user can terminate the process.
    (4-4) The left $\mu/2$ bits of b are k_b. Therefore, the symmetric key $K = (k_a||k_b)$.
    (4-5) The user gets $m = SD(K, C)$.

4 Security and Performance Analyses

4.1 Security Model

Let $\mathcal{A}$ be an adversary of probabilistic polynomial time (PPT) and $\mathcal{C}$ be a challenger. We employ the following security model [17, 25]:

IND-CCA2 Model: The model is descripted by an interactive game. Assuming $\mathcal{A}$ is an IND-CCA2 adversary, the game process is as follows:

Setup: The challenger $\mathcal{C}$ firstly determines the system parameters pp and then generates a public and private key pair (pk_{rsacp}, sk_{rsacp}) of CP. The private key sk_{rsacp} is kept secret while pp and pk_{rsacp} is public to the adversary $\mathcal{A}$.

Training stage 1: The adversary $\mathcal{A}$ makes multiple adaptive encryption and decryption queries to the challenger $\mathcal{C}$ (or an oracle).

Encryption oracle: The adversary $\mathcal{A}$ sends a symmetric key K and two distinguishable public keys $\{pk_a, pk_{a'}\}$ to the encryption oracle. If the public keys $\{pk_a, pk_{a'}\}$ is generated in setup phase and $pk_a, pk_{a'}$ are sender's public keys, the oracle returns the symmetric key information $\{v, w\}$ to the adversary. Otherwise, the oracle terminates the query.

Decryption oracle: The adversary $\mathcal{A}$ sends symmetric key information $\{v, w\}$ and two distinguishable public keys $\{pk_a, pk_{a'}\}$ to the decryption oracle. If the public keys $\{pk_a, pk_{a'}\}$ is indeed generated in setup phase and $pk_a, pk_{a'}$ are sender's public keys and the decryption is successful, the adversary $\mathcal{A}$ gets symmetric key K. Otherwise, the oracle terminates the query.

Challenge: The adversary $\mathcal{A}$ outputs a symmetric key pair $\{K_0, K_1\}$ to the challenger $\mathcal{C}$, where $|K_0| = |K_1| = \mu$. The Challenger $\mathcal{C}$ selects a random bit $\beta \leftarrow \{0, 1\}$ and creates target symmetric key information $\{v_\beta, w_\beta\}$ based on K_β for the sender a.

Training stage 2: The adversary $\mathcal{A}$ queries a number of encryption and decryption that is the same as training stage 1, but the query of $\{v_\beta, w_\beta\}$ is prohibited.

Guess: The adversary A output it's guess β', if $\beta' = \beta$, we think that the adversary $\mathcal{A}$ is successful.

The advantage of the adversary $\mathcal{A}$ is defined as:

$$Adv^{IND-CCA2}(\mathcal{A}) = |\Pr[\beta' = \beta] - 1/2|. \tag{16}$$

4.2 Security Analysis

Firstly, we show that the encryption of symmetric key K provides IND-CCA2 secure. Based on RSA assumption [14], we have the following theorem.

Theorem 1. Based on above security model, if there exists a PPT algorithm that can attack the IND-CCA2 security with advantage at least $Adv^{IND-CCA2}(\mathcal{A})$, then there exists another PPT algorithm that can break RSA assumption.

Proof: Assume that there is a PPT algorithm $\mathcal{O}$ that can attack the IND-CCA2 security. We construct a PPT algorithm $\mathcal{P}$ that can solve RSA assumption. Suppose $\mathcal{P}$

has known ciphertext C and corresponding public key pk based on RSA. Algorithm $\mathcal{P}$ runs the algorithm $\mathcal{O}$ as a subroutine to find m such that $C = AE(pk, m)$. The following steps describe the simulation process:

In the simulation, The algorithm $\mathcal{O}$ answers the adversary $\mathcal{A}$ by looking up the tables $\{\theta_1, \theta_2\}$.

The setup phase of the simulation is the same as in the security model.

In encryption phase, when the adversary submits a symmetric key $K = (k_a \| k_b)$ and two distinguishable public keys $\{pk_a, pk_{a'}\}$, the oracle chooses a random number r and computes $b = (k_b \| r)$. If $h(b) = h_b$ is not contained in θ_1, the oracle selects a random number h_b, then computes $a = (k_a \| 1^{\mu/2}) \oplus h_b$. Construct a value $\mu = ver(pk_{a'}, \sigma)$, where σ is a random number. If $h(\mu) = h_\mu$ is not contained in θ_1, the oracle selects a random number h_μ. Finally, the oracle computes $w = h_\mu \oplus a$ and adds $\{w, \sigma\}$ to θ_2. $h(a) = \mu \oplus b$ is computed and it will be added to θ_1. Return the symmetric key information $\{v, w\}$, where $v = AE(pk_a, \sigma)$.

In decryption phase, the oracle tries to find a tuple $\{w, *\}$ in θ_2, if it does not exist, the oracle selects a random number σ, otherwise, σ will be found. Compute $\mu = ver(pk_{a'}, \sigma)$, if $h(\mu) = h_\mu$ is not contained in θ_1, the oracle selects a random number h_μ. Then computes $a = h_\mu \oplus w$ and searches $h(a)$ in θ_1, if not, sets $h(a) = h_a$ that is selected randomly. Finally, the oracle computes $b = h(a) \oplus \mu$, if $h(b) = h_b$ is not contained in θ_1, the oracle selects a random number h_b. The oracle gets $\varepsilon = a \oplus h_b$.

After the challenge, a target symmetric key information $\{v_\beta, w_\beta\}$ such that $v_\beta = C$ and w_β is a random number is obtained by $\mathcal{O}$. Finally, the algorithm $\mathcal{O}$ outputs β'.

The algorithm $\mathcal{P}$ queries the decryption oracle with $\{v_\beta, w_\beta\}$ to get β''. If $\beta'' = \beta'$, $\mathcal{P}$ looks for $\{w_\beta, \sigma\}$ such that $v_\beta = AE(pk_a, \sigma)$. If $\mathcal{O}$ can break the IND-CCA2 security, then $\mathcal{P}$ can solve RSA assumption. Since the RSA is hard problem, there is no such adversary $\mathcal{O}$ can break IND-CCA2 security. Therefore the encryption of symmetric key K in our scheme is IND-CCA2 secure.

Theorem 2. The proposed DRM scheme provides message confidentiality.

Proof: In our scheme, we use AES-128 to instantiate symmetric encryption. Notice that there is no efficient algorithm can solve AES-128 so far. And based on Theorem 1, the encryption of symmetric key K is IND-CCA2 secure. In summary, the probability of the adversary obtaining the digital content m is negligible. The message confidentiality is guaranteed.

Theorem 3. The proxy server (PS) cannot get any information about the digital content of CP.

We assume that PS is semi-trusted in our system which means that PS will perform various computations honestly but he is curious. During the content publish phase, PS gets $CID = \{des_m \| l_m \| w \| v \| price \| C\}$ from CP. From Theorem 1, we have proved the encryption of symmetric key K is IND-CCA2 secure, so PS cannot obtain any information about K. From Theorem 2, it is impossible for PS to solve AES-128. Therefore our DRM scheme keeps the digital content private from PS.

Poisoning Attack. In our scheme, the malicious peer such as peer D, may send invalid or false ciphertext C' during the digital content download phase. To resist the poisoning attack, the user computes the hash of C' denoted $h(C')$, and compares it with $h(C)$ saved in advance. If two hash values are not equal, the user sends $\{h(Tag_D)\|T_{false}\|sig(pk_D, C'\|T_{send})\}$ to PS. PS checks the time stamp T_{false}, T_{send} and the signature for C'. If these are valid, PS deletes all information of peer D which is means that he cannot access to the digital content m freely. Finally, PS sends ciphertext C to the user to complete the download process.

Collusion Attack. We mainly analyze the symmetric key sharing collusion attack. A user a may share his symmetric key K to an unpaid user u. When the user u tries to access the digital content m, he needs to use secret key in cryptocurrency to generate a signature that is a payment voucher. If the user a sends his secret key to u, he must leak his part of identification code n_a in order to make u access the digital content successfully. This is equivalent to the user's identity being compromised. Therefore the attack will be avoid.

Anonymity. When a user downloads the encrypted content, he just submits a random number to complete the certification. The PS cannot obtain any real identity information from the random number. There is no identity information involved in the content access phase. Therefore the proposed protocol ensures anonymity for users.

4.3   Performance Evaluation

This section mainly analyzes the performance of our scheme and compares it with related methods [1–7]. And the compare results are shown in Table 2.

Table 2. Performance comparison

	Server load	Distributed scheme	User revocation	Not need to re-encrypt	Complexity of the billing	Anonymity
[1]	Middle	×	×	✓	Hard	×
[2]	Low	Semi	×	✓	Easy	×
[3]	High	×	×	×	Easy	×
[4]	High	×	×	✓	Easy	✓
[5]	High	Semi	×	✓	Easy	×
[6]	Low	×	✓	✓	Easy	×
[7]	High	×	×	×	Easy	×
Our	Lower	✓	✓	✓	Easy	✓

Compared to other schemes, the load on server in our scheme is the lowest. Only our scheme and Jing Feng's scheme [6] provide a function of illegal user revocation. For higher security, re-encryption method is used in [3, 7]. However, this method not only increases the load on server, but also decreases the efficiency of the scheme. Unlike these, the proposed scheme achieves the same security without the need for re-encryption. Motoki [1] provides a DRM scheme based on Bitcoin, but it's billing is complicated. Therefore the proposed scheme is practical for digital rights management in P2P network.

4.4   Efficiency Analysis

Table 3 shows the computation time of some cryptographic algorithms under the same security level. We use the Java security API to implement these operations. The implement platform is a laptop with a Intel Core i3-6100, 3.70 GHz processor. The notations T_{DES}, $T_{RSA-e/v}$, $T_{RSA-d/s}$, T_{me}, $T_{CPABE-e}$, $T_{CPABE-d}$, T_{ElG-e}, and T_{ElG-d} in Table 3 represent one DES encryption/decryption with a 128 bits [15], one RSA encryption/verification with a 1024 bits modulus [14], one RSA decryption/signing with a 1024 bits modulus., one modular exponentiation, one CP-ABE encryption [18], one CP-ABE decryption [18], one ElGamal encryption with a 1024 bits modulus [19], and one ElGamal decryption with a 1024 bits modulus [19] respectively.

Figure 5 shows the main computational cost of the proposed scheme and previous studies in [4, 7]. As shown in Fig. 5, we calculate the total computational cost for the user and the server at each stage.

We have compared the number of basic operations of the three schemes: the number of basic operation of the content publish, content purchase and content access are 10, 6 and 11 times, which is 5, 8 and 7 times in the scheme [4], and 5*N, 4*N and 3*N times in the scheme [7]. (N is the pieces which the AS breaks the content into).

Table 3. Computational cost of cryptographic algorithms

Operations	Time (Millisecond)
DES encryption/decryption T_{DES}	0.08
RSA encryption/verification $T_{RSA-e/v}$	4
RSA decryption/signing $T_{RSA-d/s}$	172
Modular exponentiation T_{me}	142
CP-ABE encryption $T_{CPABE-e}$	720
CP-ABE decryption $T_{CPABE-d}$	113
ElGamal encryption T_{ElG-e}	12
ElGamal decryption T_{ElG-d}	4

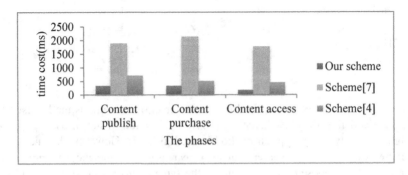

Fig. 5. The main computational cost

5   Conclusion

Aiming at protecting the digital content in network, we propose a novel DRM scheme based on P2P. Specifically, the RSA encryption algorithm ensures the confidentiality of digital content. And the symmetric key is only held by the content provider. In addition, we use the Bitcoin system for a direct and transparent payment. The content provider and the user no longer rely on the server to achieve billing. Moreover, this payment is a timely payment, i.e., when the user's payment is completed, the private key will be obtained immediately. In addition, for privacy of users, we guarantee the anonymity of users while preventing illegal users who are unpaid from accessing the digital content.

We also give a detailed analysis of the proposed scheme. The security analysis shows that the scheme can provide high security. The performance evaluation indicates that our scheme has lower load on the server and protects the privacy of users. From the comparison with other schemes, we find that the proposed scheme has a higher efficiency in practical. Anyone can utilize the scheme to protect their property.

Acknowledge. This work is supported in part by the National Key Research and Development Program of China (No. 2016YFB0800601), the Natural Science Foundation of China (No. 61303217, 61502372), the Natural Science Foundation of Shaanxi province (No. 2013JQ8002, 2014JQ8313).

References

1. Kitahara, M., Kawamoto, J., Sakurai, K.: A method of digital rights management based on Bitcoin protocol. In: Proceedings of the 8th International Conference on Ubiquitous Information Management and Communication, p. 84. ACM (2014)
2. Liu, Y., Yuan, C., Zhong, Y.-Z.: Implementing digital right management in P2P content sharing system. In: Jin, H., Rana, Omer F., Pan, Y., Prasanna, Viktor K. (eds.) ICA3PP 2007. LNCS, vol. 4494, pp. 348–355. Springer, Heidelberg (2007). https://doi.org/10.1007/978-3-540-72905-1_31
3. Petrlic, R., Sorge, C.: Privacy-preserving DRM for cloud computing. In: 26th International Conference Advanced Information Networking and Applications Workshops (WAINA), pp. 1286–1291. IEEE (2012)
4. Huang, Q., Ma, Z.F., Fu, J.Y.: Privacy-preserving digital rights management scheme in cloud computing. J. Commun. **35**(2), 95–103 (2014)
5. Zhang, J., Cai, J., Zhang, Z.: A novel digital rights management mechanism on peer-to-peer streaming system. In: Pan, J.S., Tsai, P.W., Huang, H.C. (eds.) Advances in Intelligent Information Hiding and Multimedia Signal Processing. SIST, vol. 63, pp. 243–250. Springer, Cham (2017). https://doi.org/10.1007/978-3-319-50209-0_30
6. Feng, J., Kong, R., Wang, Y.: A novel digital rights management scheme in P2P networks. Commun. Netw. **2**(4), 230–234 (2010)
7. Su, M., Zhang, H., Duy, X., Dai, Q.: A novel stochastic-encryption-based P2P digital rights management scheme. In: IEEE International Conference Communications (ICC), pp. 5541–5545. IEEE (2015)
8. Fujimura, K., Nakajima, Y.: General-purpose digital ticket framework. In: USENIX Workshop on Electronic Commerce, pp. 177–186 (1998)

9. Nakamoto, S.: Bitcoin: a peer-to-peer electronic cash system. Consulted (2008)

10. Wang, Y., Gao, J.: A regulation scheme based on the ciphertext-policy hierarchical attribute-based encryption in Bitcoin system. IEEE Access **6**, 16267–16278 (2018)

11. Tschorsch, F., Scheuermann, B.: Bitcoin and beyond: a technical survey on decentralized digital currencies. IEEE Commun. Surv. Tutor. **18**(3), 2084–2123 (2016)

12. Rogaway, P., Shrimpton, T.: Cryptographic hash-function basics: definitions, implications, and separations for preimage resistance, second-preimage resistance, and collision resistance. In: Roy, B., Meier, W. (eds.) FSE 2004. LNCS, vol. 3017, pp. 371–388. Springer, Heidelberg (2004). https://doi.org/10.1007/978-3-540-25937-4_24

13. Iwata, T., Abe, T., Ueda, K., Sunaga, H.: A DRM system suitable for P2P content delivery and the study on its implementation. In: The 9th Asia-Pacific Conference on Communications, APCC 2003, vol. 2, pp. 806–811. IEEE (2003)

14. Rivest, R., Shamir, A., Adleman, L.: A method for obtaining digital signature and public key cryptosystems. Commun. ACM **21**, 120–126 (1978)

15. National Bureau of Standards (NBS). NBS FIPS PUBS 197: Advanced Encryption Standard; U.S. Department of Commerce, Washington, DC, USA, November 2001

16. Koblitz, N.: Elliptic curve cryptosystems. Math. Comput. **48**(177), 203–209 (1987)

17. Bellare, M., Desai, A., Pointcheval, D., Rogaway, P.: Relations among notions of security for public-key encryption schemes. In: Krawczyk, H. (ed.) CRYPTO 1998. LNCS, vol. 1462, pp. 26–45. Springer, Heidelberg (1998). https://doi.org/10.1007/BFb0055718

18. Sahai, A., Waters, B.: Fuzzy identity-based encryption. In: Cramer, R. (ed.) EUROCRYPT 2005. LNCS, vol. 3494, pp. 457–473. Springer, Heidelberg (2005). https://doi.org/10.1007/11426639_27

19. ElGamal, T.: A public key cryptosystem and a signature scheme based on discrete logarithms. IEEE Trans. Inf. Theory **31**(4), 469–472 (1985)

20. Qiu, Q., Tang, Z., Yu, Y.: A decentralized authorization scheme for DRM in P2P file-sharing systems. In: 2011 IEEE Consumer Communications and Networking Conference (CCNC), pp. 136–140. IEEE (2011)

21. Reinicke, B., Cummings, J., Kleinberg, H.: The right to digital self-defense. IEEE Secur. Priv. **15**(4), 68–71 (2017)

22. Liu, J., Hu, Y.: A New Digital Rights Management Solution Based on White-Box Cryptography. https://eprint.iacr.org. Accessed 21 May 2018

23. Chen, Y.M., Wu, W.C.: An anonymous DRM scheme for sharing multimedia files in P2P networks. Multimed. Tools Appl. **69**(3), 1041–1065 (2014)

24. Andrychowicz, M., Dziembowski, S., Malinowski, D., Mazurek, Ł.: Fair two-party computations via bitcoin deposits. In: Böhme, R., Brenner, M., Moore, T., Smith, M. (eds.) FC 2014. LNCS, vol. 8438, pp. 105–121. Springer, Heidelberg (2014). https://doi.org/10.1007/978-3-662-44774-1_8

25. Hwang, R.J., Lai, C.H.: Provable fair document exchange protocol with transaction privacy for e-commerce. Symmetry **7**(2), 464–487 (2015)

LWSQR: Lightweight Secure QR Code

Lin Li$^{(\boxtimes)}$, Mingyu Fan, and Guangwei Wang

School of Computer Science and Engineering,
University of Electronic Science and Technology of China (UESTC),
Chengdu 611731, People's Republic of China
flyatlin@163.com

Abstract. Two-dimensional barcodes have commonly penetrated into our lives. QR (Quick Response) code is the most widely used two-dimensional barcode in many scenarios, such as information dissemination, online payment, account login, device authentication and so forth. Because of the openness of QR code, QR code security issues have become prominent. However, there exist challenges in designing the QR code security mechanisms. In this paper, we propose lightweight secure QR code (LWSQR), to resist the information leakage attack, QR code replace attack and malicious message attack. We divide the QR code application scenarios into two types: online scenario and offline scenario, and divide the adversaries into four types. Under five combined scenarios, we utilize the geometric pattern of two level QR code, the identity based cryptography and short signature to establish schemes of lightweight secure QR code. We have implemented these schemes and the experiment results show that these schemes are feasible in practice.

Keywords: QR code · Security · IBE · Short signature · Lightweight

1 Introduction

QR code was designed by DENSOWAVE in 1994 for applications such as vehicle tracking in industrial manufacturing [4]. Compared to one-dimensional barcodes, QR code stores information bits in two-dimensional image space, not only having greater storage capacity, but also having advantages of fast reading from arbitrary direction and so forth. QR code is used in many applications, especially smart phone-related applications. In smart phone app market, WeChat, AliPay and other apps utilize QR codes for business card sharing, cashless payments and so forth. In 2013, Google filed for a patent that uses a trusted device to scan QR codes for secure login from untrusted device [2]. QR code is used usually to encode and deliver URLs. Through scanning QR code with devices such as smart phone to link to the URLs, it greatly extends the applications on the Internet, occurring some new applications such as QR code scanning ordering food and shopping. Indeed, any devices, equipped with camera and corresponding software, could link the physical world and network utilizing the QR code as a medium.

© Springer Nature Singapore Pte Ltd. 2018
F. Li et al. (Eds.): FCS 2018, CCIS 879, pp. 241–255, 2018.
https://doi.org/10.1007/978-981-13-3095-7_19

However, because of the openness of QR code, QR code security issues have become prominent. (1) Many applications are designed improperly to store the private messages such as login credentials in QR code in plain text. It is easy for the QR code scanning devices (such as Google Glass, etc.) to obtain these private messages. (2) QR code is a type of machine-readable code, not human readable code. Once replaced or modified, it is difficult for human to distinguish from the QR codes. Criminals secretly replace the merchant's QR code of receipt of payment and spoof the users to obtain the QR code of payment to seek illegal money. The official QR codes on the popular sharing bicycle are covered by fake QR codes, leading to users'privacy leakage and mistaken money transfer. (3) Due to the difficulty for users to verify whether the QR code is credible or not, QR code could be used as an attack vector to deliver malicious messages, especially suitable for use in QRishing or malware distribution [15,16]. Even though knowing that the URL in QR code is unfamiliar, most users still access the URL after scanning the QR code [15]. Meanwhile, URL shortening service (such as bit.ly, goo.gl etc.) hides the eventual URL in QR code and nearly 8% of the URLs are shortened [13]. Thus, attackers obtain more chances to use this attack vector to get devices' higher privilege.

Secure QR code schemes based on certificate in PKI require a large storage space [9], but the capacity of QR code is limited. The RSA and DSA certificates with version 3 occupy more than 600 bytes. Even the common used DSA signatures occupy 40 bytes. Whereas, the average message bytes of common QR codes are less than 60 [13]. Longer message makes the QR code scanning process prone to be wrong. In other hand, the cost of certificate management is relatively high. As for malicious message detection, existing schemes rely on a trust third party service with query-answer mechanism to detect the message of QR code. However, the third party service is the system's bottleneck, and it is difficult to cover all the malicious messages because of the diversity of the message.

Kui Ren et al. utilize the physical nature of devices to propose a secure QR code scheme without encryption operations to resist the information leakage [17]. However, this scheme is only suitable for specific application scenarios.

In this paper, we focus on the security of the communication channel between the code scanner and the QR code (Scanner-QR Channel). We divide the QR code application scenarios into two types: online scenario and offline scenario, and divide the adversaries into four types: Adversary I, Adversary II, Adversary III, and Adversary IV. Under five combined scenarios, we utilize the geometric pattern of two level QR code, the identity based cryptography and short signature to establish schemes of lightweight secure QR code.

Contributions:

1. Utilize the geometric pattern of QR code to provide security mechanism and propose lightweight secure QR code schemes.
2. Combine the identity based cryptography and short-signature mechanisms to propose certificateless secure QR code schemes. These schemes could reduce the amount of additional data required for secure QR codes.
3. Divide the QR code application scenarios into two types: online scenario and offline scenario, and divide the adversaries into four types. Under five combined scenarios, propose lightweight secure QR code schemes respectively.

The rest of this paper is organized as follows. The QR code structure and encoding/decoding principle are introduced in Sect. 2. The QR code threat model is described in Sect. 3. We describe in detail two level QR code and Scanner-QR channel, and then propose lightweight secure QR code schemes under five combined scenarios in Sect. 4. We implement these schemes and conduct experimental evaluation in Sect. 5. The related work is discussed in Sect. 6. We conclude our paper in Sect. 7.

2   Background

For convenience, we firstly introduce the QR code structure and encoding/decoding principle. QR code is a two-dimensional image consisting of white/black blocks, divided into these components: finder structure, format information, alignment, data and error correction code etc. The version number of QR code is from version 1 to 40. QR code with version 1 consists of 21×21 white/black blocks, but version 40 is 177×177. If the version number is increased by one, the number of white/black blocks is increased by four. The error correction code of QR code is a kind of specific BCH error correction code based on Reed-Solomon codes. The error correction code has four error correction levels: L (7%), M (15%), Q (25%) and H (30%). To ensure the readability, the most commonly used QR code's version number is less than 10 in practice. However, at the 'L' level, QR code with version 10 can store only 271 characters.

QR code encoding steps consist of data analysis, data coding, error correction coding, adding mask template and module padding etc. Firstly, analyze the data format and utilize corresponding type of code scheme to encode data. QR code support Numeric, Alphanumeric, 8-bit Byte and Kanji data encoding modes. After data encoding, add BCH error correction code based on RS code. In order to improve the success rate of scanning process, utilize the mask template to generate optimal white/black blocks distribution (close to 1:1). There are eight kinds of mask templates in QR code. Each mask template is used to obtain the best mask result outputted as the final code.

QR code decoding steps consist of image preprocessing, QR code location, removing mask code, error correction, decoding data etc. After image preprocessing, the image obtained by the scanning process is converted into black/white image for the convenience of location. Through searching for the finder structure, the QR code is located. The format information could be obtained for parsing the mask template, error correction level etc. Then, utilize the mask template to remove the mask code. After error correction and data decoding, the original message string is obtained finally.

3   Threat Model

The attacks based on QR code are commonly occurring and there exist a significant amount of malicious QR codes in the network [5]. In this paper, we focus on the threat model about the QR code itself, taking no care of the threats of system applying QR code, such as scanning app's vulnerabilities, QRLJack-ing [5] etc. We will analyze the threat model from attack surface and security challenges.

3.1 Attack Surface

As shown in Fig. 1, S_i represents the ith attack surface. In the rest of this section, we will analyze S_1, S_2, S_3 respectively to model the threats and security needs.

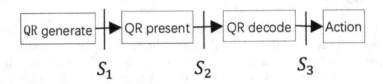

Fig. 1. QR code attack surface.

1. S_1: QR code standard does not provide authentication mechanisms. The QR code may not be generated by the claimed producer. Attackers could disguise as legitimate producers to generate illegal QR codes. Thus, the QR codes could be easily forged.
2. S_2: Attackers could modify the presented QR codes by taking some measures such as changing some white blocks into black blocks to change the message in QR code [12] etc. Meanwhile, due to the nature of QR code, the message is prone to be eavesdropped.
3. S_3: Because of lacking message verification mechanisms, attackers could utilize malicious messages (e.g. malicious URL) to implement the attack schemes such as QRishing attack [15].

By analyzing the QR code's attack surface, we could draw the security requirements shown as follows:

1. Identity authentication of QR code generator.
2. Confidentiality of QR code message.
3. Integrity of QR code.
4. Malicious message verification.

3.2 Challenges of Designing QR Code Security Mechanism

Due to the features of QR code and related applications, designing QR code security mechanism has challenges. The main features are as follows:

1. The nature of QR code itself: limited storage capacity, easily leaked message, not human readable etc.
2. Message diversity: QR code could represent many types of messages and it is a difficult issue to detect malicious ones from large unpredictable messages, e.g. detecting malicious URL.

3. The independence of function modules: the implementations of function modules (QR code generation, presentation, decoding and action) are independent, making QR code vulnerable.
4. Variety of application requirements: depending on the role of QR code in applications, the security requirements may be very different. For example, the confidentiality of QR code is unnecessary in applications of public message sharing. The different security requirements make the security mechanisms complex.

4 Lightweight Secure QR Code

In this paper, we focus on the security of the communication channel between scanning device and QR code (Scanner-QR channel). We classify the QR code application scenarios into two classes: online scenario and offline scenario and classify the attackers into four classes. We propose lightweight secure QR code schemes especially in five attacker-scenario combinations. The basic idea is utilizing geometric pattern of two level QR code and utilizing identity based encryption and short signature to provide lightweight secure QR code schemes.

4.1 Two Level QR Code

Two level QR code is as shown in Fig. 2. The two level QR code structure is based on [14], but in contrast to [14], we only embed two geometric patterns: q_1 and q_2 (represent bit 0 and 1 respectively, shown in Fig. 2) to promote efficiency and accuracy of pattern recognition. The center parts of two patterns are black block, and other parts are complementary. Let (i, j) represents the dot in $q_k(k = 1, 2)$, where $q_k = white$ or $black(white = \overline{black})$. If $(i, j) \in centerpart$, then $q_1(i, j) = q_2(i, j) = black$, otherwise $q_1(i, j) \neq q_2(i, j)$. The second level geometric patterns have no influence on the standard QR code scanning process. Meanwhile, these patterns could be used to share private messages.

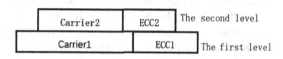

Fig. 2. Two level QR code structure.

Fig. 3. Two levels message format.

Message Encoding. It needs at least 16 pixels to represent one bit in the second level QR code. Meanwhile in order to promote efficiency and accurate of recognition, we do not embed any information in the black blocks in specific modules (such as finder module, format information module and timing module etc.). We utilize RS code to correct the errors in the second level bits. The error correction capacity in the second level QR code is same as that of the first level. Let $bits : \{0,1\}^*$ represents the second level message, $B = \{B_0, B_1\}$ represents the block pattern in first level, where B_0 stands for black block and B_1 stands for white block. Let $G = \{G_0, G_1, G_2\}$ represents the second level geometric pattern, where $G_i = i(i = 0, 1)$ stands for the embed pattern and G_2 stands for the original block. The coded second level message is: $bits\|RSenc(bits)$, where $RSenc$ stands for the RS coding function. The message format is as shown in Fig. 3. Let $M = M_1\|M_2$, where M_1 is the first level message and M_2 is the second level message. Message encoding algorithm-$MsgEncode(M)$ is described in Algorithm 1.

Algorithm 1. Message encoding algorithm

1: $M_2 = M_2\|RSenc(M_2)$
2: Utilize the standard QR code encoding algorithm to encode $M_1 : Code_1$
3: Utilize the $Template$ to obtain the embed area $B = Code_1 \odot Template$
4: $i = 0$.
5: **for** $item \in B$ **do**
6:     **if** $i == length(M_2)$ **then** break;
7:     **end if**
8:     **if** $item == B_0$ **then** $item = G_{M_2(i)}$
9:     **end if**
10:     $i = i + 1$
11: **end for**
12: According to B, generate the last QR code image $Code_2$
13: Return $Code_2$

Message Decoding. Message decoding process depends on the standard QR code decoding process. We first recognize and decode the first level QR code (standard QR code) and then based on the first level code, we decode the second level code. The captured QR code image is $Code_2$. We utilize the standard QR code decoding process to locate and to segment the QR code in $Code_2$. According to the fixed order, we extract the black blocks by executing pattern recognition to $recognize$ the second level bits. After RS error correction, we could obtain the decoded message. Message decoding algorithm-$MsgDecode(Code_2)$ is described in Algorithm 2.

The two level QR code encode/decode is as shown in Fig. 4.

Algorithm 2. Message decoding algorithm

1: Utilize standard QR code decoding algorithm to get $Code_1$ and M_1
2: Utilize the Template to obtain the embed area $B = Code_1 \odot Template$
3: $State = Failure$
4: $i = 0$
5: **for** $item \in B$ **do**
6:     **if** B is empty **then** break
7:     **end if**
8:     **if** $item == B_0$ **then**
9:         $M_2(i) = recognize(item)$
10:         $i = i + 1$
11:     **end if**
12: **end for**
13: $(M_2, State) = Rsdec(M_2)$
14: **if** $State == Failure$ **then** Return null
15: **end if**
16: Return M_2

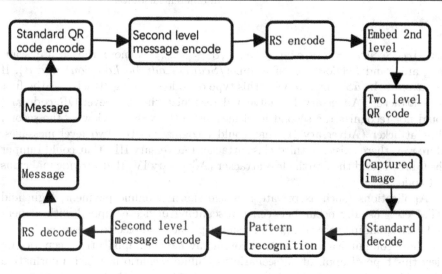

Fig. 4. Two level QR code encode/decode.

4.2   Scanner-QR Channel

As shown in Fig. 5, Scanner-QR channel is a light communication channel between Scanner and QR code. $Scanner\_adv$ denotes scanning attacker. Scanner is normal scanning party. QR code is the two level QR code presented on some media such as screen. d_{max} and α_{max} denote the valid scanning distance and angle respectively. When $d > d_{max}$ or $\alpha > \alpha_{max}$, the Scanner/$Scanner\_adv$ could not distinguish the second level pattern and could obtain nothing of the second level message, as shown in Fig. 6. Let d_1 and α_1 denote the maximum valid scanning distance and angle respectively, thus $d_{max} < d_1, \alpha_{max} < \alpha_1$.

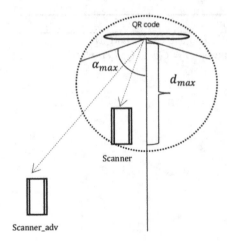

Fig. 5. Scanner-QR channel.

Fig. 6. Second level geometric pattern in different distances.

Let $AreaSecure = \{(d,\alpha)|d \leq d_{max}, \alpha \leq \alpha_{max}\}$ denote the secure scanning area, and Let location of Scanner/$Scanner\_adv$ be $Location = (d,\alpha)$. If $Location \notin AreaSecure$, we view this type of code scanning attacker as the first class attacker (Adversary I) that could recognize the first level QR code and could not recognize the second level message, otherwise we view as the second class attacker (Adversary II) that could recognize all the two level messages. Moreover, there exist the third class attacker (Adversary III) that could tamper the QR code and the fourth class attacker (Adversary IV) that provide malicious QR code.

Applications (such as private message sharing, online payment, login and OTM etc.) usually occur between the scanning device equipped with camera and corresponding software (such as smart phone) and electronic screen. Due to the short communication time and commonly network application scenario, we view this type of application scenario as Online scenario in which information leakage is a common attack. Adversary I and Adversary II all contribute to the information leakage attack. Applications such as offline payment, offline message sharing etc. usually do not require network context and in these applications, the QR codes do not change during a long time. Thus, we view this application scenario as Offline scenario. In Offline scenario, Adversary I disappear because attacker could obtain all level messages in QR code, even tampering the QR code. Adversary III and Adversary IV contribute to attacks in all Online and Offline scenarios.

According to the application scenario and attacker type, we mainly focus on these five class combinations: Online scenario- Adversary I (Scenario 1), Online scenario- Adversary I/III (Scenario 2), Offline scenario- Adversary III(Scenario 3), Offline scenario- Adversary II/III(Scenario 4) and Online/ Offline scenario-

Adversary IV (Scenario 5). We propose lightweight secure QR code schemes in these five combinations respectively.

4.3 Secure QR Code Schemes

Bilinear Mapping. Let $\mathbb{G}_1$ denote an additive group of prime order q and $\mathbb{G}_2$ denote a multiplicative group of the same order. Let P denote a generator in $\mathbb{G}_1$. Let $\hat{e} : \mathbb{G}_1 \times \mathbb{G}_1 \to \mathbb{G}_2$ be a bilinear mapping with the following properties:

1. Bilinear: $\hat{e}(aP, bQ) = \hat{e}(P, Q)^{ab}$, for all $P, Q \in \mathbb{G}_1, a, b \in \mathbb{Z}_q$.
2. Non-degenerate: there exist $P, Q \in \mathbb{G}_1$ that make $\hat{e}(P, Q) \neq 1$.
3. Efficiently computable: the map $\hat{e}$ is efficiently computable.

Overview. Let ID_g be the identity of QR code generator, ID_s be the identity of scanner, and KGC be the key generator center. ID_g and ID_s register their own identities in KGC to obtain the corresponding private keys: d_{ID_g} and d_{ID_s}. The first level message in QR code is M_1 and the second level message is M_2. σ is the signature. $MMDP$ is the malicious message detection party. PK_{ID_g} is the temporary public key. The secure QR code system overview is as shown in Fig. 7. The message format is as shown in Fig. 8. According to the application requirements, the fields in message may be different. For example, if the ID_g is known for the Scanner, it is not necessary to obtain the ID_g field in message. Similarly, other fields may be empty according to the requirements.

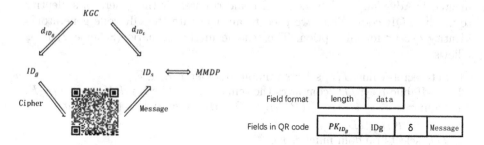

Fig. 7. Secure QR code system.   **Fig. 8.** Message format.

Initialization. We need to initialize firstly to establish the system parameters and private keys of the generators and scanners. The initialization contains two steps: Setup and Private-Key-Extract.

1. Setup: Let $(\mathbb{G}_1, \mathbb{G}_T)$ be bilinear group of prime order p and $\hat{e} : \mathbb{G}_1 \times \mathbb{G}_1 \to \mathbb{G}_T$ be a bilinear mapping. Hash functions: $H_0, H_1 : \{0, 1\}^* \to \mathbb{G}_1^*, H_2 : \mathbb{G}_T \to \{0, 1\}^n$. KGC select a random number $s \in \mathbb{Z}_p^*$, and a random element $P \in \mathbb{G}_1$. The main public key of KGC is $P_{pub} = sP$ and the main private key of KGC is s. The system parameters are $\{\mathbb{G}_1, \mathbb{G}_T, p, \hat{e}, P, H_0, H_1, H_2, P_{pub}\}$.

2. Private-Key-Extract: ID_g requests private key d_{ID_g} from KGC:$Q_{ID_g} = H_1(ID_g) \in \mathbb{G}_1^*$, $d_{ID_g} = sQ_{ID_g}$. ID_s requests private key d_{ID_s} from KGC: $Q_{ID_s} = H_1(ID_s) \in \mathbb{G}_1^*$, $d_{ID_s} = sQ_{ID_s}$.

Scenario 1. In this scenario, Adversary I could obtain the first level message in QR code but could not distinguish the second level message. Thus, we could utilize the second level geometric pattern to resist the information leakage attack. The scheme in this scenario (Scheme 1) is as follows:

1. Select a random number $r \in \mathbb{Z}_q^*$.
2. Compute the key for encryption: $key = PRF(H_1(r\|timestamp)$, $timestamp$ is for replay attack.
3. Encode the second level message: $M_2 = RSenc(key)$.
4. Encrypt the first level message:$C_1 = M_1 \oplus M_2$.
5. Decrypt the first level message: $M_1 = C_1 \oplus RSdec(M_2)$.

Security analysis: Adversary I obtains only the first level message, that is, Adversary I could not obtain the key in the second level message. If the adversary want to know the plain text, he/she must guess the right key. Moreover, due to the timestamp, the keys are different every time, so it could resist the replay attack. Meanwhile, this scheme only needs Hash, PRF, XOR and RS encode/decode lightweight operations. Thus, this scheme is lightweight.

Scenario 2. In this scenario, except for the information leakage attack implemented byAdversary I, Adversary III could counterfeit the generator's identity to produce QR code. Thus, we need to authenticate the QR code generator?s identity except for encryption. The scheme in this scenario (Scheme 2) is as follows:

1. Set-Secret-Value: ID_g selects random number $x_{ID_g} \in \mathbb{Z}_p^*$.
2. Set-Public-Key: ID_g computes the temporary public key $PK_{ID_G} = x_{ID_g}P$.
3. Sign: $\sigma = d_{ID_g} + x_{ID_g}H_1(PK_{ID_g}\|ID_g\|M_1)$, signature is (PK_{ID_g}, σ).
4. $M_1' = PK_{ID_g}\|ID_g\|\sigma\|M_1$.
5. ID_g selects random number $r \in \mathbb{Z}_q^*$.
6. $key = PRF(H_1(r\|timestamp))$,$timestamp$ is for replay attack.
7. $M_2 = key$.
8. Encryption:$C_1 = M_1^* \oplus M_2$.
9. Decryption:$M_1' = C_1 \oplus M_2$.
10. $Q_{ID_g} = H_1(ID_g) \in \mathbb{G}_1^*$.
11. Verify:
    $sig_1 = \hat{e}(\sigma, P), sig_2 = \hat{e}(Q_{ID_g}, P_{pub})\hat{e}(PK_{ID_g}, H_1(PK_{ID_g}\|ID_g\|M_1))$. If sig_1 is equal to sig_2, verify success, otherwise verify failure.

Security analysis: Although Adversary I could obtain C_1, he/she could not obtain the M_1', i.e., the adversary could not know ID_g. This scheme could also protect the privacy of the identity of QR code generator. Even though Adversary III tries to counterfeit the legal generator, he/she could not forge the signature because of the unknown private key of the generator.

Scenario 3. In this scenario, we could embed short signature into the QR code to resist attack from Adversary III. The signature scheme we adopt is the Scheme1 in [10]. The scheme in this scenario (Scheme 3) is as follows:

1. Set-Secret-Value: ID_g selects random number $x_{ID_g} \in \mathbb{Z}_p^*$.
2. Set-Public-Key: ID_g computes the temporary public key: $PK_{ID_g} = x_{ID_g}P$.
3. Sign: $\sigma = d_{ID_g} + x_{ID_g}H_1(PK_{ID_g}||ID_g||M_1)$.
4. Verify: $sig_1 = \hat{e}(\sigma, P), sig_2 = \hat{e}(Q_{ID_g}, P_{pub})\hat{e}(PK_{ID_g}, H_1(PK_{ID_g}||ID_g||M_1))$. If sig_1 is equal to sig_2, verify success, otherwise verify failure.

Scenario 4. Because Adversary II could obtain all level messages in this scenario, the geometric pattern in the second level in QR code is useless. Thus, we need to operate the message in the QR code directly to resist attacks. The scheme in this scenario (Scheme 4) is as follows:

1. Set-Secret-Value: ID_g selects random number $x_{ID_g} \in \mathbb{Z}_p^*$.
2. Set-Public-Key: ID_g computes the temporary public key: $PK_{ID_g} = x_{ID_g}P$.
3. Sign: $\sigma = d_{ID_g} + x_{ID_g}H_1(PK_{ID_g}||ID_g||M_1)$, signature is (PK_{ID_g}, σ).
4. Encrypt: $Q_{ID_s} = H_1(ID_s) \in \mathbb{G}_1^*$, $Key = PRF(H_1 g_{ID_s}^{x_{ID_g}}, C = (ID_g||\sigma||M) \oplus Key$ Where $g_{ID_s} = \hat{e}(Q_{ID_s}, P_{pub}) \in \mathbb{G}_T^*$.
5. Decrypt: $Q_{ID_s} = H_1(ID_s) \in \mathbb{G}_1^*$, $g_{ID_s} = \hat{e}(d_{ID_s}, PK_{ID_g}) \in \mathbb{G}_T^*$, $Key = PRF(H_1(g_{ID_s}))$, $ID_g||\sigma||M = C \oplus Key$.
6. Verify: $Q_{ID_g} = H_1(ID_g) \in \mathbb{G}_1^*$, $sig_1 = \hat{e}(\sigma, P), sig_2 = \hat{e}(Q_{ID_g}, P_{pub})$ $\hat{e}(PK_{ID_g}, H_1(PK_{ID_g}||ID_g||M_1))$. If sig_1 is equal to sig_2, verify success, otherwise verify failure.

Security analysis: The same as the Scheme 1 in Scenario 1, this scheme could also protect the privacy of the QR code generator's identity. Through the encryption process, ID_g is encrypted and others could know nothing about ID_g.

Scenario 5. In this scenario, we need to detect malicious QR code. The scheme in this scenario (Scheme 5) is as follows:

$MMDP$ accepts the requests for malicious message detection and responses the detection result to the requester. Meanwhile, $MMDP$ maintains a black and white list. If some identities produce malicious QR code, $MMDP$ add them into black list. ID_s applies regularly to $MMDP$ for an updated black/white list. If ID_g is included in black list, ID_s regards the corresponding message in QR code as malicious message. If ID_g is included in white list, then ID_s regards the corresponding message in QR code as clean message. If ID_g is neither in black list nor in white list, then ID_s requests $MMDP$ to detect the message and adds ID_g into the native black list when the message is detected as a malicious one.

4.4   Other Considerations

The identities attached with time stamp (such as $alice@googlemail.com||$ $current - date$) are applied in secure mail system [6] to send mails which could only be read in the future. The same identities could be used as well in our secure QR code schemes. Moreover, we could utilize the identities with limited validity period to shorten the length of signature. Because the valid period of identities is limited, we could truncate part of the signature appropriately without compromising security.

5   Experimental Evaluation

Based on the open source library zxinglib [8] and JPBC [3], we have implemented the schemes in this paper on smart phone Meizu S3 equipped with android operation system. The QR code image size is 600×600. The smart phone face the QR code on the front within the distance 0.6 m. This is a proof of concept experiment only in order to compare the efficiency of the encoding and decoding process among the schemes in this paper and the standard QR code schemes. Thus, we have not optimized the code in zxinglib and the encoding and decoding time will be a little longer than that on some practical apps such as WeChat and AliPay.

The experiment results are as shown in Fig. 9. $S_i(i = 1, 2, 3, 4)$ denotes the ith scheme, Standard denotes the standard QR encoding/decoding scheme. In Fig. 8a, the parts corresponding with the maximum encoding time 5000 ms represent the nonexistent situations. The parts corresponding with the maximum decoding time 2000 ms are also the nonexistent situations in Fig. 8b. As the QR code version increases, the time overhead of the encoding process grows faster than the decoding process. This is because the error correction decoding is easier from the high quality image than the encoding process. In the encoding process, time overheads of S_1, S_2, S_3 and S_4 are greater than the standard QR code encoding scheme, but the average cost increased by only 7.8%. In the decoding process, time overheads of S_1, S_2, S_3 and S_4 are also greater than the standard decoding scheme. The time overhead of S_1 is closest to the standard scheme with the average cost increased by only 173 ms. In comparison with the standard decoding scheme, the average costs of S_2, S_3 and S_4 have increased by only 557 ms.

Due to the storage space limitation, when the QR code version number is greater than 14, the geometric pattern in S_1 scheme is not that distinguishable than that in less version number QR code. When the QR code version is less than 12, there is not that enough space to storage data in S_2, S_3 and S_4 if we put all the fields in QR code. However, because the QR code version number is less than 10 in the majority of practical applications, S_1 scheme is feasible in practice. The extra data required in S_2, S_3 and S_4 is no more than 80 byte, so it only requires up to two more versions to storage the extra data. Therefore, S_2, S_3 and S_4 are also feasible in practice.

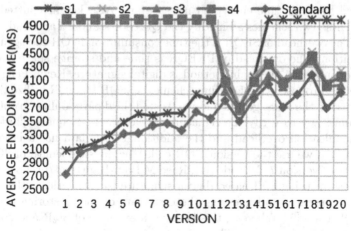

(a) Average encoding time

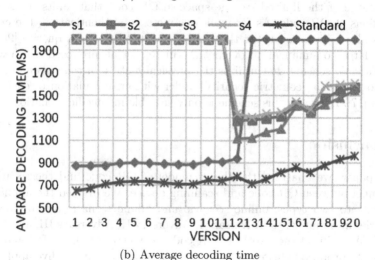

(b) Average decoding time

Fig. 9. Comparison of average encoding/decoding time.

6   Related Work

The current works about the security of QR code mainly focus on credential, integrity and malicious message authentication. As for credential, the main method is encryption including symmetric and asymmetric encryption. In 2011, Google has used symmetric encryption on the login applications [1]. Kevin Peng, Harry Sanabria et al. proposed the encryption schemes, i.e. SEQR and PKEQR [7]. SEQR uses symmetric encryption directly and the generator and the code scanner own the same key. PKEQR combines the RSA public key encryption and AES in which the message is encrypted by the AES and the key of AES is encrypted by RSA. The encrypted message and AES key are putted in the QR code. These two schemes all modify the QR code standard and lead to extra overhead. The overhead of SEQR is the time consumption in QR code generation and recognition. The overhead of PKEQR is time and storage space consumptions. As for Integrity, the main method is digital signature. Kevin Peng, Harry Sanabria et al. proposed the signature scheme, i.e. SQR [7]. SQR utilize the RSA signature to sign the message and query a trusted third party online to obtain the signer?s public key to verify the signature. However, the frequent queries have large communication overhead and the additional long data has a large space overhead. When we use the version 1 QR code, the message length of SQR will be the length of version 7 QR code [11]. Raed M.Bani-Hani et al. proposed secure QR code system using PKI-based digital signature to authenticate the identity of QR code generator and querying the certificate online or storing certificate offline in QR code [9]. Whereas, this is only an example of SQR and consumes large additional storage space. The large storage space consumption is a bottleneck because of the limited storage space in QR code that limits the security applications of QR code. As for malicious message authentication, the current schemes also rely on a trusted third party and need frequent queries [9]. This leads to large communication overhead. Kui Ren et al. proposed a lightweight secure barcode scheme that utilizes the physical feature of the screen of smartphone to establish geometric security model without calculation of encryption function [17]. However, this scheme is only suitable in specific scenarios.

7 Conclusion

In this paper, we analyzed the threat model of QR code and the security of the channel between QR code and scanning device. We divided the application scenarios into two types: online scenario and offline scenario and divided the adversaries into four types: Adversary I, Adversary II, Adversary III, and Adversary IV. We utilized the two level QR code geometric pattern, IBE and short signature to propose lightweight secure QR code schemes in the five application scenario-adversary combinations respectively. The experiment results show that these lightweight secure QR code schemes are feasible in practice. The schemes in this paper could be used in many scenarios, especially the applications presenting QR code in electronic screen. However, these schemes require a unified identity management center, and it needs to pay a big overhead to maintain a separate center. In the future, we plan to explore new technologies to overcome the limitation of storage and promote the security application of QR code.

References

1. Google experiments with new QR-based secure login. https://www.theverge.com/2012/1/17/2714263/google-experiment-qr-code-secure-login-sesame. Accessed 20 Aug 2018
2. Google Patent.http://www.google.com/patents/us20130219479. Accessed 20 Aug 2018
3. JPBC. http://gas.dia.unisa.it/projects/jpbc/. Accessed 20 Aug 2018
4. QR Code. http://www.qrcode.com/en/. Accessed 20 Aug 2018
5. QRLJacking. https://www.owasp.org/index.php/qrljacking. Accessed 20 Aug 2018
6. Secure Mail System. https://crypto.stanford.edu/ibe/. Accessed 20 Aug 2018
7. Security Overview of QR Codes. https://courses.csail.mit.edu/6.857/2014/files/12-peng-sanabria-wu-zhu-qr-codes.pdf. Accessed 20 Aug 2018
8. Zxing. https://github.com/zxing/zxing. Accessed 20 Aug 2018
9. Banihani, R., Wahsheh, Y.A., Alsarhan, M.B.: Secure QR code system, pp. 1–6 (2014)
10. Huang, X., Mu, Y., Susilo, W., Wong, D.S., Wu, W.: Certificateless signatures: new schemes and security models. Comput. J. **55**(4), 457–474 (2012)
11. Kieseberg, P., et al.: QR code security, pp. 430–435 (2010)
12. Krombholz, K., Frühwirt, P., Kieseberg, P., Kapsalis, I., Huber, M., Weippl, E.: QR code security: a survey of attacks and challenges for usable security. In: Tryfonas, T., Askoxylakis, I. (eds.) HAS 2014. LNCS, vol. 8533, pp. 79–90. Springer, Cham (2014). https://doi.org/10.1007/978-3-319-07620-1_8
13. Lerner, A., et al.: Analyzing the use of quick response codes in the wild, pp. 359–374 (2015)
14. Tkachenko, I., Puech, W., Destruel, C., Strauss, O., Gaudin, J., Guichard, C.: Two-level QR code for private message sharing and document authentication. IEEE Trans. Inf. Forensics Secur. **11**(3), 571–583 (2016)
15. Vidas, T., Owusu, E., Wang, S., Zeng, C., Cranor, L.F., Christin, N.: QRishing: the susceptibility of smartphone users to QR code phishing attacks. In: Adams, A.A., Brenner, M., Smith, M. (eds.) FC 2013. LNCS, vol. 7862, pp. 52–69. Springer, Heidelberg (2013). https://doi.org/10.1007/978-3-642-41320-9_4
16. Yao, H., Shin, D.: Towards preventing QR code based attacks on android phone using security warnings, pp. 341–346 (2013)
17. Zhang, B., Ren, K., Xing, G., Fu, X., Wang, C.: SBVLC: secure barcode-based visible light communication for smartphones pp. 2661–2669 (2014)

An Authentication Approach for Multiple-User Location-Based Queries

Yong Wang, Abdelrhman Hassan[✉], Xiaoran Duan, Xiaodong Yang,
Yiquan Zhang, and Xiaosong Zhang

The School of Computer Science and Engineering, Center for Cyber Security,
University of Electronic Science and Technology of China, Chengdu 611731, China
cla@uestc.edu.cn, abdhassan25@yahoo.com

Abstract. With the increasing use of smart mobile devices, users can
connect and coordinate with local people or events that match their interests through geosocial networking applications. This calls for techniques
to support processing the Multiple-User Location-based Query (MULQ),
which returns a group of users with k Point of Interests (POIs) based
on their locations and individual preferences. When the query processing is outsourced to a service provider capable of handling voluminous
spatial data objects, the query authentication becomes highly desirable
because the service provider is beyond the administrative domain of a
data owner. In this paper, we design an MRS-tree to index POIs, based
on which, we propose a MULQ processing and authentication solution.
We further proposed a bitmap-based dominance relationship comparison
algorithm to improve its efficiency. A set of experiments are carried out,
which shows the validity of our solutions under various parameters.

Keywords: Location-based Query · Data outsourcing
Query authentication

1 Introduction

With the proliferation of location-based services (LBSs), mobile users can easily share their real-time locations to various location-based social networking
applications, such as Facebook Place, Meetup and Google Map. Using these
applications, users can issue the Multiple-User Location-based Query (MULQ),
which returns k Point of Interests (POIs) to a group of users by considering both
their locations and individual preferences.

In data outsourcing scenarios, a data owner (DO) delegates his data to a
service provider (SP), which indexes the data and processes users' location-
based queries. In the rest of this paper, we will use the terms service provider and
server interchangeably. Because the service provider is beyond the administrative
domain of the data owner, it may return inaccurate or incorrect query results,
either intentionally or unintentionally. Therefore, *Query Authentication* [1], i.e.,

© Springer Nature Singapore Pte Ltd. 2018
F. Li et al. (Eds.): FCS 2018, CCIS 879, pp. 256–270, 2018.
https://doi.org/10.1007/978-981-13-3095-7_20

which helps guarantee query result soundness, correctness, and completeness on the user's side, is highly desirable.

Various studies have been conducted which address query processing and authentication, such as [2–4]. However, these techniques can hardly be applied to MULQ. When processing a MULQ request, the server needs to compute each user's preference. The computation results rather than the raw data are then checked against the query criteria. The data owner cannot sort or sign the computation results beforehand because the individual preferences and query locations are provided by users, they are unknown when the dataset is outsourced to the server. This dynamic characteristic causes MULQ results to differ with respect to different query locations and individual preferences. A straightforward approach is to compute the possible results, sort and digitally sign them with existing authentication techniques. Obviously, this approach would generate an overwhelming amount of data for the data owner that would dramatically increase the cost of data outsourcing. Instead, this problem requires an efficient and effective authenticated data structure (ADS) construction and verification mechanism, performed through verification objects (VOs). Our contributions include:

- We propose an MRS-tree to index POIs, based on which, we propose an MULQ processing and authentication algorithms.
- We propose a bitmap-based dominance relationship comparison algorithm to improve the efficiency of dominance relationship comparison.
- We conduct comprehensive experiments on a real dataset to evaluate the effectiveness of our solutions.

The rest of the paper is organized as follows. We review the related works in Sect. 2 and state the MULQ problem in Sect. 3. We propose an MRS-tree-based solution for MULQ processing in Sect. 4. The experimental evaluations are presented in Sect. 5. Finally, we draw brief conclusions in Sect. 6.

2 Related Work

A Top-k query ranks objects according to a specified scoring function and returns the k objects with the highest scores. Zhang et al. [5,6] devised authentication schemes for continuous location-based Top-k queries using multiple Merkle Hash Trees (MHT). For extended Top-k queries, the work [7] and [8] verify the results returned from Top-k keyword spatial queries. However, the ranking functions of Top-k queries must be specified by the users, which is impractical when the users are non-experts. Imprecise ranking functions will lead to inaccurate or even incorrect results that cause Top-k queries to have meaningless results.

Papadias et al. [9] attempted to search for a POI that minimizes the total distance between a POI and a group of query users for k aggregated nearest neighbor ($kANN$) queries. More recently, Yang et al. [10] proposed authenticated user-defined querying function processing techniques that can deal with queries over data computed by user-defined math functions. However, these queries focus on a single query user associated with a given location and ignore the problem

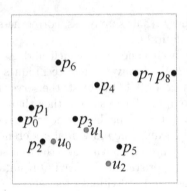

Fig. 1. An example of a POI dataset

of user's individual preferences. For one user, it is convenient to obtain results that focus on his/her individual preferences. However, using this method, it is infeasible to simultaneously consider various individual preferences from a group of users. We need more formal and flexible query processing algorithms that can find optimal results for a group of users.

Compared with the closest work in [11] and [4] the main differences lie in two folds. (1) We improve the MULQ capability that allows users expressing their individual preferences with exemplary POIs. (2) We propose an MRS-tree to index POIs and a bitmap-based dominance relationship comparison algorithm which improves the processing and authentication efficiency.

3   Problem Formulation

Without loss of generality, we consider a set of spatial POIs, Ω, $|\Omega|$=s. A POI, $p \in \Omega$, can be represented as $p = \{pid, x, y, \Theta\}$, where pid is p's identifier and x and y are p's latitude and longitude respectively, $\Theta = \{\theta_0, \theta_1, \ldots, \theta_m\}$ is p's attribute set, where θ_0 is p's spatial attribute (the sum of distance between p and all the query users) and $\theta_1, \ldots, \theta_m$ are p's non-spatial attributes (e.g. customer rating, price, etc.). Specifically, θ_0 is unknown before a query is submitted, because the distance can't be computed without querying a user's location. Each non-spatial attribute value, θ_i $(1 \leq i \leq m)$, is normalized to $[0,1]$ such that for each attribute dimension, there exists a POI $(p \in \Omega)$ whose value on this dimension is equal to 1.0. For discussion purposes, we assume that a smaller value in each attribute dimension is preferable. Fig. 1 illustrates a dataset of 9 POIs, $\Omega = \{p_0, p_1, \ldots, p_8\}$, each of which represents a POI with three attributes: *distance*, *customer rating* and *price*. The non-spatial attributes of the POIs are normalized to $[0,1]$ as shown in Table 1.

3.1   Multiple-User Location-Based Queries (MULQ)

Different from the problem statements in [11] and [4], we re-formulate the MULQ that allows users expressing their individual preferences with exemplary POIs.

Table 1. POI attributes

Pid	Location $\langle x, y \rangle$	Distance θ_0	Customer rating θ_1	Price θ_2
p_0	$\langle 1, 6 \rangle$	4.1	0.3	0.6
p_1	$\langle 2, 7 \rangle$	4.3	0.1	0.9
p_2	$\langle 3, 4 \rangle$	3.1	0.2	0.1
p_3	$\langle 6, 6 \rangle$	3.0	0.5	0.3
p_4	$\langle 8, 9 \rangle$	4.6	0.7	0.5
p_5	$\langle 10, 3 \rangle$	3.2	0.6	0.1
p_6	$\langle 4, 11 \rangle$	5.5	0.8	0.4
p_7	$\langle 12, 10 \rangle$	8.2	1.0	0.7
p_8	$\langle 15, 10 \rangle$	9.1	0.7	1.0

A MULQ can be formulated as $\mathcal{Q} = \{qid, \mathcal{U}, \Phi, \Omega, k\}$, where qid is the query identifier, $\Omega = \{p_0, p_1, \ldots, p_{s-1}\}$ is the set of POIs, and $\mathcal{U} = \{u_0, u_1, \ldots, u_{n-1}\}$ is the group of querying users. Each user in the group, $u_i \in \mathcal{U}$, recommends an existing POI, $p_i'(p_i' \in \Omega)$, as his or her individual preference. These recommended POIs forms the group preferences set $\Phi = \{p_0', p_1', \ldots, p_{n-1}'\}$. Hence, $p_i'(0 \leq i \leq (n-1))$ is a recommendation from user u_i, obviously, $\Phi \subset \Omega$. A MULQ query result set $\mathcal{R}$ is the subset of Ω with $\|\mathcal{R}\| = k$.

It is worth noting that $\forall p \in \Omega$, $p.\theta_0$ is calculated according to the locations of the users in the group:

$$p.\theta_0 = f(p, \mathcal{U}) \tag{1}$$

where $f(p, \mathcal{U})$ can be any function that denotes the spatial distance between p and the group's users, $\mathcal{U}$.

Based on these prerequisites, the dominance relationship [15] between POIs is introduced below.

Definition 1 (Dominance relationship). *Given two POIs p_a and p_b ($a \neq b$), p_a dominates p_b, denoted as $p_a \prec p_b$, if the following two conditions hold: (1) $\forall \theta_i \in \Theta$, $p_a.\theta_i$ is not worse than $p_b.\theta_i$, i.e., $p_a.\theta_i \leq p_b.\theta_i$; (2) $\exists \theta_i \in \Theta$, $p_a.\theta_i$ is better than $p_b.\theta_i$, i.e., $p_a.\theta_i < p_b.\theta_i$.*

In the above definition, the smaller the value the better POI. Taking Fig. 1 as an example, POI p_3 is said to dominate POI p_8 because $p_3.\theta_0 < p_8.\theta_0$, $p_3.\theta_1 < p_8.\theta_1$, and $p_3.\theta_2 < p_8.\theta_2$. However, POIs p_3 and p_0 do not dominate each other, because $p_3.\theta_1 > p_0.\theta_1$ while $p_3.\theta_2 < p_0.\theta_2$. Note that the dominance relationship is transitive as mentioned in [12].

Taking the individual preferences of each user in the group into consideration, assume that there is a weight matrix $\mathcal{W} = \{w_0, w_1, \ldots, w_{n-1}\}^T$, where the weight vector $w_i = \{w_{i0}, w_{i1}, \ldots, w_{im}\}$ corresponds to the attribute set Θ of Ω with cardinality $\|\Theta\| = m + 1$, and $\sum_{k=0}^{m} w_{ik} = 1.0$. For user u_i, a smaller w_{ij} indicates more emphasis on θ_j.

We formalize the preference score of a POI, p in Definition 2 and formalize MULQ on a spatial data set in Definition 3 based on Definition 1.

Definition 2 (Preference score). *Given a spatial POI set Ω with the attribute set Θ, the preference score $\Diamond(p)$ of POI p is determined by aggregating the partial scores $\Diamond_{u_i}(p, w_i)$ with respect to user u_i's weight vector w_i on each attribute θ_i of the attribute set Θ: $\Diamond(p) = agg\{\Diamond_{u_i}(p, w_i) | i \in [0, n-1]\}$.*

The preference score defined in Definition 2 is meaningful. The aggregate function (agg) can be any monotonic function such as sum, max and min. An intuitive definition of the partial score is the weighted sum of the attributes of p on the weight vector w_i, i.e., $\Diamond_{u_i}(p, w_i) = \sum_{j=0}^{m} w_{ij} \cdot \theta_j$. We utilize the algorithm in [11] to transform the group's user recommendations Φ into a numeric weight matrix $\mathcal{W}$, which provides a convenient method of expressing user's individual preferences. Given two POIs p_a and p_b, if $p_a \prec p_b$, we have $\Diamond(p_a) < \Diamond(p_b)$. Otherwise, when p_a and p_b do not dominate each other, $\Diamond(p_a) < \Diamond(p_b)$ indicates that group's users prefer p_a rather than p_b. Note that the preference score calculation can be flexibly tuned for different real-life applications as mentioned in [13].

Definition 3 (The optimal points for the MULQ results). *Given a set of spatial POIs Ω, a MULQ retrieves the set $\mathcal{R} \subset \Omega$ with k POIs, none of which are dominated by any other object in Ω and have the lowest preference score values, i.e., $\mathcal{R} \subset \Omega$ and $\|\mathcal{R}\| = k$ and $\forall p \in \mathcal{R}, \forall p' \in (\Omega - \mathcal{R}), p \prec p'$ or $\Diamond(p) < \Diamond(p')$.*

Table 2. Preference score calculation of the POIs

POI	Preference score $\Diamond(p)$
p_0	4.60
p_1	3.38
p_2	3.64
p_3	5.26
p_4	1.95
p_5	2.33
p_6	3.65
p_7	5.81
p_8	8.30

Consider the dataset shown in Fig. 1 again. The group's user set is $\mathcal{U} = \{u_0, u_1, u_2\}$. Suppose u_0, u_1 and u_2 recommend p_1, p_2 and p_3, respectively, to indicate their individual preferences. The calculated preference score of each POI is shown in Table 2. The group's users launch a MULQ with $k = 3$, according to Definition 3. The result set $\mathcal{R}$ is $\{p_1, p_2, p_5\}$ because those are not dominated by any other POIs and have the lowest preference scores, $\Diamond(p)$.

3.2 MULQ Authentication Tasks

MULQ authentication $\mathcal{Q}$ is intended to guarantee that the users always receive correct results. The server may return incorrect results either on purpose (e.g., to save computation and communication costs) or unknowingly (e.g., it has been compromised by hackers). Hence, the authentication problem is intended to provide a guarantee for the querying users that the server has executed all the queries credibly in terms of three authenticity conditions: (1) *soundness*: the returned result set $\mathcal{R}$ is the genuine MULQ result set and has not been tampered with; (2) *completeness*: no applicable MULQ results are missing; and (3) *correctness*: each POI in the result set $\mathcal{R}$ satisfies all the user's preferences.

Thus, the authentication involves three correlated issues: (1) ADS design and signature generation by DO; (2) On-line query processing and VO construction for groups of users by SP; and (3) Result verification based on the received VOs.

4 An MRS-tree-Based Solution

The brute force solution is to enumerate each combination of POIs and check whether they satisfy the conditions mentioned in Definition 3. When k POIs are selected from Ω, we would consider C_s^k combinations at the most and compute preference scores for s POIs. The time complexity of this approach is $O(m \cdot (k!) \cdot C_s^k)$. Obviously, the running time is factorial, which quickly becomes intolerable when s is large, which is typical in real spatial datasets.

To solve this problem, instead of examining each possible combination and computing a preference score for each POI, we consider them only when necessary. Therefore, we propose the MRS-tree-based solution, which consists of three stages: (1) constructing an authenticated data structure between a data owner and the server; (2) query processing and VO construction between users and the server; and (3) query results verification by users.

4.1 MRS-tree Construction

We use an MRS-tree to index the POIs for the MULQ processing and authentication. DO groups the POIs in Ω by their spatial attributes (latitude and longitude). Each POI group, termed a minimum bounding rectangle (MBR), is indexed as a leaf node of an MRS-tree with a corresponding digest and range of attributes. The digest is calculated as follows:

$$h = hash(p_1.pid|p_2.pid| \cdots |p_t.pid)$$

where $hash(\cdot)$ is a one-way cryptographic hash function such as SHA-1 [14], "|" is a concatenation operator, and p_i is the i-th POI in the MBR.

An MBR, denoted as N_i, has an attribute range, termed Θ_i^{ex}, that includes the maximum/minimum attribute values among the covered objects in each attribute dimension and is computed as follows:

$$\Theta_i^+ = \{\theta_{i0}^+, \theta_{i1}^+, \ldots, \theta_{im}^+\} \tag{2}$$

and

$$\Theta_i^- = \{\theta_{i0}^-, \theta_{i1}^-, \dots, \theta_{im}^-\} \tag{3}$$

For non-spatial attributes of MBR N_i,

$$\theta_{ik}^+ = \max_{o_j \in N_i} (N_i.o_j.\theta_k) \quad k = 1, 2, \dots, m$$

and

$$\theta_{ik}^- = \min_{o_j \in N_i} (N_i.o_j.\theta_k) \quad k = 1, 2, \dots, m$$

where $N_i.o_j.\theta_k$ represents the k-th attribute value of an object o_j covered by the MBR N_i. The $\min_{o_j \in N_i}(N_i.o_j.\theta_k)$ and $\max_{o_j \in N_i}(N_i.o_j.\theta_k)$ are the minimum and maximum values on the k-th dimension of the POIs contained by N_i, respectively.

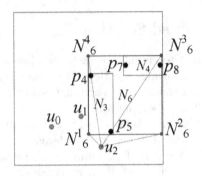

Fig. 2. The distance between MBR N_6 and user u_2

The spatial attribute θ_0^+, θ_0^- of MBR N_i is computed respectively. MBR N_i's rectangular vertexes are denoted as N_i^1, N_i^2, N_i^3 and N_i^4, referring to the red points in Fig. 2. Though these vertices may not correspond to actual POIs, they are convenient for expressing the MBRs. The spatial attributes θ_{i0}^+ and θ_{i0}^- in N_i's range of attributes Θ_i^{ex} are computed as follows:

$$\theta_{i0}^- = \sum_{j=0}^{n-1} Dis_{ij}^- \tag{4}$$

and

$$\theta_{i0}^+ = \sum_{j=0}^{n-1} Dis_{ij}^+ \tag{5}$$

where Dis_{ij}^+/Dis_{ij}^- is the maximum/minimum spatial distance between user u_j and MBR N_i. Referring to Fig. 2, Dis_{ij}^+/Dis_{ij}^- is computed as follows:

$$Dis_{ij}^- = \min(\|u_j, N_i^k\|) \quad k = 1, 2, 3, 4 \tag{6}$$

and

$$Dis_{ij}^+ = \max(||u_j, N_i^k||) \quad k = 1, 2, 3, 4 \tag{7}$$

Its preference score is computed by

$$\Diamond(N_i) = agg\{\Diamond_{u_j}(N_i, W_j)\}$$
$$= \sum_{k=0}^{m}(\sum_{j=0}^{n-1} w_{jk} \cdot \theta_{ik}^-) \tag{8}$$

Likewise, each internal node is a larger MBR that contains child MBRs, its corresponding digest, and its range of attributes. The range of attributes for an internal node is calculated according to Eqs. (2) and (3). The digest of an internal node is computed by

$$h = hash(N_1.pid|h_1|N_2.pid|h_2| \cdots |N_t.pid|h_t)$$

where N_i is the i-th child MBR, $N_i.pid$ is its identifier, and h_i is the corresponding digest, which summarizes the child nodes' MBRs and their digests.

An MRS-tree ϱ is constructed recursively by DO from leaf to root. Only the root node is signed by DO as $Sig(h_{root})$ using its private key. Figure 3 shows an original MRS-tree ϱ built from the POIs in Fig. 1.

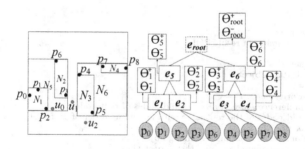

Fig. 3. An illustration of an MRS-tree

4.2   MULQ Processing and VO Construction

Before executing MULQ, we introduce another definition for dominance. Because each node in the MRS-tree has $(m + 1)$ dimensional attributes, the distance between a user and a POI is different than that between a user and an MBR. Therefore, the notion of the dominance relationship in Definition 1 is not suitable for the MBRs in the MRS-tree. The definition for the MBR dominance relationship is given below.

Definition 4 (MBR dominance relationship). *Given two MBRs N_a and N_b $(a \neq b)$, based on their attribute range in Eq. (2)/(3), if: (1) $\forall \theta \in \Theta$, $N_a.\theta_{ai}^+ \leq N_b.\theta_{bi}^-$, and (2) $\exists \theta \in \Theta$, $N_a.\theta_{ai}^+ < N_b.\theta_{bi}^-$, then N_a dominates N_b, denoted as $N_a \prec N_b$.*

Based on Definition 4, we traverse the MRS-tree from the top to down. First, a candidate min-priority heap ($\mathcal{L}$) is initiated to maintain the objects that need to be visited. Then, starting from the root node of the MRS-tree, SP calculates the preference scores of all the child objects of the root node using Eq. (8). These objects are inserted into $\mathcal{L}$ in ascending order of their preference scores. Next, SP checks the dominance relationships among these objects. If one object is dominated by another, the POIs it dominates are all dominated by the other POI. Therefore, this object will have no result POIs; consequently, it is pruned from $\mathcal{L}$ and added into S_{VO}. After pruning all the dominated objects in this child node group, SP retrieves the child nodes of the first element of $\mathcal{L}$, and calculates their preference scores. It then checks whether these MBRs are dominated by any MBR in $\mathcal{L}$. All dominated objects are removed, and the remaining objects are inserted into $\mathcal{L}$ based on their preference scores. When the first element is a POI, it is added into the result set $\mathcal{R}$. The iteration ends when the result set $\mathcal{R}$ has k elements. The objects remaining in $\mathcal{L}$ are added into S_{VO} for verification.

Algorithm 1 illustrates the details of the MULQ processing and VO construction algorithm.

Algorithm 1. MULQ Processing and VO Construction

Require:
    $\mathcal{U}$: the user set
    Ω: the POI set
    $\mathcal{W}$: the weight matrix
    k: the requested number of result POIs
Ensure:
    $\mathcal{R}$: the result set
    S_{VO}: the verification object set
1: $\mathcal{R} = \emptyset$, $S_{VO} = \emptyset$
2: initiate min-priority heap: $\mathcal{L} = \emptyset$
3: calculate the preference score of all the child nodes of root node
4: $\mathcal{L} \leftarrow$ all the child nodes of the root node with ascending order of preference score
5: **while** $\|\mathcal{R}\| < k$ **do**
6:    check the dominance relationship among objects in $\mathcal{L}$
7:    **if** an object is dominated by any other object **then**
8:       the dominated object is pruned from $\mathcal{L}$
9:       $S_{VO} \leftarrow$ the dominated object
10:    **end if**
11:    $current \leftarrow \mathcal{X}.pop$
12:    **if** $current$ is a POI **then**
13:       $\mathcal{R} \leftarrow current$
14:    **else**
15:       calculate the preference score of all the child nodes of $current$
16:       $\mathcal{L} \leftarrow$ all the child nodes of $current$
17:    **end if**
18: **end while**
19: $S_{VO} \leftarrow$ remaining objects in $\mathcal{L}$

4.3   Results Verification

MULQ, they have same result verification processing in this section. When the groups of users receive the result set $\mathcal{R}$ along with the verification object set S_{VO}, each user verifies the soundness, completeness and correctness of the results as follows.

First, each user reconstructs the MRS-tree and computes the digest of the root node based on $\mathcal{R}$ and S_{VO}, by comparing the computed digest with the original digest signed by the data owner, the soundness of $\mathcal{R}$ can be guaranteed.

Then, the users check whether the number of POIs in $\mathcal{R}$ equals the users' requested number of POIs (k). Next, the users verify the correctness of the results in $\mathcal{R}$ by examining their dominance relationships. If they are not dominated by each other, the correctness of $\mathcal{R}$ is guaranteed.

Finally, users verify the dominance relationships between POIs in $\mathcal{R}$ and S_{VO}. If (1) none of the POIs in S_{VO} can dominate the POIs in $\mathcal{R}$, and (2) the POIs in S_{VO} have worse values of $\Diamond(p)$ than all the POIs in $\mathcal{R}$, then the completeness of $\mathcal{R}$ is also guaranteed.

Algorithm 2 illustrates the verification process. Steps 2 to 5 verify the soundness of $\mathcal{R}$ by comparing the computed root digest with the original one. Steps 6 to 9 examine the number of POIs in $\mathcal{R}$. For the results in $\mathcal{R}$, steps 10 to 13 verify the correctness of $\mathcal{R}$ by examining the dominance relationships among the POIs in $\mathcal{R}$. Steps 14 to 20 verify the completeness of $\mathcal{R}$ by examining the dominance relationships and comparing $\Diamond(p)$ between the POIs in $\mathcal{R}$ and S_{VO}.

Algorithm 2. Result Verification

Require:
    $\mathcal{R}$: the result set
    S_{VO}: the verification object set
Ensure:
    $Auth$: the state of verification
1: **for** each user $u_i \in \mathcal{U}$ **do**
2:    calculate the root digest based on S_{VO} and $\mathcal{R}$
3:    **if** computed root digest $\neq$ original root digest **then**
4:        return $Auth = fail$
5:    **end if**
6:    examine $\mathcal{R}$'s size
7:    **if** $\|\mathcal{R}\| \neq k$ **then**
8:        return $Auth = fail$
9:    **end if**
10:    examine the dominance relationship between POIs in $\mathcal{R}$
11:    **if** $\exists p_i, p_j \in \mathcal{R}$ such that p_i is dominated by p_j **then**
12:        return $Auth = fail$
13:    **end if**
14:    examine the dominance relationship between POIs in $\mathcal{R}$ and objects in S_{VO}
15:    **if** $\exists p_i(e_i) \in S_{VO}$ such that $p_i(e_i)$ dominates any POIs in $\mathcal{R}$ **then**
16:        return $Auth = fail$
17:    **end if**
18:    **if** $\exists p_i \in S_{VO}$ such that $\Diamond(p_i) < \max_{p_j \in \mathcal{R}}(\Diamond(p_j))$ **then**
19:        return $Auth = fail$
20:    **end if**
21:    return $Auth = success$
22: **end for**

Again, consider the example in Fig. 1 when $k = 3$. The result set is $\mathcal{R} = \{p_1, p_2, p_5\}$, and the VO set is $S_{VO} = \{p_6, p_7, p_8, p_0, p_3, p_4\}$. Upon receiving $\mathcal{R}$ and S_{VO}, the user computes the root digest from the bottom up to obtain h_{root}, by comparing h_{root} with the signed root digest $Sig(e_{root})$ published by the data owner, the users can verify the soundness of the results. If any item in $\mathcal{R}$ or S_{VO} was missed or modified by the SP, the comparison will fail.

Next, the users verify that the size of $\mathcal{R}$ equals their requirements, namely, that $||\mathcal{R}|| = 3$. Then, they verify the correctness of the results in $\mathcal{R}$ by checking the dominance relationship of $\mathcal{R}$ (i.e., none of the POIs $\{p_1, p_2, p_5\}$ in $\mathcal{R}$ should be dominated by each other).

Finally, the users verify the completeness condition by checking the dominance relationship between $\mathcal{R}$ and S_{VO}. That is, none of the POIs in $\mathcal{R} = \{p_1, p_2, p_5\}$ should be dominated by any POI in $S_{VO} = \{p_6, p_7, p_8, p_0, p_3, p_4\}$. If the SP were to return p_6 instead of p_2, the dominance verification would fail, because p_6 is dominated by p_2. Finally, each POI in S_{VO} should have a larger $\Diamond(p)$ value than $\Diamond(p_1)$, $\Diamond(p_2)$, and $\Diamond(p_5)$, otherwise, the SP has removed correct POIs from $\mathcal{R}$ during query processing.

If all these verifications succeed, the users can be sure that the soundness, completeness and correctness of the results are guaranteed.

5   Experimental Evaluations

A set of experiments were conducted to evaluate the effectiveness of authenticated MULQ processing solutions. We used the Gowalla dataset from the Stanford large network dataset collection [15], which contains 6,442,890 user check-ins at 1,280,989 unique locations. Their non-spatial attributes are normalized to $[0, 1]$. By default, we set the fan-out of the MRS-tree to 100. The experiments were executed on a PC with an Intel Core i5-3450 processor and 8 GB RAM running Windows 7 x64 Server Pack 1. The code for the experiments was implemented and executed in JDK 1.7 64-bit. The Java Virtual Machine heap was set to 6 GB. A 256 bit SHA-256 algorithm was used.

Evaluation Metrics. We use the processing time and the consumed memory space as metrics, which evaluate the overheads of MRS-tree based-solution. The I/O time was included in the processing time, because the index was constructed from the disk directly. The consumed memory space is measured in bytes.

5.1   The Cost at the Data Owner

Figures 4 and 5 plot the index construction time and index size of the MRS-tree referring to the data cardinality. The results show that the index construction time and index size of the MRS-tree grow linearly as the dataset size increases. For 100K of POI objects, these operations require approximately 40 min, which is consistent with the experimental results of [8]. In terms of index size, for 100K of POI objects, the MRS-tree requires approximately 4.0 MB. Considering that the index construction is performed off-line and that our source code was not optimized, it is acceptable in practical applications.

5.2   The Performance Evaluations

In Figs. 6, 8, and 10, "GWMG" is the time cost of "group users weight matrix generation", and "MPVC" is that of "MUSQ processing and VO construction".

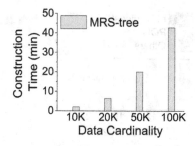

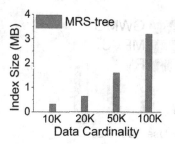

Fig. 4. Index construction time vs. data cardinality

Fig. 5. Index size vs. data cardinality

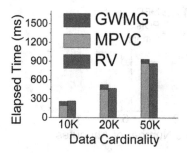

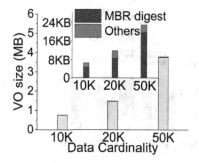

Fig. 6. Query processing time vs. data cardinality

Fig. 7. VO size vs. data cardinality

Both of them burdens the server. "RV" represents the time cost of "result verification", which is the overhead of the users.

Figures 6 and 7 show the scalability of our solution with respect to increasing numbers of POIs. For the MRS-tree-based solution, both the server CPU time and the user CPU time increase as the cardinality of the dataset grows. Nonetheless, even when the cardinality reaches 50K, their CPU times are less than 1.4 s. A similar trend is observed in the VO size. For small and medium-sized data cardinalities (e.g., smaller than 20K), the VO size is less than 2 MB, while for a large data size (e.g., equal to 50K), the VO size is still less than 4 MB. Because it does not need to compute preference scores $\Diamond(p)$ for each POI, the MRS-tree-based solution performs better, especially when dealing with large data cardinality. Obviously, the VO size increases linearly with the dataset cardinality. The determining factor is that VO is mainly occupied by POIs. The top left corner of Fig. 7 shows the remaining objects when the POIs are removed from the verification object set.

Figure 8 illustrates the overall query processing and results verification time with respect to the group user set size. Figure 9 shows the VO size with respect to the group user set size. For our solution, the time to generate the weight matrix obviously increases as the group user set size increases. In addition, a larger group user set size means a longer individual preference score computation time,

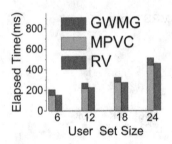
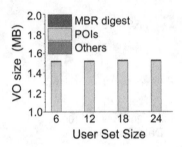

Fig. 8. Query processing time vs. group user set size

Fig. 9. VO size vs. group user set size

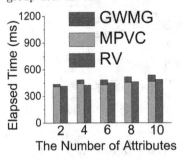
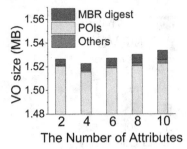

Fig. 10. Query processing time vs. number of attributes

Fig. 11. VO size vs. number of attributes

which leads to longer processing time and result verification time. Because we calculate spatial distances between MBRs and users (Eq. (6) and (7)) in the MRS-tree-based solution, the processing time rises with the increasing of group user set size. In addition, the size of VO is nearly stable. This is because no component in S_{vo} is influenced by the number of group users.

Figure 10 plots the overall query processing and results verification time with varying numbers of POI attributes. Figure 11 shows the VO size with respect to varying numbers of POI attributes. Similar to the increases in the group user set size, more POI attributes consume more time of computing preference scores, which leads to the growing trend of MULQ processing and results verification time in our solution. In addition, the time of generating the weight matrix for the group's users increases as the number of attributes arises. Note that the VO size increases from 4 to 10 in Fig. 11. This result occurs because when the number of attributes increases, the space that each POI occupies rises accordingly, which causes the VO size to rise. Nevertheless, when there are 2 attributes, the VO size does not obey this rule because two attributes make it easier to generate the dominance relationship between POIs, which leads to more POIs being pushed into the VO set.

6 Conclusion

In this paper, we analyze the problem of multiple-user location-based query processing and authentication. We improve the capability of MULQ by allowing group users to express their individual preferences with exemplary POIs. A query processing and authentication solution for MULQ is proposed. We believe this work advances practical applications of multiple-user query processing and authentication.

Acknowledgments. This work is supported by the National Key Research and Development Program of China (Grant No. 2016QY04W0802), the Science and Technology Program of Sichuan, China (Grant No. 2016JY0007), and the Fundamental Research Funds for the Central Universities (Grant No. ZYGX2016J216).

References

1. Pang, H., Jain, A., Ramamritham, K., Tan, K.-L.: Verifying completeness of relational query results in data publishing. In: Proceedings of the 2005 ACM SIGMOD International Conference on Management of Data, pp. 407–418. ACM (2005)
2. Hu, L., Ku, W.S., Bakiras, S., Shahabi, C.: Spatial query integrity with voronoi neighbors. IEEE Trans. Knowl. Data Eng. **25**(4), 863–876 (2013)
3. Lin, X., Xu, J., Hu, H., Lee, W.C.: Location-based skyline queries in arbitrary subspaces. IEEE Trans. Knowl. Data Eng. **26**(6), 1479–1493 (2014)
4. Wang, Y., Gao, S., Zhang, J., Nie, X., Duan, X., Chen, J.: Authenticating multiple user-defined spatial queries. In: 2016 IEEE 40th Annual Computer Software and Applications Conference (COMPSAC), vol. 1, pp. 471–480. IEEE (2016)
5. Zhang, R., Sun, J., Zhang, Y., Zhang, C.: Secure spatial top-k query processing via untrusted location-based service providers. IEEE Trans. Depend. Secure Comput. **12**(1), 111–124 (2015)
6. Zhang, R., Zhang, Y., Zhang, C.: Secure top-k query processing via untrusted location-based service providers. In: 2012 Proceedings IEEE INFOCOM, pp. 1170–1178. IEEE (2012)
7. Su, S., Yan, H., Cheng, X., Tang, P., Xu, P., Xu, J.: Authentication of top-k spatial keyword queries in outsourced databases. In: Renz, M., Shahabi, C., Zhou, X., Cheema, M.A. (eds.) DASFAA 2015. LNCS, vol. 9049, pp. 567–588. Springer, Cham (2015). https://doi.org/10.1007/978-3-319-18120-2_33
8. Wu, D., Choi, B., Xu, J., Jensen, C.S.: Authentication of moving top-k spatial keyword queries. IEEE Trans. Knowl. Data Eng. **27**(4), 922–935 (2015)
9. Papadias, D., Tao, Y., Mouratidis, K., Hui, C.K.: Aggregate nearest neighbor queries in spatial databases. ACM Trans. Database Syst. (TODS) **30**(2), 529–576 (2005)
10. Yang, G., Cai, Y., Hu, Z.: Authentic publication of mathematical functions. In: Proceedings of International Conference on Data Engineering (ICDE), pp. 631–648. IEEE (2016)
11. Duan, X., Wang, Y., Chen, J., Zhang, J.: Authenticating preference-oriented multiple users spatial queries. In: 2017 IEEE 41st Annual Computer Software and Applications Conference (COMPSAC), vol. 1, pp. 602–607, July 2017. https://doi.org/10.1109/COMPSAC.2017.68

12. Yiu, M.L., Mamoulis, N.: Efficient processing of top-k dominating queries on multidimensional data. In: Proceedings of the 33rd International Conference on Very Large Databases, pp. 483–494. VLDB Endowment (2007)
13. Amer-Yahia, S., Roy, S.B., Chawlat, A., Das, G., Yu, C.: Group recommendation: semantics and efficiency. Proc. VLDB Endow. 2(1), 754–765 (2009)
14. Eastlake, D., Jones, P.: Us secure hash algorithm 1 (sha1) (2001)
15. Leskovec, J., Krevl, A.: SNAP datasets: Stanford large network dataset collection. http://snap.stanford.edu/data. Accessed June 2014

Security Design

Active Shield Design for Security Chip in Smart Grid

Rui Jin[1(✉)], Yidong Yuan[1], Ruishan Xin[2], Jie Gan[1], Xiaobo Hu[1],
Yanyan Yu[1], Na Li[1], and Yiqiang Zhao[2(✉)]

[1] Beijing Engineering Research Center of High-Reliability IC with Power
Industrial Grade, Beijing Smart-Chip Microelectronics Technology Co., Ltd.,
Beijing 100192, China
jinrui@sgitg.sgcc.com.cn
[2] School of Microelectronics, Tianjin University, Tianjin 300072, China
yq_zhao@tju.edu.cn

Abstract. Information security of smart grid has received increasing attention
with more and more attack incidents. Security chip plays an important role in
smart grid, such as in smart meter and electrical terminals. Now security chip is
facing great challenges from invasive attacks, which could tamper or steal
sensitive information by physical methods. Security shield is considered as a
necessary guard to defend invasive attacks on security chips. In this work, a
divide-and-conquer and dynamic programming optimized algorithm
(DCDPOA) is introduced and a useful tool for security shield generation is
developed. A detective mechanism for security shield is also designed and
discussed in this work. Then the generated metal shield topology and full-chip
layout with active shield are demonstrated. At last, the chip is taped out to
manufacture.

Keywords: Security chips · Active shield · Detective circuit

1 Introduction

In the last few years, security chip has successfully achieved in aspects of high performance and low cost. Due to security requirements of smart grid, security chips play
an important role in electrical system, such as in smart meter and electrical terminals.
However, with the aggressively development of attack technology, security chips are
facing great challenges on protecting the security and confidentiality of sensitive
information [1–3]. It is also a critical issue concerned in smart grid. Many attack
methods have been developed, such as non-invasive and invasive attacks [4, 5]. With the
help of invasive attacks, attackers can steal or spy the sensitive information in a chip. In
recent years, many effects have been devoted into developing effective countermeasures
against invasive attacks [6–9]. Among these countermeasures, security shield has been
considered as an important protection against invasive attacks [7–9].

As shown in Fig. 1, a security shield is a mesh of dense metal wires at the top-layer
of an integrated circuit (IC) [8]. The metal wires could prevent invasive attacks,
especially Focused Ion Beam (FIB) [6], on sensitive circuits. The attacker could not

© Springer Nature Singapore Pte Ltd. 2018
F. Li et al. (Eds.): FCS 2018, CCIS 879, pp. 273–281, 2018.
https://doi.org/10.1007/978-981-13-3095-7_21

tamper circuits under the shield unless the active shield is removed or invalid. If metal wires of the shield are routed without high complexity, attackers can alter or tamper the shield easily by FIB, which is shown in Fig. 2. Many researchers focused on the routing algorithm of shield wires [8–12]. However, an algorithm with high complexity and efficiency in wire routing is still unavailable. The active shield based on Hamiltonian path has been proposed in [8, 9], which shows high complexity. But the efficiency of this path generation shows agonizingly low. Cycle Merging algorithm(CMA) [10], in which classic random Hamiltonian path was proposed, is incapable of large shield generation. So it is necessary to develop a more efficient algorithm for practical shield generation. In additional, to detect attacks, a security shield is usually connected to a detective circuit, which is designed to check the integrity of security metal shield. According to different detective mechanisms, security shield can be divided into two categories, passive shield and active shield [8]. A passive shield is checked by analogue measurement, such as by capacitance or resistance. However, passive detective mechanism is not safe enough to protect the metal mesh [8, 9]. Some alteration of the shield can not be detected. Therefore, the active shield is a more effective method to check the integrity of a shield in practice. In active detective mechanism, digital sequence is injected into shield mesh. If the shield mesh is altered or attacked, the digital sequence at the endpoint of the metal wire will be changed. Then, the detective circuit will output alarm signal.

Therefore, in our work, an active shield generation algorithm is discussed and evaluated. A divide-and-conquer and dynamic programming optimized algorithm (DCDPOA) is introduced for shield mesh generation, which has high execution efficiency and wide adaptability. Based on this algorithm, a shield generation tool is developed and employed in chip physical design. Then, the structure of a detective circuit is presented and the chip with active shield is taped out.

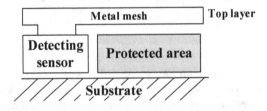

Fig. 1. The structure of active shield protection layer

 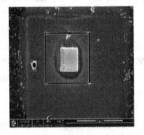

Fig. 2. FIB attack on active shield layer

The rest of this paper is organized as follows. In Sect. 2, we will present the introduction of an active shield routing algorithm and an active shield generation tool. Then, the generated metal shield topology is demonstrated. Moreover, the structure of a detective circuit is designed and discussed. Finally, full-chip layout with active shield are demonstrated. In Sect. 3, we conclude this paper.

2 Design of Active Shield

2.1 DCDPOA Algorithm

In our previous work, a high-efficient generation algorithm of random Hamiltonian path is proposed named DCDPOA algorithm [12]. To evaluate shield quality, we use the entropy as an indicator. The equation to compute the entropy is shown below [13].

$$H(C) = \sum_{d \in \{x,y\}} -P(d)log_2(d) \tag{1}$$

In Eq. (1), P(d) is the probability for the mesh path to the direction. The optimal value of the entropy is 1 bit for a 2-D shield. In Fig. 3, four mesh topologies are given, which are spiral path, Piano path, Hilbert path and random Hamiltonian path, respectively. To compare the shield quality, the entropies of the four mesh topologies are computed. The results show that random Hamiltonian path has best shield quality among the four topologies, which is 0.9955. It can be found that other three topologies have obvious rules, so attackers can easily short or break metal wires in shield layer. Once the active shield is invalid, sensitive circuits under the shield will lose protection. Because random Hamiltonian path is complex enough, it is hard to find the routing rule of metal wires within short time.

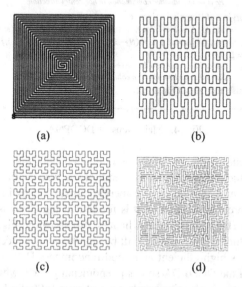

(a)   (b)

(c)   (d)

Fig. 3. Demonstration of different routing path: (a) Spiral path; (b) Piano path; (c) Hilbert path; (d) Random Hamiltonian path

Main steps of DCDPOA are shown in Fig. 4. Firstly, parameters for sub-path generation are computed. The target path can be composed of an array of sub-paths of M rows and N columns. ω, h are the width and height of each sub-path, respectively. The remained vertices are p and q, which will be merged at last step. The equations are solved to obtain suitable values. Then, the sub-paths are generated and combined. In step2, M sub-paths are combined in the vertical direction to form a high sub-path. In step3, N high sub-paths are combined in the horizontal direction to form a wide path. At last, remained vertices are merged and combined with sub-paths. The generation process is finished.

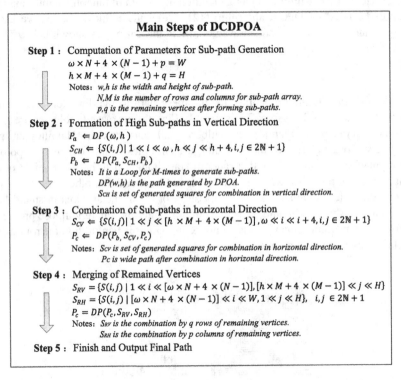

Main Steps of DCDPOA

Step 1 : Computation of Parameters for Sub-path Generation

$\omega \times N + 4 \times (N-1) + p = W$

$h \times M + 4 \times (M-1) + q = H$

Notes: w,h is the width and height of sub-path.

N,M is the number of rows and columns for sub-path array.

p,q is the remaining vertices after forming sub-paths.

Step 2 : Formation of High Sub-paths in Vertical Direction

$P_a \Leftarrow DP(\omega, h)$

$S_{CH} \Leftarrow \{S(i,j)| \, 1 \ll i \ll \omega, h \ll j \ll h+4, i,j \in 2N+1\}$

$P_b \Leftarrow DP(P_a, S_{CH}, P_b)$

Notes: It is a Loop for M-times to generate sub-paths.

DP(w,h) is the path generated by DPOA.

S_{CH} is set of generated squares for combination in vertical direction.

Step 3 : Combination of Sub-paths in horizontal Direction

$S_{CV} \Leftarrow \{S(i,j)| \, 1 \ll j \ll [h \times M + 4 \times (M-1)], \omega \ll i \ll i+4, i,j \in 2N+1\}$

$P_c \Leftarrow DP(P_b, S_{CV}, P_c)$

Notes: Scv is set of generated squares for combination in horizontal direction.

Pc is wide path after combination in horizontal direction.

Step 4 : Merging of Remained Vertices

$S_{RV} = \{S(i,j) \mid 1 \ll i \ll [\omega \times N + 4 \times (N-1)], [h \times M + 4 \times (M-1)] \ll j \ll H\}$

$S_{RH} = \{S(i,j) \mid [\omega \times N + 4 \times (N-1)] \ll i \ll W, 1 \ll j \ll H\}, \; i,j \in 2N+1$

$P_c = DP(P_c, S_{RV}, S_{RH})$

Notes: S$_{RV}$ is the combination by q rows of remaining vertices.

S$_{RH}$ is the combination by p columns of remaining vertices.

Step 5 : Finish and Output Final Path

Fig. 4. Main steps of DCDPOA

The execution time of the DCDPOA is compared with the Cycle Merging algorithm (CMA), in which classic random Hamiltonian path is firstly proposed. Wire routing with the CMA is carried out by merging small cycles into a big cycle. But according to the theoretical simulation, it is found that the CMA is not proper for the generation of a large Hamiltonian area, which is also shown in Fig. 5. With the shield area increased, the efficiency of routing will be significantly reduced. Then, DCDPOA is proposed which has high efficient and good randomness [12]. As shown in Fig. 5, the execution time of the DCDPOA shows phenomenal growth while size is up to 10^6. While for the CMA, the similar size number is just over 1600. So DCDPOA is capable of large shield generation with high efficiency.

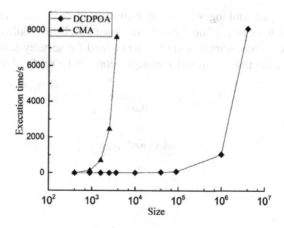

Fig. 5. The comparison of execution time between CMA and DCDPOA

2.2 Active Shield Generation Tool

An active Shield generation tool is developed on MATLAB platform (Fig. 6). As the flow chat given in Fig. 7, the procedure starts with the selection of wire path type. In the active shield generation tool, three kinds of path types can be generated. Single line path and multi-parallel lines are only routed on the top metal layer, and the main difference is the number of lines. The other path type is multi-parallel lines with order transposition. When this line type is selected, the order of lines will be changed in the sub-top metal layer at some positions. So the order of lines at start point is different with that at endpoint, which largely enhances the security of the shield. It is should be pointed that order transposition may affect the metal interconnection on sub-top metal, so the position for order transposition should be carefully selected. Then, several important parameters are defined, including the area of metal shield, the process parameters, order transposition definition and start-end points. In practical ICs, metal shield should cover

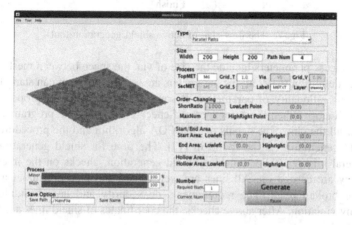

Fig. 6. Active shield generation tool

all the area except pads and logos for security consideration. The area could be defined by height and width, or by reading the GDS file from VIRTUSO tool. The positions of start-end points and order transposition can be defined for security and layout consideration. Moreover, the number of order transposition can be set for different design.

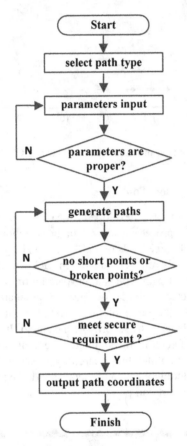

Fig. 7. The flow chat of active shield generation tool

Main process parameters include the size of via, the space between mesh grids and metal-layer definition. After all the parameters are set, the program can start. There is a check for the rationality of parameters. If some parameters are not properly set, the program will stop. When the parameter self-check completed, the program will begin routing for all the chip. The details of DCDPOA algorithm and the procedure for full-chip shield generation can be found in [12]. The time for shield generation is only about several minutes. After finishing shield generation, checks on the integrity and connectivity are carried on. All lines are well routed and placed without any short-connect or broken point. The requirements on security and layout should be met without any violation. After above checks, the coordinates of shield lines are outputted to layout tool.

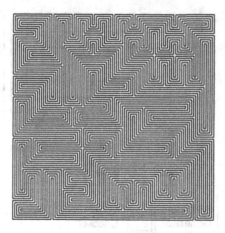

Fig. 8. The output of generated metal shield topology

The output of the active Shield generation tool is shown in Fig. 8. The graph is composed of 5 metal lines for demonstrating topology clearly here, which are generated by DCDPOA algorithm. In practical IC design, it is recommended to place more lines as shield, such as 32 lines, which are thought more security against FIB attack. All shield lines are in random Hamiltonian path. The shield lines will be placed on the top metal. The start points and endpoints are all well hid inside the wires. The order of 32 metal wires are also changed at some position. From overlook on the shield layer, it is hard to find routing rule of shield lines for attackers when generation algorithm is employed. The shield lines demonstrated in Fig. 8 will be placed on full chip.

2.3 Detective Circuits

For shield design, another important issue is the detective mechanism which is necessary for security. As described in Sect. 1, active shield detective mechanism is more practical to chip design. In an active shield, detective circuits work on monitoring the shield layer as soon as the power is on. All the endpoints of the shield lines should be connected to a check circuit. When a tamper or attack on shield happens, the check circuit will give alarm and then the chip will be reset and in safety mode. In active shield design, the digital detective mechanism is employed to dynamically monitor the condition of shield layer. As shown in Fig. 9, digital bit streams are injected into shield lines. Bit streams imported into metal lines should be random numbers. To reduce power consumption during detecting operation, digital bit streams are import into each line in successively. If all the lines are not broken or shorten, bit streams received at endpoints will be the same as that imported at start points. It should be pointed that the difference of a few bits can be ignored which is caused by signal disturb or environment noise. Due to time delay in metal wires, the clock cycle should be large enough to ensure the setup time and delay time. Another issues should be paid attention is the output load of metal lines and antenna effects of layout, which are arisen from the long length of shield wires. In practical design, the routing length of each metal could be up to several millimeters. To solve these issues, the circuits for enhancing the driving ability and weakening antenna effects should be designed.

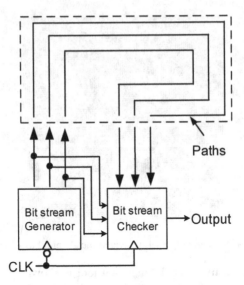

Fig. 9. Detective circuit for active shield

2.4 Chip Layout with Active Shield

At last, the layout of the active shield is shown in Fig. 10. The design has been taped out at UMC-55 nm process. From full-chip layout, the green area in center is active shield and the pads and logos are around the shield area. The shield is composed of 32 metal lines generated in random Hamiltonian path. In this chip, two mesh routing are placed. At the bottom-left corner, more order transpositions are presented which bring more security and complexity. But the space in sub-top metal layer will left less for interconnection. There will be a trade-off on area cost and security. The local graph shows the different wire routing methods of an active shield in Fig. 10.

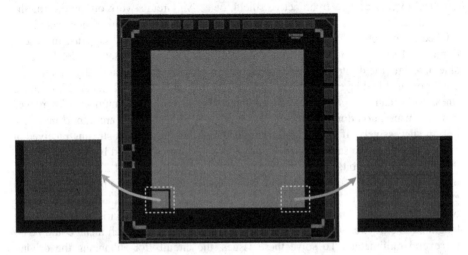

Fig. 10. Full-chip layout of active shield layer (Color figure online)

3 Conclusion

In this work, an active shield generation tool is developed with a high efficient generation algorithm, DCDPOA. The detective circuit for the active shield is designed and discussed, which could monitor any attack or temper on shield layer. The generated metal shield topology and full-chip layout with shield layouts are demonstrated. Finally, a chip with active shield is taped out to manufacture.

Acknowledgements. This research was financially supported by the science and technology project of State Grid Corporation of China. The project name is, Key Technology Research and Samper-chip Manufacture on Resistance to Physical Attacks at Circuit Level. The project No. is 546816170002.

References

1. Shen, C.X., Zhang, H.G., Feng, D.G.: Survey of information security. Sci. China Inf. Sci. **50** (3), 273–298 (2007)
2. Christopher, T.: Security failures in secure devices. In: Black Hat DC (2008)
3. Boit, C., Helfmeier, C., Kerst, U.: Security risks posed by modern IC debug & diagnosis tools. In: Workshop on Fault Diagnosis and Tolerance in Cryptography (2013)
4. Tria, A., Choukri, H.: Invasive attacks. In: van Tilborg, H.C.A., Jajodia, S. (eds.) Encyclopedia of Cryptography & Security, pp. 623–629. Springer, Heidelberg (2011). https://doi.org/10.1007/978-1-4419-5906-5
5. Kommerling, O., Kuhn, M.G.: Design principles for temper-resistant smartcard processors. In: Usenix Workshop on Smartcard Technology (1999)
6. Ray, V.: Invasive FIB attacks and countermeasures in hardware security devices. In: East-Coast Focused Ion Beam User Group Meeting (2009)
7. Helfmeier, C., Boit, C., Kerst, U.: On charge sensors for FIB attack detection. In: IEEE International Symposium on Hardware-Oriented Security & Trust, vol. 17, pp. 128–133 (2012)
8. Xuan, T.N., Danger, J.L., Guilley, S.: Cryptographically secure shield for security IPs protection. IEEE Trans. Comput. **66**(2), 354–360 (2017)
9. Cioranesco, J.M., Danger, J.L., Graba, T.: Cryptographically secure shields. In: IEEE International Symposium on Hardware-Oriented Security and Trust, pp. 25–31 (2014)
10. Briais, S., et al.: 3D hardware canaries. In: Prouff, E., Schaumont, P. (eds.) CHES 2012. LNCS, vol. 7428, pp. 1–22. Springer, Heidelberg (2012). https://doi.org/10.1007/978-3-642-33027-8_1
11. Ling, M., Wu, L., Li, X.: Design of monitor and protect circuits against FIB attack on chip security. In: Eighth International Conference on Computational Intelligence and Security, pp. 530–533 (2012)
12. Ruishan, X., Yidong, Y., Jiaji, H.: High-efficient generation algorithm for large random active shield. Sci. China Inf. Sci. (2018, to be published)
13. Briais, S., Cioranesco, J.M., Danger, J.L.: Random active shield. In: Fault Diagnosis & Tolerance in Cryptography (FDTC), vol. 7204, no. 4 (2012)

A Radio Frequency Fingerprint Extraction Method Based on Cluster Center Difference

Ning Yang and Yueyu Zhang[✉]

State Key Laboratory of Integrated Service Networks, Xidian University,
Xi'an 710071, China
yyzhang@xidian.edu.cn

Abstract. In today's information-based society, network security is becoming more and more crucial. Access authentication is an important way to ensure network security. Radio frequency fingerprints reflect the essential characteristics of wireless devices in physical layer and are difficult to be cloned, which could achieve a reliable identification of wireless devices and enhance wireless network access security. As the existing RFECTF (Radio Fingerprint Extraction based on Constellation Trace Figure) technology has some uncertain parameters and its correct recognition rate and anti-noise performance could be further improved, a radio frequency fingerprint extraction method based on cluster center difference is proposed. Combining this method with a random forest classifier, the effectiveness of the method was verified by constructing an actual RF fingerprinting system. Experiments show that when the SNR is 15 dB, the correct recognition rate of the system can reach 97.9259%, and even reaches 99.6592% while the SNR increases to 30 dB.

Keywords: Radio frequency fingerprint · Constellation trace figure (CTF)
Feature extraction · Device authentication · Cluster center

1 Introduction

Wireless networks make it possible for people to access the Internet at anytime and anywhere. Current wireless networks are found in everywhere of human society. However, their openness makes network security face severe challenges. Access authentication is an important way to ensure network security and most existing authentication schemes use MAC (Media Access Control) address or IMEI (International Mobile Equipment Identity) to identify wireless devices. This authentication method is vulnerable to the cloning attack of the attacker.

The RF (Radio Frequency) fingerprint is the result of the conversion of the received wireless signal carrying the hardware information of the transmitter of the wireless device. The tolerance effect [1] of the wireless device is the material basis it depends on. Figure 1 shows the structure of a typical digital wireless transmitter [2], among them, the device tolerance of the analog circuit part is the source of RF fingerprint generation. After the digital signal processing of the baseband signal, the signal formed

© Springer Nature Singapore Pte Ltd. 2018
F. Li et al. (Eds.): FCS 2018, CCIS 879, pp. 282–298, 2018.
https://doi.org/10.1007/978-981-13-3095-7_22

by the analog circuit will carry the hardware characteristics of the wireless transmitter. As the RF fingerprint embodies the essential characteristics of the physical layer of the wireless device, it is difficult to clone and can resist most of cloning attacks. The radio frequency fingerprint-based authentication method can achieve reliable identification of wireless devices and enhance wireless network access security at the physical layer.

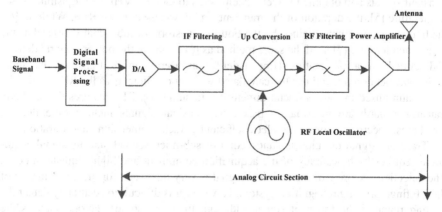

Fig. 1. The typical structure of digital radio transmitter

Currently there are two types of RF fingerprint extraction methods, one is based on transient signals and the other is based on steady-state signals. Generally, the latter is an ideal method compared with the former for its stability of signal characteristics. However, the existing scheme [3] have some uncertain parameters and its correct recognition rate and anti-noise performance could be further improved. Based on the analysis of the RFECTF scheme, this paper proposed a method for RF fingerprint feature extraction based on the clustering center difference. Compared with RFECTF, the RFF (Radio Frequency Fingerprint) features extracted by this method make the RF fingerprint recognition system have better correct recognition rate and noise resistance.

The structure of this paper is as follows: Sect. 2 introduces the main RF fingerprint extraction technologies. Section 3 describes RFECTF method and analyzes it by experiments. Section 4 introduces the RF fingerprint features extraction method based on cluster center difference. Section 5 analyzes the performance of this method and compares it with the RFECTF scheme. Section 6 summarizes and outlooks this paper.

2 RF Fingerprinting Technology Overview

The extraction of RFF features and feature sets is the key to radio frequency finger-printing technology and directly affects the performance of the entire radio frequency fingerprinting system. With different processing methods, the radio signals of the same wireless transmitter are processed differently, and various RF fingerprint characteristics for identifying the wireless transmitter can be obtained. RFF features can be classified into two categories: RFF characteristics based on transient signals and on steady-state signals.

(1) RFF extraction technology based on transient signals

All wireless transmitters have transient signals. As early as 1995, Toonstra studied transient signals and obtained wavelet coefficients to identify VHF FM transmitters [4]. In literature [5], the duration of the transient signal was used as the RFF. While in [6], the frequency spectrum obtained by the Fourier transform of the signal was used as the RFF. The literature [7] used the same method as [6] to obtain the power spectral density and defined it as a RFF feature. Hippenstiel [8] and Bertoncini [9] transform the signal to the wavelet domain and use the calculated wavelet coefficients as the RFF, while the RFF feature used in [10] is fractal dimension. In summary, RFF features that embody transmitter hardware information based on transient signals include time domain envelopes, spectral features, wavelet coefficients, fractal dimensions and duration.

Transient signal duration is nanosecond or sub-microsecond, and its signal acquisition requires high accuracy of the acquisition equipment and high acquisition costs. The detection accuracy of the transient signal is very important for the performance of the RF fingerprinting recognition system. However it is difficult to accurately detect the starting point of the transient signal, although there are some methods such as the Bayesian step change detection, frequency domain detection, threshold detection, etc. Further more, the exact detection of the transient starting point is still a difficult problem.

(2) RFF extraction technology based on steady-state signals

Steady-state signals have received more and more attentions since 2008, and many RFF extraction and identification methods based on them have been researched and proposed. Kennedy [11] first studied the steady-state signal. He derived spectral features from the preamble and used it as RFF. The literature [12] identified the wireless network card by using the modulation domain parameters, such as constellation point and frequency offset. The wavelet coefficients based on dual-tree complex wavelet transform were used as radio frequency fingerprints in [13]. Peng et al. [3] clustered the corresponding regions in CTF to obtain the clustering center, and used the clustering center as the RFF. Cui et al. [14] combined the research of radio frequency fingerprinting and the image technology and extracted two types of RFF feature, edge contour features and high density distribution features.

In short, the RFF features that embody transmitter hardware information based on steady-state signals include frequency offset, modulation domain characteristics, frequency spectrum characteristics, time domain envelope, and wavelet coefficients.

The duration of the steady-state signal is more than microseconds, which is longer than the duration of the transient signal. The requirements for the acquisition equipment are lower than that of the transient signal. The RF fingerprint extracted from the steady-state signal contains enough hardware information of the wireless transmitter and can be used to identify wireless transmitters.

3 RFECTF Method Analysis

3.1 RFECTF Method Overview

The CTF refers to oversampling the received signal at a sampling rate greater than that of transmitter and plotting the oversampled signal on a complex plane. In contrast to constellation figure, CTF contains not only the sampling points used for decision but also the variation between the sampling points used for the decision.

When the CTF is drawn, since the carrier frequency of the transmitter and the receiver have a frequency deviation, the oversampled baseband signal cannot be directly plotted on the complex plane, or the constellation figure will rotate. Peng et al. [3] explained and analyzed the phenomenon in their paper:

If the baseband signal of the transmitter is $X(t)$, the carrier frequency at transmitter is f_{cTx}, and then the signal sent from transmitter $T(t)$ can be shown as Eq. (1):

$$T(t) = X(t)e^{-j2\pi f_{cTx}t} \tag{1}$$

Ideally, the signal received by receiver $R(t) = T(t)$. Denote the frequency at receiver and the phase offset between transmitter and receiver as f_{cRx} and φ respectively, then the received signal after demodulation can be shown as Eq. (2):

$$\begin{aligned} Y(t) &= R(t)e^{j2\pi f_{cRx}t + \varphi} \\ &= T(t)e^{j2\pi f_{cRx}t + \varphi} \end{aligned} \tag{2}$$

However, in actual environment, $f_{cTx} \neq f_{cRx}$. Let the deviation between receiver and transmitter be $\theta = f_{cRx} - f_{cTx}$, then the received signal after demodulation can be shown as:

$$Y(t) = X(t)e^{j2\pi\theta t + \varphi} \tag{3}$$

In Eq. (3), the received signal after demodulation has a frequency difference offset θ, so each sampled point of the baseband signal contains a rotation factor $e^{j2\pi\theta t}$ that varies with t. It will cause continuous rotation in CTF. In order to solve this problem, Peng et al. [3] proposes a method which is shown as Eq. (4):

$$\begin{aligned} D(t) &= Y(t) \cdot Y^*(t+n) \\ &= X(t)e^{j2\pi\theta t + \varphi} \cdot X(t+n)e^{-j2\pi\theta(t+n)-\varphi} \\ &= X(t) \cdot X(t+n)e^{-j2\pi\theta n} \end{aligned} \tag{4}$$

where Y^* is the conjugate value and n is the interval between each symbol. From (4), it can be seen that the rotation factor $e^{-j2\pi\theta n}$ is only related to the differential interval n, and does not change with t. After differential process, a stable CTF can be obtained. Based on the stable CTF, Peng et al. [3] proposed RFECTF method as follows:

Step 1: The receiver gets baseband signal of the transmitter by the oversampling rate, and then performs delay and difference operations to obtain stable CTF according to Eq. (4).

Step 2: Divide the obtained CTF into $M \times N$ quadrilateral area blocks with the same size; Count the sampling points of each area block, and record values in a matrix Z, normalize all elements in matrix Z according to Eq. (5), then matrix Z' is obtained; Select a threshold α, according to Eq. (6), the elements in matrix Z' are judged to get the matrix Q after judgment.

$$Z'[m, n] = \frac{Z[m, n]}{\max(Z[m, n])} \quad 0 < m \leq M, \ 0 < n \leq N \tag{5}$$

$$\begin{cases} Q[m, n] = 1, & Z'[m, n] > \alpha \\ Q[m, n] = 0, & Z'[m, n] < \alpha \end{cases} \quad 0 < m \leq M, \ 0 < n \leq N \tag{6}$$

Step 3: Use k-means clustering algorithm to cluster elements with a value of 1 in the matrix Q to obtain cluster centers with a number T, The obtained cluster centers are arranged in anti-clockwise or clockwise phases as the characteristics of RFF.

Step 4: Store the RFF characteristics of the wireless transmitter to be registered in the RFF database.

Step 5: According to Eq. (7), calculate the Euclidean distance sum of the radio frequency fingerprint characteristics i of the transmitter and the RFF characteristics j in the RFF database, and then identify the transmitter according to the distance value.

$$S_{i,j} = \sum_{t=1}^{T} \left(d(K_t^i - K_t^j) \right) \tag{7}$$

Peng et al. [3] used the Ettus USRP N210 and CBX daughter board as the receiver, and 12 CC2530 Zigbee modules produced by TI as transmitters. According to the RFECTF scheme, extract and identify the 12 CC2530 Zigbee modules by using OQPSK (Offset Quadrature Phase Shift Keying) modulation. When artificial white noise is added and SNR is greater than 15 dB, the correct recognition rate is above 95%, and when the system's SNR is greater than 30 dB, the correct recognition rate can reach above 99%.

3.2   RFECTF Method Experimental Analysis

This section validates and analyzes the RFECTF method through experiments. The experiment was run on a 3.20 GHz Intel(R) Core(TM) i5-6500 CPU, 8 GB RAM desktop, with the Windows 7 Ultimate 64-bit operating system, and the signal processing tool was MATLAB R2017a. The transmitter and receiver are both USRP B210. The transmitted signal is QPSK (Quadrature Phase Shift Keying) modulation signal.

Transmitter uses the MATLAB Simulation module as shown in Fig. 2 to send the QPSK signal, the sampling rate is 200 KS/s. The receiver uses the MATLAB

Simulation module as shown in Fig. 3 to receive the QPSK signal at a sampling rate of 400 KS/s for a duration of 1 s. The oversampled signal and the delayed oversampled signal are respectively stored in two files. As shown in Fig. 3, the value of differential interval n is 100. The same acquisition was performed 10 times, and two files were obtained each time.

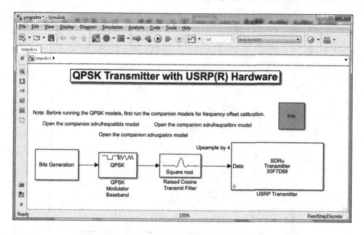

Fig. 2. QPSK signal transmission module

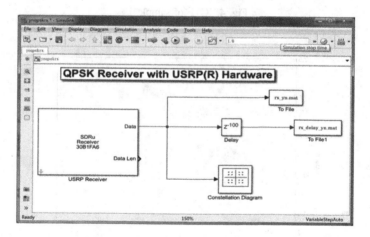

Fig. 3. QPSK signal reception module

Energy normalization and differential processing are performed on the signals in the two files obtained each time. For each sampling signals, 0 rows are removed, and the signal is divided into multiple samples by 4000 points as a sample.

Observing the CTFs of many samples, we can figure out the phenomena shown in Figs. 4 and 5. It can be seen from the two figures that there is a difference in rotation angle between the CTF of sample 1 and sample 2. From Eq. (4), we can see that the rotation factor $e^{-j2\pi\theta n}$ is only related to the differential interval n. In this experiment, the value of differential interval n is 100, and $e^{-j2\pi\theta n}$ is a fixed value theoretically. However, due to the hardware tolerance effect of USRP equipment and the experimental environment, the frequency deviation θ between the transmitter and receiver is not a fixed value. There is a certain degree of fluctuation and the two CTFs shown in Figs. 4 and 5 have a difference in rotation angle.

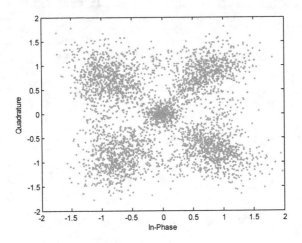

Fig. 4. CTF of sample 1

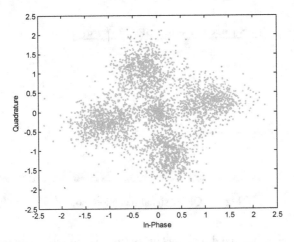

Fig. 5. CTF of sample 2

According to the RFECTF method, samples 1 and 2 are processed in the case where the number of divisions $M = N = 40$, threshold $\alpha = 0.05$, and the number of cluster is 5.

The cluster centers obtained from sample 1 is shown in Fig. 6, and the cluster centers obtained from sample 2 is shown in Fig. 7 where "×" denotes a cluster center. Comparing Fig. 6 with Fig. 7, it can be seen that there are some differences between the cluster centers of sample 1 and sample 2.

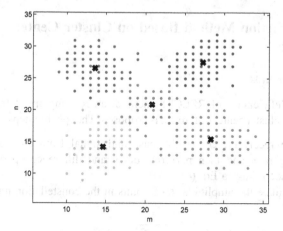

Fig. 6. Cluster centers obtained from sample 1

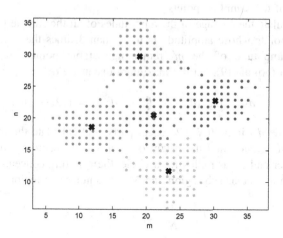

Fig. 7. Cluster centers obtained from sample 2

The RFECTF method divides the CTF into $M \times N$ small areas of the same size. When determining the values of M and N, many times experiments are needed to determine. The general values of M and N are larger. This method uses the Euclidean distance sum between the RFF features to be identified and the RFF in the fingerprint database. It requires setting a determination threshold. The value of the threshold can be obtained from a lot of experiments. In addition, the determination of the threshold α also requires a large number of experiments, which undoubtedly increases the workload.

From the above analysis, although the RFECTF scheme has achieved good recognition performance, there are still some deficiencies: (1) The selection of RF fingerprint features is flawed and needs to be improved; (2) The number of uncertain parameters is large, resulting in a large workload.

4   RFF Extraction Method Based on Cluster Center Difference

4.1   Method Details

Aiming at the deficiencies of RFECTF method, an RF fingerprint feature extraction method based on cluster center difference is proposed. The specific steps are as followings.

Step 1: The receiver receives the baseband signal from the transmitter at the oversampling rate, and then performs delay and difference operations to obtain stable CTF according to Eq. (4).

Step 2: Calculate the amplitude d_i of points in the constellation trace according to Eq. (8),

$$d_i = \sqrt{I^2 + Q^2} \; i = 1, 2, \cdots, m. \tag{8}$$

In Eq. (8), m is the total number of sample points in the CTF, I and Q are the coordinates of the sampling points.

Step 3: Calculate the average of the amplitudes of all the sample points and delete the sample points whose amplitude is more than 3 times the average value. Calculate the amplitude of the m' remaining sample points: $d'_1, \cdots, d'_i, \cdots, d'_{m'}$. According to formula (9), get the maximum distance d_M,

$$d_M = \max(d'_1, \cdots, d'_i, \cdots, d'_{m'}) \; i = 1, 2, \cdots, m'. \tag{9}$$

Step 4: Divide d_M into $N(N \geq 2)$ equal parts, and calculate the distance between each point of division and the origin of coordinates according to Eq. (10). Take $(0,0)$ as center and D_t as radius for a circle, the resulting concentric circles divide the CTF into a circular sub-region and $N - 1$ annular sub-regions, where

$$D_t = \frac{t}{N} \times d_M \; t = 1, 2, \cdots, N. \tag{10}$$

Step 5: Determine whether the number of points in the outermost annular region satisfies expression 11. If it is satisfied, the area division is completed and perform Step 7.Otherwise, calculate the average of the amplitudes of all the sample points in the outermost annular zone according to Eq. (12) and take this value as the maximum distance d_M,

$$n \geq \frac{m'}{20}. \tag{11}$$

In expression (11), n is the number of sampling points in the outermost annular region, and m' is the total number of remaining sample points in the CTF.

$$P = \sum_{i=1}^{n} A_i \Big/ n \quad i = 1, 2, \cdots, n \tag{12}$$

In Eq. (12), P is the average of amplitudes of all sample points in the outermost annular region, A_i is the amplitude of the point i in the outermost region, *and* n is the number of sampling points in the outermost annular region.

Step 6: Step 4 and Step 5 are repeated until n satisfies expression (11), and the final P is regarded as the maximum distance. The point outside the circle with radius P does not participate in the calculation of the cluster center.

Step 7: Use the k-means clustering algorithm, start from the sub-region closest to the origin, the points in each sub-region are k-clustered sequentially from the inside out to obtain Nk cluster centers. The cluster centers are first ranked according to their amplitudes and then in terms of their phase in the interval $[-\pi, \pi]$ from small to large. The ordered cluster centers are $K_1, K_2, \cdots K_k, K_{k+1}, K_{k+2}, \cdots, K_{2k}, \cdots, K_{Nk}$.

Step 8: The points inside the circle with radius P are k-clustered by k-means clustering algorithm, thus obtaining k cluster centers, sort them in the same way as Step 7. The ordered cluster centers are $(K'_1, K'_2, \cdots, K'_k)$.

Step 9: According to Eq. (13), calculate cluster center difference, and take $(\Delta K_1, \Delta K_2, \cdots, \Delta K_k, \Delta K_{k+1}, \Delta K_{k+2}, \cdots, \Delta K_{2k}, \cdots, \Delta K_{Nk})$ as RFF.

$$\begin{cases} \Delta K_1 = K_1 - K'_1, \Delta K_2 = K_2 - K'_2, \cdots, \Delta K_k = K_k - K'_k \\ \Delta K_{k+1} = K_{k+1} - K'_1, \Delta K_{k+2} = K_{k+2} - K'_2, \cdots, \Delta K_{2k} = K_{2k} - K'_k \\ \qquad\qquad\qquad\qquad \vdots \\ \Delta K_{(n-1)k+1} = K_{(n-1)k+1} - K'_1, \Delta K_{(n-1)k+2} = K_{(n-1)k+2} - K'_2, \cdots, \Delta K_{nk} = K_{nk} - K'_k \end{cases} \tag{13}$$

4.2   Method Implementation

The experimental operating environment in this section is the same as in Sect. 3. The signal processing tool is MATLAB R2017a. The wireless receiver is USRP B210 30B1FA6, the wireless transmitter is USRP B210 30F7D88, and the transmitted signal is QPSK modulation signal.

Figures 8, 9 and 10 show the main implementation of the RFF extraction method based on the cluster center difference. Figure 8 is the CTF of delayed differential signal, and Fig. 9 is the CTF after the division of the area. Figure 10 is the cluster centers obtained after clustering points in the sub-areas (for the QPSK signal, clustering of 4 clusters).

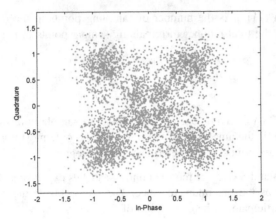

Fig. 8. CTF of delayed differential signal

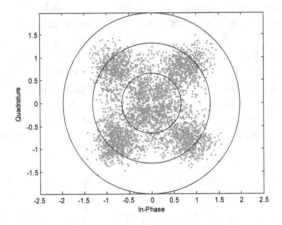

Fig. 9. CTF after the division of the area

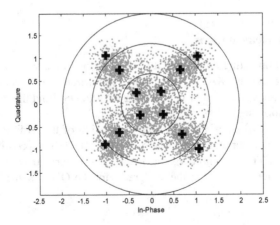

Fig. 10. Cluster centers obtained after clustering points in the sub-areas

5   Experimental Results and Analysis

5.1   Experimental Results

The experimental operating environment and processing tool in this section are the same as Sect. 3. The wireless receiver is USRP B210 30B1FA6, and the wireless transmitters are USRP B210 30F7D88, 30F7DD7, and 30F7DDE, which are the same series of devices of the same model. In addition, in order to facilitate subsequent RFF identification of the fingerprints marks the three devices respectively: the 30F7D88 device is marked as device 1, the 30F7DD7 device is marked as device 2, and the 30F7DDE device is marked as device 3. In this experiment, the signals sent by device 1, device 2, and device 3 are QPSK modulation signals. The experimental equipment and experimental environment are shown in Fig. 11.

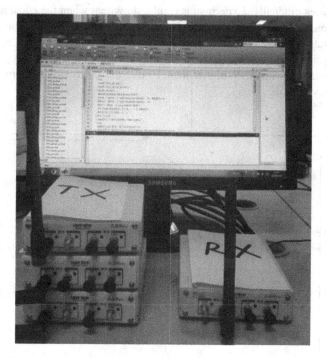

Fig. 11. Experimental equipment and experimental environment

The baseband signals of device 1, device 2 and device 3 were respectively collected for 20 times. In order to test the system performance, Gaussian white noise is added to control the SNR after energy-normalizing the received signal. Combined with the random forest classification algorithm, 30 experiments were performed on each equal number when the maximum distance equal numbers were 2, 3, 4, 5, and 6, respectively. That is, 150 experiments were performed on the five equal numbers. The experimental results with the SNR of 30 dB are shown in Fig. 12.

The experimental results show that the correct recognition rate of the system increases first and then becomes stable as the maximum distance equal number increases from 2 to 6. From the experimental results, it can be seen that when the maximum distance equal number is 4, it has a very good recognition performance, the correct recognition rate is 99.6592%, and when the maximum distance equal number is 5, the system's correct recognition rate reaches 99.6859%. When the equal number is 6, the correct recognition rate of the system can reach 99.7094%. The experimental results verify the effectiveness of the proposed scheme and highlight its good performance.

Using the same sample data set as in Fig. 12, the correct recognition rate of the system was tested at SNR of 10 dB, 15 dB, 20 dB, 25 dB, 30 dB, and 35 dB, respectively. When the maximum distance equal number is 4, in addition to 30 dB, 10 times RFF extraction and recognition experiments were performed for each SNR, and the experimental results obtained are shown in Fig. 13.

As shown in Fig. 13, with the increase of SNR, the correct recognition rate of the system increases gradually. Experiments results show that when the equal number is 4, the correct recognition rate is 95.8012% when the SNR is 10 dB, and the correct recognition rate is 97.9259% when the SNR is 15 dB. When the SNR is 30 dB, the correct recognition rate is 99.6592%. In a word, when the method of this paper is used in the environment with SNR higher than 10 dB, the correct recognition rate of the system is above 95.5%.

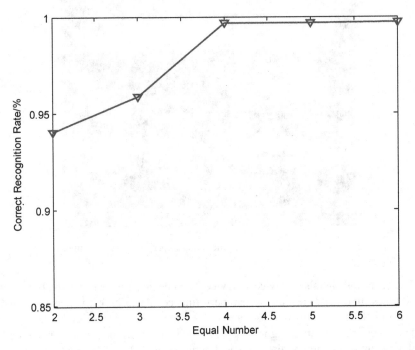

Fig. 12. Relationship between the equal number and the correct recognition rate

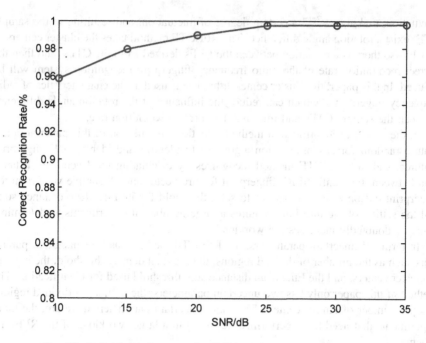

Fig. 13. Relationship between the SNR and the correct recognition rate

5.2 Comparative Analysis

(1) Comparison of methods details (Table 1).

Table 1. Comparison of methods details

Scheme	CTF	Regional division	Constellation point screening	Clustering algorithm	RFF	Identification method	Number of uncertain parameters	Correct recognition rate
RFECTF	Differential CTF	$M \times N$ quadrilateral area blocks with the same size	Elements above the threshold participate in clustering	k-means	Sorted cluster centers	Threshold of sum of European distances	4	About 95.2% (15 dB) About 99.24% (30 dB)
This paper	Differential CTF	A circular sub-region and N-1 annular sub-regions	Points outside the outermost circle do not participate in clustering	k-means	Difference of sorted cluster centers	Random forest classification algorithm	2	About 97.9259% (15 dB) About 99.6592% (30 dB)

In the selection of RFF, it can be known from the analysis in Sect. 3 that $e^{-j2\pi\theta n}$ is theoretically a fixed value, but because of the hardware tolerance effect of the USRP equipment and the influence of the experimental environment, the frequency deviation θ between the transmitter and receiver equipment is not a fixed value. There is a certain fluctuation, making $e^{-j2\pi\theta n}$ a certain degree of fluctuation, and resulting in the sample CTFs exist a rotation angle difference. The RFECTF method takes the cluster centers as its RFF, so there is a deviation between the RFFs derived from the CTFs, and then the correct recognition rate of the radio frequency fingerprint recognition system will be reduced. In this paper, the cluster center difference is used as the characteristics of radio frequency fingerprints, which can reduce the influence of the rotation angle difference between the sample CTFs and improve the correct recognition rate.

In the aspect of identification method selection, the method of this paper adopts a mature random forest classification algorithm to identify and identify RF fingerprint features, and the RFECTF method recognizes by calculating the Euclidean distance sum between the identified RF fingerprint feature vector and all sample vectors in the fingerprint database. It is necessary to set a threshold for its Euclidean distance sum, and the setting of the threshold requires a large number of experiments to determine, which undoubtedly increases the workload.

In terms of uncertain parameters, the RFECTF method has four uncertain parameters such as the number of divided regions, the regional density threshold, the number of cluster centers, and the Euclidean distance sum threshold used for identification. The method of this paper only has two uncertain parameters: the number of divided regions and the number of cluster centers. The more uncertain parameters there are, the more experiments that need to be performed, resulting in a larger workload of the RFECTF scheme.

In terms of the correct recognition rate of the system, in the case of a SNR of 15 dB, the method of this paper enables the correct recognition rate of the system to reach 97.9259%, which is about 3% higher than that of the RFECTF scheme. Under the condition that the SNR is 30 dB, the method of this paper makes the correct recognition rate of the system is 99.6592%, which is about 0.4% higher than the RFECTF scheme.

From the above analysis, it can be seen that the proposed method in this paper reduces the number of uncertain parameters in the existing scheme and improves the noise immunity and correct recognition rate of the RF fingerprinting system.

(2) Comparison of time consumption

The time consumption of the scheme is related to the number of samples when the RF fingerprint feature is extracted. It can be known from Table 2 that, when the number of samples is the same (test samples: training samples = 1:2), the method of this paper is more time-consuming than the RFECTF method. When the number of samples is less than 200, the time difference between the two methods is within 0.5 s. When the number of samples is 500 or more, the time consumption of the method of this paper is about two times or more than that of RFECTF. In practical applications, in order to make the RF fingerprinting system have a higher correct recognition rate, it is worthwhile to sacrifice some time. The implementation of the method of this paper has higher requirements on computing resources. Due to the limitation of computing resources, the experimental results in Table 2 are not very optimistic. With sufficient computing resources, it takes less time to extract and identify radio frequency fingerprint features in the enhanced solution.

Table 2. Comparison of time consumption

Method	RFECTF		The method of this paper	
One RFF feature extraction and recognition time(s) (test samples: training samples = 1:2)	50 samples	0.8478	50 samples	1.0637
	100 samples	1.4821	100 samples	1.8268
	200 samples	2.4294	200 samples	2.8316
	500 samples	5.6272	500 samples	11.1697
	700 samples	8.1829	700 samples	18.2993
	990 samples	11.5915	990 samples	30.3022

6 Summary and Outlook

Based on the experimental analysis of the RFECTF scheme, this paper points out that the radio frequency fingerprint features are not properly selected and the number of uncertain parameters is too many. In view of its shortcomings, an RF fingerprint feature extraction method based on cluster center difference is proposed. Experiments show that using the cluster center difference as a radio frequency fingerprint can improve the correct recognition rate and noise resistance of the radio frequency fingerprint recognition system. Compared with the RFECTF method, although the proposed method in this paper improves the correct recognition rate of the system at low SNR, the result is still not optimistic. How to improve the correct recognition rate of the RF fingerprinting system in the case of low SNR needs to be improved by further research in the future. In addition, the current research on RF fingerprint systems is mostly based on the experimental environment, and the actual application environment is very complex. Future research work can be carried out around the effects of temperature, humidity, various noise, and multi-path effects on the system performance in actual environments.

Acknowledgments. The Project was supported by National Key R&D Program of China (Program No. 2016YFB0801001) and the China 111 Project (No. B16037).

References

1. Honglin, Y., Aiqun, H.: Fountainhead and uniqueness of RF fingerprint. J. Southeast Univ. (Nat. Sci. Edit.) **39**, 230–233 (2009)
2. Yu, J., Hu, A., Zhu, C., Peng, L., et al.: RF fingerprinting extraction and identification of wireless communication devices. J. Cryptol. Res. **3**(5), 433–446 (2016)
3. Peng, L., Hu, A., Jiang, Y., et al.: A differential constellation trace figure based device identification method for ZigBee nodes. In: 2016 8th International Conference on Wireless Communications & Signal Processing (WCSP), pp. 1–6. IEEE (2016)
4. Toonstra, J., Kinsner, W.: Transient analysis and genetic algorithms for classification. In: Conference Proceedings of Communications, Power, and Computing WESCANEX 95, vol. 2, pp. 432–437. IEEE (1995)
5. Rasmussen, K.B., Capkun, S.: Implications of radio fingerprinting on the security of sensor networks. In: Third International Conference on Security and Privacy in Communications Networks and the Workshops, SecureComm 2007, pp. 331–340. IEEE (2007)

6. Danev, B., Capkun, S.: Transient-based identification of wireless sensor nodes. In: Proceedings of the 2009 International Conference on Information Processing in Sensor Networks, pp. 25–36. IEEE Computer Society (2009)

7. Williams, M., Munns, S., Temple, M., et al.: RF-DNA fingerprinting for airport WiMax communications security. In: 2010 4th International Conference on Network and System Security (NSS), pp. 32–39. IEEE (2010)

8. Hippenstiel, R., Payal, Y.: Wavelet based transmitter identification. In: Fourth International Symposium on Signal Processing and Its Applications, vol. 2, pp. 740–742. IEEE (1996)

9. Bertoncini, C., Rudd, K., Nousain, B., et al.: Wavelet fingerprinting of radio-frequency identification (RFID) tags. IEEE Trans. Industr. Electron. 59(12), 4843–4850 (2012)

10. Hall, J., Barbeau, M, Kranakis, E.: Detection of transient in radio frequency fingerprinting using signal phase. In: Wireless and Optical Communications, pp. 13–18. ACTA Press (2003)

11. Kennedy, I., Scanlon, P., Buddhikot, M.: Passive steady state RF fingerprinting: a cognitive technique for scalable deployment of co-channel femto cell underlays. In: 3rd IEEE Symposium on New Frontiers in Dynamic Spectrum Access Networks, pp. 1–12. IEEE (2008)

12. Brik, V., Banerjee, S., Gruteser, M., et al.: Wireless device identification with radiometric signatures. In: Proceedings of the 14th ACM international conference on Mobile computing and networking, pp. 116–127. ACM (2008)

13. Klein, R., Temple, M., Mendenhall, M.: Application of wavelet denoising to improve OFDM-based signal detection and classification. Secur. Commun. Netw. 3(1), 71–82 (2010)

14. Cui, Z., Hu, A., Peng, L.: A method of RF fingerprint recognition based on contour feature. NEtinfo Secur. 10, 75–80 (2017)

Author Index

Printed in the United States
By Bookmasters